LIFETIME LOSER

LIFETIME LOSER

JAMES ROSS

To order additional copies of this book, contact:
Xlibris Corporation
1-888-795-4274
www.Xlibris.com
Orders@Xlibris.com
36506

CHAPTER ONE

Days like today reminded J.W. Schroeder of when he was a boy learning the game of golf. The sun was as warm as the sky was blue. As most boys, he allowed impatience to permeate every crevice of his character. This proclivity for eagerness led him to cheat on a spelling test in school which in turn, spotlighted the need for his character to be molded.

Even his given name of Jerome William was abbreviated to J.W. Yet the kids in school found that pronouncing "J-Double-U" was too cumbersome and time consuming. So the initials were shortened even more to become "J Dub" and the name stuck. Such is life for an impetuous eleven year old boy.

Memories of his eleventh summer always brought a smile to J Dub's lips. His family moved to a more status-conscious neighborhood and his dad, Bob Schroeder, felt that the time was perfect for his youngest son to learn the nuances of the "gentleman's" game. This was especially so since the discovery of J Dub's cheating at school.

It wasn't long before Bob Schroeder was buying golf clubs at a nearby garage sale for his son. And, as an added benefit, the driving range was located within walking distance of their home. The advantages of being a father as well as a basketball coach and golf instructor would promise to pay handsome dividends for his son. It was time for J Dub to learn to be competitive, patient, and to respect the property of others. That summer would be pivotal in J Dub's life. He shook his head as he remembered all the times he badgered his father about golfing. A boy's patience was about as long as the blink of an eye.

"Dad, when are you going to take me golfing with you?"

"You need to learn how to hit the ball first."

"But that's so boring."

"You're not old enough or experienced enough to handle the trees, creeks, sand, and wind that the golf course is going to throw at you," his dad explained.

"I won't hit the ball there."

"Even the best do. You put your time in and practice how to hit the ball on the range. After that you can carry my clubs, caddy for me, and learn the game. When you finish reading "The Rules of Golf" then I'll let you go to the course and play."

J Dub got a chance to go to the driving range daily since his dad was teaching golf for a summer school class of kids. Each day of that summer began the same; after packing their lunch and putting some beverages in the cooler, father and son would head to the range. While some lessons are learned inside a classroom,

J Dub received his education on the driving range from his father each morning. J Dub liked to think of them as "golf-isms" that were espoused with the same fervor as a preacher delivering a sermon to a congregation.

"Show up on time, son. You don't want to be late for a tee time. Your playing buddies might get mad at you," his dad would preach, "and good buddies are hard to come by."

When J Dub got over that first ball at the driving range and took a relaxed, gifted swing, the "coach" knew he had something special. Equally as important, the "dad" realized that this could be the way for his youngest son to step outside the shadow of his older brother, Curt. Bob Schroeder was right. His multi-functional roles in J Dub's life would make the difference.

That first summer of golf for J Dub was the proverbial "necessary evil." The heat was smothering and the long, tiring work in the sunshine was monotonous. At times, J Dub wondered if the heat and humidity or his increasing frustration with the methodical approach to golf would break him.

It didn't take long for J Dub to settle into his designated spot. They had been at the range for only a few minutes when Coach Schroeder started to lecture his son.

"I want you to understand that it is unacceptable for you to behave the way that you have been at school. I won't tolerate any of it. We're going to use this summer to teach you some responsibility. You're going to learn to work hard and face the consequences of your efforts."

"But I want to play!" J Dub was exasperated. His father's insistence of taking slow, deliberate steps in learning golf wore on his patience.

"First, you're going to learn how to hit the ball. Secondly, you're going to learn the rules of the game. When you learn proper etiquette and the basic tenets of the game, then we'll take you to the course. One day you'll realize that this is more about building your character than learning to swing a club."

J Dub balked mildly, but he knew that it was useless to argue with his dad. He pondered what golf and life could possibly have in common.

"Now grab a bucket of balls and your clubs. Get the cooler and head for the side of the range," Coach Schroeder barked.

J Dub found his spot at the far end of the practice area. An old oak tree that looked like it started sprouting during the Civil War was what saved him from the blistering sunshine. He became grateful for the shade and brief moments when a soothing breeze would blow.

J Dub's regimented sessions with his father began to blossom into newfound diligence and discipline for the game. He practiced often and eventually wore all of the grooves off of his seven-iron. After that a hole started to wear through the clubface. Then the grip on the club wore out. Finally the blisters on J Dub's hands turned to calluses. J Dub learned that perfect practice made for perfect shots and that he had to work hard for his success.

When the sweat would trickle down his face and sting his eyes, he would escape to the shade of the old oak tree. It was his savior that summer. It was under the shade of that old, oak that J Dub would read his first book on golf. By the end of the summer he could recite the rules of the game.

The watchful eye of the coach knew he was molding a winner. The proud dad knew that his little boy was learning how to be a man. The constant practice and the attentive reading began to show benefits beyond learning the game of golf.

"What did you learn today, J Dub?" his dad asked.

"I learned not to cheat, to count all of your strokes, and to trust your playing partners," J Dub replied. "The game of golf is based on honesty and integrity."

Those were pretty big words for an eleven year-old. But more importantly, they were values that would be instilled in an impressionable child.

"Plus you told me not to lose my temper or cuss on the course . . . and no matter what happened to never throw clubs."

It was the swing, the swing that came whistling with dynamic force through the ball at impact! It became a thing of beauty. Time after time the ball would jump off of the club face. J Dub had molded something that could stand up under any amount of pressure. His golf years had surpassed his chronological years, tenfold. His experience hitting a golf ball would rival a veteran player. Greater still, he learned that with perseverance any accomplishment was possible.

And now, a dozen years later, the little boy had an opportunity to live his personal dream. All of the years of practice had positioned him to compete with the best young players that the game of golf could provide. That summer saw his transition from a boy to a man. This was the culmination of everything that he and his Dad had worked so hard for.

CHAPTER TWO

PGA Q-School Tournament—Texas, Early December 1983 . . .

As J Dub grew older, he noticed that "the summer of his eleventh year" had become somewhat of a melancholy memory. It was much different now than when he was a boy trying to tame his bad habits through a disciplined practice session on the driving range. Time has a way of teaching deliberation to those who experience melancholy memories such as this.

J Dub couldn't help but feel a myriad of emotions. His dad, best friend, and mentor, had succumbed to a heart attack. Coach Schroeder had been buried a few months earlier. Yet, the circle of life offered poignancy as his young wife, Marcia, carried new life. In addition to that, she was on his bag caddying for her husband during the biggest moment of his golfing career.

With the practiced obedience of a professional, J Dub literally shook off the emotional distractions and surveyed the fifty-foot downhill putt. After all, this was the one-hundred-seventh hole of the demanding PGA Qualifying School Tournament. He was in the state of Texas for the first time. This was the last of six numbing days; each day had been crammed with eighteen pressure-packed holes. One bad swing or single mental collapse could signify disaster.

J Dub had reached deep and moved into contention for the sought-after Q-School card. The top twenty would make it. Staying focused for a few more minutes meant that all of the years of hard work, dedication and determination were about to pay off.

He squatted behind the ball to read the line of the putt. A very-pregnant Marcia wobbled to stand behind her husband. They conferred about the line and pointed to a shaded area of the green. J Dub shook his head in agreement.

As J Dub placed the ball and picked up his marker, Marcia returned to the flagpole. She attended the stick as he hovered over the ball. *Come on now . . . just one good putt and I'm good to go.* With a committed stroke, he started the ball on its path.

"Come on baby. Find the bottom," J Dub shouted.

He walked after the ball knowing that he had kept his head down and had made a good stroke. *Stay cool . . . one stroke at a time. You can do it.*

"Hold your line," Marcia yelled. Her eyes intently followed the path of the ball as she lifted the pin out of the cup.

"Keep your speed, sweetheart," J Dub screamed as he tried to coax the ball into the cup.

While the ball inched toward the hole, the years and years of hard work came together in a single instant. The ball banged into the cup. As it rattled home, J Dub jumped with excitement. " . . . Yeah! Thatta baby!" he shrieked.

With one hole left to play in the biggest tournament of his life, the sound of the ball bouncing into the bottom of the cup meant that J Dub had positioned himself to take the next step into life. Marcia had a grin from ear to ear. She squinted from the bright sun at her husband and smiled as she saw him go from giving himself silent pep talks to taking on a swagger of confidence at being so close to his dream. She instinctively knew that this particular moment was as important to them as her pregnancy.

Marcia also knew that she and J Dub were meant to be together. There was no doubt about it. From the time they met on a blind date as college freshmen, she was absolutely smitten with him. That's not to say that she was the typical golfer's wife. The phrase, "Dynamite comes in small packages" described Marcia Schroeder to a tee. She was small in stature, yet somehow bigger than life. Just like her husband, she was the youngest in her family and was fortunate to have had a "proper" upbringing. Her sisters paved the way for her; much like Curt had done for J Dub. Her spunk was what attracted J Dub almost immediately. He playfully describes his wife as "full of piss and vinegar." Marcia was a pistol, and was used to getting her way.

Looking from the outside in, J Dub and Marcia appeared to be the "All American couple." They were good looking and blessed with common sense and down-to-earth roots. Marcia was glad to have found J Dub. Most of the other guys that she had dated were "book smart, life stupid" as her father used to say. Intelligence was one thing, but having a partner that could think on his feet and pay the bills was much more attractive to her than someone that could interpret the nuances of Socrates. Marcia knew she had a good man in J Dub and now it appeared he would be able to live his dream of playing on the PGA tour. That meant it would be time for Marcia to concentrate on becoming a mom and starting a family full time.

"Nice birdie, J Dub."

"That should do it, Marcia." J Dub's confidence was growing by the second. He felt really good about his game today.

"Stay within yourself. One shot at a time," she reminded him. Marcia knew how close they were. *Easy does it* she thought to herself.

J Dub handed his putter to the caddy as they walked off of the green. A smattering of applause greeted them as they walked to the next tee. Hearing the sparse applause meant he had a few fans following his round. However, his biggest fan wasn't here to see the fruition of J Dub's hard work. Although he liked to think his dad was with him, somehow.

His dream was just a breath away. J Dub walked to the center of the tee box and peered down the fairway. He reached into his back pocket for the yardage book and studied the hole. The years of practice, patience, and sound decisions were about to pay off. He looked up and winked at Marcia. "Par should do it."

Marcia could see the confidence in his eyes. But, she knew that he needed to settle down, breathe, and relax.

"Don't get ahead of yourself. Remember to just play one shot at a time."

J Dub reached into his bag and grabbed his driver and pulled off the head cover. He teed the ball up. He took one more look at his desired destination then looked down at the ball, gripped his driver, and ripped a drive right down the middle. The ball seemed to hang in the sky forever as it split the fairway in half.

J Dub grinned from ear to ear and made his way to his wife's side.

"Nice rip!"

"Caught it pretty good," J Dub replied.

J Dub's self-assurance was brimming over as they walked off of the tee box. He took a sidelong glance at Marcia and her growing belly and smiled.

"This one's for you, me, and the little one," he cooed as he patted her belly.

"Look, I'll worry about that one. You've still got some business to do out here on the course." Marcia was intent on keeping J Dub focused on the task at hand.

"We're almost home, sweetheart. PGA Tour, here we come!"

"Don't count your chickens before they've hatched. A lot can happen between now and the end of the day. C'mon, J Dub, stay within yourself!" Marcia was getting anxious.

J Dub had been on a tear. He had recorded four birdies on the back nine and stormed onto the leader board. "Knock it on the green, two putts, and the field can't catch us."

"Keep your mind on what you're doing. The other stuff can follow," Marcia warned.

"This is a dream come true, Hon!" J Dub could hardly control his emotions.

The optimistic mood changed suddenly as they approached the ball. In the middle of the manicured fairway was a deep, ugly divot. Lodged against the side of the divot was a golf ball covered in mud.

"Damn! Can you believe that crap?" J Dub said disgustedly. He was livid as he bent over to study the lie. "How can they not fix this, Marcia?"

Trying to make a positive situation out of a negative one, Marcia replied, "Maybe they were planning on putting a sprinkler head in there."

"Yeah, right," J Dub seethed. "And they thought they oughta dig up the course the week of the tournament. Some dumb, lazy caddy wasn't doing his job." J Dub's mood had darkened considerably with the turn of events and he felt his confidence slowly evaporating.

"At least you thought it was a 'he' that screwed up," she joked. Marcia was trying to keep things as light as possible.

"Let's try to figure out if we're as close to qualifying as we think we are," J Dub blurted impatiently. He wanted to know exactly where they were in the tournament. The top twenty players qualified for their Tour cards.

A nearby scoreboard showed that SCHROEDER was nineteen under par for the tournament through seventeen holes for the day. J Dub saw that he was tied with ten other players at nineteen under par. That was good enough for eleventh place. An entire slew of names sat at eighteen under par.

"Par gets us in, Sweetie. A bogey puts us on the bubble," he said. J Dub was trying hard to lift his spirits.

Marcia affectionately spoke to him in a lighthearted manner to keep him loose. "Now's not the time to make a dumbass move and burst that bubble." She tried to coax a grin out of him as she reached into his bag for a club. It was important for her to keep him as relaxed as possible. "Here's your nine-iron," she suggested.

J Dub stopped, paused, and contemplated. He grabbed the yardage book out of his back pocket and studied it intently. "That's not enough to get us there," he decided.

"Yeah, but it will get you safely out of that hole." Marcia was not a gambler. She wanted to take a sure thing.

"Yeah, but I don't want to depend on getting the ball up and down for a par." J Dub strained his eyes. He stared at the green. He tried to call upon every ounce of experience to make an intelligent decision under the stressful conditions. "We've only got one shot at getting on the Tour. We have to keep the pedal on the floor. Give me my four-iron. I'll get it on the green."

"It sounds like you are bound and determined to make that dumbass move."

"It's called talent, Sweetie," J Dub said confidently as Marcia bit her tongue. "I'm the player. I'll make the decisions." Marcia intuitively knew that it was time to shut up. She remained tight-lipped even though she felt that J Dub was rushing through the shot. She held her breath and said a prayer for him. It was time for J Dub to commit to the next swing. "I don't want any second guessing out here," he stressed.

With that, J Dub grabbed his four-iron. He stood over the ball, went through his mental checklist, and readied himself for the toughest shot of his life. All of the years of grooving his swing were condensed into a single instant. As he started the club in motion he caught the ground on his backswing ever so gently. The by-product of stubbing the earth caused his hips to release too early. J Dub came over the top with his swing and pull-hooked the ball in a direction that wasn't near the green. When he made contact he knew that he had hit the ball out of bounds. "No! No! No! Stay on the course! You lousy . . . rotten . . . son of a . . ."

J Dub slumped over. "Damn!"

He couldn't believe it. He felt physically ill as he glanced at Marcia and hung his head in his hands. The moment seemed surreal. He had practiced and played so hard to get to this point. The finality of his playing career had just sunk in. His lifelong dream had vanished . . . all in the blink of an eye.

Marcia, racked with disappointment, reached into the bag and grabbed another ball.

J Dub was heartbroken. "I guess we're going to find out now how well I handle adversity. There aren't any more holes out here to make up for that error in judgment."

CHAPTER THREE

The Treasure Chest—A Few Months Earlier On the Banks of the Mississippi River, August 1983 . . .

The Treasure Chest was a seedy little strip joint where four men had chosen to celebrate the landing of a huge account. It was fitting that they chose a converted Butler building that sat on river bottom ground near the banks of the Mississippi. The joint had beer-soaked carpet, creaking chairs and tables, a small stage in its middle and a bar prominently displayed along the side with cigarette butts mounded in each of the ashtrays. The musty odor of sweat and stale perfume permeated the air as the slow-moving ceiling fans whirred in their attempt to cool off another sticky, sultry night.

Each of the four men was a small-time operator living on the perimeter of St. Louis. The Illinois side of the river was littered with numerous small towns, each possessing a distinct and unique identity that reflected German heritage. Many of these villages were quaint little hamlets that had established a sister-city relationship with towns in Germany. These connections had arisen due to the scores of German immigrants that had originally settled on the east side of St. Louis. Walter, George, Lew, and Monty did business on the east side of the river while living in the shadows of the bigger players in the city. Plus these four found that the state of Illinois was fertile ground that allowed them to operate in any fashion that they wanted.

One of the men, Walter Hancock, was in his early forties and looked about as boring as his chosen profession of accounting. He wore glasses that seemed to find themselves tucked into several g-strings on this particular night. Looking as out of place as a virgin in a whorehouse, Walter over-indulged and boasted about how he had struck an agreement with Vern Morton to take over the books of his empire earlier in the week.

Vern had earned a nickname "Goldie" as he had done very well in life and seemingly, everything he touched turned to gold. He had negotiated contracts for railroads when real estate development caught his eye. When the World War II baby-boomers were growing up, Vern was building subdivisions and cities for their parents.

Real estate is like a lot of things in life. Once you meet with a little success, it can become addictive. Vern didn't have a few little triumphs. He had a lot of major victories. Sometimes it's called the winner's touch. And, real estate became his addiction.

Vern parlayed his vast fortune and golden touch across the country. If he wasn't buying raw acreage and renting back to farmers, he was buying apartment buildings, shopping malls, or hotels. In his heyday, Vern Morton was the man around town. He wanted to be in all of the real estate deals. However, he was starting to slow down, which was natural for a man over seventy.

At any rate, Walter had met Vern a few years back at a charity bridge function. Vern loved to play cards and was a very aggressive bidder. More often than not, he possessed the card-table savvy to bring the contract home.

On the specific night that they met, Walter was Vern's partner due to a blind draw regulation that the rules of the game required. Just because they had not played together before was no reason for Vern to back away from his traditional playing style.

The cards were dealt and Vern immediately realized that this particular hand could be the prize hand of the night. Not one to shy away from a challenge, Vern pushed the bidding to a grand slam contract in spades.

The only trouble was that Walter was going to have to play the hand. Once the dummy cards were laid down, it was fairly obvious that the contract was going to be defeated. But Walter, using his skill with numbers, figured out a way to make the bid. The rest was history as they say. He became Vern's bridge partner from that moment forward.

Their relationship blossomed. Walter gained Vern's trust, and Vern turned over the affairs of his estate to Walter.

And with that, came a victory celebration at *The Treasure Chest*.

Three local buddies joined Walter to celebrate his coup. They were George Pierce, Lewferd E. Zerrmann, and Maurice DiMonte. Maurice went by the shortened version of his last name, Monty.

George was in his late thirties and looked like a slimeball in spite of his mediocre credentials. He had gotten his law degree from a state college, which guaranteed him a career either as an ambulance chaser or as a two-bit lawyer for an insurance company. He had a penchant for chocolate snacks and had the fat ass and pudgy belly to vouch for it. George favored starched shirts, the tan European look, and a gold pinky ring squeezed onto his sausage-like finger. His black hair was greasy and slicked back. He looked like a bad imitation of a used car salesman.

Anybody trusting this guy had to have their head examined.

But George was one of those guys that always landed on his feet somehow. He was a smooth talker and had the business sense to always stay one step ahead. It was a very polished technique that he knew would serve him well.

As luck would have it, George's older brother, Norman was a local homebuilder. George was quick to realize that if Norman sold homes as fast as he could build them, then it stood to reason that the buyers would need a place to close the deal.

So, with the builders' funds and George's degree, a title company was born. George's fate as a two-bit insurance company lawyer had been realized. He and his brother hooked up with a reputable lawyer and ran some bodies through the doors while getting numerous complaints about excessive closing fees.

George knew that he would need someone to do his books. He knew of Walter and his talent with numbers and struck a relationship with him. It didn't hurt that they both had a fondness for naked women that would dance on their faces. After all, *The Treasure Chest* was known for some male bonding through the years. They thought that it was a far more entertaining place to gather for lunch than a restaurant.

Another member of the group was man by the name of Lewferd E. Zerrmann. This guy was nothing more than a big fish in a little pond that wore a mechanic's uniform with "Lew" embroidered over the shirt pocket. He was as self assured and cocky as a banty rooster. Never mind that he was relatively short in stature, Lew had a swagger and a misguided perception that women loved him. He never picked up on the fact that the women who paid him attention were working for tips. After all, the stripper straddling Lew knows that her lap dance will be more lucrative if she is quick with a compliment regarding the magnitude of his manhood.

Some of the strippers even made bets with each other to see who could get the biggest tip out of Lew. Telling lies to pay the rent was as natural to the girls as breathing. But, for Lew, he devoured the lies much like a starving man wolfing food. Yet, the lies were as substantive as cotton candy upon his tongue.

It wasn't the glamorous job, Hollywood good-looks, or dozens of cheap gold-tinted chains around his neck that solicited attention. Lew owned an auto body repair shop. The store wasn't a chick magnet and most assuredly, nor was he. It was the word around town that Lew may have his hands on more than strippers.

A few years back, Lew's father had passed away. The will instructed the executor of the estate to title a thousand acres of ground fifty-fifty to Lew and his sister. It just so happened that this acreage was situated on some of the best crop ground in the entire nation. Bumper corn crops were known to come off the black gumbo soil of the Mississippi River. Of course, it didn't hurt to have a fence line that abutted land that was owned by Vern "Goldie" Morton, either.

With the river on one side and Vern Morton on the other, Lewferd E. Zerrmann was sitting pretty comfortably for a little auto body repair guy. But you know how human nature is. If one buck makes you feel comfortable, then two bucks will make you feel twice as nice.

Lew had to figure out a way to get rid of his sister. That piece of ground was just too appealing to him to share. After all, opportunity only knocks once in a while.

After an occasional heavy lunch, Lew would drive his station wagon down the gravel road, up and over the levee, and park on the banks of the "Muddy Mississip." One of his favorite spots was under a river birch tree that would provide enough shade for a nap on a lazy, summer day.

That locale would also provide an awesome sight of the widest river in the United States. With that came a view of the local quarry, nearby railroad tracks, and scattered marine traffic in the form of barges and tugboats.

Warm summer days lend themselves to creative dreams under shade trees. And Lew had one.

Chapter Four

As Lew watched the tugboats traverse the swirling waters of the Mississippi river, he thought it would make sense to get the operators to dock their boats on his property. That way, he could get income from the crops and from the tugboat owners or the barge operators.

Increasing his income was only half the problem; the other part was related to him. There would be no sense in making plans for his income with his sister in the picture. Pure and simple, Lew needed to get rid of her to double his income. Murder was out of the question. Even a small-time swindler with connections like Lew knew better than that. Deception was legal and perfectly acceptable within the rules of almighty capitalism.

Lew looked to his mutually sleazy friend, George Pierce to help him cultivate a lucrative business deal. It seems that George had gotten to know quite a few appraisers that would be friendly to whoever was paying the bill. Before Lew signed the lucrative lease agreement with the tugboat owners, he had an appraiser low-ball the value of the farm property. With that document, Lew figured that he would get a better deal for himself in any negotiations with his sister.

After all, she had her back up against the wall. Her income was fixed as an elementary school teacher. Plus she was in need of money to erase some of her extensive medical bills that resulted from a bout with breast cancer. In typical

Lew fashion, he presented her with the lowly appraisal and then told her he'd give her thirty-five cents on the dollar to help her out.

George Pierce had the title work done before the sun went down. And Lew made the financial deal of his life. Of course it didn't matter that it occurred at the expense of his sister. All that mattered was that Lew profited, courtesy of his ravenous appetite for wealth, regardless of the consequences. The deed was quit-claimed to reflect his sole ownership in the one-thousand acre tract.

Monty was a maverick attorney in his late-thirties, the fourth and last-minute member of the group to celebrate at *The Treasure Chest* that night. He had been over at Lew's farm taking some target practice and tagged along when Lew said that it was time to go. He thought that if he played his cards right, then one of the other guys might buy him a woman.

It wasn't surprising to see these four together on a night of celebration. In some form or another, they all had reason to be grateful. The men drank their liquor until their words became clumsy and thick.

The lap dances were grinding to a halt and the girls had to work too hard for their dollar bills. It was getting late. The booze had been flowing and from the looks of their bloodshot eyes, it was time to go.

The four men staggered out of the strip club well past midnight. The fog on the river resembled a layer of pea soup resting on top of the warm waters of the Mississippi. Nothing was stirring. The air was choking off the far side of the parking lot.

"That's some racket," Lew chimed.

"It's a damn gold mine," replied George.

"Yeah, the same guy owns the hookers around here," Lew snorted. "They get you all worked up in there and want you to blow what's left on a gal out here." Lew waited for his cohorts to get into his car, pulled his station wagon out of the lot, and then drove out into the thick fog that hugged the road.

Walter jumped into the conversation. *The Treasure Chest* and the sexual innuendos had made a lasting impression on him. He could hardly contain his sexual intentions. "Wow, all they leave on is the four-inch heels."

"Right here in the Bible Belt," said George.

Lew strained his neck to see out the window. "I can't see a damn thing." The fog had reduced the visibility to a matter of feet. The heat from all of the bodies in the car had fogged up the windows to boot.

A loud thump was heard. The station wagon rocked from side to side. "Shit!" yelled Lew.

"What the hell was that?" asked Walter.

"Let's go back," whimpered George.

"It was probably just a pot-hole," Lew stated. The station wagon crept to the shoulder of the road. All four guys jumped out. George and Walter continued to the back of the vehicle. Lew ran to the front followed by Monty.

Walter eyed a black woman in the drainage ditch next to the side of the road. Her attire suggested that she was a hooker that had been working the streets. The foot or so of standing water in the ditch had soaked her dark blue skirt and pink blouse. Her red high heels were scattered . . . one on the edge of the water and the other on the shoulder of the road. The hooker's body was motionless in a small puddle of water. Her eyes were wide open and frozen in time. A gold-capped front tooth sparkled through the mist. "What are we going to do now?" Walter yelled. "It sure doesn't look like it was any pot-hole we hit."

Lew examined the front-end damage on his car. "Dammit! Look at this," Lew roared at Monty. He kicked the tire in rage. "I just fixed that." Lew began pacing and clinching his jaw in exasperation.

"We've got bigger fish to fry back here," George said.

"Let's get out of here," Lew replied.

The headlights of an approaching car glistened in the distance. "Whatever we do, let's get a move on it," Walter called in a hoarse whisper.

"We can't go. That's hit and run," George pleaded.

Lew and Monty hurried to the ditch to examine what Walter and George had found. "Leave the bitch!" Lew screamed as he checked out the body. "That's the one that gave me the clap last year." The gold-capped tooth had jogged his memory of past liaisons.

Monty put his experience as an attorney to work. "It's more like vehicular homicide. We better not leave the body here."

Lew eyed the rear of the station wagon. "Come on. Let's load her in the back," Lew urged.

With a knee-jerk reaction the four men lifted the lifeless body of the streetwalker into the tail compartment of the station wagon.

"What now?" George questioned. An alcohol-induced mood of panic had replaced good judgment.

"Will you shut up and get in? We've got to get out of here!" Lew hollered.

The four men scampered into the station wagon as the headlights of the approaching car neared. Lew stomped on the gas pedal and sped off.

"Lew! Slow down!" Monty shouted. "We've got a body in the back, for God's sake!"

"Where are we going now?" George pried.

"Head over to the river. Let's dump her in there," Monty suggested.

"It's too damn foggy out. I don't want to get anywhere near the water," Lew retaliated. The river bottom property had choked all visibility out of the night. "We need to get out of here and get on some higher ground!"

A tense moment elapsed as the men searched for an idea that could be passed along as common sense. "I know about this semi-secluded piece of ground," Walter recommended.

Lew looked at Walter in the rearview mirror for a split second while considering his options. "And . . . ?"

"It's up on the bluff," Walter continued.

Lew's eyes were fixed on Walter's as he stared into the mirror. A myriad of thoughts were racing through his head.

"That's the best idea I've heard yet. Show me the way."

CHAPTER FIVE

Vern "Goldie" Morton must have known that his days were numbered. There's just something special about that little voice that we all listen to. Call it a hunch, a premonition, or a gut feeling. Somehow, Vern knew he had to get his affairs in order.

Within months of Vern's decision to let Walter Hancock look over the affairs of the estate, Vern died of a heart attack. Now, the total affairs of the estate fell squarely on Walter's shoulders. He had a major responsibility to probate the will, manage the estate, pay the taxes, satisfy any debts, and distribute the assets.

Even though Walter was a very skillful estate planner, he worked better with live people than dead people. He had a massive mess dumped into his lap. Since he was the executor of the estate he had to look after the best interests of Margaret Morton, Vern's widow, her only child, Lucille, and Lucille's son, Matt.

Margaret had been a well-kept woman. She had met Vern right after the war. Margaret was wise enough to say and do the right things to keep him around for a few decades. She was no fool, she saw talent in her husband to spin gold out of straw and wasn't about to let it get away from her.

She had gone to an upscale finishing school and learned what to do and how to do it. Margaret could ride horses, play golf, and parachute out of airplanes in her glory years. Her years as a runway model taught her how to carry herself properly. She had been groomed to prosper in the lap of luxury.

However, her main role was to be a mother to Vern's only child, Lucille. Margaret's job was to make sure that Lucille was not spoiled by the money even though neither of them had to worry about anything financially. Of course, that was tough to do once Lucille spent some time on the east coast of Florida.

Lucille had gone to an all-girls high school. Vern and Margaret demanded that because they wanted to shelter her from boys while she was growing up.

That all changed when Lucille decided to go to college in Florida. She fell in love with the climate, practically threw away the books, and let the male college students chase her around campus.

After several party-time liaisons, Lucille met a man she wanted to spend the rest of her life with. She became pregnant and they quickly married. Shortly after her son, Matt, was born, Lucille's husband was killed in a car crash. She chose to stay in Florida and raise her son in West Palm Beach. Lucille was free to enjoy the warm weather of South Florida and try not to overspend the vast amount of money that went into her checking account every month. Lucille was fortunate to benefit financially from the proper upbringing of her mother and the entrepreneurial genius of her father without having to follow in their same footsteps.

Margaret and Lucille never wanted for money. Vern always made sure that they were amply supplied. But strange things can happen after the breadwinner dies.

The heart and soul of Margaret Morton went after Vern's death. She lost her will to live. For all of those years, she was the best friend and steadfast companion of a highly successful man. With his passing, her health deteriorated rapidly. Her weight dropped dangerously low and her lethargic moods would sink her into a depression so deep, she couldn't seem to climb out of them.

It was around that time that she got a call from Walter Hancock.

Walter operated his accounting practice out of a quaint, two-story home. The walk-around porch added a down-home feel and the tree-lined street provided the perfect setting for attracting new business. A tidy sign on the exterior read: HANCOCK ACCOUNTING and ESTATE PLANNING. The stencil on the frosted window of the front door read: WALTER HANCOCK, C. P. A., C. F. P.

Walter was very fidgety when Margaret showed up for her appointment. As she entered the door he rushed to greet her a little too loudly. "Margaret Morton! You remember me, don't you?"

"I believe so." Margaret felt she barely had the energy to speak, much less respond to such a formal greeting.

"I am the executor of your husbands' estate. We met once prior to his death."

"Mmm . . . Yes." In reality, Margaret Morton was very confused and was too proud to admit it.

Walter knew that Margaret was having a difficult time understanding simple things. He had to balance the accountability of an ethical professional with a fiduciary duty against the whims of greedy human nature. It was a wafer-thin line that he had mastered to an art form. "I have the unenviable job of settling some of your husband's affairs. It should take a bit of time, but I think that we'll manage very well for you."

"That's so reassuring." Margaret still wasn't sure about this fellow. She felt as if she were on remote control with her duties as a widow and gave into that frame of mind.

"Your husband's portfolio and his estate had a lot of land and property. So I would like to introduce you to George Pierce," Walter explained.

Lacking in professionalism, Walter yelled out the door for George. It was hard not to notice the snaky, mistrusting look on the face of George Pierce as he entered the room and met Margaret.

"George, this is Margaret Morton. Margaret, George Pierce."

"Nice to meet you, Mrs. Morton," George stated. He shook her hand and tried his best not to let her know that he really wanted to meet her pocketbook.

"My pleasure," Margaret replied politely as she noticed the diamond-studded pinky ring that was mashed onto his thick, swollen finger.

Walter continued with an explanation. "Mrs. Morton, George is a lawyer. He owns a title company where the estate has a lot of land holdings. I called him in today to meet you. We'll be using a lot of services that George can provide."

George picked up the schmoozing by laying it on thick. "Yes ma'am, I plan on working very closely with Walter to dispose of some of the assets in your estate. Does that sound agreeable to you?" he asked in a condescending tone. He was doing his dandiest to be as charming as he could to the old lady as he forced a flashy smirk.

"I suppose so. Vern had always trusted Walter. If Walter suggested this meeting, then we can proceed." Margaret was far too nice and worldly to be mixed up with these two and was in too confused a state to realize the caliber of men they really were.

"Based on your substantial holdings, we will be in constant touch with you, Mrs. Morton. One of the first things I would like for you to do is sign this power-of-attorney form," replied George. He pushed a form to Margaret. He hoped that his blasé manner wouldn't raise any suspicions from her.

"What do you want me to do with this?" Margaret asked.

George's anxiety caused him to blurt out a hurried response. "Just sign it!" He immediately caught himself and gave Walter a quick look as if to say, *I'm okay* . . .

"Vern always warned me about a document like that," Margaret mentioned. "He told me to never sign a power of attorney form." That was the one thing that she did remember explicitly and didn't mind reinforcing the point.

An uneasy moment expired. Walter and George exchanged glances. George, who seemed to have an answer for everything, was speechless. With his eyes, he gave Walter a look. *You're the one she trusts . . . Do something!!!*

"Well, uh, if you don't want to sign that, uh, Mrs. Morton, uh, then that will make our job of carrying out the wishes of your, uh, deceased husband a lot more difficult," Walter adlibbed.

"Why, no, I have no intention of signing a power-of-attorney form," Margaret insisted.

George and Walter swapped looks again. "Okay, then well, we'll deal with things as they come up," Walter had an idea. "We do have to pay some money to the government. Would you sign this tax form?"

"I'll sign that," Margaret agreed. "Vern always told me to pay what was owed to the government."

A slight sneer crept across George's face. Walter pushed a tax form to Margaret. After a momentary pause she reached for a pen. In a matter of a few trusting seconds Margaret Morton signed her life away.

CHAPTER SIX

Through a series of shrewd and highly questionable business moves, Lew had amassed quite a few assets. He had figured out that obtaining owner-financing agreements from some older land owners and renting the acreage back for a percentage of the crops was a pretty good gig. It had become even more profitable when the storage bins were located next to his barn on ground that he owned.

If cash got tight to make payments, he could always use his chameleon-like sales ability to stall off an elderly note holder. Or, he could blame his misfortune on some less-than-favorable weather conditions to renegotiate the loan. In his opinion, the old land owners were much easier to deal with and more forgiving than the asshole bankers.

Those days on the banks of the Mississippi watching the trains go by also put a few fruitful ideas into Lew's head. He concocted a plan to buy property from the railroads. Lew had befriended a retired railroad executive who had explained a dilemma the rail line was facing.

The company had abandoned several lines and the railroad tracks were sitting on ground that was virtually worthless. However, Lew figured that it had value to whoever was on either side of the rail. Many times, the right-of-way, or easement, went right through a farm field. Often times, the same owner was on both sides of the tracks.

With the help of the retired exec, Lew purchased the rights to the abandoned rail line. He then contacted the neighboring property owner and literally raped them into buying the property back just to cross their own farm field.

It wasn't like putting a gun to a person's head, but psychologically, it was just as effective. And he profited handsomely off of that scam.

During the middle part of his life, Lew's maneuvering started to provide him with a very comfortable lifestyle. He had acquired a large, ranch-style home. One storage bin became two and two became four and four became eight and so on.

The rent for the property was coming to him in the form of corn, wheat, and soybeans. The bins were needed to bank his profits. By doing it that way Lew could wait until the commodities market was to his liking. There was no sense selling corn at a buck eighty a bushel if he could wait until the time was right to get double that.

And that was what Lew did. It seemed to be a fairly effective way to get around Uncle Sam, too.

When Lew needed a new barn to replace the old, rotten one, a mysterious fire that destroyed the barn and a few old tractors was blamed on a lightning strike. With a little help from his insurance friend, the new barn was paid for.

To protect all of these assets, he decided he needed a security gate to complete his fortress. The electronics were soon in place and up went the eight-foot tall, moving wrought-iron gates. He had the only farm in the area with a protective entry to screen out traffic on his driveway.

Lew even finagled a way to keep it all through two disastrous divorces.

On this particular morning, he sat at his kitchen counter and sipped a cup of coffee. Standing near him was a skanky-looking brunette, fifteen years his junior. She buttered toast at the breakfast island and was clad only in panties and a t-shirt. It appeared that she had been a conquest from the previous night.

Even a young toy like that couldn't erase the misery from Lew's face. He was a balding old man who wore tinted sunglasses despite being indoors. Every day, he wore the same thing; his trademark mechanic's uniform with "Lew" stitched over the shirt pocket. Lew was a miserable SOB and nothing would change that.

Scattered across the top of the breakfast island was an assortment of pills. They seemed to represent an escape from reality for Lew. His neurotic obsessions bordered on the edge of paranoia. He was especially proud of the jet black, velvet, ring holder which he had nicknamed "Nirvana." The contents of the elaborate case were known only to Lew and the container never left his presence.

The morning paper was spread across the counter. On this specific morning the local sports headline read: J.W. SCHROEDER FALLS ONE SHOT SHORT.

The body of the article continued with, "After landing in a divot on the 108th hole of the grueling PGA Qualifying Tournament, Schroeder pull-hooked the next shot out of bounds . . . ."

The article caused Lew to pause. The headline caught his eye before he really comprehended the goldmine he had discovered. He floated into deep thought and suddenly his eyes flew open wide as he grabbed his phone. He grunted into the receiver, "I think we got our boy, Monty."

Maurice "Monty" DiMonte was on the other end of the line. He was a piece of work. His hardened look seemed twenty years over his given age. His rock-hard pot-belly would rival that of the most serious beer drinker. He wore his thinning hair in carefully combed strands pulled into a ponytail that was patterned after a rock-star idol. To say that he was not particularly pleasing to the eye would be an understatement.

His desk was cluttered with files and documents. The office was in as much disarray as his personal hygiene and his attire.

"Monty" was the person that Lew always called for advice. Monty had a childhood buddy that aspired to be a political figure. Right out of law school he got involved in his friends' campaign. They won the election and he became a force in local politics. Lew was attracted to Monty because of his connections.

Most people in that position would put on a pretty straight face. But Monty seemed to get a lot of enjoyment out of crossing over the line. He always thought that he was above the law and didn't mind going into uncharted territory. That was especially true if he felt like he was protected or could wield his political influence to escape with the spoils. He was addicted to the power of being well-connected.

"Get him up here," Monty urged.

"How much time do you need?" Lew asked.

"The incorporation documents are boiler plate docs."

"Huh?"

"Standard, simple, basic shit," Monty curtly responded as he became impatient with Lew's questions. "I don't need any time to put it together."

"Damn, you're quick! Give me a day to meet with George and Walter," Lew replied. "We need to go over some title and accounting stuff too."

Chapter Seven

Humble, Texas—Mid December, 1983 . . .

J Dub and Marcia were stuck in a double-wide trailer. Their hopes of setting up a little nicer living arrangement were dashed when J Dub knocked the shot out-of-bounds on the last hole of the PGA Q-School Tournament.

So, Plan B went into action. J Dub decided to stay put in Humble for the winter. No sense in battling the winter in Illinois when he could be hitting balls in milder weather. He applied for a job at the local driving range during the day and for a little extra cash he found work at a truck stop near Interstate-45 a few nights a week. It would be a sore reminder of his errant decision during the tournament.

J Dub sat at the kitchen table tweaking their budget and guesstimating maternity expenses. *Marcia has a few months to go before she delivers* he mused as he calculated his meager projected salary for the next several months and compared it to their expenses. *Damn!* J Dub knew it was going to be a struggle when he looked at the numbers. He sighed and rested his head in his hands. He couldn't get the picture out of his head of what could have been when he rushed through his shot at the Q-School Tourney.

"Dammit," he said to no one in particular.

Marcia was sitting in the living room looking out the window as she sipped her decaf tea. She saw J Dub sitting in a heap at the kitchen table and knew he felt badly about their predicament. She was struggling herself to keep her mood light, which was not the easiest thing in the world to do when you're nearly six months pregnant. She cursed her raging hormones and began to feel sorry for herself.

She jumped suddenly as the unruly neighbors raced the car engines next door. Irritation set in. It was one thing to be startled and an entirely different thing to be aggravated. At different times of the day and night, Marcia heard the rednecks gunning their engines as they worked on their wrecks. Their slobbering yells were a constant reminder of the non-stop beer guzzling. Pabst Blue Ribbon cans littered the park. She was already sick of it and they had just moved into this mobile hell hole.

An annoyed glance at J Dub was all it took to convey her thoughts regarding their living conditions. *Four years of college and now THIS* she angrily fumed to herself. She wanted to pick a fight with J Dub, but thought better of it. She knew her pregnancy was wreaking havoc with her emotions and she tried to think of something else. Marcia knew that J Dub was a good man; she would just have to trust him that things would turn around.

One night right after the qualifying tournament, the floor heater started to sputter as they were finishing dinner. The evenings were damp and cool and managed to seep into every crevice of the trailer. It seemed like whatever could go wrong, would go wrong right now for the young couple. "You need to get that fixed," complained Marcia.

"Yeah, I know. The car is leaking oil and we have a baby on the way, too," J Dub said in a frustrated tone.

"What are we going to do?"

"It might be time to give up the dream," conceded J Dub.

"You don't want to do that," urged Marcia. She suddenly felt guilty for complaining so much.

"It's another ten-month wait before the next qualifying tournament. We need to get out of here. The driving range doesn't pay squat, I'm up all night at the truck stop, and we're gonna have a new mouth to feed," J Dub moaned.

"Things will work out just fine, Honey. Normally when one door closes another one opens up."

"Yeah, but I can't wait that long for the next door to fly open," J Dub complained. "I need to make something happen . . . and soon."

"Things will work out how they're supposed to work out. Be patient. Let's get through the winter and get the baby born." No matter how trying times would become, Marcia always looked for the silver lining. It's just that her hormones weren't cooperating with her lately.

"But I'm getting antsy. The energy is there, the desire is there, but I feel like such an idiot . . . such a failure," J Dub complained. He was dangerously close to spilling tears, as he admitted his vulnerability to his wife.

Marcia took a moment to hug her husband. "You're the same guy now that I fell in love with a few years ago. Sure, a better decision could have been made out on the golf course, but it didn't happen that way." Marcia knew that her husband ached to have that shot over. She did her best to comfort him.

"I toss and turn all night reliving that shot," J Dub grumbled.

"It happened that way for a reason."

"Then that reason better slap me in the face pretty soon."

"It may not happen that fast. Just go to the range and keep your game in shape. Let me worry about this," Marcia stated as she patted her belly.

"Yeah, but I need to make something happen. This is not where I want to be right now in my life," J Dub moaned.

"Relax. Neither one of us is where we want to be right now, but we're in this together. Accept it. Take things a day at a time," Marcia urged as she held his chin in her hand.

J Dub grinned. "You won't bail out on me, will you?"

"I'm not leaving you, J Dub, just because you made a dumbass move out on the golf course one day." She paused to reflect. "Although I was tempted when you told me, 'I'm the player. I'll make the decisions'," Marcia mocked him. "You are aware that you married a feminist, correct?"

"Yes, dear . . . you'll never let me forget it!" J Dub smiled at his wife and suddenly grew quiet. "If Dad would have seen that . . ." J Dub's voice lingered until he shook his head.

"He would have chewed your butt," Marcia added.

"He taught me better than that. It wasn't a positive way to handle adversity on the course," J Dub rambled.

"Don't worry about it. Next time you'll listen to me." Marcia broke into a big smile. She knew that she had given him excellent advice on the course before he knocked the wayward shot out of bounds.

J Dub grinned back and chided her. "I must really be slipping to new depths to be forced to listen to a girl out on the golf course."

"I've been on your bag long enough to know that you should have taken the nine-iron," Marcia stressed.

"Why didn't you stop me?"

"I learned long ago that you can't stop a Schroeder when they get to thinking one way," Marcia said. "Plus you didn't want any 'second guessing out there', remember?"

"I thought for sure that four-iron would get the ball out of that divot."

"You're too good for your own sake. An average player would have just chipped out."

"You'll forgive me?"

"I guess I'll keep you around!" Marcia teased. "But let's see how you handle the misfortune of not getting your tour card."

"Good. I'll figure out what we'll do next," J Dub promised.

Marcia pulled J Dub close to her, wrapping his arms around her and whispered, "Come here, you," and they shared a lingering, soft kiss.

CHAPTER EIGHT

George Pierce drove up to Lew's gate. He grunted his name through the intercom system and waited as the gate opened. As he traveled down the driveway the gate closed behind him.

George was the kind of guy that was always looking for an angle. He was a real con man and rotten to the core. His moral fiber didn't contain many scruples.

They say "birds of a feather flock together" and "you can't change the spots on a leopard." Both applied to these characters. George and Lew found each other. Neither was going to alter their behavior.

Their common bond was power and greed. Both wanted to achieve that goal using other people's money. They learned their lessons in capitalism early in life. The difference between these two guys and most successful entrepreneurs was intent. Together, their evilness was like glue. And their bond was tight.

Lew waited outside his house as George pulled to a stop. "Did everything go okay, George?"

"We got what we were after."

"You're kidding?" Lew was amazed that George could obtain Margaret Morton's signature so quickly. "That fast?"

"There was no problem. She's damn near dead," George said viciously. His sinister chuckle signaled evil intentions. "I wasn't there two minutes. I pushed the power-of-attorney form in front of her and she balked. But then Walter got her signature on a tax document. She signed it before it stopped moving across the desk," George gloated.

"When do we start?" Lew probed.

" . . . Right away. How's your loan coming?"

"Joe, down at the bank, said I have to find somebody with golf experience before the bank will approve the loan. I have to find some kid willing to bust his ass from dawn to dusk and not steal from me," Lew explained.

"Got anybody in mind?"

"Yeah, I got a line on a local kid that's down in Texas now. He just got out of college and missed his chance at the tour. I need to see if he might want to run a golf course."

"How much time do you need?" George inquired.

"Deed it over to me right now and I can make a quick trip to Texas," Lew suggested.

"I want my cut first," George demanded.

"That might be six months off. I'm going to try to get the kid up here. We need to keep the business rolling and generating some cash flow."

"Give me a few days to work with Mary Jean," George mumbled.

Lew's smirk indicated that he didn't mind the delay. "No problem. I'll need some time to see Walter and pay a visit to the kid in Texas. Hell, I still need to find him."

CHAPTER NINE

Walter Hancock really wasn't a bad guy. At least he had some semblance of a conscience, a quality that some of the guys he socialized with lacked. One of Walter's problems was that he assumed the stereotypical persona and lifestyle of an accountant and needed some cheap thrills to feel important.

After getting his accounting degree, Walter continued for his MBA. Then he passed the CPA exam and got hired by a 'Big Six' accounting firm. The long hours in the downtown office weren't really his cup of tea. He always used to joke that sitting in his cubicle was like sitting in a beige prison. But he was good at what he did, so he sat in his beige prison debiting his credits.

That was until he got in with some executives at one of the large corporations. They had been making a killing in their company stock and stock option programs. Walter figured out a way to shelter their income and cut their capital gains.

He wasn't afraid to do that. He would push the envelope when it came to saving a client a buck or two from Uncle Sam. One thing led to another. A friend referred a friend and so on and so forth. Before long, Walter had assembled quite a little book of "Who's Who" that he was representing which increased his value as the ultimate asset for any company . . . at least one that wanted to make money.

He broke away from his staid job at the accounting firm and opened up his own little one-man accounting office. That's the American way. But for Walter it meant that he would have the liberty to stretch the rules a little farther and increase his value that much more.

He was the type of guy that was dangerously influenced by others. Being out on his own doomed him because it allowed him to meet characters that had wicked objectives. And Lewferd E. Zerrmann had a knack for finding the four-leaf clover in a field of grass.

Walter liked operating out of the older two-story Victorian home. The kitchen was convenient for his continuous snacking. The various rooms were put to use holding reference books, past files, and tax returns. There was paper cluttered everywhere! That was the way that Walter liked to function.

When Lew came through the door, Walter was snacking on a doughnut. He looked up to peer over the glasses resting on his nose.

"Did you get that French whore scent out of your clothes yet?" Lew asked as he grabbed a seat.

"Man, that's some powerful shit. I stopped at the quick trip and poured orange soda over my head so that my wife wouldn't notice," Walter quipped.

"We've got to do that again real soon," Lew suggested.

"Find me a large account. I'll buy."

"Speaking of which," Lew uttered, "George said that everything went well during your meeting with Margaret."

"We got her to sign a tax form. I'm not sold on trying to do things this way," Walter said as he lapsed momentarily back into his accountant mode.

"Who the heck is going to know? The old lady is out of it. Just make sure she gets her allowance," Lew persisted.

"But it just isn't right."

"What difference does it make? Who cares if it is a cash asset or a property asset?" Lew ranted.

"I don't have the authority to start moving assets without her permission."

Lew's powers of persuasion didn't stop until he got his way. "She gave both of you her signature. She trusts you. Let's make a deal."

"Yeah, but . . ."

" . . . You're the executor of the estate, aren't you?"

Walter nodded but was clearly uncomfortable with the way Lew was pressuring him.

Lew continued, "I want to get that ground."

"Then I'll have to get it appraised," Walter stated.

"Screw that. It takes too long."

"I have to get fair market value for the estate. It's my fiduciary duty," Walter advised. He was accustomed to more subtle "creative accounting" than Lew's deal.

"Then I know just the appraiser to use," Lew suggested.

"Besides you'll need it for your bank loan."

"Yeah, but I've been thinking about that."

"Is the bank giving you a hard time?" Walter asked.

Lew dodged the truth. "There are some issues."

"What are they telling you?" Walter pressed for an explanation.

"First off, they want somebody with experience running the place," Lew stated.

"And you don't know crap about golf," Walter surmised.

" . . . And could care less about it. I want the land," Lew simply stated his objective.

Walter stepped right into Lew's world of thinking. "The financials won't support a very high price."

"I was hoping you'd say that." Lew was in a buyers' mode.

"But I owe an obligation to my client," Walter explained.

"Screw the client!" Lew hollered.

Justification was one item that Walter could fudge about without feeling too guilty. "We do need to dispose of some things . . ."

"Why don't you owner-finance me?" Lew suggested.

Walter smiled and said, "You took the words right out of my mouth."

"Let's draw up a contract." Lew frothed at the mouth.

"Not so fast. I've got to get George involved too."

"Make that land disappear from the books," Lew proposed.

With a grin Walter said, "I'm pretty creative."

If Lew was going to wheel and deal he wanted to make sure that he maintained the upper hand. "Then make sure that it's a favorable price."

Walter took the bait. "Go and line up your kid. I'll need a few days as well to get everything set up with George."

CHAPTER TEN

Mary Jean Graham was one of those women that could turn a man's head. She had gotten divorced after she had met George Pierce, although one had nothing to do with the other. She was in her early thirties and had the body of an aerobics instructor. It was easy to see why George had recruited her to work for him.

She knew her strengths and accentuated them to the delight of males who cared to notice. One day her hair would be up, the next day it would be down. If she wore business slacks early in the week, she would have on a skirt later in the week. The constant was that whatever she wore was tight and magnified her gorgeous figure. Her body language made her outfits even more appealing. A hot-blooded male had trouble concentrating when she was present.

Anything that Mary Jean possessed in the body department was missing between her ears. Even though she was as friendly as she could be, her thought process was a little scattered. But, no matter what George told her to do, she did it with a smile far more sophisticated than her intellect.

Mary Jean knew the value of non-verbal communication and was very effective mitigating any hard feelings or confusion that might arise from a closing. George really did find a diamond in the rough with Mary Jean. She had the country girl naiveté and city girl moves to get what she wished. George found a faithful employee in Mary Jean and took care in grooming her for his needs.

The day after George had met with Walter and Margaret he approached Mary Jean at the receptionist desk. He had a copy of the tax form with Margaret's signature. "Good morning, George. Did everything go okay yesterday?" Mary Jean asked.

"It couldn't have been any better!" George answered. "In fact I've got a little project I want you to start on."

"And what might that be?"

George handed her a file. "I have a signed tax form for an influential account. I want you to take this document and copy it. For the next several days I want you to start practicing how to write the signature of Margaret Morton."

" . . . Margaret Morton of the Morton family?"

George nodded.

"How neat is that?" Mary Jean exclaimed.

George had the grin of a kid that had just taken candy from a baby. "When you get it perfected, let me know," George insisted.

"I can't sign for her and notarize."

"Sure you can. When you sign her name to the power-of-attorney form that I'm going to give to you then we'll be able to do anything that we want," George rationalized. He winked at Mary Jean. "We're going to be awfully busy the next three to six months."

Mary Jean looked at George with a bewildered look. "What are we going to be doing?"

"You always wanted to live the good life, relax, and work on your tan on a tropical island, didn't you?" George inquired.

Mary Jean flashed a devious smile. She had always known that she and George would eventually end up together. Yet, Mary Jean still looked a little confused. Even though they had been lovers for quite some time, George was still her boss and she wasn't about to dispute what he was saying. After all, he was the expert.

"Just make sure that it's a perfect match," George continued, "and we'll march a lot of closings through these doors. The estate has condos in Southern California, a ranch in western Nebraska, apartments in Tulsa, a hotel in downtown St. Louis, lots of acreage in Southern Illinois, and shopping centers in Louisville, Nashville, and Denver. All of it needs to be sold."

Mary Jean nearly spit out the sip of coffee she had just taken. "Can we get all of that property sold that quickly?" she stammered.

"If you can get her signature perfected we can." George paused for a minute and reflected on his next admission. "You know, having a law license, the majority of the stock in a title company, and a faithful employee almost gives me a license to steal," he commented with a smirk.

Mary Jean glanced at him out of the side of her eye and grinned. George leaned over and kissed her forehead.

Chapter Eleven

Valley Trail Driving Range—Humble, Texas, January 1984 . . .

Vince, the owner of the VALLEY TRAIL DRIVING RANGE, held a soft spot for golfers competing in the qualifying tours and snapped up J Dub the moment he applied for the job. His research indicated that he was a 'good guy' and noticed that he had a very pregnant wife that was depending on him as well.

He was happy to give him a job for as long as he wanted to stay, although he knew he wouldn't stay long. Humble is not the sort of town most people settle down in and take root. The range wasn't anything special by any means; and the range itself occupied a field that seemed to flood every third year or so. When the water would come up, Vince had a habit of leaving the balls on the ground and taking off for Houston to enjoy a long weekend. Vince knew that the golf circuit was filled with "wanna-be's" that missed a crucial shot and needed a short term job to save enough money to get back home. Thus, he was pleased to give J Dub an opportunity.

The pro shop was nothing more than a trailer. The parking lot was a gravel dust bowl. Most of the synthetic grass mats were weathered so much that they were rendered useless. The golfers, more often than not, chose to hit off of clumps of grass that sprouted from the barren clay soil.

The range was located outside of Houston and most of the golfers that stopped in were on their way either to or from the big city. It offered a great situation for J Dub. In between the customers, he could work on his game and still keep a watchful eye on the trailer and lot.

In the days following the disappointment of the Q-School tournament, J Dub was having a difficult time readjusting to life as a driving range pro. He was frustrated by the turn of events and had no idea which direction his life was headed. So, he turned to what he knew best . . . practice on the range.

To the non-golfer or the social golfer, life on the range is incomprehensible. Most people get a set of clubs for Christmas and head to the golf course to play golf. Others get invited to fill out a scramble a couple of times a year and just hack it around.

For the serious golfer however, life on the range is a necessity. To the low handicappers and the pros, hitting a bucket of balls is an absolute.

The skilled players understand that perfect practice makes perfect shots. To find the sweet spot on the club every time takes years and years of hard work. To groove a swing means hours of repetitive motion that only the pro can understand.

J Dub went back to the corner of the range to pound ball after ball. He worked on driving the long ball. He fine-tuned the precision of his approach shots. He mastered the delicate touch of the chip shot. He practiced the pace of his putts. Each drill was performed with consistency and skill from the many years of practicing. He had mastered practice to an art form and it showed.

His mood wasn't the same though. On one of his first few days back from the tournament things became doubly frustrating. It was warm for an early day in January. The wind blew the dust from the gravel parking lot across the range. The mosquitoes and flies seemed to breed in the trailer.

J Dub was servicing a customer when an old Ford station wagon with Illinois plates and front-end damage pulled onto the lot. It came to a stop. Lew Zerrmann got out of the car, looked around in an arrogant way, and in a crass manner, spat on the gravel.

As was customary, Lew was dressed in his mechanic's outfit. The boots and the work pants didn't really lend themselves to the golf environment. After he sized up his surroundings, Lew continued into the trailer and waited as J Dub wrapped up a transaction with a previous customer.

Nothing was going right for J Dub at this time of his life. As he bent over for ice, the scoop snapped in the ice bin. In frustration, he fired the scoop into the trash can. He placed the cup under the soda dispenser and hit the refill button. The soda canister ran dry and splashed soda all over him. J Dub hurriedly grabbed a towel to dry off and placed it into his hip pocket.

As he dropped a token into the golf ball dispenser to prepare a bucket of balls for the customer, he accidentally knocked the container over. With balls bouncing across the floor and around the trailer, J Dub chased them down and refilled the bucket. After the customer left, he threw the towel in frustration against the wall.

J Dub noticed Lew in the back of the trailer. "It's been a rough week. What do you need?" J Dub asked.

"Lessons," Lew answered.

J Dub laughed in Lew's face. It's not too often that someone out of the blue walks into an off-the-beaten-path trailer and asks for lessons, especially in January. J Dub looked at Lew's thinning hair and noticed his advancing age. "It's kind of late for you, isn't it?"

"I need to learn how to win at the game of golf. That's the only thing that counts with me," Lew explained.

J Dub was all too familiar with the lesson that he had just been taught at Q-school. "It doesn't always work that way."

"What do you mean?"

"Just because you get lessons and you want to win, doesn't mean that you're going to be successful," J Dub clarified.

"It should increase my odds," Lew implied.

"Maybe," J Dub hinted. "Then you need to factor in the elements like the hills and water and sand and wind . . . not to mention your own mind."

Lew looked around the place, glanced outside, and replied, "You better make that just water, sand and wind. There doesn't appear to be a hill in sight from where I stand. What do I need to get started?" Lew inquired.

"Twenty years would help," J Dub smirked as his irritation grew. "Why now? Where have you been all of your life?"

"Busy with real estate," Lew responded.

J Dub looked out the window at the banged-up Ford station wagon with out of state plates and glanced back at Lew dressed in work clothes. " . . . Yeah, right. Who do you think you're fooling? What brings you from Illinois?"

"I'll get to that in a minute. I'm interested in lessons at the moment." Lew was taken aback a little. He didn't expect to be belittled when he walked into the trailer. He was used to people kissing up to his backside. "Golf looks like a great game," Lew continued.

"Sometimes it can be . . . sometimes not. But I guess what's most important is the lessons in life that you take away from the game."

"Like what?"

"You've heard the expression, 'It's not whether you win or lose, but how you play the game,' haven't you?" J Dub asked.

Lew nodded and said, "Then it might not be right for me."

J Dub found the answer to be very curious. "Why is that?"

"I could care less how I play the game. I play to win, period," Lew stipulated.

"Then maybe golf isn't suited for you," J Dub said. "It's a gentleman's game."

"What the hell is that?" Lew laughed.

"It's a sport that requires a lot of principles in life like honesty, integrity, and respect. That's not to mention politeness and patience," J Dub replied.

"You don't need to preach that crap to me, kid," Lew stated adamantly.

J Dub was getting aggravated. "Then you really don't want to learn how to play, do you?"

"Sure I do. Get me set up with some clubs, a bucket, and a few lessons," Lew insisted.

J Dub glanced at the pair of boots that Lew was wearing. "You could use a pair of golf shoes, too," he quipped.

Lew looked down at his work boots and agreed, "Those, too."

"Got time to practice?" J Dub probed.

"Who's got time for that?" Lew asked. "I just bought a golf course. I told you that I play to win. I need a cram course in how to play so that I can be the best player on my own place."

J Dub forced a laugh at the ridiculousness of the situation. "Life hasn't thrown you any three putts?"

Lew was getting tired of J Dub's questions. "Look, kid. I never lose. In any deal that I make I come out on the winning side. Let's keep it plain and simple. Teach me how to play the game," Lew insisted.

"If you're willing, then maybe I can help out."

"In more ways than one, I hope," Lew mumbled under his breath.

"What's that supposed to mean?" J Dub asked.

"Would you rather be in a sand trap or the fairway?"

"Either one is better than a divot," J Dub joked.

Lew was puzzled by that comment.

J Dub brushed it off and said, "Never mind."

Lew didn't want J Dub to know that he had read the article in the newspaper and had realized what the reference meant all along. "It may have been the best thing to ever happen to you," Lew proposed.

"Why do you say that?"

Lew was a master of catching people off-guard and switching them to his way of thinking. "You know, you might be just the kind of guy I need," he thought out loud.

"Good. I told you I'd give you lessons," J Dub maintained.

"No. No. I told you I would get to the reason I am here from Illinois."

J Dub was puzzled. "Why?"

"You can tell I don't know much about golf," Lew admitted.

"No kidding."

"How long have you been here?"

"A few months I guess," J Dub responded.

"You seem to work well with people."

J Dub was intrigued by the direction of the conversation. "I try."

"Is this what you want to do the rest of your life?" Lew inquired.

"Not really. It's just a place to park myself until my next opportunity comes along. At least I can still practice my game down here. It beats the cold back home at this time of the year," J Dub rationalized.

"Would you want to help me out with more than just lessons?" Lew asked.

"What did you have in mind?"

"Like I said, I just bought this golf course," Lew explained.

"Okay. Good for you."

"I need somebody that knows what they're doing to run it," Lew continued.

The very thought piqued the interest of J Dub. However, he was in no mood to give away his services. "What's in it for me?"

"I need someone that's honest with the cash." Lew's paranoia seemed to always be centered on money.

"Why is that . . . so you can sleep at night?" J Dub pried.

Lew nodded his head. "I won't tolerate somebody ripping me off," Lew maintained.

"That's one thing my folks taught me not to do."

"Good. That's real important to me."

J Dub looked Lew in the eye. He sincerely wanted to get away from the driving range and hoped that a head pro job would open up at a nearby course. "What did you have in mind?"

"The word on the street is that a very talented, hot-shot golfer is looking for a head pro job," Lew confided.

"I've got a few resumes and a couple of applications out there," J Dub admitted.

"So I've heard. I'm thinking that you can move back to Illinois and be my partner. That way you won't steal," Lew suggested.

J Dub's interest had turned genuine. The very mention of becoming a partner in a golf course operation stirred his juices a little.

"You can come in, get a little slice of the pie, run the place for a few years. When it's time for me to move on, I'll sell the place to you," Lew proposed.

"Then put it in writing," J Dub demanded without blinking.

"You'd be interested?"

"Golf is all I know. Of course I'm interested. But I'm also a married man. I have to run all of this by my wife," J Dub clarified.

They studied each other carefully. "It would be a great opportunity for you two," Lew insisted.

"I want to stay in golf and the tour is out for now. This place isn't where I want to park myself for very long," J Dub confessed. "There is more to life than giving lessons as a teaching pro at a driving range."

Lew dropped a token into the ball dispenser. He had forgotten to place a bucket under the machine. Golf balls bounced throughout the trailer. J Dub turned to Lew in disbelief. *What kind of an idiot am I getting involved with?*

"Ahhhh . . . forget the lessons for now. We have more important stuff to discuss," Lew concluded.

CHAPTER TWELVE

Over and over, J Dub's mind was playing the scenario of moving to Illinois and becoming a partner in a golf course property. It was easy to get lost in thought when he grilled. His eyes squinted as the billows of charcoaled smoke chased him from one part of the grill to the other as he plopped the patties of hamburger meat on their raw sides. J Dub had to admit to himself that the one thing that he really liked to do was barbecue on the outside grill. He had fashioned a nice sized pit out of an old thirty-gallon drum of oil. It didn't matter if it was hamburgers or pork steaks, chicken breasts or filets, J Dub could cook. Plus, it seemed that everything tasted that much better if he kept his throat moist with a generous swallow of beer now and then.

There was just something missing at the trailer park. And that was called atmosphere. Dirty little kids were playing in the dust. Clothes would flap in the breeze off a line strung between trees. Puddles of water from the frequent rain showers of southeast Texas would sit for weeks and act as a breeding ground for mosquitoes. Even the community mail box was constantly vandalized. J Dub looked around taking the scenery in, hoping that it would be the last bit of "Humble" pie he would have to eat for awhile.

As he flipped the burgers that evening, Marcia came out of the trailer to bring J Dub a beer. She swatted flies with a fly swatter on the way to her husband.

It was hot and humid, even as dusk was overtaking the huge Texas sky. Both glistened with sweat as they silently prayed for the slightest breeze to blow, which never came. She yelled her mosquito fatality count to no one in particular, "One down, a few thousand to go." The fly swatter had been discarded rapidly after a couple of misses. A rolled-up newspaper seemed to be much more effective and covered more ground.

J Dub snickered. "Go get some dog crap and maybe you can get ten or twenty at a time."

"Is it hot, or what?" she asked as she wiped the perspiration off of her brow.

"Maybe we can get out of here pretty soon," J Dub said.

"That went out the door when you didn't take the nine-iron."

"You won't let that go away, will you?" he said with a smile.

Marcia walked over to kiss him. Affectionately she said, "It was your dumbass decision. What were you thinking about?" She had hoped to impress upon him the fact that stubbornness can be a detriment as well as an asset.

J Dub grinned and shook his head in dismay. He changed the subject as quickly as he could. "I had a bit of a surprise today," J Dub mentioned.

"A golfer came by to hit balls?" Marcia asked sarcastically.

He smiled at her. "We had a few."

J Dub watched his wife swing the rolled-up newspaper at another pest. "Well, are you going to tell me?" Marcia asked.

" . . . About what?"

"The surprise you had today!" Her temper easily flared in this miserable weather.

"Oh. Yeah. It was the weirdest thing," J Dub started the story when a mosquito landed on the back of his neck and took a blood-thirsty gulp. The smack of his hand behind his ear clapped across the lot. "Let's get inside so all of these insects won't eat us to death, Marcia," J Dub stated as he smiled over his shoulder at his wife. She was swinging the newspaper rapidly and wildly. J Dub took the burgers off of the grill and they entered the trailer.

They crammed around the undersized breakfast table. Marcia had thrown a vinyl, red-and-white checked table cloth on it. It looked like something from the truck stop where J Dub had been working nights. Pork and beans, potato salad, and sliced tomatoes were Marcia's treat for the two of them this evening. J Dub made sure that he squirted a generous supply of ketchup on his hamburger.

"So tell me what happened today, J Dub," Marcia said.

"It was nuts . . . just a bad day all around. Nothing was going right. And then this guy dressed in work clothes and driving a beat-up station wagon came in," J Dub volunteered in between bites of food.

"Probably to tell you that you just won the lottery?" asked Marcia, tongue-in-cheek.

"No. He started talking about winning this and winning that and how much of a big shot he was. Then he wanted me to give him lessons," J Dub explained. "He looked like a clown . . . right out of the old jeans and tennis shoes crowd."

J Dub chuckled to no one in particular. It had been a standard joke in their family that the guys that didn't know anything about the etiquette of golf always showed up at the golf course dressed in jeans and tennis shoes. "This guy didn't have a clue about golf. He didn't know a three-wood from an eight-iron, let alone a Top-Flite from a Titleist."

Marcia was growing impatient with the golfisms and finally asked, "So what happened?"

"I started talking about the principles of the game and how they applied to life . . . just the general philosophy stuff. Then he said he didn't care about any of that because he didn't play by the rules anyway," J Dub revealed.

Marcia inquired, "Did you send him packing?"

"No. He's in a little bit of a jam. He really needs some help," J Dub went on to explain.

"Tell him the psych ward is in the next county," Marcia countered. She continued eating her tomatoes and potato salad but something in her gut told her this guy was a whacko.

J Dub carried on. "He goes on to say that he just bought this golf course and he doesn't know a thing about golf. He watched me taking care of a customer and thought that I was being real helpful. Then he said that he was interested in getting a guy over at his place that wouldn't steal from him. He wanted to know if I would be interested in being his business partner in this golf course that he was buying."

"How ridiculous is that?" Marcia exclaimed. "Going into the golf business and not knowing a thing about it. And why would he make a comment like that about 'not stealing' from him? C'mon, J Dub . . . use your head. Why would he drive down from Illinois to ask YOU to be his partner? I mean, I love you and all that, but c'mon, he must be nuts."

"I thought so too, but he wants to know if I'd be willing to give it some consideration. He wants me up there in two weeks," J Dub halfway grinned. "I'm thinking real seriously about it."

Marcia came unglued. "What? Don't you think you're rushing into this? Did you even get his name?"

"Yeah, I've got all that stuff."

"Then you better call Curt," Marcia advised, knowing full well that J Dub's older brother would help. "Let him check the guy out. He can make some phone calls and do some checks on him. I'm not convinced about this guy from what you've told me." She stared at her husband in disbelief, but could see the hope in his eyes. Marcia backpedaled a little and relented, "We'll want to make sure that we're protected if that is what you want to do."

"Anything that Curt can dig up on him would be great," J Dub said to his doubting wife.

Marcia butted in. "I told you. This guy sounds like a whacko!! We'll need more than a few checks that Curt can make." She was extremely skeptical as she placed a slice of tomato in her mouth. She read her husband's face as she chewed her food. "Are you crazy? If you go into business with the guy, then we'll have to think about sending *you* to some nut house."

J Dub took a bite from his burger. "Maybe this is the opportunity that we've been waiting for," he reasoned as a huge glob of ketchup splattered on his plate.

"Are you going to give up your dream?" Marcia asked in reference to J Dub's dream of playing on the PGA tour.

"You know, Hon, we've got some applications out there." J Dub's rational side was hard at work. "The guy must have talked to some of the local guys in the St. Louis area and went about finding me. I'm torn . . . but we're going to have one more mouth to feed around here pretty soon and have you looked at where we're living? This isn't exactly how I pictured things as we bring a baby into our lives." J Dub's jaw began twitching as the frustration consumed him. "It's just happening so quickly. I mean, why me, of all people?" He swallowed a spoonful of pork and beans and chased it with a generous helping of potato salad. "Sometimes life works like that. If nothing else, I'll be doing what I love to do."

"I don't know. We've had too many changes around here lately. I don't know if I can go through all this in my condition. I don't want to move right now," Marcia cried as if the trailer park was the real solution to their housing needs.

"If it's not us, it will be somebody else," J Dub replied. "Besides, I want to get the heck out of this hole that we're in."

"It sounds too good to be true," Marcia stated as she chastised herself silently for sounding so vulnerable. She hated feeling this way; she liked to be in the driver's seat.

J Dub wanted to make the move. His efforts were geared toward swaying his life-partner to agree. "It won't be much different than the range. He wants me to watch the register."

"That means your weekends will be gone," Marcia whined.

J Dub nodded. "But that would have been the case if I made the tour."

"There's a big difference between a pro running a golf shop and a professional on tour and you know it," Marcia complained.

J Dub knew where Marcia was headed with that comment. "You mean money-wise?"

Marcia nodded her head. Not that she was money-hungry, but having some money would eliminate a lot of their worries. It would provide some stability and peace of mind for both of them.

"At least we won't have to travel from stop to stop. We can stay put for awhile," J Dub offered.

"But your dream was my dream," Marcia pleaded.

"We'll just have to put it on hold for a little while," J Dub stated. He was clearly faced with a life-changing decision. After he took a final swig of beer he crushed the can. "You know, from a business standpoint and a real estate perspective, it might be a decent move. Let's make sure that there is a buy/sell agreement and a partnership arrangement that is spelled out. I want to look at the contract and all the other documents beforehand."

"I don't know if this is the right time to walk eighteen holes in a thunderstorm with a stranger," Marcia added.

"Let's put the tour on hold," J Dub rationalized. "There is supposed to be a driving range at the course. I can still practice there," J Dub said. He was more than willing to move down a different road in life. His own eagerness even surprised him. Things weren't adding up, but he felt like he needed to strike while the iron was hot.

"I want more details. I'm leery about jumping into this too quickly. I want to see the contract, any agreements, what he wants out of you, as well as what your hours are going to be," Marcia demanded.

"We'll get some help with that. Between your dad and Curt, we'll get the right advice. This could be the deal of a lifetime," J Dub suggested. He looked deeply into the eyes of his wife. "Marcia, you always said that when one door closes another one opens up." He paused to reflect on what he had just said. "Maybe this is it."

Marcia was less than thrilled. "I wish you'd have taken the nine-iron."

CHAPTER THIRTEEN

First week of February, 1984 . . .

George, Walter, and Lew sat in the conference room of FARMBELT ABSTRACT & TITLE COMPANY. Doughnuts and a pot of coffee were readily available to extend hospitality toward the guests. For the health-conscious customers low fat cookies and hot chocolate were on hand also. Walter had placed himself in a very compromising situation and was more than a little fidgety on this specific morning.

"Can we get this thing closed today?" Lew asked as he jammed half of a doughnut into his mouth.

George slid a contract in Lew's direction. "Here's the contract for the sale of the golf course from the Morton Estate to Lew Zerrmann. The signature on the power of attorney form is a perfect match," George explained.

Walter chimed in with a slick grin. "It comes with a very favorable price. You can put my tip in a briefcase and leave it on the back porch." He wanted to emphasize that his conciliatory negotiation had come with a hefty cost.

Lew nodded his head in agreement. He forced a sly, devilish grin and then raised a question. "How's it going to come down?"

Walter replied, "What we've done is have the estate enter into an owner-financing agreement with you, Lew." Walter shoved the loan papers toward Lew.

George added, "We'll wait until you've been up and operating for a year and can qualify for a bank loan. Then we'll take the funds from the bank and disburse them."

"I'll show that the property assets are going away on the books and it will become a note receivable," Walter made clear.

George slid another document toward Lew. "Here's the legal description and survey of the property."

"Good. That gives us time to incorporate the business," Lew said as he examined the documents, knowing that the incorporation would protect him personally from his business.

"It can't get any easier than that," Walter stated. "Is everybody happy?"

George and Lew shook their heads with approval. Both flashed a sinister smirk at each other.

"They got copies of everything two days ago, right?" Lew asked.

George and Walter both nodded.

"They should be here any minute. I hope that everything was to their satisfaction. I need somebody that knows what they're doing to run the place," Lew said.

Meanwhile at Curt Schroeder's office . . .

Curt did the best he could to check out all there was to know about Lew Zerrmann. He made a few phones calls and nothing seemed to indicate that the guy was not on the up-and-up. The one thing that seemed like a positive at the time was that Lew had a fondness for real estate and his most recent acquisition was thirty miles from Curt's office.

Curt was older than J Dub by a couple of years. He wasn't anything special, but J Dub worshiped his older brother. Curt would blaze the trail and J Dub would follow. Curt had been a fair athlete in his own right while the two boys had been growing up. Since their dad had been a basketball and golf coach, athletics and the lessons that could be derived from sports had been instilled in them at an early age. Curt concentrated on baseball and football, but didn't quite have the size, commitment, or talent to take it to the next level. After Curt graduated from high school he watched as his little brother led the golf team to three straight State championships.

When J Dub chased his dream of playing on the PGA tour, Curt was busy getting his real estate license. He later got involved in banking and commercial lending. No matter where their path in life was headed, their dad made sure they applied the lessons they had learned on the athletic field. However, there comes a time when every little boy has to give up his dream and go to work in the real world. Curt had chosen real estate and lending; J Dub was at a crossroads.

Marcia had taken all of the paperwork to her father's lawyer and everything checked out. Actually, the buy/sell agreement between the parties was very fair. There were provisions that covered many situations. A formula for establishing value was spelled out.

Lew was the majority stockholder in the corporation and J Dub was the minority stockholder in the corporation. It was agreed that the two parties would operate under an 80/20 split. It was a fabulous opportunity for J Dub to build the business and ultimately buy the business once Lew decided that he wanted to sell it.

On the road from Texas . . .

It was a bright, sunny, crisp morning as J Dub completed the last leg of his journey from Humble, Texas with a U-Haul in tow. Marcia did all that her condition would allow her to. Days earlier she put a lot of the little things in boxes while J Dub and an acquaintance had cleaned out the double-wide and loaded the few possessions that J Dub and Marcia had into the U-Haul.

"I hope that everything works out okay. We don't know this guy at all," J Dub said in an excited, but anxious way.

"If he turns out to be a jerk, then you can always get out of the deal. Just keep hitting balls," Marcia deadpanned.

J Dub grinned from ear to ear. If there was anything he loved to do, it was pounding ball after ball on the driving range. "There's no problem with that. I just hope that we're not walking into something that doesn't make any sense," J Dub stated with caution as if to reinforce his major decision. Marcia's anxiety seemed to grow with each passing mile marker. "Okay, honey. Try to force a little smile," J Dub said. He grinned at his wife across the car seat.

Marcia was clearly apprehensive. "I'll be really pissed off if he screws us."

"Let's go full force through that open door and make the best of it," J Dub said. He clamored with excitement. He had flown up, met Curt, and had driven to see the place a week earlier. They felt that even though the course was run-down and the clubhouse was in need of repair, a wonderful business opportunity existed for J Dub and his family. It seemed that for the first time in a long time, things were turning around.

J Dub and Marcia went down the road and traveled to the banks of the Mississippi River. The directions to the title company were perfect. The young couple had a budding business opportunity awaiting their arrival. In short order, J Dub and Marcia parked their U-Haul in front of FARMBELT ABSTRACT & TITLE COMPANY.

The office of the title company was located in an older home near the business district of town. It appeared that it had been someone's residence at one time, but had been converted into a business as the town expanded.

J Dub and Marcia entered the door. Both of them were apprehensive about the sudden turn of events. J Dub's adrenalin was overflowing. Marcia's skepticism was presented as a nervous mother-to-be.

With the energy and chirpiness of a baby robin going after a worm, Mary Jean greeted them. "Good morning! You must be the Schroeder's."

"We're here for a closing," J Dub mumbled as his stomach began to tie in knots.

Marcia looked around and checked out every little nook and cranny of the place. She eyed some artificial plants and whispered to J Dub, "Even the plants are fake."

"Just relax. Everything will be fine."

"Gag me," Marcia said.

"Don't let Lew hear that. We don't even know the guy. It might turn him on." J Dub returned the deadpan expression and gave her a lightning-fast wink.

Mary Jean made an offer. "Can I get either of you any coffee or doughnuts?"

They declined. "We had something on the way," Marcia answered.

"Where did you come in from?" Mary Jean probed.

"All the way from Texas," J Dub responded. "It's been like a tornado the last couple of weeks."

Mary Jean beamed. Her enthusiasm was infectious. "Are you excited?"

"Why sure. This is a big deal for us," replied J Dub as he began to loosen up a little.

Mary Jean noticed the advanced stage of Marcia's pregnancy. "When are you due?"

"I still have a few more weeks."

George popped his head around the door. The minute his eyes hit Marcia's, she felt something was wrong. He had that look about him that signaled that his intentions were for him and not them. "Hi, I'm George Pierce. Come on into the conference room."

He extended his hand to J Dub and they exchanged pleasantries. Marcia nudged J Dub from behind and shook her head no to warn him. He looked a little perturbed. J Dub was concerned by the cold feet that Marcia was experiencing. He jerked his head toward the conference room, gave her a frustrated look, and followed George.

As they entered the conference room, Lew stood up and eyed Marcia. "J Dub was right! Wowee! He said you'd be my best daughter-in-law!"

Marcia forced a grin and patted her belly. She turned to J Dub and in a condescending tone asked, "Have you already picked the godfather, too? My, what a lucky girl I am." The whole process had been moving too quickly for her satisfaction.

J Dub made light of the situation and covered for his wife. "This pregnancy thing has her worked up a little." Marcia shot J Dub a dirty look and forced a smirk for the group.

Forced laughter filled the room.

"I guess we're all stuck together for a while," Marcia conceded.

Lew was ready to get down to business. He grabbed a chair and sat down. "J Dub. Marcia. Are you two youngsters ready to make your first million?" Lew cried.

Marcia was cynical. "I'll believe that when I see it."

Lew continued, "This is an opportunity of a lifetime for you two."

J Dub replied, "We couldn't be any happier." As he mockingly smiled at his wife, Marcia turned to glare at her husband.

Lew was oblivious to the banter that the young couple had exchanged. His mind was focused on closing on the property as quickly as he could. "You've met George. He owns the title company and is doing the closing for us. Walter Hancock will be our accountant, J Dub."

Walter stood to shake hands with the young couple. "This transaction will be beneficial to a lot of parties."

Lew shoved a document toward J Dub. "We've got some paper work to take care of. This is a partnership agreement that I had my lawyer draw up."

"Can we look at it?" Marcia asked.

"It's just simple, basic stuff. It's easy to understand. It's the same document that you got for review a couple of days ago," Lew countered matter-of-factly. He wanted to get the formalities out of the way.

"I just want to make sure," Marcia replied with a hint of aggravation. She took copies of the document out of a manila envelope and compared the verbiage. J Dub and Marcia flipped through the pages.

"Here's the contract with the seller, and the financing agreement, and the legal description of the property as well as the survey," Lew hurried. "George did the closing statement."

George and Lew pushed several documents toward J Dub and Marcia. They flipped through the pages. Once they were satisfied that all the documents were the same as what they had reviewed they wrote their signatures.

"Now we've run all of this by our lawyer. If he suggests any changes at a later date, then there won't be a problem?" declared Marcia.

" . . . Absolutely. No problem. We can always amend," replied Lew. He stood and extended his hand. "Congratulations! Let's go look at the place!"

J Dub turned to Marcia. "It's probably not a bad idea to go look at whatever we just paid a million bucks for." As crazy as it sounded, even though J Dub and Curt had driven by the place and given it their blessing, Marcia had never seen the property.

Marcia mocked him more than ever. "You got that right. I've witnessed my share of dumbass moves over the last few months."

Chapter Fourteen

Crazy things happen in life. The last few weeks had provided a roller coaster of emotions for J Dub and Marcia. It started with the highs and lows of that fateful day on the golf course during the qualifying tournament which morphed into the opportunity to become self-employed.

But to go into business with a total stranger and buy something for a million bucks, sight unseen, was going over the top. Now, Marcia was about to crawl into a banged-up station wagon that had a wrecked front-end just weeks before delivering a child.

As luck would have it, the trip to the course was short and uneventful.

Lew pulled the car around the corner and they entered the parking lot. A broken-down sign propped against the base of a tree read: PRAIRIE WINDS GOLF COURSE. The sign looked weathered. It appeared as if the previous management group had let the maintenance on the grounds slide.

At first glance, the place was a disaster. Weeds were everywhere. The parking lot was a mixture of pot holes, gravel, and torn-up asphalt. The cart barn needed to be painted and had a loose door flapping in the wind.

The telltale sign of trouble ahead was in the first glimpse of the clubhouse. Shingles were falling off of the roof. A wrought-iron railing was loose. The guttering was detached. An upstairs window was broken and served as a nesting spot for as many sparrows as the eye could count.

It looked like the two-story frame home was built during the Depression. The balcony in the rear had a broken support beam and was falling down. A large crack in the foundation allowed a view of the lower level. A pump for a water-well was just yards from the front door.

"Welcome to your new home, J Dub," Lew crowed.

Marcia was disgusted. "I thought you said we were going to live the country club life," she barked to Lew. She didn't know if she felt like puking or smacking J Dub into next week for rushing into this deal. But then again, she didn't exactly stop him as she cursed her own naiveté.

"It needs a little work," Lew said sheepishly.

"As in a couple of million bucks," replied Marcia as she cursed silently to herself.

"Calm down, Honey. The golfers spend most of their time out on the course. We'll spit-shine the place," J Dub said as he tried to console his wife.

"Have at it. I'll be nursing."

"Now calm down you cute little thing," Lew stated in as comforting of a tone as he could muster. He took the opportunity to pat her belly and flashed a devilish grin.

"Hey. Keep your hands to yourself. That's off limits," J Dub said as he scolded Lew.

Lew was startled that J Dub would react that way. He couldn't blame the young husband for being protective of his very-pregnant wife. "Sorry. That was completely out of line." He could tell the young couple was completely overwhelmed from the closing and seeing the place in shambles.

Marcia glared at him. "I'll say it was."

J Dub changed the tone of the first visit and said, "What kind of shape is the course in?"

"We can hop on a truck and go see," Lew answered.

"Does the equipment work?"

"Heck if I know," Lew replied.

"We need to check that out and see if the carts are charged."

Lew was in love with the land deal and was ignorant to all of the other details that went into running a golf course. "Make the golfers walk," he demanded.

J Dub was mildly offended and aggravated by the gullibility of the statement. "You can't do that! If we open up and aren't ready to service the public, then they'll never be back."

"Throw down some fertilizer and cut the grass . . . that's all they need," Lew said.

J Dub's ire was on the rise. "There's a lot more to it than that. We'll need water and good greens mowers and cart paths."

"That's not to mention a new clubhouse," chimed Marcia.

"Let's not spend the money before we get it," stated Lew.

"If we don't get this place in a lot better shape, then there won't be any money to spend," cried J Dub. He wasn't too concerned about the clubhouse and parking lot. What mattered most to the golfers was the layout of the golf course and the condition of the fairways and greens. He had heard that it was an enjoyable course to play.

A stray bull terrier puppy sauntered up the road and across the parking lot. The dog's fur was matted down. It appeared that it had missed several meals. Its tongue was sticking out and the dog was panting heavily from the walk up the hill. Upon seeing J Dub, Marcia, and Lew the wag of the tail went on overload.

" . . . Lookee there! Our first customer," shouted J Dub. J Dub coaxed the puppy over to the group. The dog was in need of a drink of water and some serious tender, loving care. *This dog is in about as good a shape as this golf course*, thought J Dub as he obligingly scratched behind his ears.

Lew grabbed a blanket out of the back of the station wagon. "Let's roll out the red carpet."

J Dub responded, "He's not quite par for the course. So we've got our first Bogey." With that statement, a name was born.

Marcia, J Dub, and Lew prepared a bed for Bogey in the cart barn. They poured a bowl of water for him. Bogey took to J Dub like they were long-lost friends. Bogey vigorously licked J Dub's face. He rolled over on his back so that J Dub could scratch his distended belly.

Bogey had beautiful markings. The bridge of his snout had a patch of white. Even one eye was surrounded by light-colored fur. His shoulders were firm. His chest was solid. His paws indicated that he would be adequately able to support an above average amount of weight. It was apparent that when he filled out and reached maturity he would be a strong dog.

Marcia could see how happy her husband had become. She knew that he needed this change and offered up words of encouragement. "It looks to me like there is only one way to go . . . and that's up. I guess the future is bright after all."

"We'll have this place up and running in no time," replied J Dub. Bogey lapped at his face.

"I just hope that you two can get along. There's going to be plenty to do," Marcia conceded.

CHAPTER FIFTEEN

It has often been said that one of the best ways to get to know someone is to marry them. One thing was certain—J Dub and Lew were married to each other, in business anyway.

Another thing was certain. J Dub knew who he was. His intent was to take the principles of golf that his dad had taught him such as honesty, integrity, patience, respect, and apply them in business to his partner and the customers. His view of the business was long term.

Lew, on the other hand . . .

. . . Well, let's just say that every book has a story. Lew had his story and was sticking to it.

Even though the place needed a lot of work, J Dub saw tons of potential. He was excited for the chance to be self-employed and he was up to the challenge of fixing the place up and attracting customers. Lew had told him that one of the reasons that they had gotten such a good deal on the purchase of the golf course was because of its deteriorating condition.

Of all of the personal property items that came with the course, the item that J Dub had an eye on the most was an old, Ford pickup truck. Anxious to appease his new partner, Lew instantly made the decision to give the truck to J Dub. It leaked a quart of oil every couple of days, but it was transportation that helped J Dub get from his new apartment to the course and not much else.

J Dub's adrenalin level was overflowing, so there was no problem for him to get up at 4:45 in the morning and be at the course before daybreak. Solitude can accompany those moments right before sunrise and offer some of the most joyous and memorable minutes of the day. At that time of the morning, J Dub always had a "best friend" that was happy to see him.

The first morning on the job, J Dub pulled the battered pickup onto the lot and parked it next to the cart barn. He instinctively unlocked the cart barn and Bogey greeted him with a jump in the air and a wagging tail. It's always healthy to know that someone loves you.

J Dub picked him up and hugged him. Bogey rolled over onto his back for J Dub. That was a clear indication that he wanted his belly scratched. The dog would constantly wag its tail and have the energy of a litter of puppies. J Dub regularly made sure that there was plenty of food and water in Bogey's bowls. For a stray that staggered onto the parking lot, Bogey had turned himself into a country clubber.

If J Dub walked into the pro shop, then Bogey was on his heels. If J Dub pulled carts out of the barn, then Bogey was on the seat beside him. If J Dub went to the driving range to hit balls, then Bogey would accompany him and watch. Bogey might as well have been J Dub's shadow. They fell in love with each other.

It became obvious from the first day or so that the place to be at sunrise was the pro shop. A large picture window provided a good look at twelve of the holes on the course. The clubhouse sat on a small rise above most of the course. J Dub could pretty much see all of the activity on the golf course just by looking out of the picture window.

More importantly, however, was the beautiful view to the East that the picture window provided. Looking out that window provided a gorgeous view of the expansive irrigation lake on the golf course. Behind the lake was a tree line. Every clear morning, the orange sun would peek out above the tree line and cast its beauty over the lake.

In the early morning there were long shadows. Fog would sit atop the water. The wispy clouds would quickly burn off under the heat of the sun. On most mornings Mother Nature would provide, at no charge, a priceless moment to jumpstart the heart.

The shooting pulsations of water from the sprinklers would glisten in the morning sun. Deer would graze near the banks of the lake and could be seen through the misty haze at daybreak. Honking geese would signal their arrival and land on the water. The rabbits and squirrels would dart through the underbrush. The robins would circle for their daily meal.

Even the man-made machinery took on a beauty of its own. At that time of day the golf course maintenance people could often times be seen riding a smoke-spewing tractor as they cut the grass on the greens or manicured the fairways.

J Dub never had a problem getting his butt up and out of bed. He enjoyed the early-morning moments with Bogey as well as a cup of coffee. The orange reflection of the sun shining across the lake at sunrise was enough to energize the dead.

The entire facility needed a complete overhaul in the first few days of operation. The pro shop had a counter that doubled as a sign-in area and a bar top. Whoever worked the cash register was also responsible for serving drinks and snacks to the paying public. On the busier days two people were needed to work the counter.

The beer cooler needed to be cleaned out and recharged with Freon. The beer taps had to be sterilized and brought up to code. The refrigerator needed a thorough scrubbing. Even the hot dog roller grill required some minor service.

J Dub quickly put his personal thumbprint on the office located off to the side of the pro shop counter. He brought in quite a few boxes that contained plaques and trophies that he had won in various events as well as assorted memorabilia that had accumulated over the years. The trophies went in the bookshelves. The plaques went on the wall. Personal pictures went on his desk. There was even a framed newspaper headline that read: J. W. SCHROEDER FALLS ONE SHOT SHORT. It found its place on the wall behind his desk.

It took J Dub a few days to get everything moved into the office. Running a golf course operation wasn't what he had dreamed of as a kid, but it wasn't a bad thing either. He had an opportunity to remain involved in golf. Plus he had a tremendous chance to set his family up for life.

One of the first things that Lew insisted on doing was hiring a bookkeeper. They interviewed several younger ladies due to Lew's penchant for females. Although he wasn't necessarily the apple in every woman's eye, Lew did like to have them around.

They settled on a gal named Julie. She was right out of junior college and from the surrounding area. Julie had recently turned twenty-one. The great thing about her was that she wasn't over-qualified for the position. By completing two years of junior college, she had qualities that both Lew and J Dub thought were admirable. However, Julie didn't have the full college credentials that would lead to raises and a job promotion.

Julie was quite a catch. They both felt that she would fit in very well with a predominantly male customer base. She was feisty and assertive. Her quick wit reflected her Midwestern roots. Not only would she be able to manage the books and pay the bills, but she would be able to help J Dub work the counter in the pro shop. It would be a Monday through Friday type of position which allowed for her to have her weekends free.

Lew and J Dub thought that Julie would be a perfect fit. It had been encouraging for both of them to sit down and discuss the various applicants. After talking about the pros and cons they mutually decided on Julie and she was hired.

In one of those first few days that the golf operation was open for business, Lew stopped in early. If he wasn't eager to start the improvements, he at least feigned excitement. "Where should we start, J Dub? This looks like it could keep both of us busy for quite a while."

"Golfers are here to golf, Lew. We need to get the course fixed up."

"Then let's get out there."

"Can you handle the register, Julie?" J Dub asked.

Julie smiled. "I'm sure that I can manage, but replacing you is asking a lot. Lew speaks so highly of you," Julie said as if she had practiced her politics. There was no doubt that she wanted to get off on the right foot with the guy that she would be working with on a daily basis, but at the same time refrain from "kissing up to him" right off the bat.

In a similar fashion, J Dub wanted to score some points with Lew. "Winners say the right things, Julie." Lew gushed with contentment. In those first few days it sure looked like everyone was going to enjoy working with each other.

It was off to the golf course during those first days for Lew and J Dub. One of the first projects that the two of them embarked on was erecting a fence. J Dub quickly found out that Lew was an excellent supervisor. He would sit in his pickup truck, listen to country and western tunes, and make sure that the temperature control button functioned properly as J Dub worked his backside off.

J Dub got to where he could operate a post-hole digger pretty well. The two of them found out that if J Dub dug the hole, then Lew would help get the post anchored. It was going to be back breaking work for J Dub, but he was the more youthful and energetic of the pair. Together they would string the length of fence.

With work that needed to be done on the greens and the tee boxes, J Dub thought that putting up a fence was far down the priority list. After several days of digging in the hard soil and wearing out a pair of gloves J Dub turned to his partner. "Why is it so important to get this fence up right away?" he asked.

"We need to mark our territory," Lew responded.

"It's a golf course. All we need to do is put out-of-bounds markers up."

"I don't want the golfers getting into the neighbor's crops," Lew replied. The boundary of the golf course was surrounded on three sides by farm fields. The neighboring farmers had planted either wheat, soybeans, or corn.

"We can put up a sign telling the golfers that the farm field is private property."

Lew was adamant about what he wanted. "I want the fence up to protect our land."

"What do mean by that? It's only a field of grass."

"In case there is any dispute, we'll be able to win in court," Lew answered.

That's an odd response J Dub thought. He didn't want to jeopardize the relationship that was in its infancy. It wasn't too long after that and the fence line was installed. After the fence was completed Lew admired the work that was completed. "We did a good job, J Dub." Lew was quick to take credit for most of the work that J Dub did.

"Now I want you to get these in the ground too." Lew reached into the back of the pickup truck and handed J Dub numerous signs that read: NO TRESPASSING, NO HUNTING, NO SWIMMING, NO FISHING, NO UNAUTHORIZED PEOPLE, and NO CONCEALED WEAPONS.

"And make sure that this one gets put up by the pro shop." Lew handed J Dub a sign that read: NO BEER (unless bought in the pro shop)

"We don't need to put all of these signs up out here. This is a golf course," J Dub countered.

"We need the people to know that it is ours and that we make the rules," Lew insisted.

"Do you think that we're going to have convicted felons on a daily basis and regular turkey shoots?" J Dub thought that a facetious response might drive home a point.

"Just do as I say," Lew stated stubbornly.

J Dub sarcastically threw out another idea. "Let's be sure to get one more sign made."

"Did I forget one?"

"Yeah, you did. Where is the one that says that no whizzing in the woods is allowed?"

J Dub was at a loss for what to do. He was becoming extremely frustrated with Lew and this didn't bode well for a long and prosperous partnership. He got the signs posted around the golf course. It sure didn't look like it was going to be a welcoming site for the golfers, however. Nor did it look like it was going to be a friendly place to visit.

CHAPTER SIXTEEN

It didn't take J Dub very long to network out to the golfers. He got up early and shook as many hands that he could. He made a conscientious effort to be as friendly as possible to everyone that came through the door. In a very short period of time he had gotten a lot of players to feel comfortable. Several of the guys became regulars. Most of them were retired fellows looking for a place to hang out away from home.

On one of those early mornings a warmer-than-usual day in February signaled that spring was right around the corner. J Dub got an unexpected visitor just moments after unlocking the pro shop door and opening up for business.

"I heard that some new ownership had taken over this joint," a gravelly voice announced the instant the door slammed shut.

"We closed on it less than a week ago," J Dub offered. "What can I do for you?"

"My name is Earl. Me and my buddies used to play here all the time until the conditions got so bad, we had to leave."

"We hope to change all of that," J Dub volunteered.

"Good! We always did like the layout," Earl chimed back.

"Do you have some guys that you normally play with?" J Dub pried. He knew that it was vital to cultivate regular business during the weekdays, especially for a public golf course operation.

"I'm sure that I can arrange to get eight or ten guys over here pretty often if you can cut us a deal or two," Earl suggested. All of his golfing partners were on a fixed retirement income and he knew that every little bit helped.

"I'm sure that we can find some nice ways to accommodate a group like that," J Dub countered. "Repeat business is the name of the game."

"Good!" Earl exclaimed. "That's the type of working relationship we'd like to establish. I can get all kinds of players to come back over here."

"Whatever it takes, Earl. We'd love to have you."

"Would you have a part-time job available?" Earl was on a roll and wanted to keep it going. It seemed like the new kid was genuinely sincere.

"Hey, I grew up playing golf. I know how it is. We need to have guys like you around here. And that goes for your buddies, too," J Dub proposed.

A relationship was born. "Easy Earl" was more or less the ringleader or spokesperson for the group. He was in his early-seventies and was an ornery, opinionated son-of-a-gun. Earl was quite a golfer in his heyday and could still shoot his age on most days of the week. He took a liking to J Dub on that very first meeting and insisted that a few of his old-time buddies made it a point to show up at Prairie Winds.

To return the favor, J Dub hired Earl on a part-time basis. It was J Dub's philosophy that the weekends took care of themselves, but the week days were what separated the successful operations from the ones that struggled. So Earl was put behind the counter three days a week for no more than a half day. He was quite a sight behind the counter as he wheeled his oxygen canister with him as he fetched drinks and snacks for customers. It wasn't past Earl to put some time in as a starter on the first tee box on the weekends. When he rode around the course as a marshal he was easy to spot. The guys that hung out in the snack area used to joke that a hair bomb must have blown up from inside Earl judging from the nose, ear and body hair that popped out from every orifice. That, and Earl always carried his fishing poles with him. He would often stop at a lake, throw in a line, and take a break for a half an hour or so.

J Dub knew that thriving public golf course operations couldn't afford to pay much out in salaries. It was far more profitable to hire a retired guy, let him have a little responsibility, and give him free golf. So, Earl was good for business and felt like he was part owner in the joint.

Rollie wasn't quite as old as Earl. He was in his late-sixties. After serving in the war he had come back to operate the family business which was a distributor for electronic parts. When he got to retirement age, he sold the business and settled into his "golden years".

As is true with most guys, there is always something that bugs the daylights out of you. Rollie possessed a few of those traits. During the war he had a mortar explode a few feet from his head. He survived, but lost about ninety percent of the hearing in his left ear.

Over the years that problem developed into a twofold problem. One, he couldn't hear worth a hoot. Two, he never shut up. Rollie would talk incessantly, even when hitting his golf ball. That would drive the guys nuts. And on top of that he was in constant motion. Rollie was the only guy that they knew that could hit a ball and still be walking. "Good for the ticker" he would always say. He was the only guy on the course that wore a sweatshirt every day of the year including summer because he was 'cold'. He was deaf and had heart problems that caused poor circulation in his legs, despite his support hose. Sometimes the guys would call him "Broadway Rollie" referring to Joe Namath's infamous panty hose commercial in the early seventies.

Like Rollie, BT was in his late-sixties. He was a tall, lanky ladies' man. In spite of his awkward body build, he always came to the course in a sleeveless sweater and pressed trousers. He was a neatnik and always looked "prim and proper" as Marcia used to observe. In his younger days, BT played professional baseball but only made it to the higher levels of minor league ball. His big chance came when a player on the major league roster got injured and the club called down to the minors for a replacement. However, BT was hurt at the time so never made it to the big leagues.

He went into education and helped out as an assistant coach in football and baseball. After making a career of that, he retired and existed on a school pension. Everyone at the club knew that BT was as tight as a wound-up rubber band. The guys normally played for quarters and inevitably BT would usually show up with little or no cash in his pocket. One day BT had lost fifty cents and did not have the money to pay off his loss. The guys wouldn't let him leave without settling his debt. So, BT wrote a check for fifty cents just to get out of the clubhouse. From that point on his nickname was "Checkbook."

Fred was a red-necked, red-headed, blue-collar night foreman at the local car manufacturing plant. To say that he was an opinionated, country boy with a flat top wouldn't do him justice. He had a chest that resembled a beer keg and a belly to match. Never in a million years would he be able to wear a button-down shirt. His double chin had turned into a triple chin. His freckles were large and massive and every bit of hair he had was bright orange. His skin by comparison was almost as light as an albino. If he was out in the sun for a period of time, his complexion would turn fire-engine red. Even his eyelashes screamed orange which made his blue eyes appear even more watery and lighter blue.

Everyone knew when Fred was coming. He wouldn't merely walk, he would waddle. The strut he had was to keep his arms from rubbing his body and his legs from chafing together. Fred would occasionally play an even-par round of golf just to prove that golfers come in all shapes and sizes.

Paul was in his mid-sixties. Of all the guys in the group, he commanded the most respect. He had a distinguished look and frequently was referred to as a silver fox. Anyone that needed advice or assistance would get in touch with Paul. He was dependable, honest, and a straight-shooter. He was an ex-military officer and lived off of a sizeable U.S. government pension. Having a military background instilled a sense of order and neatness that affected him to his older age. You could count on Paul to have freshly starched and pressed slacks with a smart looking golf shirt and matching spit-shined golf shoes. J Dub guessed that Paul must have cleaned every spike in his golf shoes each morning to pass an inspection. Hence, Paul was such a perfectionist that he often times bordered on being nauseous. His travels across the states had afforded him the opportunity to hone the skills of his golf game. Paul was a talented golfer that would shoot par golf almost every day. His perfection carried over to his swing and course management.

Elia was Paul's barber. His family had survived the bombings and turmoil in Beirut, and shortly thereafter made the trek to the land of opportunity. No one knew exactly what Elia did. However, he was known for carrying a ton of cash and an electric razor in his bag. Elia complained that no matter how often he shaved, he still had a five o'clock shadow. He called it "The Nixon Curse." Maybe it was his Middle Eastern custom to carry that much cash or maybe he just pocketed the cash from haircuts. No one knew for sure what he did, except he did a lot of shaving.

There were several unusual things that made Elia loveable. He had caught a lot of shrapnel in Beirut as a young adult and when complications set in, a good portion of his colon was removed. On more than one occasion, Elia crapped in his pants out on the course after eating a hot dog at the turn. To complicate matters, he only had one testicle. When he first started to play golf he took a ricochet off of a tee marker at the driving range. The resulting damage to his scrotum necessitated an embarrassing medical procedure.

Paco migrated to the United States from Chihuahua, Mexico. He originally crossed the Rio Grande, got employment, and ultimately obtained U.S. citizenship. Paco was not a stranger to work. He started his own landscaping company and then recruited his brothers, cousins, and nephews to work for him. A huge toothy grin was a regular visitor to his face that accentuated his marble-brown eyes.

Due to his choice of work, Paco was a hearty soul with a strong back. His strength was always a surprise since he was borderline skinny. Paco wore faded jeans and sneakers with a white t-shirt and light blue windbreaker. He also wore a simple gold cross that hung from a short chain around his neck. He could hit the ball a mile and the boys kept asking him back. For an immigrant, Paco caught onto to the American way of life quickly. He blended in well with the boys.

Finally, Curt became an invitee to the group. J Dub told him that there was a pretty good game at the club and that he should make it a point to join in. So, more often than not, Curt started to hang around with the guys, too. They encouraged him to show up for the daily golf games and Curt had a tough time not accepting.

These guys became a fixture at Prairie Winds. You could count on a good portion of them being there every Saturday and Sunday morning as well as several days a week. "The boys" didn't have much to do during the day. They would meet early in the morning, share their coffee and doughnuts, and play a round of golf. Most days they were done with their round by lunchtime. Then they would hang around the clubhouse and play backgammon and gin until it was time for supper.

Chapter Seventeen

March 1984 . . .

The business had only been open for a few weeks. Everything that had been going on between J Dub and Marcia had all been focused on J Dub. It was J Dub trying to get on the PGA tour. It was J Dub buying a golf course and getting into business with a stranger.

Marcia was getting tired of it all. She had been carrying a baby for quite a while and was feeling resentful about not being noticed. Her pregnancy was nearing completion. Her irritability was multiplying by the second.

As they were cleaning up after dinner one night J Dub said, "Lew is some guy. He sure is taking care of us." He was appreciative of the fact that Lew had given him an interest in the business, the old pickup, and a fair amount of responsibility.

Marcia had already grown sick of Lew and her pregnancy wasn't making things exactly easy for her, knowing that J Dub was literally at Lew's disposal. She was in the mood to spar. In mid-thought, she blurted, "That's a bunch of bull. He's taking care of himself."

"He's already talking about the time when . . ."

Marcia interrupted, "Oh, please! Lew is talking about how he has you wrapped around his stubby little thumb." She was still fuming and ready for an argument with J Dub.

J Dub looked at his wife in surprise. "What was *that* all about?"

Marcia furrowed her brow and pointed at her bulging belly with both hands. "*This* is what it's all about, big boy! I am sick of not being able to sit down in a chair like a normal person. I'm disgusted with this continual backache. Why won't *this* nine pounds of baby come out?"

J Dub tried his best to hide his chuckle as he saw his very pregnant wife giving him the mother of all dirty looks. He forced a slight grin as she waddled back and forth throwing silverware into the kitchen drawers and slamming them shut. He could tell she was beyond pissed off. J Dub nervously rubbed the back of his neck. "It shouldn't be much longer, Hon."

As Marcia dried off a spatula she waved it in J Dub's face. "It's been all about you. You try blowing up like a balloon and have a baby kicking your bladder at all hours of the day. Look at this!" She showed him her swollen fingers with her wedding band squeezing her left ring finger.

"It's been a tough stretch for us."

Marcia was offended by his reference. " . . . Us? *Us?* I'm sorry. I don't see you carrying nine pounds of baby! What about me? I have to sleep sitting up! Everything I eat gives me indigestion. There's nothing the doctor can give me to make it any better! This damn heat rash around my waist is killing me. I look like I have baseballs for ankles!"

"What did the pediatrician say?"

"He's said any day for a week."

"Did you tell him how miserable you are?"

Marcia mustered the best exasperated look she could and shot it squarely at her husband. *I know he didn't just ask me that. He must think I'm some ignorant fool!* She fumed. "Yes. Dammit!"

Marcia was getting to the end of the road with her pregnancy. She had been absolutely thrilled to become pregnant. Her two older sisters had already delivered babies and she wanted to experience the same joy that she had heard about. When the news of her pregnancy was announced her mom had been ecstatic. An incredible feeling had overcome Marcia. She was going to experience the same feeling that all of the other females in her family had experienced. In fact, the whole pregnancy had been an incredible occurrence. She had met the right man. Having a baby seemed so right, so good, and so pure.

Perhaps it was a woman's intuition, but Marcia knew that she was pregnant from the moment of conception. She didn't want to believe the intuitive feelings that were prevalent, but deep down inside she knew that she was pregnant. Then, when she had missed her period and the doctor had confirmed the pregnancy, Marcia was not surprised at all. She was calm and thrilled. She felt as if this was the reason she had been placed on earth.

From the moment that Marcia had heard the doctor confirm her pregnancy she felt as if her life had taken on a whole different meaning and magnitude. She had become deliriously happy and excited only to be overcome by anxiety and fear worrying about the health of the unborn child. The pregnancy had filled her with joy and contentment for the most part. She very much wanted to be a mom.

J Dub knew that his wife was tremendously excited about bringing another life into the world. He did not want to see his wife be so uncomfortable and unhappy. "We can have it induced."

"Ya think?" she sarcastically shot back.

"Why sure."

"Well, DUH!" Marcia growled. The shout caused an immediate release of energy. At that instant Marcia felt her water break.

Marcia looked down and saw a huge puddle on the floor as she steadied herself by the counter. "Dammit! I just mopped the floor!" she whined. J Dub grabbed his wife and started walking her to the car.

"It's going to be fine, Marcia. I'll mop the floor later, ok? Let's get you to the car," he soothed. Marcia's hormones were shot. She began to half cry and half whine.

Marcia was leaning heavily on her husband as he grabbed her hospital bag. "J Dub? Do you swear the baby is coming out? Really?" she sniffled.

"With any luck it will come out in the delivery room and not in this truck. Hang on." J Dub and his wife sped off to the hospital leaving a cloud of smoke from the burning oil. The worn out shocks magnified every bump.

J Dub rushed Marcia into the emergency room of the hospital and began to excitedly explain what was happening. A very bored looking nurse seated at the information desk continued reading her latest romance novel. Without looking up she handed J Dub a clipboard of forms to complete. As she droned her instructions he tried to politely interrupt her to get immediate attention for his wife.

"Complete these forms. Please note that pages twelve and thirteen are front and back. It's mandatory to initial and sign on each page."

"Miss? My wife is about to have a baby! I don't have time to complete all these forms. Miss? Did you hear me?" J Dub was starting to get irritated now. He finally saw a couple of nurses walking by and asked them for help.

The nurses wheeled Marcia into the delivery room and gave J Dub some scrubs to change into. J Dub and Marcia were finally in place to have their baby as the doctor instructed Marcia when to push.

"Oh, Marcia! I love you so much, Honey!" J Dub could hardly contain his excitement as he held his wife's hand and coached her on breathing techniques. The anesthesiologist looked at the print out of the machines that were hooked up to Marcia's belly.

"Hang on, Mr. Schroeder, she is about to have a major contraction."

"Why are you telling me, to hang on when my wife . . ." J Dub stopped in mid-sentence, fell to his knees, and screamed in excruciating pain. The anesthesiologist and a nurse jumped to J Dub's aid and helped to pry Marcia's nails from his forearm. Before they knew it, the exhausted couple welcomed their bundle of joy into the world.

~ ~ ~

The birth of a child was a beautiful experience for J Dub. His wife had delivered a gorgeous, healthy, baby girl. They named her Gail. A lot of the emotions that had been flowing through Marcia hit J Dub the minute his first child was born.

From that moment on, life changed for J Dub. Marcia was right. Up until then J Dub's world had been centered on golf and making the tour. Gail changed all of that. She brought a new type of joy to him that could not be put into words.

The first time he held his baby daughter was almost a religious experience. Up until then she had only been connected to Marcia. But now, as he held her, the power of being a part of bringing new life into the world nearly made him collapse. The bond that he felt was incredible and he instantly fell in love with his new daughter.

It was as if the dream of Tour school was a distant memory in the rear view mirror. That vision did not count at all anymore. Now it was all about being a family man and providing the very best that he could for his newborn.

CHAPTER EIGHTEEN

The next day . . .

Bogey jumped into J Dub's arms the minute the cart barn door sprang open. It was as if he knew that J Dub was a new father. J Dub took the pre dawn moment to bond with his energetic little buddy. Things seemed to be perking along fairly well. J Dub and Marcia had completed the move into their apartment. The boxes were unpacked. Now they had a new addition to the dinner table. Life in the Schroeder household was good. And, it was mostly due to their beautiful daughter, Gail. Marcia was more comfortable physically. She was now free to enjoy her one-on-one time with her daughter during the day while J Dub was at the course.

J Dub opened the door to the pro shop and watched as Bogey did his best imitation of being a guard dog. He flipped on the lights, turned off the security system, opened the cash register, and started making coffee. He turned on the small television behind the counter to check the weather forecast for the day.

As J Dub sipped on his first cup of coffee, Julie came through the door. "How's the proud papa this morning?" she blurted as she dumped the newspaper and junk mail on the counter.

"Good morning, kiddo!" J Dub rang out. They chit-chatted as J Dub recounted the scene in their kitchen right before Marcia's water broke. Julie laughed so hard her eyes were tearing and her laughs began to be accentuated by snorts.

"That Marcia is a hoot!" she giggled. "I guess that's just nature's way of saying *that nine pounds of baby needs to come out!*" Julie and J Dub yelled in unison as they laughed together. J Dub felt a kinship with Julie. Besides himself, she was the only one that had noticed the idiosyncrasies about Lew. She genuinely liked Marcia and seemingly liked J Dub a great deal. He viewed her as more of the kid sister he never had rather than an employee. Some of the guys even commented on how much they favored one another. Julie was the girl next-door type . . . pretty, smart as a whip, and nobody's fool.

Julie finished preparing the bank bag for the daily deposit and J Dub announced that he was going to the bank and would be back shortly. By then most of the regulars were in their usual seats drinking coffee and eating doughnuts. Julie watched as Curt walked in. He waved hello to her with a big smile on his face. She smiled and waved back and remembered when she told him once how he and J Dub looked exactly alike. He smiled and only said, "Yeah, but J Dub is the boy wonder." Just a quiet way an older brother brags on the accomplishments of a younger brother.

The guys were getting torqued up on the coffee. They were laughing and teasing Fred with every doughnut bite. It seemed as if he was on a mission to bust his navel out of his belly. J Dub returned and, after slamming the door to his old truck, could hear even from the parking lot all of the guys laughing and talking in the pro shop. He smiled, shook his head at his good fortune, and walked inside with the empty bank bag.

"Hey guys! I've got an announcement to make!" Curt stood raising his Styrofoam cup of coffee. "Say hello to J Dub . . . The proud new daddy of a healthy, beautiful baby girl!" Whooping, hollering and whistles of congratulations ensued as someone handed J Dub a box of some of the thickest cigars he had ever seen. He promptly stuck one in his mouth and began furiously puffing on it until the billows of smoke poured out of the other end.

"Thank you! Thank you!" J Dub shouted.

"Hey, Senor J Dub! Mucho congratulations on the new bambino!" Paco yelled.

"Awww, J Dub, there ain't nothing like it. That little girl is going to have you wrapped around her little finger for the rest of your life! And, you're going to love it." Easy Earl was getting surprisingly misty as the others chimed in on the congratulations. J Dub never had so many handshakes or slaps on the back as he did that day. He loved every second of it.

The stench of the cigar was getting to J Dub so he put it out while continuing to joke and crow about his growing family. Julie refilled complimentary cups of coffee all around. "If only we had some Baileys to put in the cup of joe, huh guys?"

Julie casually glanced over at the front door and saw Lew about to walk in. She leaned over to J Dub's ear and whispered, "Lew's here." Her senses immediately warned her of trouble. She walked to her office and began her bookkeeping duties for the morning.

J Dub tried to get a reading from Lew's face as to whether he was in a good mood or not. The unpredictability of Lew's moods had caused Julie to invest in a huge bottle of Pepto Bismol tablets that were stored behind the counter. She and J Dub joked about popping Pepto as if it were going out of style. They had only worked together a short time but she could already read his *I have a headache* look or *Lew has been on my butt* look. She joked that she could spot it coming down the fairway.

"Hmmmm. Let's see what we have in the ole drawer today," Julie thought aloud. "I've got your Pepto, the purple pill, your Mylanta and some Alka Seltzer to boot. Oh wait, I also got some BC Powder. God awful to swallow, but it works. Pick yer poison, J Dub."

"You have enough medicine in your drawer to open a pharmacy, girl!"

"Yeah, yeah . . . what's yer poison?"

"BC Powder, I guess. Sheesh, I hate taking that stuff."

"Take a BC Powder and come back strong, yes indeedy," Julie wisecracked as she mimicked W. C. Field's classic cigar hold and sing-song conversational beat. J Dub couldn't help but laugh.

Lew walked in and did a quick headcount to see how many green fees should have been collected. The guys hanging out in the pro shop were nothing but an annoyance to him. But, he knew that it brought in money, and that is what was important. Lew opened the register and began counting. He quickly slammed it shut with irritation. "J Dub! Get over here!" he barked.

"What's up, Lew?" J Dub had worked there long enough to know that Lew would find a way to rain on the parade. He was a little perturbed that he had to come in and be so abrupt about everything.

"Where are the green fees?" Lew growled. "These guys can't just sit here all day drinking up coffee! I need people to play!"

J Dub's celebratory mood darkened as he tried to explain again to Lew that the guys were good for business. Lew just didn't get it. Just as J Dub and Lew were about to get into it, a group of golfers came in for their tee time. J Dub greeted the foursome and said, "Hi guys, you must be Paul's friends." He shot an *I told you so* look at Lew. "Come right over here gentlemen. Lew is the owner and will ring up your fees for you. I'll bring the carts around front."

Lew grunted an obligatory hello. He began punching the numbers on the register waiting for the sale to add up. After several uncomfortable and unsuccessful minutes, Lew was getting aggravated and began hollering for J Dub.

"I'm coming," J Dub announced. He cleared out the jumbled mess of numbers that Lew punched in and correctly rang up the sale.

"You better hang on to this one, Lew!" one of the golfers joked. Lew's face began to turn red from anger and embarrassment. The golfers exited the pro shop, loaded up their carts and drove to the first hole. J Dub shut the cash drawer and started to walk away.

"Wait, open it back up," Lew demanded. J Dub opened the drawer and looked at Lew as he thumbed through the twenties and grabbed some out of the till.

"What are you doing?" J Dub wasn't quite sure if what he saw was really happening.

"We both need some pocket change. The tax man gets too much as it is." Lew stuffed a crumpled twenty into J Dub's shirt pocket. "Here. Now take Marcia out to dinner." Lew turned and walked outside.

J Dub stood dumbfounded. *He's been skimming the till, that, s.o.b.* He walked over to Julie who was adding a long list of numbers on her ten-key adding machine. "Have you ever noticed?" J Dub began.

Julie interrupted, "That Lew comes in and takes money whenever he wants to?" They exchanged glances. "Why, yes. I have." She was disgusted with his antics and ethics too. As she hit the total key on her machine she looked up at J Dub and quietly said, "Sorry, I thought you knew."

J Dub simply stared at Julie and shook his head. It's as if they could communicate with each other without speaking.

"Yeah, that's such an in-your-face way of doing it. I'm sure he'll come up with something else before long." Julie thought for a moment and asked, "J Dub, does he think we are just absolute idiots or what? I can't even think about it or I'll get mad, and we don't want that, right?" She smirked at J Dub.

"Yeah, I've heard something about hell hath no fury like a woman scorned," J Dub half heartedly laughed. Then they both were quiet. There was nothing else to say.

CHAPTER NINETEEN

A few weeks later . . .

In spite of Lew's one-time withdrawal from the cash register Prairie Winds continued to thrive. The relationship between J Dub and Lew was complicated. Even though a general mistrust of each other had developed, they both realized their dysfunctional need for one another to make the business perk along. J Dub understood the game; he realized what the golfers wanted and expected and he was very affable with the customers.

The phone rang at seven in the morning as J Dub was busy opening up. "Prairie Winds," J Dub announced through the receiver.

"I just wanted to make sure that you had the place opened," Lew's voice said from the other end of the line. It was a familiar, but clumsy, reminder to J Dub that he was second in command behind Lew.

"Everything's under control," J Dub countered. *Now you're free to roll over and go back to bed*, he thought.

"I don't want you standing around. Take out the trash or rotate the beer in the cooler," Lew ordered from the other end.

"Yes sir," J Dub cordially responded. "I sealed the parking lot and striped it last week. There's a lot to do around here, you know."

"Just make sure it gets done," Lew demanded. It was if he didn't want anyone to short change him on the salaries that were paid out.

"As a matter of fact, I'm heading out to the course after lunch to work on a special project," J Dub volunteered. Some weeds had overgrown in a creek that traversed a fairway and J Dub planned on taking a weed eater out on the course to clean up the excess growth.

J Dub didn't mind doing all of the odd jobs. They gave him an opportunity to get outside and be on the course. Plus he felt that the business would be his one day and every little bit that he did now built a stronger foundation for the future.

Later that day after the players were on the course and the pro shop was running smoothly, J Dub changed out of his golf attire and put on some shorts, a t-shirt, and work boots. "Keep an eye on things," J Dub said to Julie. "I'm going to clean up the creek on number three." There had been several complaints from the players about the weed growth that was occurring in and around one of the creeks that traversed the third fairway. The maintenance crew had been pre-occupied doing odd jobs and it was still too early in the season for the student help to swing into full force.

J Dub went down to the maintenance shed, grabbed a weed eater, and headed off to the job site. The players had been right. It seemed as if everything with a root system was growing in the creek bed that crossed the fairway on the third hole. The weeds were so tall that the players couldn't see across the creek to the green.

Into the creek went J Dub. He had the weed eater on overdrive and was sending stalks, leaves, and buds flying everywhere. The sweat dripped into his eyes. Some remnants of the weeds covered his head and face. Grass clippings covered his t-shirt and shorts. His allergies kicked in causing him to sneeze.

Lew eased his motorcycle to a stop on the edge of the creek bank. "What the heck are you doing down there?" He grimaced at the sight of J Dub.

"A lot of the guys wanted the weeds knocked down in this creek," J Dub replied.

"We can get one of the kids to get in there and do that."

"They won't be out of school until a few weeks from now. It's no problem. I'll just knock these weeds down and this will speed up play," J Dub rationalized.

"If you keep doing this kind of stuff, then you'll have the place shaped up in no time," Lew stated.

"The guys were complaining that it was taking too long to find a ball if it rolled into the creek, plus the weeds were getting so high, some of the guys couldn't even see over them."

"Why didn't you fire up the brush hog?" Lew asked.

"I thought about it, but the creek banks are too steep."

"Can we get a tractor to clean it up?" Lew inquired.

"I don't think that it will shave it very close. It's too vertical in here."

"Can we spray it?"

"The Department of Natural Resources will be down here in no time if they ever find out," J Dub explained. He was well aware of the controls that the state placed on some chemical applications.

"Who will tell them? It's private property."

"Why take the chance? It's no big deal to hack them down this way."

"They'll be back up in a few weeks," Lew mentioned.

"Then we'll send the kids down in here at that time."

Lew tried his best to get J Dub away from the grunt work, but J Dub was too conscientious to let the weed problem get out of hand. "You're doing a good job. Keep up the good work."

Rather than pull away at that instant, Lew guided his motorcycle over to the shade of a box elder. He parked his vehicle and polished the chrome. Lew had a penchant for motorcycles. To him the golf course was a place where he could get off the road and race his cycle up and down the cart paths and across the fairways. On more than one occasion Lew would have fun on his motorcycle weaving in and out of foursomes and making a racket.

"You shouldn't be out here on that thing," J Dub yelled over to Lew.

"What else is this land good for?" Lew yelled back.

"A lot of the players have been complaining about the noise that it makes."

"I'll do what I want. This is my place."

It was true. Lew was the principal owner of the golf course. No one could dare tell him what to do. The old man riding over the course on a motor driven bike was ridiculous and smacked of disrespect to any paying customer. But Lew didn't care. It was his place and he felt as if he could do what he wanted to do. Lew was in the moment of enjoying himself and decided he would let J Dub worry about the customers. After all, he had what he wanted.

Lew was not a "people" person by any stretch of the imagination. He depended on J Dub to give first class treatment to the clientele and he needed his expertise on what to do with the course. Lew, despite his lack of people skills, was very good with equipment and machinery. It seemed as if the only items that he could relate to were the inanimate objects, such as tractors, mowers, and motorcycles, as well as dozers, scrapers, and backhoes. It didn't take much for Lew to look at an engine to see why it sputtered. A mechanic's world is black and white. His hands may be rough with calluses but the formula never changed in fixing an engine. People on the other hand, weren't quite so easy to figure out.

"Hey J Dub, you've been working your tail off around here. Go ahead and take off early today."

"Okay, I will as soon as I finish up this creek."

Lew pulled off and gunned the engine of his cycle. The muffler noise disturbed the tranquility of the golf course.

J Dub stopped working for a second. His eyes followed the trail of the cycle as he became even more exasperated with Lew's antics on the course. He couldn't help but wonder what would compel anyone to take a joy ride on a motorcycle across a golf course.

It wasn't much longer before J Dub wrapped up the work in the creek and walked into the pro shop. He was hot and sweaty and covered with weeds. "Keep the old fart busy and out of here," Julie said. J Dub chuckled and thought about how Lew's eccentricities drove both of them crazy.

J Dub reached for a glass of water. "He's got more BS projects . . ." and bit off his thought to keep from getting even more annoyed.

" . . . than the government," Julie concluded. "Just keep him away from me." She handed him an envelope and mockingly held her hands up in surrender. "He told me to give this to you. I don't know anything, I just work here."

J Dub wiped his brow on his sleeve and slid his work glove off his hand with his teeth. He opened the envelope to find a note from Lew. In the envelope was a set of keys. He glanced out the window to see Lew's old pickup sitting in the parking lot.

"What's he up to now?" asked Julie.

"I got after him for having that motorcycle out on the course."

"Then what?" Julie pried.

"He told me to mind my own business. Now he gave me his old pickup," an amazed J Dub said. "Try to figure that one out."

"He's about as tough to read as a newspaper in Braille," Julie commented.

"The minute you think you have him figured out, he pulls something different out of his hat," J Dub replied confused.

"He either doesn't want us to know too much about him or he doesn't want to be predictable," Julie commented.

"It makes it tough to function when you don't know what side of him is going to shine on any given day," J Dub replied.

" . . . On any given day?" Julie shouted. "You don't know what you're going to get from him at any given minute. He can change his mood quicker than a runway model can change her clothes."

J Dub chuckled to himself. He loved the way that Julie could assess a situation and come up with a witty analogy, a real spitfire from the South. "We're all in this together. I guess we'll have to get used to it. As much time as we spend together, we need to keep peace in the family," J Dub compromised.

"Whatever you say," was all Julie managed to comment.

"The way he likes to control will have us all on an emotional roller coaster before this ride is done."

CHAPTER TWENTY

Later that spring . . .

J Dub peered out the window of the pro shop and noticed Marcia parking their car. He had a grin from ear to ear as he rushed to help Marcia open the door. She had Gail in one arm and a picnic basket in the other.

"Well, lookee there," J Dub exclaimed.

"I thought that you might like some lunch," Marcia said with a glistening smile. She was getting out of their apartment more and more now. Gail was getting old enough to travel around town a little better. The family situation had been steadily improving for J Dub.

Marcia had resumed the catering activities she had started when they first got married. She put things on hold for a few months during the latter stages of her pregnancy and the early weeks of Gail's life. However, Marcia started taking on a few light jobs that would give her the opportunity to make an extra buck or two for the family.

Today, she decided to kill a couple of birds with one stone. Not only could she bring some lunch to J Dub, she could bring Gail to the golf course for the first time. It gave J Dub a great opportunity to introduce his little girl to the boys.

J Dub gave his wife a peck on the lips for her thoughtfulness. In so doing he grabbed Gail out of her arms. "Hey guys, here's my little girl," J Dub shouted to the boys that were congregated around a table in the back of the pro shop.

Fred shouted back from the rear of the room, "Teach him how to putt, J Dub. That's something that we cain't do!" he belly laughed long and loud as he pounded the table with his meaty fist, laughing at his own wit.

"What does pink mean?" asked J Dub as he mugged a ridiculous face at Fred. It was obvious that Fred did not notice that Gail was dressed in pink and was not a little boy. The boys in the back laughed it up at Fred's expense.

Lew and Julie walked out of the office. Lew was a very adept chameleon. He couldn't stand kids. It must have been because they would generally take the focus off of him when they were in the room. Lew did not take kindly to anyone that didn't recognize his considerable status in life.

"What have we here?" Lew asked with feigned excitement.

Since Lew had asked, J Dub took the opportunity to introduce his daughter to his boss. "Gail, meet big Lew." He took an instant to sneak in a subtle compliment to Lew.

"Born with a silver spoon in her mouth," Lew responded. With that he took the occasion to tickle Gail's belly with the hopes of making a new friend.

Gail took the moment to let Lew know exactly how she felt. After an infectious giggle, she let out a big burp and spit up some formula. Lew didn't know quite how to act after Gail's reaction. He yanked his hand back and rushed for a towel as he muttered his disgust.

All the boys in the back got a big charge out of Lew jumping back from Gail. They couldn't resist the opportunity to laugh at him. Lew glared in their direction.

To divert attention away from Lew as he wiped the soured mess off of his hand, Marcia chimed in, "Who wants a sandwich?"

J Dub couldn't resist the temptation. "I can't pass up home cooking."

He reached for the stack of dollar sandwiches that Marcia brought with her into the pro shop. Lew grabbed a sandwich from the basket. "You didn't have to do that," Lew stated as he took a bite.

"It's nothing. They're left over from a catering job that I did," Marcia replied.

To the surprise of everyone in the pro shop, Lew stopped in his tracks. He glared at Marcia and asked, "Is that what I am to you, an afterthought?"

He threw the sandwich into the trash can and stormed out of the pro shop.

"What was that all about?" asked Fred from the back of the room.

"Can you believe that?" responded J Dub.

"Is he Dr. Jekyll or Mr. Hyde?" asked Easy Earl.

Marcia was both embarrassed and furious. "He can't be serious."

"It's like that every day around here," Julie noted. "You never know what mood you're going to catch him in."

"All I can tell you is it is better that you guys deal with him than me. How can you deal with that kind of behavior?" Marcia shot J Dub an exasperated look.

Julie replied, "It's as tough as the bark on an old oak tree."

"We've just learned to accept it and move on," continued J Dub. "It's easier for us to ignore it than bring it to his attention and start a confrontation."

"Is that what you have to put up with on a daily basis? It's bad enough when he acted so repulsed by Gail's spit-up. What kind of a man is he? Jeez Louise, she's just a baby," Marcia retorted.

"It comes with the territory. He's the boss. It's his place and he can act any way he wants to, I suppose," J Dub replied.

"Well, you can stand here and put up with it, but our little girl doesn't have to. C'mon, Gail. Let's put you down for a nap," Marcia cooed as she headed for the door.

One by one the sandwiches disappeared. The boys didn't let them go to waste. The mood in the pro shop returned to normal.

"I guess his ego couldn't stand that a baby was getting more attention than him," Rollie laughed in between bites.

"Yeah, and she sure wasn't as impressed with him as he had hoped," BT chuckled.

CHAPTER TWENTY-ONE

Later that summer . . .

The two men shared a hearty laugh as the Mercury Marquis made a left turn onto the blacktop driveway. Maurice (Monty) DiMonte had always wanted to drive a nice car. However, he chose to scale it back a bit from the expensive, luxurious sedans so that he wouldn't bring too much attention to himself.

Monty was a lawyer that a person wanted to have on retainer. To operate successfully in a capitalistic world, some people think that it is necessary to have a lawyer on their side who is not only willing to bend the rules a little but who offers suggestions on how to without arousing suspicion. In his eyes, that was the difference between a two-bit lawyer and one on retainer.

Monty would do it in a heartbeat. To some it is called crossing over the line, to others it might be unethical behavior. Monty didn't care what it was called; he would do what was required to win.

He wasn't necessarily that bright or astute. Monty had gone to a private Catholic law school that was more or less reserved for people that had the connections to get accepted. Once in, it was a given that three years later a law degree would be handed over.

It didn't really matter that it would take multiple attempts to pass the bar exam. Once a lawyer is licensed the public gets a glimpse of what their true personality is all about. Some go to work to uphold the law. Others pursue civil lawsuits. A few concentrate on divorces. Several go into corporate America. A number go into private practice and become commissioned salespeople looking for the next meal.

It's the last kind that Monty migrated toward. Many can misuse their credentials and bend the rules to work toward their advantage. Monty was all about making connections and getting things to work for him rather than against him. He prided himself on knowing people in high places and getting things done with a phone call. He liked to think of it as "working smarter, not harder."

The passenger in Monty's car that was the source of all of the laughter was Raymond Parsons. He was a polished jokester and more often than not had a quick quip for any happenstance that occurred in everyday life. The two couldn't look more opposite. Raymond was a little older than Monty. He was clean cut and had weight that was proportionate with his five foot nine frame. The freckles on his face made a good match for his thinning, red hair which accentuated his hazel eyes. Despite his age, he gave the appearance of a more youthful man. Raymond was soft-spoken, but was very ambitious when it came to receiving favors. In fact, when it came down to it, Raymond was nothing but a whore that would take anything beneficial that came his way.

The two had known each other since grade school. Raymond had been best friends with Monty's older brother. The older boys were inseparable during their younger years and would always let Monty tag along. So, in a way, Raymond developed into a little bit of a father figure for Monty. While their years didn't separate them by much, Raymond always had the quiet nature of being the eldest which was more noticeable when they were younger.

Raymond had preceded Monty through school. However, when he got out of college, he took a job working for the union that handled the workers at the nearby steel mills. That led to a short stint as a lobbyist for the coal miners union. After several years of hard work, he became a trusted asset for the unions. With their backing he ran for a seat as a local congressman and won. His constituents loved the wide-eyed innocent look that seemed to be indelibly etched on his face.

So, the two of them renewed their friendship in their adult years. A congressman with union affiliations and a lawyer with questionable ethics spelled possible disaster. The two became best friends and Monty oiled the political machine of Raymond. Their association was the very definition of synergy. It was a lethal combination and most importantly, lucrative.

The Marquis rolled to a stop at the electronic gate that seemed to weigh several tons and was equipped to stop a loaded eighteen-wheeler. It had been programmed to be activated by a remote control device that Lew utilized. An intercom system had been placed at the gate for the guests to use.

Monty had been over to Lew's residence on many, many occasions. He was such a trusted friend to Lew that he should have had his own remote device by now to let himself enter. However, Lew couldn't bring himself to lose control of the entrance and always made Monty go through the same exercise as the rest of the people.

"Lew. It's Monty. Let me in."

"I can see you through the surveillance camera."

The massive gate pulled back from its locked position and slid open to allow the Marquis to enter. A white rail fence surrounded the entrance to the property. An electronic, barbed-wire fence was intertwined with it and further insulated the perimeter of Lew's property. Majestic oak trees had been planted years before and their foliage made for an impressive entrance to the property. The driveway was about two hundred yards long. It took a circuitous path to the home and emptied into a large parking area to the side of the garage. It seemed to always carry a fresh coat of sealer.

Over the years Monty had traversed this route mostly to save Lew from lurking trouble. Not everything that Lew had done up to this point in his life could be construed as "lily-white." His love for money was unparalleled and Monty was well aware of that. Lew was an extremely greedy man and would do anything to accomplish his objectives. That included bending the rules and associating with people that could help him get what he wanted. It was not above him to cheat to get ahead or, for that matter, break the law to prosper.

To an outsider, Lew's behavior was similar to that of an eight-year old little boy that never matured through adolescence and into adulthood. All of the attention had to be centered on Lew and he had to have his way. If someone crossed his path, then a vengeful Lew would take the necessary steps to remind the perpetrator who had the upper hand.

These traits had allowed Lew to do well for himself financially and his residence was the envy of many. His home was equipped with all of the modern conveniences and up-to-date security devices. His compound included about thirty acres and was improved with a new barn, several storage bins, and a grain elevator. Monty had successfully helped Lew navigate two divorces through which Lew managed to come out of with what could be considered lucrative victories.

Monty, who was the main reason for the profitable settlements, inched the Marquis down the driveway toward Lew's home. Each visitor seemed to feel the same eerie mood as they neared Lew's front door. Even good friends could feel a cloud of creepiness. It always seemed like Lew had an ulterior motive for every meeting. This day was no different. Something sinister was in the air as the Marquis neared its parking spot.

Lew, through a variety of dubious maneuvers, had become the largest single property owner in Raymond's district. A greedy land mogul coupled with political influence and skillful legal moves added flammable fuel to an already deadly mixture. As the two men got out of the car Lew approached to shake their hands. "Ray. Monty. Welcome to the Big Z." Lew had affectionately placed the nickname on his own property.

"Thanks for having us over," replied Raymond as he pumped Lew's hand.

"Where do the years go? It seems like we were doing this yesterday," added Monty. He packed a slug of Redman chewing tobacco into his jaw.

The three men strolled to the barn. Lew had a variety of rifles stored inside. Monty and Ray each picked out a shotgun. Lew was always the one that looked for an advantage. He took the opportunity to grab an automatic assault rifle. Even in a practice situation he had to control the outcome. In a twisted and demented sense Lew needed to prove to Monty and Raymond that he could knock out more targets.

"What the hell?" demanded Monty. "We're only out here to take a little target practice."

"You're always looking for that extra kicker," added Raymond, as he carefully eyed Lew.

Lew got a lot of satisfaction knowing that he could bend the rules of fair play and get away with it. "We'll see who's got the best shot now," he said with a grin. His desire to be the best and to win any competition bordered on being nauseous.

Behind the barn was a skeet machine. They proceeded to shoot at clay pigeons launched against a beautiful blue sky. The clay pigeons didn't stand a chance against the assault rifle, but fared a little better against the shotguns that Monty and Ray fired. When they were finished they left the barn and walked back to the car. "My thinking is that with some help from the Federal Land Bank we can do that project on that piece of ground. What do you think, Monty?" Lew asked suggestively.

"That is gonna be a tough one to pull off," Monty responded.

"The key is getting someone else to pay for it . . . some sort of federal grant or something like that," Lew insisted. "The deal becomes a slam-dunk winner if we can get someone else to fund the money."

"I like your thinking, Lew. The money is out there. We'll figure out a way to get our hands on it," Ray added.

"Don't worry about the ground. I have that angle figured," Lew volunteered. "A lot of land has been deeded to me lately. Now I have to figure out how to make it profitable."

"Give me a couple of days to figure this out," Monty said.

"You're in good hands, Lew," Ray chimed as he extended his hand to Lew. "Thanks for having us out today."

"I've got plenty of ground. Don't worry about that," Lew said as he reinforced the point about the land. They shook hands. Monty and Raymond got in the Marquis and drove off. Lew watched with excitement knowing full well that he had tactfully planted the seed for future income.

CHAPTER TWENTY-TWO

Near the end of the summer . . .

Even though the sky had started to lighten, the sun hadn't made it to the horizon as J Dub pulled his pickup truck into the parking lot. J Dub's working world *was* the golf course. His routine was clearly established. It was hard to tell Monday from Thursday or Saturday from Wednesday. The days became weeks and the weeks became months. But at dawn there were a lot of worse places to be.

Fred's banged-up, used Cadillac was already in the lot when J Dub pulled up along side it. Snores could not only be heard reverberating across the parking lot, it seemed like the entire car was shaking. If J Dub didn't know better he would have thought that Fred was trying to suck all of the air off of the golf course.

Rather than awaken him, J Dub gently closed the door to his pickup and tiptoed to the cart barn. The minute the door slid open Bogey jumped into J Dub's face and showered him with slobbery kisses. It appeared that his wagging tail was actually moving his head from side to side. As J Dub pulled the carts out of the barn, Bogey jumped into the seat beside him. Bogey would follow so closely at J Dub's heels that he would occasionally get kicked in the snout. The bond that they established was enduring. When Bogey tilted his head it was as if he understood every word that J Dub spoke.

J Dub unlocked the pro shop and was firing up the coffee pot when a bleary-eyed Fred sauntered in. "You're up early this morning," J Dub said tongue-in-cheek.

"Us old-timers can't sleep," Fred said in between yawns.

"You could have fooled me by the way you were gasping for air a minute ago," J Dub laughed.

"We want to get our round done by ten-thirty today. That way we can beat the heat," Fred announced. "Besides, there's a big card game back in the clubhouse at lunchtime."

"What are you playing for . . . quarters today rather than dimes?" J Dub asked with a snicker.

"Ha, ha, ha," Fred said facetiously. "It's too early for your humor. What are you going to do today?"

"Probably the same old stuff. Julie will get in shortly and Lew will call to check on us."

One by one the gang made their way through the pro shop door. In short order they picked their playing partners and headed for the first tee.

Right on cue a few hours later Lew showed up ready to complete a couple of tasks. J Dub and Lew both knew that it would take several years to get the property exactly how they wanted it. J Dub's emphasis was on improving the golf course. After that the clubhouse, parking lot, cart paths, and irrigation system needed an influx of money. Lew, on the other hand, was solely interested in getting as much money into the bank as possible. "Is the sign finished yet?" he grumbled. His impatience came off as a sign of discontent.

"I'm glad that you asked," J Dub answered. "Follow me." He led Lew around to the back of the clubhouse. J Dub enjoyed working with wood. He had completed the finishing touches on the new sign for the golf course. PRAIRIE WINDS GOLF COURSE had been carved into a piece of wood and the sign was ready to be erected at the parking lot entrance. The lettering gleamed with bright red paint. A fairway had been painted green. A lake on the sign was royal blue.

"It looks nice. You did good," Lew said carefully so that his compliments wouldn't go to J Dub's head. "Let's get it up."

Naturally, J Dub worked the post-hole digger to get the holes dug. After the posts were secured, the sign was fastened. There remained one more essential task.

Their final action to christen the golf course was to erect the flagpole. After digging the hole, mixing the concrete, and hoisting the flagpole into position, the golf course was finally ready to show off its improvements to the public.

"Now we've got a decent product to sell. This place is screaming for business now!" exclaimed Lew with a definite amount of pleasure.

"We still have a ways to go, but everything seems to be a lot better than what it was," J Dub chimed. "Even though we've been open for a few months, I guess now we can have our official grand opening."

"Not yet," Lew hollered over his shoulder as he walked to his pickup. He grabbed an American flag out of the cab of his truck, hooked it to the rope, and hoisted it up into the gentle breeze. "There's nothing like the good 'ole USA," Lew said with a grin.

"Where else could a guy go from rags to riches?" J Dub asked.

They shook hands knowing that this business opportunity could be fruitful for both. "J Dub, you're like the son I never had. You're the best partner a guy could hope for."

"My worst shot looks like my best one now."

Lew beamed. He went back to his pickup and retrieved a package that was wrapped in newspapers. "Here's something else."

Lew peeled the newspaper off of his newest surprise. He unfurled another flag. This one read: PRAIRIE WINDS GOLF COURSE.

"We'll fly this one under Old Glory," Lew stated.

"You've got a winner's touch, Lew. Nothing gets past you."

Lew hooked the golf course flag to the rope and hoisted it to fly under the American flag. "The whole world oughta love us now!" Lew yelled. His normally somber mood had taken a back seat to a rare, jubilant feeling. He was so proud of the golf course flag. It had been a total surprise to J Dub.

Lew and J Dub shook hands again and hugged each other. At that moment, despite their ups and downs, their bond could not have been tighter.

"Be sure to take good care of things today. I've got to run off to another appointment," Lew said hurriedly as he jumped into his pickup truck.

Just as farmers can look at the land and tell when crops should be laid in the ground, Lew knew the seeds of suggestion had already been cultivated with Monty and Raymond regarding his land. Now it was time to develop those seeds into his cash crop.

As if following a beacon, the Marquis returned to Lew's driveway and slowly drove through the gate once permission to enter was granted. However, this time Monty was alone. As was his custom, Lew approached the car the minute that Monty pulled up to park. "You're always out here by the time I get parked. Do you have something inside that you don't want me to see?" asked Monty.

"You know better than that, Monty. The camera at the gate keeps an eye on things," Lew replied. "Nothing is inside that gate that doesn't belong inside that gate."

"Do you need protection over and above what the camera can see? You probably need more eyes with all of the land that you've got and now the golf course."

With a smile Lew added, "You know I do. You're aware of all that land that has come my way."

"If you need help watching over it, then I can have that arranged."

"That piece of land down South is eight hundred acres. It's not growing much from a yield standpoint," Lew hinted.

"How can Raymond and I help?" Monty inquired.

"I want to put a cash crop on it."

"How do you plan on doing that?"

"The field is totally secluded. The river is on one side. Railroad tracks block it on another side. The bluff protects it on the final side. There's only one way in and I have an electronic system protecting that."

Monty probed for more information, "What did you have in mind?"

"I need to be aligned with the right people."

With a grin, Monty replied, "We've got that covered."

"The planting of the crop is simple. We'll put twelve rows of corn on the perimeter of the field. Every other row is corn on the interior of the field," Lew continued.

" . . . Holy shit!" Monty was in awe of the suggested plan.

"With a special spray we can block the infrared camera in case anybody gets suspicious. No one will be able to get onto the property to detect what's going on."

"How are you going to distance yourself from the law?" an inquisitive Monty asked.

"That's where you and Raymond come in. We'll have to hide money."

Monty was all ears.

"We need to set up several corporations with post office boxes for addresses. We can deed the property back and forth to muddy up the property ownership," Lew proposed.

"Maybe even get a corporation or two from abroad?" Monty suggested. "I could be the registered agent."

Lew smiled. "I like the way you think."

"That way you can still keep access to the property."

"That's better yet," Lew said with an evil smirk.

"What's our cut?" Monty asked.

"I'm thinking that it should be a sixty-forty deal," Lew surmised. "I need for you to cover my ass and help with the distribution connections. Can you get it done?"

Monty nodded. "Consider it taken care of. You know that we can do that."

"We've tried running the numbers for a few years, but that's so hot and cold. This will be a lot more lucrative than the bookmaking stuff. We can have a couple of bad weekends with the games and take a hit. This will keep the bucks coming in until George gets the offshore 800 number set up. This should be real steady income for us," Lew implied. "You know . . . a more positive cash flow."

Monty smirked. The dollar signs were already becoming visible in his head. Raymond was using his connections to secure a lucrative loan for Lew from the government. With the ground, Lew was off and running in the marijuana trafficking business.

CHAPTER TWENTY-THREE

The next spring—U.S. Attorney's office in Illinois . . .

The newly appointed prosecuting attorney, Brian Moore looked like the poster boy on a Wheaties box. He had excelled in sports through high school and college. His bio read like a Who's Who and defined his personality and appeal which garnered an impressive circle of friends. After graduating from college he went on to get a law degree from one of the most prestigious law schools in the nation—Virginia.

He married his high school sweetheart and started a family. His life was a model for success. His perfect conviction record was two percent better than the federal government's ninety-eight percent average. Brian was a young-looking man in his early forties and was on a fast track to a sensational career. It was no surprise that law enforcement took notice.

The government came knocking right after his graduation from law school. After a number of victorious decisions, Brian was promoted to an U. S. Prosecuting Attorney. To some the boyish good looks and the immaculate haircut were odious. However, for those that are in need of help from a federal level, those same qualities were reassuring that the good guy always wins.

The April showers sprouted the May flowers. The daffodils and jonquils were in full bloom. So it was that spring morning when Lucille Morton and her son, Matt sat in front of Brian Moore. "We had no idea," Lucille sobbed.

"We thought that we still owned the property," Matt continued.

"Whoa. Wait a minute," Brian interrupted. "What are you talking about?" Brian was clearly caught off-guard by their conversation.

"We're the heirs of the Morton Estate," Lucille said. "We live in Florida."

"For several years our family has had an accountant named Walter Hancock handling our affairs," added Matt.

"He had been managing our property for all of this time," continued Lucille.

"But we've come to find out that we don't even own very much of it any more," said Matt.

"How can that be?" asked Brian.

"Walter is the executor of our estate," explained Lucille. "He would give us monthly, quarterly, and yearly statements."

"What we thought that he was managing, he sold!" Matt added angrily.

"Without our authority," Lucille cried.

"I don't understand," Brian replied.

"We don't either," Matt conceded.

"The best that we can figure out is that my mother must have signed a power-of-attorney document before she died," Lucille volunteered. "But that doesn't sound like anything that she would have done. We talked about it all the time. Daddy had strongly advised her not to do anything along those lines."

"And Walter Hancock took it upon himself to sell our property off," Matt added.

" . . . Without our permission!" Lucille exclaimed. "He must have had a bogus power-of-attorney document."

"We don't know where to turn," Matt carried on. "There doesn't seem to be any branch of law enforcement that we can use."

"It's too big of a deal for the state," Lucille stammered.

"And the local yokels and highway patrol can't understand our dilemma," Matt included.

"And you think that some federal laws were violated?" Brian surmised.

Matt and Lucille both nodded their heads. "Where else can we go?" Lucille inquired.

Brian shifted his attention to the window. He looked out at the gorgeous foliage and its radiant colors. He pondered his next question. "What do you think happened?"

Lucille responded adamantly, "We think that we may have been victims of a forgery!"

"It might be more of a situation for civil court. We just handle criminal matters out of this office," Brian rationalized.

"If it is grand theft or grand larceny, would that make a difference?" Matt probed. "Those certainly are criminal offenses."

"Wait, before the word criminal is used in this conversation, with all due respect, was your mother cognizant of her actions when she visited this executor of the estate?"

"Of course she was!" Lucille snapped.

"Do you have proof of that? Did either one of you accompany her to this meeting with this Hancock fellow?"

Both Matt and Lucille looked at each other and dejectedly admitted no.

"The reason I ask that is because any attorney involved in this case would." Brian sat back in his chair and fixed his stare upon the Morton heirs. He finally conceded. "Something just doesn't feel right here. I'll tell you what; let me get one of my assistants on it. Maybe it is a situation that can be investigated by the FBI."

"We want to find out what happened," Lucille said. "What we thought was a sizeable portfolio of property has been whittled away to nothing."

"Not only do we not have the property, but we didn't get any money for it either," Matt admitted.

"How can that be?" Brian wondered out loud. "If the property is no longer in your possession, then you should have gotten money for it. Did you check all of your bank statements to verify that no deposits were made?"

"I checked all of the bank statements for the estate as well as our personal statements to make sure a deposit wasn't made into the wrong account." Matt admitted.

"We feel like fools," Lucille sobbed.

"Let me put one of my white-collar experts on the file. It sounds like we are going to need someone that understands a financial statement and a tax return. My office will look into it," Brian assured them.

CHAPTER TWENTY FOUR

Prairie Winds Golf Course—that same spring . . .

The days, weeks, and months continued to pass by. The chief concern for J Dub was running the business. All of his energies were concentrated on getting the golf course operational on a day-in and day-out basis. It was quite an undertaking to have the facility open for business from dawn to dusk, seven days a week, during every kind of imaginable weather condition. Running a successful golf operation was hard work and took a lot of hours.

J Dub had no idea who the heirs to the Morton Estate were . . . let alone Monty and Raymond Parsons. Nor did he care. His new family was keeping him busy when the golf course would allow. It was tough on him to get up every day in darkness, service the public, and return home to the demands of Marcia and Gail. But not once did he complain. He loved the work that he was doing, the boys, and Bogey . . . and he most certainly loved his wife and daughter.

On one of the days Rollie approached J Dub in the pro shop about having a special tournament. "You know J Dub, all of us regulars have really taken notice as to how nice you've made this place."

"Well, thanks Rollie. I'm glad that you fellas are enjoying your days around here," J Dub replied.

"I'm good friends with some higher-ups over at Children's Hospital. Would you guys like to host their charity tournament?" Rollie asked.

J Dub was excited about the chance to host a prestigious event. "We're trying to build the business up. That would be the perfect clientele to have over here."

"Let me hook you up with the guy running the charity event. They're looking for a place to play."

Soon thereafter Children's Hospital agreed in principle to a ten-year pact to have their annual fund-raising golf event at PRAIRIE WINDS GOLF COURSE. J Dub considered that a major coup for the blossoming business. It takes a fair amount of money to play golf. J Dub thought that throwing out the welcome mat for a group of financially stable doctors was an excellent way to build repeat business.

"If you're going to start attracting those types of people, then you have to do something about that idiot on the motorcycle," Easy Earl complained. "We've got more golfers bitching about that than any single thing around here." Easy Earl had a way of getting to the point with J Dub.

"I know it Earl. I've mentioned it to him several times," J Dub sighed.

"What sort of hillbillies would do something like that? This is a golf course, not a dirt bike track," Earl continued. He was clearly frustrated.

"He totally disregards the golfers," agreed J Dub. "And it looks so unprofessional."

"You know what he says . . ." Earl continued.

"Yeah, it's his place and he'll do what he wants."

"But I'll tell you right now, it is making a lot of the players mad around here," Earl ranted. "And it's such a shame. This is a fun place to play a round of golf."

"Let me work on it."

To say that the motorcycle issue was straining the relationship between J Dub and Lew would be understating the obvious. Lew spent a lot of his spare time atop the highest hill on the course dilly-dallying around. It was customary for him to race his motorcycle down the hillside, with muffler blaring, on a regular basis. Naturally, Lew paid no attention to the players on the course who were primarily out there to enjoy some of the solitude that a golf course can provide. The roar of his motorcycle was meant to be a subconscious reminder that he was always there, always watching.

One morning, Lew roared off of the hill and made a beeline for the parking lot. He cruised into a spot near the front door of the pro shop. Lew had pre-determined that an area by the front door was off limits to vehicles. Parking in that spot was the best way for him to announce to the world that he was on the premises. After parking his cycle, he sauntered into the pro shop.

All of the boys were in the back at their table playing backgammon and gin. The talk varied from simple reminiscing to the world affairs to current events. Bogey had developed a certain comfort zone with the boys. On most days the dog would nap nearby. After all, it was like he was one of the guys anyway.

"Why don't you guys do something constructive? Is that all you bums have to do today?" Lew said in a condescending tone as he entered the pro shop and glanced at the table in the rear of the room.

Rollie was not going to take any static off anyone. He was a war vet that had worked his tail off after the war. His disposition was normally pretty sour. He fired back, "I worked all of my life to enjoy this and I don't know why it's any of your concern since my money is padding your pockets."

Fred, who was never at a loss for speaking his mind, added, "We know you don't do squat. All you do is sit up on that hill and stroke your engine."

Lew quickly got defensive. "That's a crock of crap. I work every minute of every day just to get ahead in this world. Do you know that I have to work the first eleven days of every month for free? It all goes to the government. Uncle Sam gets way more than his share."

Easy Earl had been around the block a few times. He was no spring chicken. He'd heard it all since he'd kicked tires all of his life on a car lot. "You probably screw him too. Don't come in here and throw your crying towel our way."

The fact that the boys had bonded so well and enjoyed a great deal of camaraderie had always irked Lew. "You guys need to go get a life instead of playing games all day," Lew yelled across the room to the boys. He then turned his attention to Julie. "What's the tent for?"

"We're hosting the Children's Hospital tournament tomorrow," she said.

"Why didn't anyone tell me?" Lew asked, oblivious to the day-to-day activities scheduled for the golf course.

"There's a lot of stuff that goes on around here that you're not aware of," Julie lashed out. "We can't go running to you every time a decision needs to be made." Julie had a way of putting Lew in his place. She bit her tongue to not offer more words of wisdom to Lew. *Where is J Dub? He needs to get this old fart off my ass,* she mused.

Lew glared back at her. "It's my place. I certainly have every right to know what goes on around here."

Julie rolled her eyes as she passed Lew and muttered an uninterested *"Whatever"* under her breath. At that instant, J Dub walked into the pro shop with Mel Parker. Mel was a huge, gregarious man that towered well over six and a half feet. It appeared that he obviously hadn't missed too many meals either.

"Lew, I'd like for you to meet Mel Parker. He's the hospital administrator for Children's Hospital," said J Dub.

Mel smiled heartily and looked down on Lew. He delivered a crushing grip to Lew's hand when they shook. Even though he was an innocent, "teddy-bear" type, Mel's huge frame towered above Lew and intimidated him.

"Lew Zerrmann."

"We are so grateful for the donation. The gift that you're providing will benefit children's health in so many ways," stated Mel.

Lew nearly flew into a fit in the pro shop. A very awkward moment passed. Lew caught himself and meekly mumbled, "Yeah . . . well, I just love kids." He offered the comment in a mocking tone.

Mel had several last minute duties to take care of before the tournament so he gracefully bowed out of the conversation. He turned to J Dub and said, "It looks like we're all set. See you tomorrow." With that he nodded to everyone and waved goodbye. Mel quickly left the pro shop.

The door barely closed and Lew turned to J Dub and shouted, "When did we donate the golf course?"

J Dub found Lew's reaction very mysterious. He replied matter-of-factly, "You made a ten-year commitment to them for their fund-raising drive."

Lew did his best job of acting as if he was unaware of the obligation and flippantly asked, "You mean they're not paying for the course?"

J Dub shook his head and tried to keep his temper in check. "No. You agreed to donate the course one day a year for their fund-raising drive. You mentioned at the time that it would be a helluva way to get a write-off from taxes."

Lew was furious. "You need to remind me of these things! That's one less day a year that I can make money."

"You said that the write-off would more than make up for that."

"That's not a good practice for us to get into. It hurts our cash flow too much."

"Lew, it's one day, for crying out loud, anyway it's over and done with now," J Dub stated.

"Do we have a signed agreement with them?" Lew asked.

"It was a gentleman's agreement."

"What's that supposed to mean?"

"It was a handshake agreement," J Dub said in an exasperating way. *Leave it to Lew not to know what being a gentleman is*, he thought.

Lew pondered the statement. "Then we might be able to get out of it."

"If so, then our reputation would be shot," J Dub hinted.

"I don't like that deal."

"Then you shouldn't have made it," J Dub challenged.

"We need to get out of that."

Julie had done most of the preparations for the scramble tourney. She was bursting at the seams. "Get a grip, Lew! My God! It is one freaking day! Your precious cash flow won't be affected that much." She was disgusted by the talk of canceling the event. *Only Lew would pitch a fit about a one day charity event for children* she muttered as she turned to storm into her office.

Lew couldn't help but follow her butt as she walked off. He chased after her as if he was on a mission. "You fill out that outfit so well," Lew leered. "You look delicious." Over the previous few months he had been becoming very forward with his advances toward her.

"Oh, pleeeeeease," pleaded Julie. "Don't even go there."

"I've been thinking. I'm getting up there in years. I need someone to take care of me." As Lew inched closer to Julie he continued, "You need a Sugar Daddy to take care of you." He rubbed his arm against her breast.

Julie jumped away and said, "You come any closer and I'll kick you so hard you'll cough up things you ate as a child, and don't think I won't do it! I ought to sue you for sexual harassment!"

Lew was offended and taken aback by her reaction. With a defensive tone he replied, "Then give me a check for fifty thousand. I just finished doing all of the work on the fifth tee box."

Julie exclaimed, "I can't do that! That's illegal!"

An angry Lew grabbed the checkbook away from her and made a point to cop a feel by rubbing his arm against her breast again. He started to write a check. "I'll run my business how I see fit," Lew insisted. "Get used to it."

Julie grabbed her purse and stomped out of the office.

CHAPTER TWENTY-FIVE

The Next Day at the Golf Course . . .

"Alright, Julie. The course is in great condition. It looks like we're ready for the tournament," J Dub said proudly to his trusted assistant.

"And all of it was done without one bit of help from Lew. What a butt hole," Julie commented. The two of them stood together peering out the picture window as the sun was rising. "J Dub, the course looks more manicured than my nails. If I didn't know better I would swear that you were trimming the course with scissors last night," Julie remarked as they both admired the beauty of the course.

"How do you know I didn't?" J Dub asked with a quick wink.

Julie smiled and started walking toward the coffee machine. Over her shoulder she asked, "I'm going to fire up the coffee pot, want some?"

"Nah, I'm good for now. There are more important things to digest." A couple of hours later, J Dub squinted toward the entrance as he heard traffic begin for the day. He scurried over to the parking lot to direct the processional of luxury cars. A Mercedes-Benz led them, followed by a Jaguar, followed by a BMW on so on. Cadillac's, Lincolns, and even a Porsche and a Lexus dotted the asphalt spaces.

J Dub had hired a lot of kids to assist the players upon their arrival. "Alright everybody, as the cars pull into the lot and park be available to load golf clubs into the carts for our players, ok? Make our guests feel welcome!" Everyone participated, including Marcia, who had made dozens of baskets of sandwiches for the group. Julie and a group of volunteers made sure that drinks were flowing in the circus-like tent and that all the activities were going according to plan.

J Dub checked in with Julie frequently and was pleased with the progress they were making. "You did a fantastic job, Jules. This event is going off without a hitch."

"Thanks, J Dub," Julie said. She accepted the compliment shyly; a nice comment from him meant more to her than a lifetime of "atta girls" from Lew because she knew he was sincere in his praise. She had worked hard for it, too.

Promptly at ten o'clock the event started. J Dub was paired with Mel and two doctors from the hospital. Dr. Peterson was a younger doctor in his forties and Dr. Thompson was somewhat older. They shared a passion for golf and genuinely wanted to try to win the tournament. So Mel "stacked" his team by inviting J Dub to be their "ringer." Mel thought that it was necessary to have someone in their group that could be counted on.

As with most scramble tournaments, the holes were crammed with golfers. The play was very slow and there were long waits between shots. Of course, much of the slow play was because these golfers were busy working all day and didn't get out often enough. Playing quality was sub-standard to say the least but that was to be expected on a day like today. To a lot of them it was a day off from the pressures that were associated with a normal work day at the hospital.

Mel's team got off to a very good start. They had six birdies on the first seven holes, thanks in great part to J Dub's solid swings. He could flat play the game of golf.

The foursome hit a little bit of a snag on the course and was forced to go through a minor delay on the eighth tee box. Mel stood back as J Dub prepared to hit a drive. "Let's see the master hit one into the stratosphere!" Mel yelled. J Dub smiled and continued with his concentration. He adjusted his grip to really lay into the ball. The doctors stood completely silent as they studied his technique up close. *POW!* J Dub connected with the ball on a perfect swing. The doctors were amazed and Mel let out a low whistle of deep admiration for J Dub's obvious natural talent. "Do you think that you'll ever try the tour again?"

J Dub was flattered by the attention but nonchalantly shrugged his shoulders saying, "That was a dream of mine at one time. Running this place is my everyday vision now."

Mel persisted. "Don't waste that God-gifted talent that you have, son."

"I had my chance and it didn't work out. That door closed. Marcia was pregnant and a new door opened up," J Dub volunteered.

"How many hours a week do you put in here?"

"Somewhere in the neighborhood of seventy to eighty," J Dub replied.

"That sounds like an emergency room doctor," cracked Dr. Peterson.

J Dub smiled. "You know, when you think about it, the work environment is pretty nice. Almost all of the people are out here are on their day off and they're in a good mood."

"But with those kind of hours, you won't see your kids grow up," Mel stated.

J Dub took a philosophical tone. "There are different ways to win in life, Mel. This is my way of setting my kids up down the road."

With that, a drink cart approached the tee box. Three girls dressed in short shorts and v-shaped halter tops occupied the seat. It was obvious that they were enjoying a day on the golf course. The weather was picture perfect. A cool breeze was blowing and the sun felt warm on bare skin—this was San Diego, wasn't it?

The driver, Amy, was an attractive young woman in her mid-twenties. She had light brown hair tucked neatly into a visor and her halter top was positioned to accentuate her ample cleavage. "Who wants a drink?" asked Amy. She flirted with Mel and the two doctors. "I know at least one of you wants one. Come on, don't be shy!" She smiled and winked at Mel in particular.

Mel was a functional alcoholic. He had risen to a respectable level within the hospital despite his penchant for partying. Everyone at the hospital was aware that Mel had a weakness for vodka. In his defense, Mel was able to resist drinking on the job. However, the minute that his work day was over it was common knowledge that he could be found at the local watering hole.

His love for a cocktail would many times lead to a cab ride home and a bright red nose the next day. The powers-that-be would turn their heads because Mel ran a very profitable operation. His infectious personality and towering stature made it next to impossible to dismiss him. When Mel replied, "I'll have a Peach Snapple!" everyone on the tee box grinned.

Dr. Thompson immediately turned to the other members in his golfing group. His comment was sort of a signal to the others that things could get out of hand, "Uh, oh."

Mel was quite proud of the drink girls that he had recruited for the day. He had gotten permission from J Dub to bring his own cart girls from the hospital to serve drinks to the golfers on the course. "J Dub, these ladies are three nurses that work at the hospital. I'd like for you to meet Amy, Beth, and Carin. And make sure you say Cuh-wren."

As Amy handed the Peach Snapple to Mel she said, "Here you go La-La."

J Dub started laughing. " . . . La-La? Where did that come from?"

"Two more Peach Snapple's and you'll see," stated Dr. Thompson. "He'll be in La-La land."

"You never told me that you had a nickname," J Dub jested.

Mel enjoyed the fact that his peer group knew about his addiction. He grinned affectionately at Dr. Thompson. Of course there was no way to tell how many drinks Mel had under his belt at this time of day. The playing partners in his group figured that Mel had probably started at breakfast since this was his day off. Mel turned to the girls and asked, "How are the tips running today?"

Beth was a cute brunette. "We're not making anything, Mel. It looks like we need to get the players loaded."

"You know that these doctors are heavy tippers ladies. Fill 'em up."

The girls were anxious to serve the golfers. They ran around the drink cart waiting on the players. Mel sneaked off to his golf bag and pulled out a quart of Grey Goose. He took a thermos bottle out of his golf bag and mixed the vodka with the Peach Snapple.

Mel grabbed a couple of hands full of ice out of the drink cart and packed the cubes into his thermos. He shook the humongous cocktail before taking a healthy swig. "You know, I've been thinking. We need to figure out a way for you girls to increase your tips. Why don't you girls get those tops up?" Mel said with a devilish grin to the three cart girls.

He pulled his shirt out of his pants and tried to lift it over his head. The shirt got caught on his head. That, coupled with the effect of the vodka, put Mel in a ridiculous position. His ample belly overlapped his belt buckle and he stumbled.

As he staggered around with his shirt over his head Carin said, "We can't do that out here. We're decent girls."

Mel got out of the mess that he was in and pulled his shirt down from his head. He replied, "Decency doesn't have a thing to do with being entrepreneurs.

If you're afraid to show those puppies, then what do you say we buy some belly shots?"

Beth was the adventurous one in the group. She hopped into the golf cart and spread-eagled across the seat. "I'll go for that!"

Mel licked his chops. "That's my kind of girl!"

Mel ran to his golf bag and grabbed the Grey Goose. He handed it to Amy. Amy acted as if she had played this game before. She poured the vodka on Beth's lips. The liquid cascaded down Beth's chin, across her throat, and through her cleavage. The vodka formed a puddle in Beth's navel.

Mel couldn't resist himself. He dove into Beth's navel and lapped up every drop. He rose with an impish grin on his face, peeled off a twenty dollar bill, and gave it to Beth. Feeling proud of his accomplishment, Mel yelled, "Next!" He was obviously starting to feel the effects of the vodka.

"My turn!" shouted Amy. She jumped into the cart and sprawled across the seat in a similar fashion. Carin grabbed the vodka bottle.

The whereabouts of Lew Zerrmann were unbeknownst to the group that was frolicking on the tee box. He had retreated to his safe haven—the highest point on the golf course. Lew sat atop his motorcycle, under the large shade tree, and surveyed his domain. Through his binoculars he noticed a commotion in the distance.

With an ornery spirit, Lew revved the motorcycle down the hill and headed across the golf course. He was oblivious to the golfers that were busy making their shots. The muffler on the motorcycle echoed across the property. It blared out of control until he screeched to a stop next to the tee box where the drink cart was parked. As he slid to a halt, Lew caught Mel as he lapped vodka out of Amy's navel. "What the hell is going on here?" Lew demanded.

Amy grabbed a twenty dollar bill from Mel and reveled in the good fortune that the day had suddenly offered. She innocently said, "We're giving belly shots for tips. It beats serving drinks for a dollar."

A disgusted scowl encompassed Lew's face. He grabbed the vodka bottle from Carin and turned to Mel. "Where did this come from?"

Mel glanced up from the compromising position that he had found himself. With vodka smeared all over his face he replied, "It goes great with Peach Snapple. You ought to try some!"

Every party needed a pooper. Lew was determined to fill that role on this day. With newfound morality, Lew barked, "That's it for you guys. Your day is over and so is this charity." With a swift motioning of his hands, Lew told the golfers and the girls to get into their carts and drive back to the clubhouse. "Take it on in. Head back to the clubhouse. This is my place and I won't tolerate this kind of behavior out here."

As they started the long trek back to the clubhouse, Mel turned to Dr. Peterson and exclaimed, "What an asshole."

"Some people just don't get it," Dr. Peterson replied.

Amy, with tears in her eyes, turned to J Dub and cried, "It's my day off. All I was trying to do was make a couple of extra bucks for my kids."

J Dub, out of fear for retaliation from Lew, could only say, "He's the boss."

The girls drove off behind Mel and the doctors. J Dub turned to Lew and bristled, "They were just having some fun."

" . . . With their own booze!" Lew yelled.

"We're trying to build the business, aren't we?" J Dub persisted.

Lew tipped his hand as to what was really irritating him. "Then they can pay for it!"

"It's their day off from work. Let them have some fun."

"Not at my expense!"

"Oh, give me a break!" J Dub continued. "You were dead set on ruining this event from the beginning, weren't you? Well, congratulations! Take a victory lap! Your motive is as transparent as your business sense!" J Dub was fuming, but he sensed that he had better keep his mouth shut before it got him into more trouble with Lew.

Lew glared at J Dub then mounted his motorcycle and gunned its motor to a deafening pitch before squealing off.

CHAPTER TWENTY-SIX

In the days that followed J Dub's frustrations were reaching the boiling point. He hated to bring his problems home to Marcia, as he knew her probable solution to the matter. He had worked too hard and invested too much. He had an ally in Julie, but if he brought her down, then things really would be miserable at work. That left Bogey to listen to J Dub's ranting and venting about Lew. With a simple cock of the head, Bogey became J Dub's sounding board. J Dub took Bogey to the driving range and would hit one ball after the other while cursing Lew. Somehow, J Dub felt that Bogey was the only one that really understood his circumstances.

J Dub avoided Lew as much as possible. Lew became more obsessed with his motorcycle, painstakingly polishing its chrome. He touched the body of the motorcycle with the hand of a lover and subconsciously patted it in a sexual way. "We're not going to let anyone or anything happen to our land, are we gorgeous?"

Lew whispered sensually. As he stroked and caressed his bike, he looked off into the distance of his clubhouse. He smiled an evil smile and carefully finished polishing his motorcycle.

The days went by. The weeks and months went by. And, soon the seasons would pass. J Dub was faced with a couple of challenging situations. He worked for a partner that constantly reached for power and control. He tried to work within the confines of those demands and tried to balance his work life with his family life.

The real joys for J Dub were at home. He cherished the time that he could spend with his daughter yet, in some ways, a chasm was developing in him. He enjoyed the time that he spent with his newborn but the hourly demands of running the golf course were present too. He enjoyed every minute of being a father, a parent, and a husband, but he knew that to fulfill that pleasure he had to be successful bringing in the money that could afford those privileges.

In spite of the conflict that had occurred between home and work, J Dub had developed a love for his job. It was great to be around the guys. It was wonderful to be self-employed. Plus he had a bright future and watched the business expand. Sure, the moments around Lew became stressful at times, but J Dub decided to overlook those instances and look at the whole picture instead.

Marcia also had seen her opportunities expand. She loved every minute of being a mother and a parent and a wife. She felt as if she had delivered on her purpose on earth by bringing new life into it. Marcia felt the joy that only a mother could feel and became very protective of Gail.

A few months after Gail was born, Marcia returned part-time to her catering interests. It was the sort of job that allowed her to be a stay-at-home mom and earn extra income for the family. She was constantly nagging at J Dub about the number of hours that he was putting in at the golf course. Not only were weekends peak business times for J Dub, but the amount of hours that he was expected to be at the course during the week were growing, too.

While she was understanding of the demands placed on J Dub, Marcia still wanted J Dub to be around the house more to help her with Gail and her catering business. Marcia was becoming increasingly irritable and defensive about the growing demands Lew placed on J Dub.

"Can't you get some more time off to help me?" Marcia asked one night.

"I don't want to jeopardize my relationship with Lew any more than I have to," J Dub replied.

"The golf course is more important to you than your wife and daughter?" Marcia asked. She readied herself to spar with her husband and his ridiculous reply.

"No, I didn't mean it that way." said J Dub. "We'll have a wonderful future if I can play my cards right."

Marcia was frustrated. She wanted more attention from her husband that she was receiving. "And you want me to do it all around here? J Dub, in case you didn't realize, it takes time and effort to make a household run and to take care of a baby."

"Aw, come on, Honey. We knew when we took the deal that it would mean a lot of weekends on the job," J Dub groaned.

"Yes, but not every waking hour, indefinitely! When was the last time you had a weekend off? You haven't! That's not realistic, J Dub."

"We're both learning a lesson on what he's all about. With some of the stuff that he's pulled lately, I don't even know if I know the guy."

"Well, I do!" Then she made mock introductions. "J Dub Schroeder, meet Lew Zermann, the asshole! Mr. Asshole, meet my gullible husband, J Dub!"

Conversations of this sort always sent J Dub into a despondent mood. The aggravation was etched all over his face.

"I'm sorry if living our lives interferes with Lew's plans, but that is just too damn bad," Marcia angrily responded. She was used to speaking her mind and letting the sarcasm fly at her husband when she was angry. But she saw a look in J Dub's eyes that made her stop and settle her temper.

"Look, I don't like it any better than you. I know that is hard for you to believe, but I am struggling here. Give me a break, will ya?" J Dub quickly turned his head and rubbed his neck. "I'm trying to think about our future. It's our family's future, Marcia!" He could feel his eyes stinging with tears and quickly wiped them away.

And so it had become for J Dub. Lew was a demanding, non-compassionate partner and Marcia wanted her husband back. No matter what he did he couldn't seem to make anyone happy. J Dub was being torn in two directions. One hand told him to work his backside off for a promising future and the other hand told him to spend more time with his family.

"I guess there isn't any use in discussing this. There doesn't seem to be a simple solution," Marcia offered. "Come here," and she took her husband in her arms and let him hold her for as long as he wanted while she rubbed his back.

CHAPTER TWENTY-SEVEN

Eleanor Hackett was one sharp cookie. She had braved and defied the odds of growing up shy and physically awkward in a dysfunctional home. Her father was a weak and fearful man who succumbed to the allure of leaving his family when responsibility for them loomed too large.

That left Ellie and her mother and older sister to fend for themselves. The three of them had to band together to make the household work. With that environment thrown into their laps Ellie was forced to grow up in a hurry. She rapidly developed an affinity for a dollar. The trio had to watch every penny that came in and went out. This step in her life built a foundation of strength that she found noticeably absent in what she perceived were her adversaries . . . men. When asked about her dad as a child, she famously responded, "Make no mistake. I had a father, not a daddy. There is a distinct difference."

As she matured Ellie's body kept growing and growing. She never did possess much "eye appeal" and was constantly ridiculed by the kids at school. When her body started to grow and fill out she turned into a very large woman. In high school, Ellie was nearly six feet tall and weighed well over two hundred pounds. Her hardships and awkward moments in life proved to be the perfect ruse for her future success.

While the other kids in high school socialized and enjoyed their teenage years, Ellie became anti-social and hit the books. Her life was destined for great things and attending the prom wasn't on her action plan even if someone would have asked her. Living the life of a misfit allowed Ellie to develop a keen interest in defending the underdog. She developed a firm understanding of accounting and continued on to get her MBA in college. After that, Ellie enrolled in law school and got her law degree. At the ripe age of twenty-seven she had earned the right to place "Esquire" behind her last name along with taxation expertise.

The government took notice of her ability during a summer internship. After attaining her law credentials Ellie went to work for the U. S. Attorney's office. Her area of expertise was tax accounting and white-collar crime. She could tear apart a financial statement or a tax return and expose a crook in a matter of minutes. Her tenacity made the little guys squirm and she quickly earned a reputation for sending people to prison. After all, white collar crooks were prone to have their hands in the proverbial cookie jar either financially and/or legally. She made sure she was an expert at both.

"Ellie, wait up! I want to talk to you about a situation I am working on," Brian Moore shouted to her in the hallway. More quietly he said, "I've talked to a mother and son that believe they have been fleeced of their estate. I took a brief look at the circumstances, and I can't determine what the loophole is. Interested?"

"Who are the victims?" she asked.

"Does it make a difference?"

"Well, no. But if this is a small claims gripe, then my current workload won't permit it."

"It's the Morton estate," Brian advised.

Ellie chomped at the bit. "Of course I'll help! You say you looked for all the obvious issues?" she inquired as Brian nodded emphatically. "Let me look at the particulars. If necessary I may bring in the FBI and IRS just in case," she reasoned.

"This is what I found out, Ellie. The title company where the closing was done for this property is now defunct. There aren't any escrow records, earnest money receipts, or tax records. Brian advised. "A guy by the name of Lewford E. Zerrmann purchased the property. He formed a corporation to possibly cover his tracks. All the docs were done by licensed, accredited professionals. The FBI had nothing on the fraudulent deed claim. According to the estate the tax returns don't show any capital gains on any IRS records."

"To go one step further I asked for info on George Pierce, Walter Hancock, and Maurice DiMonte, as well as Raymond Parsons. Even though some of these men are known to us, they all had a hand in this transaction at one point or another." Ellie nodded and jotted some notes.

Brian could tell by the look in her eyes that he had gotten her attention. "On the surface, everything appeared to be in order. Lew had even taken a minority partner named J. W. Schroeder in to run the business. I can't put my finger on exactly what happened, so I am bringing it to the expert."

Ellie smiled and thought for a moment. "Brian, one small thing doesn't make any sense to me. Let me take care of it and I will get to the bottom of it."

"That's what I was hoping you would say," Brian offered.

~ ~ ~

Several days later . . .

Brian and Ellie spent a lot of time together. Not only did they work together behind the scenes prepping for a case, but they often worked hand in hand in front of a judge and jury in the courtroom. As they were wrapping up a different case and preparing to leave the courtroom, Brian turned to Ellie and said, "Once again, congratulations are in order. You're a true master at figuring out how the crooks try to hide details in these white-collar crime cases. As my top assistant, you're still undefeated."

Ellie was not that impressed.

"You've won six in a row without a loss for my office, Ellie."

"These small-time guys are easy, Brian. I'm bored."

As they walked down the hall, she brought Brian up to speed on the Morton case. Ellie was clearly nonchalant. She casually said, "The investigation turned up something interesting. It might be time to move in a different direction."

"What's that?"

"It looks to me like there have been some money laundering activities taking place."

"Who's the culprit?" Brian asked as his curiosity was piqued.

Ellie stopped in her tracks, paused, and looked him in the eye. She said, "Maurice DiMonte."

Brian responded in a manner that was not expected. "Don't go after Monty, Ellie."

"May I ask why not?"

"He's a good friend of Raymond Parsons. Don't go there," Brian warned.

"Well, it may be too late for Mr. DiMonte."

Brian was visibly upset with the news that he had just heard. Raymond Parsons was a political friend of his and the two of them had done political favors for one another over the years. Maurice DiMonte was the attorney for Parsons. He didn't want to strain that relationship. There were too many political functions that Brian and Raymond attended together. "You're my top assistant, Ellie. Err on the side of caution."

"DiMonte is a lawyer with a lot to lose. I want to know what's going on. He and Parsons and Zerrmann have been up to something."

"Be careful. They play to win," Brian advised.

"I want bigger fish. I'm calling DiMonte in. They're not above the law," Ellie countered. "Don't worry about me, I can handle myself."

CHAPTER TWENTY-EIGHT

Sometime later . . .

Lew was a skilled and polished predator. He had it all figured out pretty early. He had gotten a sucker for a partner and he intended to work him to death. Actually, that was a pretty good strategy. Lew was good at delegating and he had found the perfect person that would obey. J Dub had a wife that expected him to be responsible and he had a mortgage payment and a child to provide for. J Dub wasn't going anywhere.

Lew knew very little about being a "people person' and even less about golf. He was tight with the dough and he would leave it to J Dub to bring the cash in. Lew couldn't stand to be in the clubhouse socializing with the customers. It made him feel too uncomfortable.

It seemed as if Lew's only hobby was learning how to control people and situations. That sort of power was about the only thing that gave him pleasure.

He had no wife. He had no children. He had no faith in an almighty power. His self-centered conduct led to very destructive and evil actions. Even the number of friends he had was restricted because he tended to use everyone that he met for alternative motives.

One of his few friends was Monty. Their liaison had developed into a relationship of convenience more than anything else. The bond between them went way back to their grade school years. Like a lot of people, their connection had seen its ups and downs. In a sad and sick way these two guys needed each other. They both had taken advantage of the "bottom feeders." Being true capitalists had made them that way. Lew had a knack for living on the edge and taking advantage of every little nook and cranny that was available to him.

Monty was there to help Lew out of his little jams. Without Lew, Monty would have no purpose. Without Monty, Lew would not be as bold and brazen with his scams. So, even though their connection had been tested, they migrated instinctually to each other for the next challenge.

Lew was inside his compound reading *The Rise and Fall of the Third Reich* for the umpteenth time when the electronic buzzer went off signaling that a guest was at his gate. After granting access he heard a car approaching his driveway area. He smiled, dog-eared his book and walked to the nearest mirror to check his comb over. With everything in order he walked outside to greet his guests.

Lew sucked in his gut a bit and pulled his trousers up well past his belly button. He wore his customary shirt with "Lew" embroidered over the shirt pocket. His pants fit snugly around his balls and, being short, exposed his white socks. He strutted around like a tomcat prowling a back alley looking for discarded fish.

Somehow, Lew must have sensed what to wear. Out of Monty's car jumped a woman in full biker attire. She was in her early forties and could have been mistaken for a grandmother in her late fifties. Her cotton candy-like, bleached blonde hair exposed dark roots. She had a large gap between her two front teeth and walked like she had been sitting on a fire hydrant all weekend. She had a little wrinkled pooch of belly that jiggled atop her belt buckle. Her caked-on makeup highlighted her eyelashes, thick and clumped with old mascara. The black leather was two sizes too small for her bulging thighs and expanding buttocks. Though sadly ironic, Lew was catching her at her best.

Glowing and smiling, Monty said, "Lew, I'd like for you to meet my ex-wife, Lois."

"It's hard to believe that we've never met after all of these years," Lew said.

After an obligatory handshake and a quick smile Lois gushed, "Monty's told me so much about you." It was as if Monty had prepared her in advance to throw out the compliments to Lew. She immediately made Lew feel as if he was larger than life by her submissive behavior. She knew how to flirt and use body language to attract a man.

Lois had gotten pregnant when she was seventeen. The father was fifteen years older than her at the time and the families more-or-less forced them to get married. She gave birth and raised a daughter in a loveless marriage.

That was until her daughter was thirteen or so.

Her husband had a quadruple bypass. He had smacked her around a little and put on sixty pounds, so while he dealt with his health issues, she played around on him. He found out about her liaisons and filed for divorce.

As things turned out, her attorney for the divorce settlement was an aggressive slimeball named Maurice (Monty) DiMonte. They worked an agreement out that, simply put, was nothing but functional under the barter system. She got a few dollars of cash in the settlement and Monty got plenty of sexual favors for his fee.

After the divorce was finalized, Monty and Lois flew to Nevada and returned as husband and wife. He drank heartily and often, put on some weight, and suffered from erectile dysfunction after a few years of marriage. Basically, they couldn't do each other any good. She liked to please her man and Monty couldn't get it up.

By looking at them, it shouldn't have come as any surprise. Monty had a gut that lapped over his belt and wore his thinning hair in a ponytail. Monty smoked, chewed, drank and every night snored loudly. Lois was lily-white in color. She had a belly of her own with stretch marks and abundant cellulite. They had become so disgusting to each other after Monty's inability to perform that they couldn't bear sleeping in the same bed. Eventually they agreed to sleep in separate rooms.

Finally, after about eight or nine years they had called it quits. Lois had been through the wringer. She didn't work, had latched onto other men for survival all of her life, and was faced with a body and looks that were in sharp decline. She needed a new mark.

Lew smiled at her like a blood-thirsty Bassett hound. He spat on his hand to mat down his comb over. As he sucked in his gut to make a better first impression, Lois spotted Lew's motorcycle which was parked nearby. She walked over to it and began stroking the seat suggestively. It looked like she was giving somebody a hand job, or wanted to.

Lew immediately reacted to her aggressiveness. He seized the moment with, "We'll have to go for a spin."

That brought a provocative grin from Lois. The gap between her two front teeth suggested that she couldn't wait to grab Lew by the hand and drag him to the nearest mattress.

"You two may have more in common than we ever did," observed Monty. Even though they were no longer husband and wife, they had remained friends. He hoped that she would find a man that could satisfy her sexual appetite. It was easier to fix her up with someone than to listen to her gripe about how middle-aged men were lousy lovers.

Lois flirted with Lew as hard as she could. Her attention was directly focused on the cycle and the man that could start it up.

It had been a few years since Lew had experienced that kind of sexual attraction. He sucked in his gut a little more until his face became flushed. He stuck out his chest even further. Whether she wanted him or his motorcycle or his pocketbook was secondary. The fact that he was getting the brunt of the attention from a female that he had just met was what mattered most.

"Take good care of her, Lew" Monty called out. "Hey, by the way, that ball-busting federal bitch is after my ass good," replied Monty. Ellie Hackett had been prying into the affairs of Monty with a steadfast resolve.

"Just keep your mouth shut and we'll win. Everything will be fine," Lew said. With his forefinger and thumb, Lew made a motion as if to zip his lips together as he cranked up his motorcycle.

"That's easy for you to say. The heat is off of you," Monty retaliated.

Monty had done a nice job setting them up together. With his work finished he got into his car and drove off. Lois took a seat on Lew's cycle. Monty and Lew shared so many things in life that it came as no surprise that they would share a woman, too.

Chapter Twenty-Nine

Early summer—1986 . . .

Seasons passed and the more things changed, the more they remained the same. J Dub was continually caught between a rock and a hard place trying to run a profitable business and running interference for Lew. The boys adopted Prairie Winds as their second home and spent every day together. Their routine was as constant and predictable as a timer. They met for coffee and doughnuts in the morning and played early rounds of golf with Bogey nearby.

Bogey grew up on the course oblivious to the luxurious lifestyle he was afforded. He was playful and accompanied the boys on their rounds of golf each day. He managed to occupy himself with swimming in the pond and chasing butterflies and birds when the golfing action was slow. Such were the lazy days of summer when a pooch could nap under a shade tree as the warm breezes rustled the leaves overhead. The weather was absolutely perfect and the golf course had the profits to prove it.

"We've been rolling in the cash this year," Lew commented to J Dub one day in the office as J Dub counted the proceeds for a bank deposit.

"We've been catching a lot of breaks. The weather has co-operated and we've been getting a ton of repeat business," J Dub conceded.

"We might as well own the bank," Lew said as his eyes stared at the stack of money on the desk in front of J Dub.

"It's nice to get ahead of the game a little bit. Some of the pressure goes away," J Dub agreed. He could finally see that all his hard work was paying off handsomely.

"I've been talking to some of the neighbors. We've got an opportunity to pick up some more property," Lew proposed. He couldn't stand the thought of the money sitting idly in the bank. He wanted to get his hands on it.

"What do you want to do?" J Dub inquired.

"You can't go wrong buying land. It looks like we have the staying power now. I'd like to start buying up the neighbors and maybe build another one of these. Then we can put houses on any of the property that is left over," Lew projected.

"If that's what you want to do, then we have the money to pull it off," J Dub stated.

"Can you run and manage two courses at the same time?" Lew probed.

The thought of expanding the business thrilled J Dub. He began to envision the two courses and eventual condominiums and homes surrounding the golf courses. His family would be setup for life. "Of course! Let's go for it if that is what you want to do." The look on Lew's face suggested that he had something up his sleeve.

Their plans for expansion took off immediately. They had taken that summer's proceeds and bought an extra forty acres of land adjacent to the property. Cash was paid for the property and Lew negotiated crop rights with the seller that would allow the seller to get the soybeans off of the field before winter came. However, something happened before the seller could harvest the crop. It started raining. And it rained. And it rained.

Lew got impatient. He had wanted to make an improvement to the course which called for the construction of a small lake. Lew was bored and had nothing to do. The beans were late coming off of the field, and the rain would have filled up the lake had it been built.

So Lew started the work anyway. That didn't set well with the seller because it meant a lower yield and a few bucks out of his pocket. Things got mighty tense around the golf course for a few days with Lew's various threats and his refusal to reimburse the seller for his loss.

It came to a head one morning when Elmer, the seller, came busting through the door of the pro shop. J Dub stood at the register. "Where is that son of a bitch?" Elmer demanded.

Elmer was all of about five foot six and one hundred and thirty pounds. He was frail, but ornery. He wore wire rimmed glasses and had on bib overalls and a green, John Deere hat. His twitching jaw established his unbelievable frustration.

"Whoa, Elmer, who are you looking for?" J Dub asked as he looked up from the counter.

"You know who I want! Lew! He built that sepia-ass pond before I finished getting my beans off of the field."

J Dub tried his best to diffuse the situation. "We bought that ground from you."

"And I had a reasonable time to get my crop off of the land."

"I guess that Lew thought you were taking too long," J Dub theorized.

"I still had the crop rights."

"He wouldn't mess you up on purpose," stated J Dub, defensively.

"Bull patties! I want some money for those beans that he ran over. If he doesn't get it to me today, then I'll come over here and spray Roundup all over his greens!"

Elmer was livid. He continued, "I've had enough of him trying to get every little bit of advantage on this deal. I want my money! This is one part of the deal he isn't going to win on!"

The boys in the back shook their heads in disbelief. The amount that was being disputed only amounted to a few hundred dollars. Lew had been too cheap to pay for the damage that he caused and Elmer was about ready to have a coronary artery explode over a few bushels of soybeans. It was instances such as these that brought J Dub back to reality on the difficulties of dealing with Lew's antics.

"Get it taken care of or I'll do it for ya!" Elmer yelled as he headed out the door.

In his haste, Elmer bumped into Coach Thomas who was coming into the pro shop. The Coach was an attractive black man that stood about six foot four. He was in his thirties and a very athletic man. Elmer's small frame did not stand a chance against the muscular physique of Coach. He bounced off and continued out the door.

Coach Thomas had earned All-America honors at a Division Two NCAA University. He could shoot the eyes out of a basketball. After leading his team in scoring during his senior year, Coach gave the semi-pro circuit a try. A couple of years of long bus rides and third class travel took its toll. Coach hung up his sneakers and took a job coaching the local high school.

He was an avid golfer and had a regular tee time with his friends at Prairie Winds. That had come courtesy of some promotional work that J Dub had done. J Dub thought it would be beneficial to business if discounted fees could be offered to school teachers. So he distributed school passes to teachers. It was more of a goodwill gesture than anything else. The teachers would have the opportunity to play for perhaps eight to ten weeks in the summer. Any play in the spring and fall was limited due to the daylight hours that dwindled after school let out.

That idea caught on. Coach always had a standard tee time. He would usually bring two of his buddies and, more often than not, golf with another black man named Thomas Jefferson Booker. Booker was in his early thirties also and had played college basketball with the Coach several years back. He was a very handsome and physically fit man too. Their competitiveness was keen and their friendship strengthened because of it.

On this particular morning Coach and Booker and a couple buddies came through the door only to nearly be knocked over by the little tornado exiting the pro shop. "What stirred up that little hornet?" Coach asked J Dub.

J Dub just shrugged it off. He really wasn't in the mood to share the golf course problems with the customers. J Dub changed the subject. "Hey, your basketball team did pretty well at the state tourney this year, didn't they?"

"I was proud of them. They really came on at the end of the year."

"I saw where they fell just one basket short."

Coach was proud of the effort that his team put forth. "Yeah, but they showed a lot of heart. It really makes you feel good, if you know what I mean."

"That's got to be a rewarding feeling," J Dub concurred.

A smug look of achievement overwhelmed the Coach. "Say, I've got something for you," Coach said as he handed a pan of brownies to J Dub. "My wife's recipe is the best!"

"We'll put these to good use, won't we guys?" J Dub yelled across the pro shop. "Are there four of you today?" J Dub asked as he wrote their names on the sign-in sheet.

"Yeah, here's my school pass," Coach replied.

Lew and Lois walked into the pro shop only seconds after the transaction took place. With the sight of the four black men in the pro shop, Lew stopped in his tracks. He stared at the foursome and gave them a menacing glance. His mood quickly turned to business and Lew headed straight to the sign-in sheet to see if the foursome paid.

As he counted up the number of players, Lew noticed the pan of brownies. He grabbed one and took a bite. With a mouthful of food, Lew mumbled, "These are great!"

"Coach's wife made those," J Dub said.

The Coach beamed with pleasure. In that instant Lew finished counting the number of players that had teed off. He looked aghast and spat the brownie onto the floor at Coach's feet. He feigned a choking cough. "It must have gone down the wrong pipe," Lew stammered.

"Bullshit," Coach said as he took a step toward Lew. Coach had been around long enough to know when a racial gesture had been made toward him. He had grown up in the projects and had survived a tough childhood. He didn't want to relive the same discriminatory action that he had experienced as a young kid.

Booker quickly raised his eyebrows and stepped between the two. Their desire to win went way back to their college days on the court and Booker knew that his friend was in no mood to take that kind of behavior from Lew.

The Coach settled himself down and calmly turned to J Dub. "Why don't you hand them back to me so I don't get sued?"

J Dub grabbed the pan of brownies and handed them to Coach. The Coach was still frothing at the mouth to continue the confrontation, but glared at Lew instead. Lew defiantly stared back, confident that this massive man wasn't going to touch him. The foursome headed out the door and off to the first tee.

After they exited the pro shop, Lew turned to J Dub and said, "J Dub, you can't win with that type around here. We weren't meant to mix with those people. Keep them off the premises."

~   ~   ~

Lew would retreat to the sanctity of his hill more and more, especially when there was a disagreement or some sort of conflict. Now he had a companion and a built-in ally. Lois was in need of someone to take care of her so she would normally always accompany Lew on the ride to the top of the hill.

After the confrontation with the Coach in the pro shop, Lew and Lois took off for the hilltop. The blaring muffler echoed across the course as he powered the bike to its destination. It was meant to be a constant annoyance for anyone within earshot and a not so subtle reminder of his supremacy over the golf course.

Under the tranquility of the shade tree, Lew would preach to Lois about how good he had it. "This is the best view in the whole county. No one can tell me what to do," he would say. "This is all mine," he would appear drunk with his own power as they looked down on the golf course below them. Lew would talk to Lois as if she was an inanimate object.

It didn't take long for the Coach and his playing partners to come into sight. "Well those sons of bitches . . ." he muttered under his breath as he squinted down the fairway at Coach and his group walking the course. The more they seemed to be enjoying themselves, the more infuriated Lew became.

With Lois sitting behind him on the cycle, Lew glanced over his shoulder with a look of disgust. "Watch this, Lois. Time to make those assholes run," he countered. He grabbed the remote control device and hit a few buttons. The sprinklers were activated. Water sprayed all over the green where the Coach and his buddies were putting.

"Hah! Look at'em run! They're not so tough! They'll think twice before messing with me," Lew shouted. He glanced over his shoulder with a pleased grin on his face. Lois hugged him tighter. She returned a pleasing grin and laid the side of her face on the shoulder of her new best friend. The power that Lew possessed appealed to her.

"We'll fix this problem," Lew said.

With that he raced down the hill and raced the motorcycle toward the green where the Coach and his playing partners were toweling off. When Lew and Lois arrived, the foursome was approaching the next tee box.

"Can I see your receipt?" Lew asked.

"We're playing on a school pass," Coach replied.

"You still paid, didn't you?" Lew persisted.

"Yes we did . . . at a reduced rate."

"Then I need to see your receipt."

"J Dub didn't give me one," Coach said.

Lew spoke defiantly. "Go get one or you'll be told to leave."

"Can't you just call the pro shop?" Coach asked.

" . . . I guess I could, if you were the *right* kind of customer," Lew replied.

"You mean right color, don't you Cracker?" leered the Coach.

"If the shoe fits . . ." Lew said and smiled his evil smirk. Each of the men glared at the other and Lew knew that Coach was not going to get physical with him. "Listen you ninety-nine. It wouldn't look so good in the newspapers if a high school coach were to beat up a white man, on a peaceful day at the golf course, now would it? I'm thinking that it might even get ya fired. What do you think, Lois?" Lew patronized his dim witted girlfriend as she smiled her sickening smile to the Coach. "Hell, a big strappin' fella like yourself, might even be tempted to rough up Miss Lois, here. What a shame." Lew locked his eyes with the Coach for several moments.

Finally Booker intervened. "Pick your battles, Coach. It's not worth it."

With that statement, calmer heads prevailed. Coach turned to his playing partners and said, "I'll be right back guys." The Coach hopped into a golf cart and began the long trek back to the pro shop.

Lew felt the power and control of the situation. After all, he was on his own turf and could make his own rules and do what he wanted. The minute that Coach got out of sight he turned to Booker. "And Leroy, you can bet I'll make sure that all you others paid, too."

Booker had to bite his lip to keep from turning a nasty situation into a brawl. Lew returned to his motorcycle and screamed away. Lois hugged her man tighter than ever.

J Dub was in the pro shop working the counter. He had just dealt with the Coach and glanced out the window to see Lew racing across a fairway. *Right on time*, he thought to himself. He went to the coffee machine and placed the pot of coffee into the microwave and heated the pot to the boiling point.

As Lew reached the parking lot J Dub returned the hot pot of coffee to the burner. Seconds later, Lew strolled through the front door. He continued to the coffee machine and poured a cup of coffee.

"What was all of that nonsense with the Coach?" J Dub inquired as he made a concerted effort to keep his cool.

Lew did his best imitation of playing dumb. "What are you talking about?"

"You know exactly what I'm talking about."

Without checking the temperature of the coffee in the cup, Lew took a sip and spat the hot coffee out all over the floor.

"That's getting to be a habit with you," J Dub said with a very slight smirk.

Lew rushed to the nearest water faucet. "Dammit! What did you do?"

"I microwaved it so it would be the way you liked it."

Lew glared at him. J Dub nonchalantly turned and headed toward the door. On the counter was a sign that J Dub had started to make. Lew glanced at it and asked, "What are you making?"

"It's only a sign for the parking lot," J Dub answered.

The sign on the counter read: RESERVED FOR BLACKS . . . NIGHTS ONLY

"We can put it in the far corner of the lot," J Dub offered. He had done his best to be passively aggressive without entering into a confrontation with his partner.

As if he missed the total point, Lew replied," If they come in here at night, they'll steal us blind. I don't want them in here period."

J Dub walked out the door in total disgust.

CHAPTER THIRTY

At home later that night . . .

Marcia's catering business kept her occupied but there were plenty of times that she found herself daydreaming while doing monotonous tasks. Such is the case when making hundreds of meatballs. She began to think about when she first met J Dub. A smile came to her lips as she was reminded of their romance. She knew he was the one. *That was one beautiful man*, she mused.

She knew the deal was sealed when J Dub kissed her for the first time. Marcia always prided herself as being a woman that wasn't easily impressed. Yet, when his lips softly caressed hers that first time, her knees almost buckled. She had never met a man that could kiss the way J Dub did. She also loved the way he accepted and loved her true self. He wasn't afraid of a strong woman like other men. That made him all the sexier to her. No doubt about it, she had it bad for J Dub. As she watched her hands make the meatballs over and over, she audibly sighed. She was so frustrated with her husband's absence at home. The more she thought about it, the more she became upset.

"Hi Hon, it's me," J Dub called as he shut the front door. Marcia glanced at the clock on the wall and noticed the time. *He gets home later and later,* she fumed as she continued making meatballs.

"I'm in the kitchen J Dub, making meatballs," she called out. He came in to the kitchen and wrapped his arms around her waist and nuzzled her neck.

"Could you use some help? I'm a master cook, remember?" He cheerfully volunteered. J Dub wanted to forget about the day's events.

"Thanks, Honey," Marcia tried to overcome her frustration with her husband's job. J Dub took the completed meatballs and began cooking them. "These are kind of large, aren't they? You won't make any money on this item," he offered. That was it. The straw that broke the camel's back.

"Who are you to tell me what I can or cannot make money on?" Marcia snapped back at him.

"I was just offering some advice. They look awfully big."

"What are you, an accountant now?"

J Dub shook his head. This had been brewing for quite some time. Marcia was very resentful of the hours that J Dub had been spending at the golf course. Ever since he told her that Lew demanded he work weekends and four out of five weekdays, there had been a tension in the air. He had very little time to spend with Marcia and Gail.

She threw a bag of chips at him. "You've been around him too damn much. You're starting to talk like him." Her feelings about Lew festered until they bubbled over.

"He's teaching me about business, I am trying to build a future for our family," J Dub reasoned.

"Bull! J Dub, if you keep the pace you are right now, neither your kids nor your wife is going to know who you even are. Do you really want that? Do you want Gail growing up not knowing what it's like to have a father?" Her eyes pierced through him. "Well, do you?" Marcia was adamant and wasn't backing down.

Without waiting for a reply, she quietly reminded him, "This job may cost you a wife and a family." J Dub stared at his wife and she maintained her point. He dejectedly hung his head and said nothing further. There was nothing else for either of them to say.

CHAPTER THIRTY-ONE

Early Fall—1986 . . .

Ellie Hackett had been trying her best to get to the bottom of the fraudulent deed claim that the Morton heirs had talked to Brian Moore about. The FBI couldn't come up with anything conclusive to help the government's case. At the very best it appeared as if the government might have a circumstantial case, but that wasn't good enough to try to go for a criminal conviction.

However, based on grand jury testimony and the available evidence, Ellie was fairly convinced that something had been taking place between Lew Zerrmann, Maurice DiMonte, and Raymond Parsons. She just couldn't put her finger on it and no one was talking.

The government had no idea about the small pot farm that Zerrmann had been harvesting. Nor did they have any inkling that it even existed. The farm was very well hidden. It was surrounded by the river thanks to a bend in the channel and a levee that carried railroad tracks as well as a large bluff.

It was difficult to get to, let alone discover.

Yet, on the other hand, DiMonte had been getting his hands on some cash and had been stashing it away in investments. Ellie originally thought that it might be campaign funds that had been coming into the Parsons coffers, but that turned up empty.

The only recourse available to Ellie was to call DiMonte into her office and try to get him to talk. It was a bright, colorful, autumn day when DiMonte appeared in her office. He reluctantly took a seat opposite her desk. She suddenly got up, walked over to the window and peered out at the lovely pastels that covered the grounds and dotted the nearby countryside.

"The reason I asked you in today, Maurice, is because your name surfaced during an FBI investigation of Lewferd E. Zerrmann," she blurted.

"And?" was all that Monty could muster.

"We didn't receive any glowing reports." She studied his movements as she returned to her desk. She had been taught to keep an eye open for any movement or nervous twitch, just in case she struck a sensitive nerve. With a touch of uneasiness, Maurice fidgeted with his hands.

As she took her seat behind her desk she said, "We don't have enough to make anything stick on your associates."

Maurice sat stoically. He didn't even blink.

"But we do have enough evidence on you for money laundering activities that can put you away for quite some time."

Maurice locked eyes with Ellie. He glared at her. He clenched his jaw tightly and worked the muscles in his cheeks.

"We would like for you to tell us what you know," she continued.

Tense seconds ticked away. Ellie studied every move that Maurice made. She had no idea what to expect. His eyes fixed on hers once again. After clenching his jaw a second time, Maurice exploded. "What do you think I am? Some snitch or something?" He gave her a defiant stare. "Go play with a cucumber!"

Ellie was shocked. Never in all of her years of law enforcement had she been insulted so brazenly. After an awkward pause, she gathered her bearings. In a soft-spoken tone Ellie appealed to Maurice's common sense. "You're a lawyer with a lot to lose."

Maurice sat with his arms folded and glared back at her.

After a pause she continued, "Maybe ten to twelve years of your life."

The silence was eerie.

She was unrelenting. " . . . Certain disbarment."

Monty looked fiercely at her without blinking.

After another moment of silence Ellie persisted. "Monetary fines."

That was followed by a yawn and a disinterested demeanor from Monty.

"We can make it easy on you," Ellie said persuasively.

Maurice stared at her. "I have nothing to say," he replied.

"I'm prepared to indict and prosecute," Ellie persevered.

Insubordinate and rebellious, Monty bellowed, "Prove it!"

CHAPTER THIRTY-TWO

Walter Hancock was, by nature, a nervous type. He was especially jumpy on this particular morning as he awaited the arrival of Lew Zerrmann. Walter had taken the Zerrmann account after a referral from one of his clients. Naturally, when Lew had purchased the golf course, the accounting and bookkeeping affairs of the business went to Walter also.

Walter's wife, Nora, couldn't stand Zerrmann. She had met him briefly at an open house over the holidays one year and had found him disgusting, lewd, and despicable. She warned her husband about getting involved with Zerrmann.

Walter lived on the edge however. Rather than live as a victim buried in a deep rut, he would seek out those who provided the risk that was missing in his life and profession. Lew Zerrmann filled the bill on both counts.

Over the years, Walter had developed a clientele base that was extremely loyal to him. He was smart, knowledgeable and educated. He knew the IRS Code backwards and forwards. Walter prided himself on staying current with the yearly tax changes. He would attend all of the seminars and continuing education classes that were offered on an annual basis. Early on in his career he had developed an attitude that indicated that he wasn't afraid to live in the gray area that goes with the territory that the IRS had established. It was his opinion that the IRS established deductions for a reason. It was up to him to justify those reasons to a client. Perhaps that explained his nervousness on this morning.

After all, they had been involved in a little bit of deception a couple of years earlier. As Zerrmann walked through the door, Walter handled the pleasantries quickly with ease. After a couple of exchanges, Walter got right to the point. "How is the golf course business?" he asked.

"We're making money hand over fist," Lew replied.

"The kid has worked out for you?"

" . . . Like I never imagined. He's practically living there."

"Watching over the money, I presume."

Lew nodded and forced a grin. "But I have to figure out a way to get my hands on it," Lew stated. "We decided to buy some more ground, but I want the rest of it for myself."

Zerrmann had just gotten the scare of his life. The feds had been asking him all kinds of questions and he had to depend on his friends to stay quiet. The last thing that he wanted was for someone to find the marijuana stalks on the field that he owned down south. He had quickly taken a disc to them and plowed them under. Lew sanitized the field the best that he could and put a legitimate crop on the ground. In so doing, another problem had been created. He lost his supply of cash. Lew's greedy nature was what had precipitated the call for the meeting with Walter.

"I hope that you don't intend to just take it," Walter suggested.

No, nothing like that," Lew said. "But I can't stand to pay taxes. That's a total waste of money."

"That's the price we all have to pay to live in this great country of ours," Walter replied.

"Don't give me that bullshit." Lew's cockiness had progressed to the point where he thought that he was invincible.

"I'm just yanking your chain," Walter laughed. "At least I found out that you were human after all with a real, live heartbeat."

"You found out. Now figure something out," Lew blurted impatiently.

"Well, the easiest way to get to it is to create an expense to offset income," Walter offered.

"That'll make the business less profitable."

"Don't be naïve."

"What are you talking about?" Lew pried.

Walter liked it when he had a rare advantage over Lew. "Think about it."

"I have! An expense is a charge against income. I'll make less money," Lew stammered.

Walter grinned and shook his head. "The corporation will make less money."

"And that means me."

"Not necessarily," Walter continued.

"What are you getting at?"

"Like I said, think about it," Walter suggested. "What is it you like to do on the golf course besides play golf?"

"I can't stand the game. It's a total waste of my time," Lew revealed.

"Okay, then what else do you enjoy doing?"

"I don't mind the odd jobs."

"What does that entail?" Walter probed.

"I'll move some dirt for a tee box or fix a creek or repair a sprinkler leak. We just purchased some additional ground. J Dub and I are talking about building a new golf course. That would keep me occupied for a while."

"What do you use to do that work?"

"The dozer, backhoe, or scraper depending on what we want to accomplish."

"Is that machinery that you own?" asked Walter.

"Yeah, it's my stuff."

"Then why don't we have the golf course pay you for your work?" Walter offered.

"It already does."

"But we categorize that work as a capital improvement. Let's expense the work out," Walter hinted.

"Why do it that way?" Lew wondered.

" . . . So that we can get the golf course income to you!" Walter exclaimed. He was getting a charge out of leading Lew down an obvious path, but keeping him in the dark at the same time.

"You've lost me."

"Look, we'll create a machinery lease expense account. The machinery lease expense money will go to you for the use of your machinery," Walter explained.

"Will I have to pay income taxes on that?" Lew asked.

"Of course, on your personal return," Walter replied. "However, doing it that way funnels all of the business income to you."

Lew paused for a moment to think through Walter's logic.

"All we have to do is stay below the threshold of what the IRS looks for. We don't want to throw up any red flags," Walter explained.

"So, we create an expense for the corporation that offsets any income that it brings in?" Lew volunteered out loud.

"That's pretty much it. That way you can get your hands on the cash without bringing attention to any kind of skimming scheme," Walter justified. "The expense will actually be a bill from you to the corporation to pay you for the machinery that the corporation is leasing from you."

Lew thought for a second about what he had just heard. "I always knew that you were brilliant," Lew admitted.

Walter smiled and said, "The trick is not throwing up a red flag. Don't get too greedy."

Lew smiled and uttered, "When can we start?"

~   ~   ~

It didn't take long for Lew to put his newly-discovered plan into action.

Life at the golf course and in the pro shop had developed its routine. The number of guys showing up in the morning would vary from day to day. It would depend on what errands needed to be run or what doctor's appointment had to be met or whose back needed a rest.

To J Dub and Julie, this was their home away from home. It was a standard pattern. These guys were like "family" to J Dub and Julie. Relationships were formed, bonds were created, and deep ties were established. They all watched out for each other.

That's not to say that disagreements didn't occur or arguments break out. Any differences that did take place were normally settled in quick order. The standard jokes were a topic of conversation as well as the daily news. One could almost always count on some sort of a prank on a weekly basis.

It was obvious to all who was running the show. J Dub was the man. He was there from dawn to dusk, darn near every day. Julie was his "right hand man" so to speak. The two of them ran the business and made the decisions on the day-to-day stuff.

They could expect a phone call or a quick visit from Lew toward the end of the morning hours. He liked playing the owner and would come by frequently to stir up the pot. He didn't know a thing about golf, couldn't stand the guys most of the time, and stopped by long enough to get his ego stroked. Actually, things went a lot more smoothly in his absence. However, he felt that he needed to make an appearance from time to time mainly to check on the money that was coming across the counter.

So it didn't come as any surprise when he walked into the pro shop one day and said, "J Dub, come on into the office. We need to talk about a few things."

J Dub turned the counter over to Julie and followed Lew into the office. "What's on your mind?" he asked.

"I've been doing some thinking. Maybe it's about time we started making some improvements to the golf course. We can start buying up the neighboring property, but if we don't take care of our bread and butter, then the cash that's coming in might slow down."

"I've always felt that we needed to put some money back into the course."

"There has to be some things that we can do to improve the place."

"Several of the tee boxes can use some work. We need to get sprinklers and water to some of the areas that are too dry. Plus some of the creeks need to be worked on."

Lew was quick to agree. "That sounds like stuff that I can handle."

"We need to do some basic repair out on the course," J Dub said. "If we don't put a little something back into the place, then the guys will start griping," he continued. "I really don't want to listen to the negative stuff all of the time."

"I've got the equipment and the machinery to do the minor jobs," Lew volunteered.

"Do you have the time?" J Dub asked. "You always seem busy."

Lew felt like he needed to justify why he needed to do the work. "Those are little jobs that I can do on my own time. I can do the work and bill the course for my services. If we went on the outside to have the work done, then we'd have to pay somebody. Plus, I'll be able to do the work at below market rates and give us better quality on the job."

"That sounds good to me. We need to get some minor things done around here," J Dub replied.

"What needs to be done first?"

"We need to get a sprinkler line installed in some of the areas where the rough is burning out."

And so it was. Lew's plan went into action. He would bring some heavy-duty equipment over to the course and piddle around on one of the holes. Over the years he busied himself with all sorts of little odd jobs.

Additional sprinkler lines were installed. Rock was hauled in to reinforce creek banks and solidify cart paths. Lew would tinker with the tee boxes. He would move some dirt and create some mounds in various places. A tree spade replanted a variety of trees. A small pond was built. Older trees were trimmed. If greens needed to be rebuilt, then Lew and his machinery were quickly on site.

All of this work on the course pleased J Dub. He felt that, finally, things were getting done on the golf course. "Well, would you lookee there! Ole Lew looks like he is finally doing something around here!" declared Fred.

Easy Earl squinted in the distance, "It's about time. This place is really shapin' up." J Dub smiled at the consensus of the room and continued with his own work inside the pro shop.

Meanwhile, Lew would borrow the greens superintendent or some hourly workers or even J Dub, for that matter, to help with the various odd jobs. Whether it was a bulldozer, scraper, high-lift, or backhoe, the equipment was on the golf course. Any number of machinery operators was around to see that the work got completed.

Whatever appeared very innocent on the surface was just a smoke screen for what was going on behind the scenes. To a casual observer, Lew was doing a lot for the golf course.

For those involved, Lew wasn't carrying his weight. It was not uncommon to see him pull the machinery onto the job site and supervise the hourly underlings. He then would retreat to the shade of a tree and sit in the air conditioning of his pickup truck. He would doze on and off as the country music played in the cab.

He had a pretty nice racket going. The jobs were going to be awarded to him. No competition was allowed to bid on the work. All that he would have to do was fill out a bill, present it to the golf course, get paid, and cash an attractive check.

Upon completing a job Lew would simply march into the pro shop and instruct Julie to meet him in the office. In fact, one day the boys were shooting the breeze in the pro shop. J Dub was working the counter with Julie.

Paul asked, "Have you seen the one that he's been hauling around here lately?"

J Dub replied, "Lois?"

Fred was never one to shy away from a wisecrack. He said, "She's been thirty-nine so long, she has two sons that are older than her." The gang in the pro shop erupted into laughter.

"Can you imagine what she looks like in the morning without that makeup?" Elia asked.

Rollie couldn't resist an opportunity to chime in. "My wife is over seventy and looks better than that thing Lew rides around with."

The boys reveled in their light-hearted moment. The pro shop door opened and Lew barged in. The boisterous energy left the room. Lew turned to Julie and said, "I need to meet you in the office."

Rollie yelled across the room, "Who have you been screwing today?"

Never the one to be one-upped by anyone, Lew responded, "Did that yesterday."

"Then what are you doing around here?" Paul asked.

"I had a big project on the course. You guys will really like that improvement."

"What did you do, plant a tree?" Fred asked. The guys chuckled at Fred's sarcastic wit. They knew that whatever Lew did was with a minimal amount of effort.

"No, I did the creek work over on number three," Lew answered not knowing that he was the butt of their humor.

"If you're going to be out there, then why don't you cut the greens once in a while," Rollie yelled.

"Then maybe we'd be able to make a putt," Fred added.

"They get cut twice a week," Lew answered. "That's more than enough. I've got to keep my payroll in line. And you know how gas prices are."

"That's a real profound statement coming from a guy that doesn't know a driver from a sand wedge," Fred chided.

"Or a Maxfli from a Callaway," BT added.

Lew turned to Julie and said, "Come on Julie. I don't have time for this crap."

They both headed into the office. "Here's my bill for all the work that I did out there," Lew said as Julie grabbed a seat behind her desk.

"What did you do?" she asked.

"We hauled some rock in to cut down on the erosion. Then I leveled off part of the tee box, put in two sprinklers, and laid down the sod," Lew answered.

In reality, Lew did next to nothing. The greens superintendent and a couple of hourly workers did the work. The only thing that Lew did was tap the rocks down into the bank of the creek with the shovel of the backhoe. The others hauled the dirt, spread it evenly, and put the sod in place.

Julie grabbed the checkbook out of the desk drawer and asked, "How much do you want?"

Lew gave her the bill. Julie looked at it and with a gasp blurted, "Sixty-five thousand dollars!"

"That should cover my time and expense. I want you to code it to a new machinery lease expense account that we're going to set up," Lew stated.

"That won't fly with the accountant."

"I've already taken care of that."

"We've only got seventy-five thousand dollars in our checking account. We need some money to stay afloat," Julie replied.

"We'll be fine. The cash flow is strong. Now hurry up and write me the check," Lew demanded.

"You have to be out of your mind," Julie responded firmly.

"Just do as you're told. This is my business and I'll do whatever I want."

With that, Julie shook her head helplessly and wrote out a check for sixty-five thousand dollars to Lew. Lew took the check and smiled at her. "Now, Sweet Cakes, that wasn't so hard to do, was it?"

Julie looked at him with a half-hearted look of disgust. Lew turned and walked out of the office.

CHAPTER THIRTY-THREE

The following Saturday morning eight of the boys were playing golf. They divided their group into two foursomes. Curt, Paul, Paco, and Elia were in the first foursome. Fred, Rollie, BT, and Easy Earl were following them.

Saturday mornings were especially busy at Prairie Winds. That's not unlike most golf courses around the country. It is imperative to stay on time. Normally it took a few holes for the crowd that surrounded the first tee box to thin out and a reasonable pace of play to ensue. This particular Saturday was no different than most.

Once the crowd thinned out, Julie spoke to J Dub about Lew's billing of the company. "J Dub, I don't know if you are aware of this or not, and maybe it's none of my business . . ." J Dub could see that she was visibly upset.

"Go on, Julie. It's okay," he coaxed.

"Lew has been billing for all the work he has been doing around the course and he is charging unbelievable amounts of money for it," she blurted out.

"What's an unbelievable amount?" J Dub casually asked as he swallowed the last bit of his soda.

"Sixty-Five thousand dollars."

J Dub spit out his soda in disbelief. "Yeah, that's pretty much what I thought too," Julie dryly added.

Later in the round . . .

As they walked off the second green and headed for the third tee box, Curt casually spoke facetiously to the other guys in his foursome. "Now we get to witness the sixty-five thousand dollar improvement that was made on this hole. J Dub told me all about it."

"What are you talking about?" Elia asked.

"Lew said that he fixed this tee box. He wanted all of us to have a better golfing experience," Curt continued with his tongue in cheek.

Paco examined the tee and exclaimed, "He hasn't done much of anything!"

It was fairly obvious to the naked eye that next to nothing had been done. True, some small improvements had taken place, but a sixty-five thousand dollar enhancement was out of the question.

"What a rip-off," Elia blurted. "I could have gotten a shovel and done this with my own two hands for that kind of money."

"He'll be here in a minute. You can bet that he wants to get our approval. That poor guy needs to have his ego stroked. He's watching us from somewhere," Paul stated.

It was a known fact that Lew would be somewhere on the course during the weekend mornings. He couldn't stand the boys, but felt as if they were the most likely people to tell him how great he was. True to form, Lew was watching the foursome. He and Lois were on his motorcycle and were peering at the foursome from a distance. Lew was very proud of the work that he had done on the third tee box. He felt the need to hear the accolades from the regular crew. He needed to know that his accomplishments met with their acceptance.

Like a lawnmower cutting the grass at sunrise, the roar of the motorcycle muffler broke through the peace and tranquility of the golf course. "Here he comes," said Elia.

Paco's eyes searched for the sound. "Looks like he has his trophy babe with him," replied Paco.

Lew steered the motorcycle through and around several groups of golfers. He skidded to a halt at the third tee box. "What do you fellas think?" he asked.

Elia was unimpressed and acted nonchalantly. "About what?" he asked.

"All that creek work I did. Look at all of that rock that I laid in there," Lew responded. Lois was eager to make her man feel as if he had accomplished something. She had her hands wrapped around Lew and gave him a hearty squeeze.

To the boys, it appeared that only a few rocks had been laid on the creek bank. Whatever work had been done was nothing to get too excited about. Paco broke the silence and said sarcastically, "You do real good work, Lew. Did you place them in there one by one?"

Lew had to thump on his chest a little. "Yeah, putting those rocks in there will cut down on the erosion. When we'd get a good rain the water would come roaring down through here."

Paul felt the need to challenge Lew a little and said, "I've been over here after a good rain and the water in that creek wouldn't be two feet deep."

Lew stood up to Paul and said, "But if it was left uncontrolled, it would eventually wash away this tee box."

Elia wasn't about to let his friend and golfing partner take the heat. He looked around at the weeds, sparse grass, and unevenness of the tee box. It was apparent to the golfing group that if the tee box got washed away then maybe the course would be in better shape. "Maybe if it got washed away that would be a good thing," Elia added.

"Yeah, this tee box ain't flat either," Paco added. As a Mexican immigrant Paco knew a little about landscaping.

The comment had just gotten out of Pace's mouth when a huge chunk of earth broke off and fell into the creek. Several rocks cascaded down the bank and splashed into the water. "Watch it Paco!" yelled Elia. "Don't get swept away into the river!"

All of the boys started laughing at Lew's expense. Lew couldn't stand that the quality of his work was being disputed. He revved up his cycle and peeled off. In the process gravel from the cart path was sent flying.

The boys had nothing to say, so they chuckled to themselves. Lew really thought that he had made a major improvement to the golf course. In reality it was all going to be washed away.

The boys hit their drives and continued with their round of golf.

CHAPTER THIRTY-FOUR

Lew was as devious and conniving as J Dub was honest and trustworthy. The two struggled to co-exist with their obvious differences. Lew didn't trust anyone. Some saw this as an indicator of his own lack of trustworthiness. Regardless, he was intent on protecting his interests in the golf course and land. Lew knew there was one man involved in the mix that was familiar with the day-to-day operations and was onsite from sunup to sundown. That man was J Dub. To Lew, there was an obvious need to mistrust him.

Later that fall Lew spent a morning with Lois perched on the hilltop counting golfers that walked past. Lew had a pad and a pen and marked down each and every player that went by. Most of the players went off the first tee by one o'clock in the afternoon, so Lew's day was pretty much over right after lunch.

When things started to slow down Lew raced back to the pro shop. After he parked in his favorite spot in front of the door, he busted into the pro shop with Lois following closely behind. He made a fast track to the sign-in sheet and starting counting the number of players that had teed off. J Dub watched as Lew counted the number of names on the sign-in sheet. The sheet was Lew's idea in the first place and was his way of having a checks-and-balances system in place for his business.

After comparing the number of names on the sign-in sheet to the number of players that had been marked down on the pad, Lew said with a highly suspicious tone in his voice, "Nobody played for free, did they?"

"What are you talking about?" an innocent J Dub offered.

The moment of truth had arrived. Lew eyed J Dub warily. His suspicions told him that J Dub wasn't registering all of the players. Worse yet, his fears indicated that J Dub was pocketing money from his partner. Before making an accusation that would strain their relationship, Lew paused to think. "Nothing," he replied.

The seed had been planted and the damage had been done. The implication was that J Dub had been stealing money out of the register. In reality, nothing could be further from the truth. Lew had the most honest partner that a guy could hope for, yet he felt the need to test the water in an area that wasn't harmful.

The next day . . .

Julie was at her desk preparing the bank bag deposit for J Dub when a repairman walked in. He resembled Lew in that his name "Chuck" was embroidered on his work shirt.

"Can I help you?"

"Yeah. Got a work order to install a camera," Chuck replied as he handed a copy of the order to Julie for verification.

"But, we didn't order a camera to be installed. Maybe it's for another golf course?" Julie offered.

"No, lady. Got the call this morning. The guy that ordered it is Lew Zerrmann. You know'em?" Chuck was growing impatient.

Julie sighed, rolled her eyes, and okayed the work to be done. After Chuck installed the camera over the register, he tested it and made sure that the till and the person handling the money could be seen at all times.

"Thanks, lady. Tell yer boss the work is done, will ya?" Chuck grunted as he lumbered out of the shop.

Sarcastically, Julie waved goodbye, "Ta-ta, Chuck. Will do."

When J Dub walked into the shop, Julie was at the register with a total look of disgust.

"What's the matter? What did he do now?" J Dub asked.

"Oh, I suggest that when you ring in the golfers' fees, you had best smile real purty." Julie offered.

"What?" J Dub was confused.

Julie nodded her head to the camera in the corner ceiling and advised, "Smile, you're on Candid Camera."

"I don't freaking believe this," J Dub replied as he stared at the camera with hands on his hips.

"If that isn't a statement of disrespect, then I don't know what is," Julie added.

"He doesn't trust us," J Dub said. He was flabbergasted and felt betrayed.

The insinuation from the previous day had blatantly become an accusation. The fact that Lew felt the need to check the actions of his partner smacked J

Dub hard in the face. If Lew couldn't trust his partner, then J Dub wondered if the partnership was doomed from that day forward.

And now, to be accused of stealing in a very indirect way, J Dub felt violated. His honor and reliability were being disputed. It was a feeling that J Dub knew would forever stick in his mind as a contributing factor toward any rift that might occur between the two partners in the coming years. The suggestion by Lew that his partner was stealing so angered J Dub that he set a plan in motion to cause the action to backfire.

CHAPTER THIRTY-FIVE

After Ellie Hackett's decision not to prosecute Lew and his cronies on the fraudulent deed claim, Brian Moore felt the need to call the Morton heirs into his office.

It's tough enough to get the feds to even investigate something. They are like every other understaffed business out there. A local prosecuting attorney's office may get upwards to two to three hundred tips a week that need to be investigated.

Because of a shorthanded work force and a lack of man hours to investigate, a prosecuting attorney's office has to "cherry pick" the cases that it can go after. No matter what they say publicly, the prosecutors go after the high-profile cases that make a big splash in the news and remind the public that "Big Brother" is alive and working well in America.

If a tip comes into the feds on an obsolete and vague criminal charge, then the prosecuting attorney's office practically wants the evidence gift-wrapped to them. That way they can finish the job at hand, get a quick and easy victory, put another notch in the "win" column, and move on to the next crime.

What appeared on the surface as an open-and-shut case when it first surfaced turned into an albatross around the neck of Ellie Hackett. A series of legal challenges attacking Statute of Limitation concerns as well as insufficient forensic detail regarding fraudulent deed claims pretty much backed Brian Moore and Ellie Hackett into a corner.

The evidence that they had gotten did not give the government a clear-cut chance for a victory. The investigation had cost the government several hundred thousand dollars. After compiling all of the evidence and running it by the internal legal minds, the government felt as if the chance for conviction was no greater than fifty-fifty.

To a federal prosecutor those odds are a death wish. Rather than pursue an uphill battle and an uncertain outcome, it is usually recommended that a tenuous case not be prosecuted. After reviewing the evidence, pouring through the deposition testimony, and failing to get a grand jury indictment, Brian Moore and Ellie Hackett had no choice but to let the crime committed against the Morton heirs fall through the cracks of the justice system.

The time had come to call the Morton heirs and explain to them what had happened. Brian and Ellie were business-like and matter-of-fact in their approach to the meeting. Brian started the meeting off the best that he could after Lucille Morton and her son, Matt, arrived in his office.

"We've got the proverbial good news, bad news scenario," Brian started.

"Start with the bad news," Matt offered.

"We've decided not to prosecute," Brian continued.

"What?" Lucille deadpanned. Tears started to form in her eyes.

"You've got to be kidding," Matt said. "That's not right! What happened?"

"We conducted a very detailed investigation," Ellie explained. "We think that improprieties existed, but whatever happened will be next to impossible to prove in a criminal court of law. All of the evidence is purely circumstantial. We don't have any hard core, solid proof that we can hang our hat on."

"We lost several thousand acres of land," Matt persisted, "along with other property."

"As far as we can tell through the investigation, everything was performed in accordance with the law," Ellie retaliated.

"But we didn't receive any money for the property," Lucille blurted as she began to weep.

"The tax returns bear that out," Ellie agreed. "No capital gains had been recorded on your tax returns that the accountant filed. But we can't prove that the transaction was illegal."

Brian and Ellie truly felt sad and disappointed for the heirs. The goal of every prosecutor is to see that justice is done. In this case, nothing more could be done.

"As I stated when you first sat down, we do have some good news," Brian offered.

"No news can be good after what we just heard," Lucille said.

"One of Zerrmann's associates will be facing criminal charges," Ellie stated. "The investigation led us to some unlawful behavior."

"What did he do?" Matt asked.

"We can't talk about the case due to the sensitive nature of it," Ellie continued.

"How can that be good for us?" Lucille questioned.

"We'll have to see where it leads. Right now no one is talking," Ellie explained.

"And in the meantime, we've been cleaned out," Matt said frustrated.

"Look, our goal is to see that the bad guys are brought to justice. We have a service and a duty to perform for the American public," Brian retaliated.

"It's just that we can't catch all of them," Ellie added.

"Some of them fall through the cracks for various reasons," Brian said as he and Ellie tried to explain the difficulties in bringing people to justice.

"What can we do now?" Lucille asked.

"Something was going on, but we won't be able to get a conviction in a criminal court of law due to the nature of the crime," Ellie answered.

"Your best recourse may be a civil suit," Brian stated.

"The burden of proof is not as great in that court as it is with us," Ellie continued.

"And all the while, someone can steal property, control it, occupy it, and the burden of proof is on us to get it back?" Matt persisted.

"That doesn't seem right . . . or fair," Lucille said as her tears turned to anger.

"Sometimes that is the way it is," Ellie stated.

"We don't like to see criminals get off the hook any more than you do." It was the only solace that Brian could extend to the heirs.

"This is a very confusing and complex situation," Ellie added, "especially if no one talks."

"So the expense of an investigation needs to be funded by us now," Matt stated.

"With no guarantees that we'll get our property back," Lucille stammered.

Brian and Ellie reluctantly nodded their heads. "At least the burden of proof will be lighter," Ellie said in the most consoling tone that she could offer.

CHAPTER THIRTY-SIX

J Dub was still seething from the video camera incident later that night when he helped Marcia with some prep work for a catering job that was scheduled for the next day. It was one of the rare times when they were able to spend some quiet time together. He placed bananas, apples, and oranges in baskets to simply help out. J Dub was more than glad to spend a moment or two doing the time consuming things that Marcia needed to have done, so that she could devote her time to creative issues.

J Dub hoped that this time together would be conjugal instead of an argument session. After a long hard day J Dub wasn't fond of what seemed to be entering the picture on a more frequent basis. J Dub asked a thoughtful question after the baskets had been prepared. "Do you need any more help with this tomorrow?"

Marcia's reply was curt. "What if I did? You would be at the course kissing Lew's butt rather than helping me. Don't ask if you don't mean it."

"It's my job to be at the golf course. You keep forgetting that the course will be ours one day."

"If things don't improve around here, then the money from my jobs will contribute to the down payment on my next house."

J Dub kept his silence in an effort to calm the situation down for a moment. It was bad enough that he had the hassles with Lew all day; he didn't relish coming home to hear how unhappy his wife was. It wasn't like Marcia to make casual threats and such permanent ones made him feel even more vulnerable.

"What are you talking about?" J Dub inquired.

"I don't like the fact that I'm second fiddle around here."

"Marcia, that doesn't make any sense. I'm up before dawn, working until dusk to provide for us and our family," J Dub retaliated.

"And I'm getting the short end of the stick. It's safe to say that you're putting in way too many hours up there and not spending nearly enough time around here," Marcia complained.

Feeling the frustration of trying to balance time on the job with family life, J Dub pleaded with his wife. "What am I supposed to do? We have bills to pay. Somebody has to put in the hours in the pro shop to get the job done. I can't be two places at one time."

"It just seems like your priority is the golf course."

"It's a big part of my life, no doubt. But it's for our future. It'll be ours some day."

"I'm not so sure that we have much of a future. If things don't improve around here, then I don't know if you'll be included in my future."

"Oh come on, Marcia." J Dub was in no mood to deal with these issues on the home front. "You've known all along about the time demands that the golf course would require."

"I understand that J Dub. Asking me to live alone for all intents and purposes, even though we are married, take care of our child and run a catering business by myself is unreasonable. You and I are going in opposite directions. We're growing apart. If things don't change, then I'm going to make my current life as a single parent permanent."

Marcia's comments hit J Dub square in the stomach. He despised fighting like this and felt as if he was on foreign ground. He had put too much into the course to throw in the towel now. He stepped outside to sit on their porch. He stared at the moon and finally pondered to himself, *Now what?*

~   ~   ~

U. S. Attorney's Office—Next Day . . .

The day of reckoning had arrived for Maurice DiMonte. He and his cronies had decided not to talk. It is hard to defend yourself with the silent treatment. However, some defense attorneys prefer to keep their clients off of the stand rather than subject them to some tough questioning.

Ellie Hackett was ready for him and had quite a little dossier compiled to convict him. She wasn't about to let him wiggle his way out of this jam.

DiMonte was a bright, but shrewd, lawyer. He made the decision early in his career to step over the line and associate himself with an undesirable element. His plan was that he was basically above the law and that no one would be smart enough to catch him.

Through a series of, or better yet, a maze of electronic transfers, DiMonte had shifted, hid, altered, broken up, and reallocated millions of dollars of funds. To muddy the waters and create confusion, DiMonte had withdrawn funds, redirected monies, and minimized transmittals over and over again in an attempt to hide what was taking place. There was no doubt that reclassifying transactions was his forte'.

Ellie Hackett caught him with his hands all over the transactions. In her mind he was tied to Lew Zerrmann and Raymond Parsons but she couldn't tie them to DiMonte. So she did the next best thing. She got what she could.

If DiMonte wanted to take the fall and protect his buddies, then that was his call. And so it was.

When the gavel came down and DiMonte got nearly twelve years, he practically went into shock. He couldn't believe that a person with his status in life and his connections could be convicted as a first time offender and be required to serve a prison sentence. After all, he had been a prominent lawyer in the area. He had political connections that would be able to bail him out of difficulties. He couldn't fathom that the case against him would hold any water.

However, as is often the case with white-collar criminals, they believe that they are above the law, so to speak. That may be the situation for those that don't get caught. However, for those that do, the government wants to know what happened. His reluctance to talk further complicated his position.

As DiMonte was led past Ellie on his way out of the courtroom, he had one last opportunity to talk to his prosecutor. In a whisper that was barely audible, he lip synced the words, "You fucking bitch."

It was the only bit of "come-uppance" he could muster for the woman that took a decade of life from him. After all, that was what it was going to amount to. Federal sentencing guidelines require that people convicted must serve at least eighty-five percent of their time. The length of time that he would have to serve was depressing news. But equally as depressing was the facility with which he was going to have to serve his time.

CHAPTER THIRTY-SEVEN

1987 Golf Season . . .

The daily shenanigans continued at the golf course. Different things happened on different days, but a few things stuck out in J Dub's mind better than others. J Dub would be hard pressed to forget the day that he was helping a couple of his regular players after their round. He had been walking from the cart barn to the pro shop when the two old-timers, Harold and Ferell, both in their sixties, stopped him.

Bogey was following closely behind him as he strolled over to their car. His easy-going nature was so deeply embedded in J Dub's character, that it was a knee-jerk reaction to assist the old timers with their golf bags. He placed them into the trunk of the car.

"Did you fellas shoot your age today?" J Dub wondered. It was always a good sign for an elderly man to post a score that was identical to his chronological age. The closer to par, the better, was their mantra.

"Maybe by the fourteenth hole," was Harold's disgusted reply. All of them enjoyed a hearty chuckle at the familiar golf course humor.

As they were laughing it up and visiting, Lew pulled his motorcycle onto the scene. Lois, wearing white hot pants, a bright pink tube top, and stiletto heels sat with her legs spread behind him. The wind had exposed and magnified her dark roots and the nickel-and-dime sunglasses she wore made her look like a figure out of a comic book. Being the anti-social person that he was, Lew bypassed all the pleasantries of making a customer feel welcome.

He immediately parked the cycle next to the group, peered into the basket attached to the back of the cart, and turned to whisper something to Lois. He eyed a number of golf balls and reached into the basket to grab one.

Harold was cleaning out the golf cart, changing shoes, and putting his watch back on. He took offense to Lew grabbing the golf balls and asked, "What do you think you're doing?"

"Where did you get those golf balls?" Lew queried.

"I found them on the course," Harold replied.

"Yeah, we found them in the woods and the lakes," Ferell added.

"That's golf course property and I want them back," said Lew. To him that meant money out of his pocket. He reached into the basket and started to stuff golf balls into his pants' pockets.

"Get out of there! I found them!" exclaimed Harold. He hurried to the back of the cart.

J Dub tried to stave off an ugly confrontation. "Leave them alone," he said as he turned to Lew.

"Those balls belong to the golf course and I'm taking them back," stated Lew.

"My ass you are!" Harold yelled as he pushed Lew away from the basket.

Golf balls started to bounce on the parking lot as Lew lost his balance. A small scuffle ensued between the Harold and Lew. Bogey started to bark and growl as he sensed Lew's aggressive behavior. Lew scurried after the balls.

"What kind of a jerk are you?" Harold demanded of Lew.

"I want my property back," Lew insisted.

Ferell added, "I've never seen anything like this. J Dub has taken good care of us over the years. I'll be darned if I ever come back. This is my last time!"

"Take the damn balls!" Harold yelled as he reached into the cart basket, grabbed a handful of shag balls, and threw them in Lew's direction.

Lew chased after the balls and stuffed them in his pockets. Bogey barked uncontrollably at Lew.

"Let's get out of here," Ferell said to his golfing buddy as they entered the car. They backed up and drove off of the lot.

After stuffing the balls into his pockets, Lew chased after Bogey who was barking louder and louder. He tried to kick the dog after it started to nip at his pants.

"Stop it, Lew! Jeez! What are you trying to do? Get rid of all our customers?" J Dub asked as the two irate customers exited the lot.

"We can clean these up and put them in the fishbowl for resale. Every little bit helps," Lew replied.

"What kind of idiot are you? We lose two regular players so that you can make fifty cents!" J Dub was incredulous.

"You can't let the customers run your business, J Dub."

"Yeah, Bogey. Better to lose all our customers than miss the chance to sell golf balls for fifty cents," J Dub muttered sarcastically to the dog knowing full well that Lew was in earshot. He began to walk across the parking lot and toward the clubhouse.

"If you want something to do, quit bothering the customers and fix the first tee box! In the meantime, I'll check with Jules to see if she can break the bank for that small of a job," J Dub mockingly yelled over his shoulder to Lew.

Not only had Lew done a good job of alienating J Dub, but he had roused Bogey's animal instincts and set them on edge. It was as if the dog could sense his evil intentions. Lew's behavior toward Bogey was a far cry from J Dub's and the animal sensed wickedness.

Not more than thirty minutes later another customer issue came to the forefront. Even though the business continued to be profitable, Lew seemed to be at the center of another chaotic episode. Four young men, all in their twenties, had paid in the pro shop and continued out to the course for a nice relaxing day of friendly competition and camaraderie. As they were waiting to hit their drives on the third tee box the sounds of Lew's muffler broke the calm serenity of the golf course.

Perry turned toward the other members of the foursome and said, "How in the world are we supposed to tee off with that racket going on? Look at that idiot out here. Have you ever seen anything like it?"

Will was by the ball washer and said, "Doesn't he know that this is a golf course? Motorcycles out here should be outlawed."

Stan was digging into his bag for another golf ball and replied, "That's half the reason I come out here. I want to get away from all of that stuff."

"I don't know who the heck he thinks he is, but he's headed our way. It looks like he's got some babe out for a joyride," stated the fourth member of the group who was nicknamed Tutti. He happened to be a large, heavy-set, red-headed, country boy that liked to drink a few beers while playing golf.

Not only was the sound of the muffler annoying, but Lew's constant weaving between various groups of golfers was distracting and dangerous. It was hard to say what his motivation was other than feeling he had to be the marshal of the course. That was difficult to fathom since he didn't know anything about the sport. At any rate, he was speeding over to the foursome of young men who were equally as content to keep playing golf and enjoy their day in the sun. With Lew's arrival on the tee box that was all about to change.

"What's in that cooler?" Lew stammered.

Tutti replied, "Beer."

"Did you buy it in the clubhouse?" Lew inquired.

The foursome shook their heads.

With that response, Lew bolted off of the motorcycle and grabbed the cooler as Lois steadied the bike. He popped the tabs and started pouring the beer on the ground.

Tutti had already had a few and was known to have quite a thirst for a beer or two on the golf course. He wasn't in any mood to see the iced down beverage flowing across the cart path. "Hey! It's hot out here!" he exclaimed. "Cut it out!"

"Listen, Porky. I own this place. I'll do what I want," Lew replied.

"Then so will I!" Tutti yelled back as he reached into his bag for a golf club. "Get out of here before I wrap this around your neck! I'm thirsty!"

With a hot red head and a thirst to match, Tutti chased Lew back to the motorcycle. The club was cocked to make solid contact. Lew was genuinely scared by the actions of the kid and with good reason. He kicked started the cycle, waited for Lois to hold on tight, and popped a wheelie as he sped off.

"What a jerk!" Perry exclaimed. "How are we supposed to enjoy this round with that kind of nonsense going on?"

"I don't know, but it's too nice of a day to throw in the towel. Let's forget about it and keep playing," said Will. So, the young men continued playing. Two holes later the earlier incident was nearly forgotten when one of them noticed a police car with lights flashing coming down a fairway.

"Can you believe it? First a motorcycle and now a cop car," Stan said as he stood over his ball to take a shot.

"On a golf course," exclaimed the bewildered Will.

"That wacko called the cops!" yelled Perry.

Within seconds the police car rolled to a stop near the young men. A young-looking, rookie police officer as well as Lew and Lois exited the car. As they headed for the group Lew stammered. "The red-headed one came after me with a club." Lois nodded her head.

The police officer was clearly faced with a dilemma. Being out on a golf course was out of the ordinary for starters. However, his allegiance was to the business owner that was making the complaint. "Is that true?" the officer asked the foursome.

Tutti tried to defend himself against the absurdity of the situation. "He came up to us and started pouring our beer out!"

"That doesn't give you the right to go after him with a lethal weapon," the officer replied.

"I wouldn't consider a golf club a lethal weapon," the red-headed, country boy pleaded.

"In certain situations it could be," the officer insisted.

"We were out here playing golf and that guy came over and started bothering us," Perry interjected.

"It's his property. He can do what he wants," continued the officer.

"Not on my dollar bill. This will be the last time we come here to play golf," Will said.

"Let's go in for questioning," the officer stated.

"Right now?" Stan asked in total disbelief. He was ready to hit his next shot.

The officer was as serious as could be. He nodded his head affirmatively.

"Can't we finish our round?" Will asked inquisitively.

The officer shook his head no.

Perry then made a request. "Can we get rain checks for the holes that we didn't play?"

Clearly caught in an impasse, the officer nodded toward Lew. "You'll have to ask him."

Lew had the law on his side. He was feeling awfully secure and felt that he was in entire control since he had the needed backup in his hip pocket. "It's not raining today, boys. We don't need your kind around here."

The four young men found themselves in disbelief with the ludicrousness of the circumstances. Their relaxing round of golf was being turned into a trip to the police station. Tutti grabbed a can of beer and shook it vigorously. He popped the tab and sprayed beer in Lew's direction. "Now it's raining, asshole" he said.

Lew and Lois scurried for cover and raced to the security of the police car.

"We might have to look at resisting arrest charges now," the officer countered.

J Dub and Julie had been working in the pro shop when they saw the police car speed through the parking lot and head down the fairway. They couldn't leave the pro shop and the cash register unattended, but both knew that Lew had found the trouble that he had been looking for. Now the police car was returning from the golf course with two golf carts following closely behind. "It sure doesn't look like the punishment fits the crime," Julie said to J Dub as she peered out the window.

"What in the world has he done now?" J Dub asked. He bolted out of the pro shop, with Bogey in pursuit, and ran toward the police car as it was entering the lot.

Lew quickly got out of the squad car and yelled at J Dub, "See what happens when they take their own beer!" Bogey began to growl at Lew.

J Dub stood in stunned silence. He then tried to defend the golfers the best that he could. "It's ninety degrees out."

"They get drunk and cause trouble."

"Did you put the radar gun on them or something and catch them speeding?"

Perry shouted from a golf cart. "We want rain checks!"

Lew reprimanded J Dub and said, "Get rid of them." The tone in his voice caused Bogey to bark and growl.

J Dub was at a loss for words. Lew chastised J Dub some more and asked, "When are you going to win some of these battles?"

"It's all about control with you, isn't it?" J Dub retaliated. "Why did you get the cops? We could have handled this in-house."

Lew's matter-of-fact reply was menacing. "There comes a point in life where you need some back-up. Even Hitler needed the Nazi army."

The comment caught J Dub off-guard. He was taken aback and dazed at the reference to Hitler. The remark scared J Dub. He had to pinch himself and wonder what motivated his business partner. "What are you talking about?" J Dub asked as he tried to redirect the conversation.

Lew's eyes were in an icy stare as his lips curled slightly into a sinister smirk. The moment was frozen in a surreal atmosphere. It was as if the comment about Hitler turned Lew on.

After a momentary pause, J Dub continued in a mild manner. "We need to keep customers around . . . and the first tee box still needs to be fixed." He walked off as Bogey barked at Lew. J Dub continued to the pro shop and was immediately quizzed by Julie.

"What did he do this time?" Julie asked.

"He kicked those kids off the course for bringing their own beer. Not only that, it looks like they have to go down to the police station."

"Is he pressing charges?"

"I guess. The cops wouldn't bother coming out here unless he was serious about having them arrested." J Dub shook his head. It was as if the business would take one step forward and two steps back. "But that's only half of the problem."

"What else did he do?" Julie inquired.

"He made some perverse reference to Hitler," J Dub stated.

"Hitler? What did he say?" Julie pried.

"He said something about needing backup like Hitler had the Nazi army."

"Does he think that he is some sort of power freak that is the reincarnation of Hitler?" Julie wondered out loud.

"I hope not . . . but the way that he controls and intimidates, he must think that way."

"Hitler slaughtered hundreds of thousands of people," Julie uttered. "That's disgusting."

J Dub nodded and had a resolved look in his eyes. "I better learn a little more about my partner. If I don't watch out, then he might slaughter me after he gets done slaughtering this business."

CHAPTER THIRTY-EIGHT

Lois was settling in at Lew's home. In a strange and twisted way she was a nice complement for him. It was hard to tell if she was a passive person or just acquiesced to his every whim and wish. Lew's insecurities came to the forefront in their relationship but she allowed him to dominate.

She had learned to live resourcefully. It was easier for her to make her way by letting the men in her life tell her what to do. That was how she had survived. By allowing men to dictate what she could or could not do, Lois had been exposed to a lot of situations that had made her develop into a full-fledged woman.

To say that she was bi-curious would have been a misnomer. Lois was not curious anymore; she had crossed over a long time ago. In fact, Lois had grown to prefer women. To her, they were much more passionate, gentle and soothing than a man. However, she was wise enough to know that a man could provide her with the means to make her liaisons with other women possible.

And so, Lew and Lois found each other. She needed him to survive and thrive. He needed her to act out his kinkiness and to balance his insecurities.

Lew was a demented, perverted, controlling person. Those traits carried over to the bedroom. One of his fetishes was sniffing panties. In his younger days when he was trying to get a lot of notches on his bed post, he had developed a passion for collecting souvenirs.

One of his conquests had left a pair of panties behind and Lew was forever hooked after that. He had placed that pair of underwear in a Tupperware container and visited it repeatedly when the sensors went off on his sexual appetite. When his libido would get the best of him, Lew would visit the container, take out the panties, smell their crotch and masturbate to the memory the panties provided.

Over the years he had the opportunity to collect many panties. Lew had gotten so meticulous with his collection that he had purchased a separate container for each pair of underwear. Each container was labeled so that he could associate a name with the scent. He had even gotten to the point where he dated the occasion. The souvenirs were mementos of his most pleasurable achievements.

To take his passions to the next level, Lew built a shrine in the lower level of his home. Not only did the room house his immense collection of women's underwear, but he furnished it with bondage equipment and sado-masochistic devices. It was in this self-anointed shrine where Lew discovered that wearing a pair of silk women's panties gave him an out-of-control erection.

Time after time, Lew would retreat to the room and pull a keepsake out of a Tupperware container. He would drown himself in the aroma, fondling, sniffing and jerking off until he came. In a sick and perverse way, his behavior was animalistic, like a male member of an animal species marking his territory.

This ritual turned Lois on. She would come alive when he would mention the room and his wild intentions. In a way, they were both predators and they used each other to accomplish their own sick objectives. Lew gave Lois free reign to sleep with other men or women if she wanted. Because he wanted to control her, he let her do whatever she wanted to do sexually. His extra reward for giving her freedom came when she would bring other women back to share with him.

The sexual relationship between Lew and Lois progressed. With each succeeding liaison the sexual pattern developed a familiar flavor. Lew would start out by donning a pair of women's panties, and then he would sniff a pair from his collection and masturbate. He encouraged and persuaded Lois to recruit her women to the sex room where he could watch and be watched. All parties would participate in a ménage-a-trio and Lew could then add a pair of panties to his growing collection.

Lew's perversion probably grew from his intense hatred of women. He had been burned by two failed marriages. Neither ex-wife allowed the controlling nature and both got out of the union as quickly as they could. Lew carried the scar they left behind.

So he took his anger out on the next batch of women that entered the picture. Lew had found a perfect match for his desires. Lois needed to be told what to do. She needed a dominant force in her life. When Lew suggested that she recruit women for his sexual pleasure, Lois was eager to jump at the opportunity.

Together, they made a lewd and twisted pair.

CHAPTER THIRTY-NINE

Lew's off-handed remark about Hitler continued to motivate J Dub's cautious approach toward his partner. It never failed to amaze him that in spite of Lew's antics, the course was still making money. He knew it was due to his conscious effort to keep Lew away from the course as much as possible. The guys and Jules trusted J Dub to do things by the book. No doubt about it, life in general would be so much easier with Lew out of the picture. As J Dub readied the course for the day's golfing, he found himself releasing a heavy sigh as he thought about his partner. He walked inside the clubhouse, said his hellos to the fellas, and then poked his head in Julie's office.

"How are we looking this month?"

Julie had just tallied a long list of numbers on her calculator and totaled it. "We're looking great, J Dub! It was another great month, money-wise."

J Dub grinned from ear to ear and saw Lew walking toward him. "We had another great month, Lew," J Dub announced.

"So I hear, where's Julie? I want to get your input on some ideas that I have."

"Knock, knock," J Dub announced as he and Lew sat down in Julie's office.

"What's up?" Julie was just as cautious as J Dub when it came to Lew sitting in her office unannounced.

"With all of this money in the bank, what would you two think if we re-invested some more of it into land?" Lew asked.

"What did you have in mind this time?" J Dub countered.

"We have an opportunity to acquire fifty acres of property that is adjacent to number thirteen," Lew replied.

"We'd be foolish not to buy that," J Dub said. "It would fit in with our long-range plan. We're going to need to acquire it sometime if we want to expand the business to thirty-six holes."

"As long as our cash-flow needs are met through the winter months and we have money left over for real estate taxes, then I don't see any problem with that," Julie added.

"Let me put the deal together and I'll get back with you," Lew concluded.

That quickly, Lew put his next plan into action. Like a chameleon he deftly applied his sales skills to his waiting prey and negotiated an attractive purchase price per acre. The contract was drawn up quickly, concessions were agreed upon, and the farmer signed without as much as a flinch.

~   ~   ~

The next part of the plan necessitated a meeting with Walter Hancock. Lew rarely did anything without consulting his accountant. "Walter, it's been a while. How has life been treating you?" Lew asked shortly after entering the accountant's office.

Walter was forever worried about the secret that the two of them had been keeping for several years. "I'd be feeling a whole lot better if we hadn't gotten in that mess together," he reminded Lew as he peered over his bifocals.

"Quit worrying about that," Lew followed. "That's over and done with. No person on this earth even misses someone like that. As far as her next of kin are concerned, she just ran off and never returned."

"Yeah, okay Lew. It's not easy for me to do. We ran over a person and it's hard for me to forget," Walter whined. "That's especially so since I'm hearing through the grapevine that Monty is running into some trouble."

"I told you to forget about it. The body is buried on property that I own. It's in the middle of the woods. Nobody will ever find it," Lew said trying to calm him. "What trouble?" he asked as an afterthought.

"Never mind," Walter said. He was not entirely comforted by Lew's words and was clearly upset and nervous about being forever connected to Lewferd E. Zerrmann.

Lew felt the need to reiterate the point. "Look, it was an accident. She was just a hooker with no family. No one misses her. There haven't even been any missing people notices," Lew replied in his best hand-holding tone.

Walter Hancock had a lot more of a conscience than Lew Zerrmann would ever have. "Do you have any remorse at all? God, Lew. You just amaze me sometimes." It was times like these that made Walter uneasy about being in business with Lew. There were always strings attached which made things messy sometimes.

"If we come out and admit to it now, then we'll all go away for the rest of our lives. Let things be. Don't turn over stones that don't need to be turned over," Lew persisted.

Walter locked gazes with Lew. He knew he was fighting a losing battle and no amount of reassurances from Lew was going to ease his conscious. He decided to let it go.

"Keep your mouth shut and nobody will ever know," Lew demanded. He wanted to move on to a more pressing topic. "I need for you to help me out with something else."

"Good Lord, what now? What are you going to get me involved in this time?" He was agitated enough with Lew for one afternoon, but knew he would be convinced to participate.

"I had an opportunity to buy fifty acres of ground from Buford Ludwig. He was farming the ground just to the east of the course," Lew explained.

"What do you need me for?" Walter was mystified.

"George is gone. He used to do all of my title work," Lew stated.

"Is he still at your place in Tortola?" Walter queried.

Lew nodded. "He and Mary Jean are watching the place for me. We've had quite a little offshore bookmaking operation going for a few years now."

"I don't want to hear anything about that!" Walter shrieked in disbelief. "I didn't hear you say that."

"Quit being such a puss."

Walter shrugged it off. His professional ethics knew better. "It sounds like the two of them are the ones that made out like bandits. It sure would be nice to get out of here and live the good life in that kind of climate," Walter moaned. He was clearly miffed that Lew arranged for George to get out of town and had agreed to house him at his island retreat.

"Don't worry about that stuff. George was coming out of a divorce and was at a different stage in his life," Lew reasoned.

"And I'm stuck here, more or less at the mercy of you two. It's not the best situation for me and my family to be in," Walter sulked. The longer he mulled over the situation he was in, the angrier and more resentful he became.

"Quit your whining. We all know what the deal is. I need for you to help me on this next deal." Lew plainly wanted to move on to the new subject matter.

"Tell me about it," Walter said curtly.

"I negotiated a favorable price per acre from Buford. The ground is probably worth twice as much as what I told him I would pay for it," Lew explained. "I got a great buy on the contract."

"Something tells me that I shouldn't be too surprised at that," Walter replied with a touch of skepticism in his voice.

"The golf course has the money to pay for it," Lew continued.

"That's important," Walter deadpanned, shaking his head.

"Since I negotiated such a good deal, I want to have the golf course pay market price for the ground," Lew reasoned.

"And where are you going with all of this?" Walter asked.

"I want half of the property titled in my own name," Lew replied bluntly.

"How are you going to get away with that, pray tell?" Walter asked not hiding his sarcasm. He was anxious to see what was working in Lew's mind.

"What I'd like to do is get the golf course to pay for the property. Then at closing have half of the property titled in my own name. That could be my commission, more-or-less, for putting the deal together," Lew clarified.

"Then we'll have to declare commission income on your tax return," Walter replied, finishing Lew's train of thought.

"I don't want to do that!" Lew shouted.

"Will you please calm down? I have other clients in the waiting area! If you don't want to do it that way, then your basis will be affected."

"What are you talking about . . . basis?" Lew wondered out loud.

"You're going to have an asset put in your name. No money will be paid for that. When it comes time for you to sell it, then your capital gains tax will be a lot higher," explained Walter.

"I don't ever plan on selling it."

"You say that now, but there will come a day when you will have to pay the piper," insisted Walter.

"I'll worry about that when the day comes," Lew rationalized.

"What about J Dub?" Walter was aware that Lew had a naïve business partner.

"He'll never know. For all I care, he can think that we're buying fifty acres. There won't be any way for him to find out otherwise unless he goes down to the

Recorder's office. He's not that sharp," Lew added. "Besides, he's running the place and will be too busy with the day-to-day stuff to worry about what I'm doing."

"You're disgusting."

A smug and cunning grin spread over Lew's face. "You've got to get ahead in the world someway."

Walter shoved his bifocals on top of his head and rubbed his face in frustration.

"Now listen," Lew continued, "I need for you to get the legal descriptions on the deed taken care of in George's absence."

A look of disdain shrouded Walter upon the reminder that George was on a tropical island without any worries. "And you want me to do your dirty work again."

"You're the licensed professional," Lew said in an expressionless tone. "I'm just being a good businessman. You want my account, don't you?"

Walter nodded. "I may admit to that, but sometimes I don't."

"Then do as you're told. I'm calling the shots on this thing."

CHAPTER FORTY

Whooosh-Crack! J Dub had a bucket of balls beside him and was pounding one ball after the other onto the driving range. Bogey took his place clear of J Dub's swing and watched his master with his soulful eyes as they followed his swing from top to bottom.

J Dub paused as he noticed that the last swing was not his best. He squinted toward the far end of the range to see how far he had driven the ball. Even on his worst day he was better than most golfers that came to the club.

"Bogey, what am I supposed to do? If it isn't Marcia being so angry with me at home, then it is Lew at work. It's like you're the only one that's on my side." Bogey cocked his head with interest at the sound of J Dub's voice.

Whooooosh-Crack! "Damn it!" J Dub cursed his lack of concentration and continued his conversation with Bogey. "As a businessman, I should be thrilled. The course is doing really well financially. But, I have a partner that has a fixation on Hitler and is driving customers away. And, here I am cleaning up his messes and he doesn't even appreciate it." J Dub looked at Bogey who walked up to him and nuzzled his leg.

"Thank God for you, boy," J Dub whispered to his dog as he scratched him behind the ears, much to Bogey's delight. "Get back over there. Don't want to hit you by mistake," J Dub coaxed Bogey.

Whoooosh-Crack! "Lew is just making things extremely tense around here, boy. He's just always got to be in control." *Whooosh-Crack!* "I hate that I am part owner and I have to walk on egg-shells around him. It's driving me crazy!" The more J Dub ranted the harder and farther his club hit the balls.

"Honest to God, I feel like if I make or say one cross word, I'll be out of a job. One miscalculation and my career might be over in the blink of an eye! I can only imagine what the other employees must feel like. So, for the sake of my family's future, I have to stay on his good side. I don't know what it is, Bogey, but I get a feeling that Lew has his bases covered." J Dub smiled at Bogey as he obediently stood out of range and wagged his tail at each swing. "You think every swing I do is great, don't ya boy?" J Dub knelt down and played with Bogey for awhile and decided to call it a day. "That's the key, isn't it? Just don't make any waves with Lew. Thanks for being a good listener little buddy." The dog licked J Dub's face and hands in affirmation.

After his enlightening conversation with Bogey, J Dub knew that he should just do his job and stay out of Lew's way. Yet, he couldn't help but rack his brain trying to think up an idea that Lew would admire in a sick, demented way, yet, at the same time, pimp Lew. Then it came to him one morning on the way into work. J Dub was just too damn mad to 'play nice'.

J Dub was fond of the "oldies, but goodies" style of music. His radio dial was tuned into the station that broadcast the sounds of the sixties and seventies. A song named "Big Shot" by Billy Joel blared through the speakers. Instinctively, J Dub began singing along with the music, "*. . . Because you had to be a Big Shot, didn't ya, Ya had to prove it to the crowd . . .*" He stopped in mid lyric and laughed in spite of himself. *By George, I think you got it*, he chuckled.

"I know I said that I would mind my business and stay out of Lew's way, but this is just too tempting. Sorry, Bogey," J Dub apologized. The dog barked and wildly wagged his tail in approval. "Yeah, now I know why they call you man's best friend. You agree with everything I say, don't ya boy?" J Dub laughed.

"We can give ole Lew a taste of his own medicine, can't we little buddy?" J Dub laughed and began planning on making a 'special' place for Lew to park out front. *Let's see, if I put the Big Shot sign right in front, everyone can enjoy the inside joke, when in reality, the vehicle, whether it was a motorcycle, sports utility vehicle, or pickup truck would get in the way of the traffic coming in and out of the front door. Oh this is beautiful*, he smiled to himself.

J Dub was good at making subtle, little signs. He made a sign that read: BIG SHOTS ONLY, RESERVED FOR LEW. He then rolled out an eight foot by eight foot piece of Astroturf and glued that down by the front door. J Dub proceeded to lay a piece of hose across the Astroturf and hooked it up to a set of stereo speakers.

Any object that rolled over the hose would send a signal to the music and "Big Shot" would blare through the speakers. That device would indicate Lew's arrival. It would also give everyone within earshot a huge chuckle.

A few days later . . .

The regular boys were sitting in the pro shop after finishing up an early round of golf. They were at their table in the back of the pro shop settling up their bets. J Dub and Julie were both working the counter.

Golfers were always coming through the door and the phone was constantly ringing. Between taking greens fees, booking tee times, fixing sandwiches, and serving drinks, there was quite a bit of hustle and bustle for the two of them.

Fred was the jokester of the group. He yelled at J Dub from the back of the room, "J Dub, were you in here the other day when that blonde asked Julie if she could buy some green golf balls?"

"No, I must have been outside."

"Julie said, 'Green golf balls? The grass is green.' And the blonde says, 'That way they're easier to see in the sand.'"

All the boys got a kick out of that and started rolling with laughter. J Dub couldn't help but snicker himself.

The beer was starting to flow pretty rapidly through the regulars. BT didn't want to be outdone. Shortly afterward he sauntered up to the bar and asked Julie for another beer. As she was pouring the ale, BT asked her, "When is your dad getting out of jail?"

" . . . Jail?" Julie responded. "My dad's not in jail. Why did you say that?"

"Wasn't he the one that stole the stars from the skies and placed them in your eyes?" BT grinned. He was quite the crooner in his younger days and had used that line on many unsuspecting women during his bachelor days.

"That crap may have worked in your heyday, but it won't work on me now," Julie said as she smiled back at him. "I appreciate the effort though, you owe two bucks!"

BT gladly reached into his pocket and paid for his beverage. He had gotten the opportunity to flirt a wee bit with Julie whose smile and quick wit radiated throughout the room.

Just then Marcia walked through the door. Gail's face lit up with a bright smile when she saw J Dub. She ran to her daddy.

"Hey, girl!" Marcia called out to Julie. Marcia, already heavy in her second trimester, waddled over to J Dub for a kiss. Their three-year-old daughter tugged at her daddy's pants' leg.

Julie was astonished about Marcia's condition. "J Dub, you never said anything about that!"

J Dub shrugged. "We try to keep our personal life at home." He winked at Marcia.

"Are you able to drink leaded?" Julie inquired as she turned back to Marcia.

"Are you kidding? This ain't my first time at the rodeo and any doctor that tells me I can't have caffeine . . . well, let's just say it will get pretty ugly." Marcia quipped.

Jules laughed and poured coffee as Marcia effortlessly bellied up to the counter and sat on a nearby stool. "Is the next one a boy?" Julie asked quizzically.

"We don't want to know," Marcia replied.

"At least you could start preparing. Don't you want to know if you should start buying pink things or blue things?" Julie continued.

"We'd just as soon keep it a surprise," Marcia said as she smiled at Julie.

"Well, one thing's for sure. You'll definitely have nine pounds of baby!" Julie and J Dub shouted in unison. Even Marcia began to cry she laughed so hard.

"Big Shot" echoed throughout the room. The boys in the back stopped their cajoling and Marcia jumped in her seat. She was startled at the loud music. Julie glanced at J Dub and rolled her eyes. She instinctively knew that the mood in the pro shop was about to change. Gail started to cry.

"Yeah, me too, Gail," Julie said before Lew walked in.

Lew busted through the doors of the pro shop singing the words to "Big Shot." His boastful and jovial mood diminished when he noticed that everyone in the pro shop was enjoying themselves. It was disruptive!

He stopped, grinned at himself, and announced," That sounds better and better each day." Everyone stared at him as if he was a pathetic, pitiful excuse for a human being. After glancing around the room Lew stayed true to form. He looked straight at J Dub and declared," Coffee break is over. We have some work to do, J Dub."

Gail was still whimpering even though J Dub was holding her in his arms. She had gotten a small cold and was in an irritable mood. "Gail needs medicine. Can we add her to the insurance policy?" J Dub asked Lew.

Lew stopped dead in his tracks. He glanced at J Dub who was holding Gail. He noticed the coffee cup in Marcia's hand. His eyes shifted to her bulging stomach. "Your wife stops in here for a free cup of coffee and now you want me to pay for your screwing?" Lew chastised him.

A hush fell over the room as everyone looked at J Dub, then to Marcia. For one brief moment, Marcia's eyes grew hot with tears. Then, true to her hormones, she got up off the stool and strode deliberately over to Lew.

"What did you say, Mr. Big Shot?" Marcia challenged.

"Oh God, I think she's gonna blow," Julie cringed.

"You heard me! You expect me to pay for the sick kid and the one that's about to pop out of your belly? Ya ever heard of birth control lady?" Lew angrily replied.

"Yeah, I have Mr. Big Shot. Let me just say this much. You're the first person I ever met where the best part of you slid down your Daddy's leg. So don't lecture ME about birth control!" Marcia was sparring for a fight and was ready for Lew.

J Dub handed Gail to Julie and went after Lew who was backing away from Marcia.

"Don't you ever, and I mean ever, speak to my wife or family like that again. You got me?" J Dub shouted. He shoved Lew backward toward the door. "Go on! Get the hell out of here. The sight of you sickens me!"

Lew looked all around and realized that he was the most hated person in the room.

"GET OUT!" J Dub screamed as he reached for the nearest object which was a stack of magazines and mail and threw them at Lew's head. Lew angrily turned around and stomped out of the room.

"That sorry piece of . . ." He stopped short of using profanity. Everyone in the room was glad to see that J Dub finally had mustered up enough nerve to stand up to the ego maniac.

However, in Lew's eyes, he had been publicly embarrassed in front of a lot of people. He would never forget that moment.

Chapter Forty-One

Eight years later—1995 . . .

The old adage, 'The more things change, the more things stay the same,' rang true for the Prairie Winds golf course and those that frequented the club. Lew was still a proverbial pain in every sense of the word, which resulted in J Dub pounding a bucket of balls in frustration while Bogey wagged his tail in approval after each swing.

Marcia gave birth to two more children. The second child was another beautiful baby girl. Her name was Carrie. Four years after that she gave birth to a son, named Nick. J Dub had always wanted a son and now their prayers were answered at last. The family plan was in full gear at the Schroeder household. J Dub and Marcia normally had every minute of every day spoken for.

J Dub had made a commitment to Marcia to give up his weekends at the golf course, and he kept that end of the deal. Bolstered by Marcia's catering income and in spite of Lew's stinginess with the profits of the business, J Dub and Marcia managed to scrimp and save enough money to buy a home.

~ ~ ~

Eleanor Hackett aggressively worked her way up the ladder of jurisprudence. She became a governmental guru in prosecuting white-collar criminals. Her success rate garnered countrywide attention. She conducted national seminars and trained federal law enforcement officials on what to look for in tax returns and financial statements. The Attorney General of the United States called her away on a special prosecutorial assignment that lasted two years. Upon her return she was appointed the United States Attorney for her District.

Walter Hancock continued to fret over his role in the cover-up of the hooker's death. The fact that he was remotely involved in the death of another person gnawed at his conscience. He remained a steadfast ally to Lew, despite the nagging from his wife, Nora, who was oblivious to the secret that he kept. Walter knew the tax code backwards and forwards and seemingly stayed one step ahead of the IRS in handling Lew's accounting affairs. He managed the account for a minimum monthly fee. Of course, because of his role in the killing, Lew controlled the actions of Walter. Whenever his fidgety nature would get a little out of control Lew would more or less bribe him into a sense of false reality.

George Pierce enjoyed his time in exile on the island of Tortola, the largest island in the British Virgin Island chain. In an elaborate barefoot ceremony on the beach, he and Mary Jean Graham, twenty years his junior, got married. They re-established themselves, kicked back a little, and house-sat Lew's paradise retreat. The money that he had fled to the islands with seemed to have an eternal supply.

Maurice DiMonte went off to a federal prison in Colorado that was famous for housing white-collar criminals. He appealed his conviction and used the prison library to research ways to get back at Ellie Hackett. If nothing else, those efforts kept his mind preoccupied and served as a way of survival behind the bars.

The popularity of Raymond Parsons soared. He was re-elected every two years and his constituency grew at an alarming rate. Not only did he carry a powerful stick in local politics, but he became a major player in the U. S. House of Representatives. The one thing that you could count on from Raymond was the loyalty that he gave to those that supported him over the years. Lew Zerrmann was an early supporter and was always given preferential treatment from his office.

One of the final pieces to the puzzle was the Morton Estate. The heirs, mother and son, had been swindled. Law enforcement wasn't too keen on getting to the bottom of such a complex case. Their case was so unlike a bank robbery. With a bank heist the surveillance camera frequently captured a suspect in the throes of committing a crime. But with a crime like fraud, all of the circumstantial evidence needed to be pieced together. From a forensics standpoint, the methods of obtaining and providing proof beyond a reasonable doubt are totally different. When a scam is committed the entire diabolical scheme needs to be restructured.

After the initial disappointment from the U. S. Attorney's office, Lucille and Matt set out on another course of action. Even though it was next to impossible for the government to get a conviction, they realized that their case could be easier to prove in the jurisdiction of a civil courtroom.

Something happened that they didn't count on. Getting an attorney to bring a civil suit against Lew Zerrmann turned into a major undertaking. Lew Zerrmann was very connected in the political circles around town and he was no stranger to the courtroom either. For them to obtain an attorney Lucille and Matt needed to list the different accomplices that they felt had defrauded them.

Lo and behold, they found that nearly every law firm they approached could not take their case due to a conflict of interest. What they also soon learned was that attorneys are really no different than any other practical businessman in the world. Lawyers and law firms look at the complexities of the case and assign a rate of success to it. If a lawyer doesn't believe there is at least an eighty or ninety percent chance of succeeding, they simply will not take a case on a contingent basis.

The major law firms all passed on the case for the Morton Estate for one or both of those reasons. That created a dilemma for the Morton's. They felt as if they had major civil damages, but no one to turn to for help. They clearly needed a stroke of good luck. Acting on a referral from a friend of a distant relative's acquaintance, the Morton heirs stumbled upon a proprietary office. That was when Dennis K. Sneed entered the picture.

Dennis K. Sneed had an office that was located on the second floor of a rehabbed historical building. He operated a one-man show. The office environment promptly bore that out. His name was stenciled on some frosted glass that comprised the top half of his office door. Lucille and Matt knocked and poked their heads around the door after a voice yelled, "Come on in!"

Lots of times initial meetings can leave lasting impressions. Lucille and Matt weren't disappointed. It wasn't difficult for them to stop in their tracks as they entered Denny Sneed's law office. Boxes and law books and papers were stacked and strewn around the room in a manner akin to the destruction left by a tornado. In fact, Denny had to throw some papers off of a chair and onto the floor just to offer Matt a place to sit.

Denny Sneed was in his mid-forties. He was considered a maverick attorney in the legal community because of previous civil lawsuits that he had filed. Early in his career he was quite rebellious and undoubtedly controversial. Denny was the third of four sons born to Melvin Sneed, a wealthy landowner and farmer in southern Missouri. Denny had a solid family upbringing. He followed his two older brothers off to college and strayed a little from the conventional path.

Like most college kids, he experimented with smoking pot and occasionally stayed up cramming all night while pumped full of uppers. However, his love was playing the bass guitar in the hottest band on campus. He had let his hair grow halfway down his back and he let his creative juices flow. Besides strumming the bass guitar he dabbled with songwriting.

Somehow he stayed on course and made it through law school. From gazing at the certificates on the wall it was hard for Lucille and Matt to determine if his accreditation came from an online university, a mail-order house, or an actual law school. Nevertheless, Denny had passed the bar exam and was licensed to practice law.

The pictures that adorned the wall revealed another surprising tidbit about Denny. He had met a foreign exchange student from Bombay, India. They dated, fell in love, got married, and adopted two babies. One was a Vietnamese girl and the other was an Ethiopian boy. To add to this unique lifestyle his wife had influenced him to get involved with yoga and meditation.

In a nutshell, Denny had a wider range of life experience than most. He had gone from a privileged youngster, to a pseudo-hippie, to a responsible law student, and ultimately to a non-traditional family man practicing Far Eastern customs. It was quite a journey.

Denny's ego was huge, unparalleled. He would often walk into the courthouse wearing a wide brimmed cowboy hat. As Lucille and Matt looked around the room, they noticed it hanging on the hat rack. The brim must have been eighteen inches in diameter and atop it was what looked like an inverted coffee mug. That hat was Denny's trademark piece of attire in addition to his usual jeans, t-shirt, and sneakers.

"We need some help," stated Matt.

One other distinguishing characteristic about Denny stood out. Before he would answer or comment he would look at the client with the wide eyes of a fascinated child. His facial expression would resemble that of a person with chronic constipation. It was almost as if he was letting the time lapse away and he was counting up the dollar signs on the invoice that was to be generated.

For one not familiar with this trait, it was a revolting few moments before Denny would produce a response. All the while Lucille and Matt were wondering if Denny had dirtied his drawers. His breathing became slow and deliberate. It appeared that he had lapsed into a surreal state of meditation before he would elicit a response.

As Denny walked to the window to ponder his next comment, Matt said, "We believe that we were defrauded and swindled out of our property by a group of people that were involved with a fellow named Lew Zerrmann."

Denny raised his eyebrows and was instantly curious. Coming from a family that controlled a lot of land in their own right, Denny took an immediate interest in their story and quickly decided to take the case. A couple of trust fund babies had found the non-conforming, eccentric rebel that they had been searching for. Plus he knew a little about law.

From the beginning of their union with Denny, Matt and Lucille realized that not only would they be overmatched in court, but they also would have to do most of the investigative work by themselves. Yet they were determined to create havoc and get to the bottom of the hoax that had befallen them.

All the while, with the efforts of this trio occurring mainly behind the scenes, Lew Zerrmann continued to behave in a manner that was oblivious to their efforts. He had gotten away with the scam of a lifetime and it was his feeling that the Statute of Limitations had run its course.

Over the past ten years since meeting, Lew and Lois had established themselves openly as swingers. They were a sexually active couple that played in threesomes, foursomes, and groups. Lew's appetite for the elicit was insatiable and when it came to sex, there wasn't much he was opposed to, including having sex with the wives of married men.

His self-indulgent, immoral behavior spun out of control at times. Lew truly believed he lived the good life and that no one could stop him or attempt to bring him down. Because of his political connections he had insulated himself well. To those outside his circle of connections it seemed like Lew had truly become too big for his britches. He had literally become a big fish in a little pond . . . and actually believed that he was untouchable.

CHAPTER FORTY-TWO

Summer of 1995 . . .

Walter Hancock was every bit as edgy now as he was on the night that he was included with the crew that buried the hooker. Back then the alcohol had somewhat of a numbing effect. The years seemed to have a way of making him more eccentric and more assiduous. Perhaps it was his price to pay for keeping the dark secret. After all, he was the only one in the group that seemed to have a conscience. All the others were dead of emotion.

As the years passed along, he became more and more precise with his routine. Every day he would arrive at his office at exactly 7:30 a.m. He would immediately go to the kitchen area and make a pot of coffee. While the coffee was brewing he would visit the restroom and make sure that every strand of hair on his head was in place.

He would then drink one black cup of coffee, read the morning newspaper, and follow that with a cup of coffee with one creamer and one tablespoon of sugar. Then he would pick up a pencil and idly tap his desk as he gazed out the window. Something was going on inside his head—either that or he was going insane.

Lew Zerrmann burst into his office one morning in early June and disrupted his routine. The pencil in Walter's hand sounded as if it were keeping the beat to a song. "What are you so nervous about?" Lew asked.

"The property has served its purpose," Walter declared. "Get rid of it."

Lew was not impressed with that reply. He just shrugged his shoulders nonchalantly. "Quit worrying about things. I've taken care of everything," he stated.

Walter blew up. " . . . And that is exactly what I am worried about! My life and future is in your hands. It's not exactly the way I envisioned things would be when I reached this stage of my life."

Lew couldn't stand being lectured like a child in elementary school. He was used to always calling the shots and getting things done his way. Walter was relentless. He was starting to vent his years of resentment.

"Get the damn thing sold!" Walter exclaimed in a voice that was clearly frustrated. He had allowed himself to be controlled by Lew Zerrmann for nearly fifteen years and he clearly was not pleased about it.

Lew got up from his seat, went to the kitchen, and poured a cup of coffee. Even when he was getting a lip thrashing he was inconsiderate. "You know how fond I am of ground," he said when he returned to his seat.

"We've been dodging a bullet on the golf course for years!" Walter continued. He was making reference to all of the creative accounting that the two had started when the business was in its' infancy. "All that stuff is going to catch up with us one of these days."

"You know, I've kind of gotten to the point in my life where I like the place," Lew replied indifferently. Lew wasn't about to let a wimpy accountant gain control of the conversation. It was clear that he was going to dig in and show Walter who was making the decisions. He sat up straight in his chair and firmly crossed his arms.

Walter didn't take lightly to the body language. "Look, dammit! The books are cooked. Your skimming is out of control. If you don't watch out we'll throw up a red flag and trigger an audit."

Lew's cockiness was reaching new heights. He had gotten away with the tax scam for so many years he thought that he was immune to any kind of governmental action. "We've beaten them all of these years. They don't want a little old man like me. If they thought that something was up, then they would have stopped us a long time ago."

"Why take that chance? Different administrations go after different things," Walter rebutted. "Why do you have to continually think that you are above the law?"

"Every small businessman does the same thing that we're doing. It's the American way. The IRS knows that and just turns their head," Lew rationalized.

"But your greed is getting out of hand. The course has declared a negligible amount of income. The expenses are exceeding the income at a ratio that is going to set off a computer program," Walter replied.

"Hey, it's not cheap to live any more," Lew responded defiantly.

"Just find a new piece of dirt and move on," Walter stated with frustration. He was visibly exasperated with this client.

"You know how tough it is for me to do that. Once I get attached to something . . ."

"Sell the damn place!" Walter interrupted.

"Dammit, Walter, relax! You're going to give yourself a heart attack."

"No. You're the one that is going to give me one."

A grin came over Lew's face. "That was what I came in here to talk about this morning," Lew conceded.

"What? Heart attacks?" Walter forced a smirk of his own.

"No. I've been giving some thought to selling the business to J Dub," Lew stated. He finally looked like he wanted to have a meaningful conversation with Walter.

"It can't come soon enough. For the measly fee you're paying me to keep the books, it's not worth the risk for me to put myself on the firing line," Walter said.

"If I sell the place, then I want top dollar for it," Lew blurted.

"That's going to be tough. The business hasn't been making any money. The income approach on any appraisal will bear that out," Walter countered.

Lew was getting into an area with which he was unfamiliar. "What about the land value alone?"

"Well, maybe. It depends on how it is zoned," Walter replied.

"There's a power line easement, and an oil pipeline, and some ground that's in a flood plain. I can't imagine it can be worth any more than what normal agricultural ground is selling for," Lew retaliated.

Walter was an expert in dealing with numbers. They were going down a path that was very familiar to him. "You have three different appraisal methods. They are income, market, and cost. Any appraiser will have to make adjustments. Those are regulated. If the checks and balances system is flawed then it won't add up."

"Hmmm . . ." Lew wanted to hear whatever information was available, especially if it affected his pocketbook. "What are you getting at?"

"Look, we can easily figure what the cost of the ground is. That takes care of the market approach. We can figure out how much it would cost to build a golf course if we had to replace it. That's the cost approach. The only thing that concerns me is the income approach. Your track record with that business doesn't show any net earnings," Walter reasoned.

"If I'm paying an appraiser I'll just tell him what I need," Lew volunteered.

"It doesn't work like that! An appraiser is licensed by the state. They're not going to put their livelihood on the line to line your pockets."

"It worked on you, didn't it?" Lew started messing with the rational thinking that Walter's brain was programmed to generate.

"Is that your solution to everything?" Walter asked incredibly. "Pay people off?"

"If I hire him then he should do what I tell him," Lew responded. His arrogance was off the chart. In Lew's world everybody and everything had a price.

"You are something else," Walter gasped. "The appraisal is normally ordered by a buyer or the bank for the buyer. It's there to protect someone from overpaying."

"J Dub won't know," Lew reasoned.

"The income approach is loaded with holes due to the skimming," Walter was relentless in driving home his point.

"J Dub will pay anything for the place," Lew insisted. "He's got too much of his time and his heart into the place."

"The bank may not let him."

"Then I'll finance him myself."

"You always have to have your way, don't you?" Walter conceded.

"It's my last big score. I have to get top dollar for the place. If it means I have to pay some appraiser to get that done, then so be it," Lew said adamantly.

"Just get it done." Walter was at the end of the rope. "Quit wasting time."

"With what I've been through, this is nothing. I'll find some appraiser that has a family to feed, slip him a few bucks under the table, and get a value that I deserve. Then I'll find some banker that is only interested in covering his ass," Lew persisted.

Walter could do little but stare incredulously at the man who was speaking such absurdities. "You are something else."

"Don't worry. I'm good at getting things taken care of," Lew said with a devilish grin.

" . . . Yeah. That's what I'm afraid of. Just get it done before you-know-who comes knocking," Walter stated. He realized that his common sense approach was going nowhere with a shady figure like Lew Zerrmann.

CHAPTER FORTY-THREE

It didn't take Lew long to put his plan into action. He had stumbled across an out-of-town appraiser years earlier when he refinanced the debt on the golf course. At the time he had gotten clearance from the bank to use the fellow and now he saw an occasion to renew their relationship.

Several years earlier Lew had been running short on cash. So he thought that it would be an ideal time to take advantage of attractive interest rates that were present in the economy. The appraiser that the bank had recommended specialized in golf course appraisals. Lew made the initial contact with the gentleman over the phone and was surprised at how anxious the appraiser was to travel nearly six hundred miles to do a property appraisal.

At the time, Lew figured that he might as well kill two birds with one stone. Not only would he be able to take advantage of the low cost of money that was available, but he also saw it as an opportunity to replenish a checkbook that was getting depleted. He worked with the appraiser to get an inflated value on the business. He then refinanced the property and took several hundred thousand dollars of cash out of the business.

Back then, that money went into the golf course checkbook. He quickly raided the cash flow of the business under the guise of the machinery lease account which he had set up with Walter.

Lew knew exactly who to call to get an inflated value on the business and he didn't waste any time in doing so. He knew that he would be able to tell his appraiser buddy exactly what value he wanted and the appraiser would jiggle the numbers to make things work.

The next order of business was to tell J Dub that he wanted to sell the golf course. Even though years had passed, things had been quite tense at the course. Each morning J Dub came in and greeted the regulars and Julie. But there was a glimmer of mistrust that shrouded his eyes each time Lew walked into the shop. Not wanting to arouse his suspicions, Lew decided over the years to lay low with J Dub. He didn't want to push him too hard, especially not now.

"Julie, I'm gone to the bank in case Lew is looking for me." J Dub replied as he zipped the bank bag sealed.

"Yep," Julie chirped as she poured another round of beers for the guys. J Dub walked out of the shop and the screen door clapped behind him. As if on cue, Lew drove his cycle up to his favorite parking spot the minute J Dub's truck went out of sight. He entered the pro shop.

"Did you need J Dub? He just left to go to the bank," Julie offered as she walked past Mr. Big Shot.

"I'm aware he's gone, I was waiting for him to leave. C'mere when you get through serving the drunks," Lew replied as he headed out the door and to the rear of the building.

Julie rolled her eyes in aggravation and served the beers to the group. "Sorry, guys. I guess Lew forgot to tell me he was the voice of morality around here," Julie quipped sarcastically. The guys snickered and went on with their card game. Julie followed Lew to the rear of the building.

"Now don't say anything to him," Lew whispered as he placed his fingers to his lips.

"You know I can keep a secret," Julie said.

"I'm not so sure about that," Lew countered as he looked over his shoulder. "He'll be back any minute."

"Here he comes now!" exclaimed Julie as she noticed J Dub pulling back into the parking lot. "That was quick."

"Go get him," stated Lew.

Julie ran out to the parking lot and greeted J Dub. She escorted him to the rear of the building. "What's going on back here?" J Dub asked.

"Happy birthday!" Lew yelled as he ripped the tarp off of an object.

Underneath the tarp was a brand new, three-wheeled, John Deere Truckster. It was an all-terrain vehicle that would allow J Dub to travel rapidly across the golf course. The vehicle would be able to serve multiple purposes and was exactly what J Dub had had his eye on for months. "How did you know that is what I needed?" an amazed J Dub exclaimed.

"The word got out, I guess," said Lew proudly.

Julie noticed a stencil on the side of the Truckster and ran to feel it. On the side of the Truckster was a decal that said J Dub. She turned to Lew and in a surprised tone said, "You didn't tell me about that!"

J Dub remembered the incident that had happened years before with the boys and the cooler. He kept in mind Lew's penchant for chasing down golfers on the motorcycle. "I guess now we can set speed traps," he quipped. "We'll both have a vehicle to run after them with."

As puzzling to figure out on his bad days, Lew was equally as puzzling on the days that he meant well. "I've been way too demanding of you. This is just my way of saying 'Thank You' and well, sometimes I have a big mouth," Lew said as he brilliantly played his hand to J Dub.

"Well, thank you. I really appreciate that." J Dub stated as he turned to shake Lew's hand. Lew noticed that the hardness in J Dub's eyes toward him was starting to fade. That would serve his purpose well.

"Let's go back inside and get something to drink," Lew suggested as the three of them headed for the pro shop door. The boys were sitting in the back playing cards. Bogey's years were advancing and he was taking a nap. He had gone eighteen holes with them earlier in the day. What had once been an overabundance of energy had now turned into a little bit of a struggle. When Bogey was a young dog it was not unlike him to run all over the golf course when the boys went to play a round of golf. Now, he would run for the first few holes and then walk the remaining holes. He would search for shade and a lot of the times Bogey would jump into Easy Earl's cart and ride.

The normal chit-chat was taking place, followed by an occasional disagreement. The old-timers were getting ornery and set in their ways. "Hey, old man, when are you going to take up the game?" Easy Earl yelled from the back of the room toward Lew.

"I haven't got time for it. Been too busy making money," Lew responded.

"You're just like all the rest of those idiots," Rollie chimed. "Spend all your time worrying about money and don't have time for any friends."

"Isn't making money what it's all about?" Lew countered.

"For fools that don't know any better," Fred said as he seized the opportunity to chide Lew.

"I'm trying to make something out of myself," Lew declared. "My achievements speak for themselves. That's why people look up to me and I command the respect that I deserve."

Easy Earl got a lot of delight in kidding Lew. He added, "Do you think if you die with the most toys, you win?"

All of the boys erupted with laughter.

"Yeah, well . . ." Lew couldn't stand being the butt of the joke. He retreated to the sanctity of the office. "J Dub, come on in here."

J Dub followed him into the office. "I've got something that I'd like to discuss with you. Can you be at my home tonight at seven?" Lew inquired.

"I don't think that Marcia has anything planned."

"Good, I'll see you then."

It had been several years since J Dub had been to Lew's home. Something big had to be coming down. Lew usually reserved his home for grand occasions. For all J Dub knew maybe Lew was going to announce his marriage plans to Lois.

J Dub made the short drive over to Lew's home just as the sun was setting. He stopped at the electronic gate and got clearance to enter. After Lew opened the gate for him J Dub pulled his pickup truck down the driveway. Dusk had already fallen. On this particular night the surroundings took on an eerie calm.

Lew greeted J Dub at the door and invited him in. J Dub was shocked to see what appeared to be three hundred guns and rifles stacked up in a pile by the door. J Dub had always known that Lew was a gun collector, but leaving the guns heaped in a pile on the floor by the front door seemed a little odd.

On the wall opposite the pile of weapons hung a six by six foot Swastika. The Nazi flag stunned J Dub. It seemed that the references that Lew had made to Hitler in the past carried a little more substance after seeing what was draped on the dark paneling. "What the heck are you into?" he asked.

"Oh, don't pay any attention to that. It's just a little hobby of mine," Lew said as he brushed aside the question. "Come on down to my lower level."

J Dub stumbled down the stairs and entered a dimly lit bar area. The dark, walnut paneling on the walls added to the creepy atmosphere. The macabre setting sent chills down J Dub's spine. The darkness reminded him of death. Lew didn't bother to increase the light in the room and the bar remained dark. The air was stagnant. As J Dub pulled up a stool, Lew offered him a soft drink.

Lew could be very persuasive when he wanted to be. He was a skilled manipulator and effectively disguised his true agenda. The bait had been set in the trap earlier that day. "You know J Dub," Lew started. "I've been looking back on a lot of things that have happened in my life and I've come to the conclusion that I am not any good at handling the people part of this business."

"I think that we all have realized that for a while," J Dub agreed.

"You and Julie have done such a great job of running my business over the years."

"Well, thanks. We've tried, but it hasn't come without a lot of hard work," J Dub conceded.

"It originally hurt my feelings when the two of you didn't want me around there," Lew explained as he watched J Dub's reaction closely.

J Dub didn't necessarily buy into that statement. He knew that Lew had other things going on and had always treated the golf course like it was a secondary investment in his life. "We realized early on that your interests weren't in being a 'hands on' type of partner. Plus, you didn't know much about golf and let's just say that customer service isn't your strong suit. That's the reason you brought me into the picture." J Dub's bluntness surprised even himself, yet, he knew he was speaking the truth.

"Deep down, I always knew that you were right. I knew that from a long range perspective you needed me to stay away from the customers," Lew admitted.

"It's no secret. We've always known that it is probably good if you just stayed away," J Dub replied.

There was a momentary pause and Lew asked, "How about forever?" J Dub had no idea what Lew was referencing. "I'm tired of all the BS," Lew confided.

"What are you getting at?" J Dub asked as he studied his partner. "What you're saying is nothing new. You never did care much for golf and all of the camaraderie it provided," J Dub confessed. He raised his drink and took a sip.

Out of the blue Lew blurted, "Give me five million and it's yours."

J Dub choked on the drink and spit the beverage across the bar. After all of the years as business partners the news that Lew wanted to finally sell the business to J Dub came as a big surprise. As Lew scurried for a towel, J Dub continued. "Five million dollars? Are you nuts?"

"It's time for our buy/sell agreement to kick in," Lew said.

"The business can't be worth that. Is that your pie-in-the-sky offer or something?" J Dub asked skeptically.

"That's a helluva deal for you and your family," Lew pleaded.

" . . . Maybe for you! Give me some time to sort through some things," J Dub said. "There is no way the course is worth that much money. Not to mention all the work I have put into it. That should be considered too. I've gotta think this through." He looked Lew in the eye, got up, and left. J Dub wasn't sure if Lew wanted to sell him the business or make a good deal for himself. It was hard to tell whether or not Lew had something else up his sleeve, or genuinely wanted to move on with his life.

CHAPTER FORTY-FOUR

The first order of business for J Dub was to break the news to Marcia. Finally, after all of these years, the time was near to break away from Lew and get on with their lives. He thought that the perfect time to tell Marcia was, casually, over dinner. J Dub wanted his brother, Curt, to be there also. Curt had been so instrumental in helping the two of them get started. J Dub thought that it would be appropriate for Curt to hear the news at the same time as Marcia.

He fired up the barbecue grill the next evening. He felt at home when the barbecue grill was throwing off smoke and the flavor of the charcoal was permeating the air. Grilling hamburgers made him feel as comfortable as the driving range. Both places were where J Dub could truly relax.

The three children were playing in the backyard, well away from any conversation that was about to ensue. Marcia placed a tablecloth on the picnic table. Curt searched the cooler for a beer.

"Curt, Marcia, he's ready to sell," J Dub blurted out. It had been twenty-four hours since Lew had broken the news to him. He couldn't hold back his excitement any more. Marcia ran to hug her husband. She had been wanting for her husband to distance himself from Lew for years. Curt rushed to shake his brothers' hand.

"It's what we've always dreamed about," J Dub declared.

The news hit Marcia hard after the initial shock. She stopped celebrating and cried. "Now I'll never see you."

In a way she was right. If J Dub put in a lot of hours now, then the recent news would mean that her husband would be responsible for running the business during every daylight hour. Of course, he was pretty much doing that now anyway. "Sure you will," J Dub replied. "We'll hire someone to help with the hours."

Marcia kissed her husband on the forehead. She said, "I've always thought that you were in way over your head with that guy."

"I learned a long time ago to just let him have his way. Then I could normally get what I wanted from him," J Dub stated. He felt as if all of the years of playing his cards right were now going to pay handsome gains.

"I haven't trusted him for years and I'll be glad when he stops lording over you" Marcia declared.

"Get the financial statements and tax returns. I'll help you out," Curt offered. Curt had been involved in real estate financing for a number of years and was comfortable providing advice to his younger brother.

There's something about that guy that I don't trust," Marcia reiterated.

"I know what you mean, Marcia. We all can see it at the golf course," Curt added. "None of the guys take him too seriously."

"Everything will be fine," J Dub stated in a reassuring tone, purposely leaving out the price tag that Lew wanted for the place. He had decided to let Curt take a look at the returns and financial statements and deal with the issue then.

"Yeah, right. I'll believe that when I'm signing papers at the closing table," Marcia said cynically. "I'm going to have to see it to believe it."

CHAPTER FORTY-FIVE

Unbeknownst to J Dub, another force was hard at work. The Morton heirs, Lucille and Matt, behind the guidance of their new, aggressive lawyer Dennis Sneed, had begun their own investigation into the affairs of Lew Zerrmann. They felt like they had been defrauded nearly fifteen years earlier. Perhaps Marcia's words were a foreshadowing of events to come.

Even though the government couldn't find enough evidence to try and convict Lew Zerrmann and his associates in a criminal proceeding, the heirs and Denny Sneed felt as if they could muster enough support to get a case heard in civil court. One main obstacle stood in the way for them. It was not a small problem either. It was the death of Margaret Morton, who had died shortly after signing the tax form in Walter Hancock's office.

~   ~   ~

Everyday life continued at a snail's pace at the golf course. J Dub was naturally excited at the opportunity to finally purchase it. His enthusiasm was bubbling over. A day or two later, the boys were at their back table playing backgammon and gin. Some golfers had just paid and had left the pro shop. While J Dub was fiddling with the register Rollie yelled from the back of the room. "Hey J Dub, when you get to be our age you should never pass a bathroom without stopping, you should never trust a fart, and you should never waste an erection."

All of the boys howled in laughter. "If you don't get rid of that asshole partner of yours, then you won't see our age," Easy Earl chimed.

"We're working on that. He finally decided to sell it to me," J Dub said with a smile that glistened from ear to ear.

"J Dub, that's the best news of the week," BT howled. One by one the guys came up to J Dub and congratulated him on the opportunity.

A mini-celebration ensued. The accompanying noise summoned Julie out of the office. "What the hell is going on out here?" she asked inquisitively.

"J Dub is going to buy the place," Elia stammered in his deep Middle Eastern accent.

"Maybe now we'll be able to get the first tee box fixed," piped in Paco.

"It's about time we got an owner that understands the needs of a golfer," Fred added.

All of the boys were shaking hands and slapping each other on the back. "Yeah, well, we'll see about all that. You guys calm down before one of you drops over from a heart attack," Julie stated.

"Don't rain on our parade," Fred continued.

"Yeah, this is a day to celebrate," Elia added.

"Yuck it up all you want," Julie said. She turned to J Dub and continued, "I need to tell you something."

"Right now?"

Julie nodded. "I don't think it should wait." She turned to head back into the office.

"Big Shot" boomed through the speakers. Julie stopped in her tracks, glanced at J Dub, and rolled her eyes. Life had been going fairly smoothly in the pro shop. The last thing that the two of them wanted was for Lew to pop in. "Can it wait?" asked J Dub reluctantly.

Julie let off a frustrated sigh. "It's going to have to," she replied.

Lew and Lois entered the pro shop. It was obvious that they had been out for a joyride on Lew's motorcycle. Lew hummed the tune of "Big Shot." He had a wind-blown look and wore his sunglasses. Lois wore a way-too-tight pair of hot pants, a halter top, and a leather vest. No matter how hard she tried she couldn't return to her glory years. She was twenty years too old and thirty pounds too heavy.

As was his customary procedure, Lew rushed over to the sign-in sheet. He acted as if he and J Dub never had a conversation about the business changing ownership. Lew quickly counted the number of golfers that had teed off. It was hard to predict whether or not he had been on the golf course counting the number of players or if he had been out enjoying the countryside. His unpredictability kept J Dub on guard. With the amount of responsibility that J Dub had, he hated to have Lew always looking over his shoulder. "Our play looks slow today, J Dub," Lew exclaimed.

"Is there any wonder?" J Dub was continually frustrated by Lew's actions to the golfers. "The weather is too hot for a lot of players and the other ones you've already run off the course."

The boys in the back were still in a jovial mood from the news that they had just received. BT shouted to Lew. "All of the days should be this slow!"

Rollie continued, "If the weather is as hot as what was just in here, then . . ."

"Did you see the knockers on that blonde?" Fred butted in.

"The redhead wasn't too shabby either," BT stressed.

"What are you guys talking about?" Lew's curiosity had gotten the best of him.

Elia volunteered, "Two coeds were in here about forty-five minutes ago."

"They about stopped three hearts," Paco said.

"And made my pacemaker skip," Rollie added.

Lew considered himself to be quite the ladies man. It didn't matter if Lois was in his company or not. If there were some young and pretty women that he could exercise his influence with, then he was going to go for it. "Where did they go?" Lew inquired.

Fred couldn't stand Lew. They had had several run-ins over the years. Most of their conflicts centered on Fred's relaxed lifestyle. Lew was a task master and couldn't stand to see someone that got enjoyment out of life. "Out to play golf, you moron. What the 'hail' else do you think they would be doing here?"

"Was it just the two of them?" Lew asked. His juices were flowing like a teenager. The thought of two college coeds on the golf course sounded terribly exciting to him.

"No, they had four guys with them," BT answered.

Lew immediately scolded J Dub. "Dammit, J Dub. We can't have more than two people to a cart." His personality couldn't help but chastise the very person that looked after him the best.

"Two of the guys said that they would walk," J Dub said as he tried to defend himself.

"I'm sure about that," Lew replied facetiously. "You know better than that. We can't have more than two people in a cart because of insurance purposes," Lew said as his harping continued. "Come on, Lois. We need to see what's going on out there." Lew bolted out the door with Lois in quick pursuit.

Rollie immediately jumped to his feet and recognized that a good time was about to be had by all. "Let's go guys. It's time for some fun. They oughta be on hole number four by now."

The boys scrammed out the door. J Dub felt as if things might get out of hand. He turned to Julie and said, "Keep an eye on things. We'll talk later."

A miniature caravan traveled down the first fairway. Lew raced across the golf course on his motorcycle. Lois had her arms wrapped around his waist with a death grip. Four golf carts filled with the regular guys bounced their way behind the cycle in quick pursuit. J Dub, with Bogey aboard, gunned the Truckster to keep up.

Exactly as Lew had surmised, each coed was in a cart, flanked by two college kids. All of them appeared to be in their twenties. As so many before them, they were trying to have a pleasurable time on the golf course. All of that was about to be altered as Lew raced to a stop next to one of the carts. "What do you fellas think you're doing?" Lew inquired.

The first college kid was not too impressed. It wasn't an everyday occurrence to see a guy on a motorcycle while playing a round of golf. "What's it look like, old man?" he stated. "We're playing golf." Every simple question called for a simple answer in his book.

After peering at the motorcycle the second college kid felt justified about asking for more information from the man that had questioned them. "What are you doing? Who are you and what do you want?"

Lew felt compelled to stand his ground and wield what he thought would be considerable power to an unruly bunch of college-aged kids. "I'm the owner," he declared, as if that was going to make an impact on the youths.

"Is that supposed to mean that we're in deep trouble?" the first college kid asked facetiously.

The coeds were stunningly gorgeous. One was a blonde and the other was an auburn-haired beauty. Both were tall and long-legged. Their tanned bodies made every hot-blooded man with a heartbeat salivate.

Their attire wasn't suitable for the golf-course but no one had the mettle to suggest that they change even if they had something to change into. Each wore tight short shorts that exposed a little of their butt cheeks, and it was clear their ample breasts had been augmented. They were knockouts and college life had taught them how to handle men. They were both very adept teasers. Their good looks could intimidate most guys, and their brains made it a pleasurable game for them. If Lew thought that he was going to walk into this crowd and use his "bully" tactics on them, then he was about to find out differently.

As Lew was trying to wield his authority, the blonde sauntered over to the motorcycle with every intention of rescuing her friends from any harassment. She admired the machine. Lois flirted with her. Lew turned his head to admire her figure. His eyes roamed over every inch of her body. She literally stopped the conversation. In a very innocent quality the blonde deadpanned, "Hey, that's cool. I've never seen a motorcycle on a golf course before."

Lew seemed oblivious to the comment. Despite her physical attributes, Lew tried with all of his might to not be swayed by her body language. He was not to be deterred from the task that he had in front of him. "Insurance doesn't allow three to a cart," he blurted, albeit a little sheepishly.

At about that time the boys and J Dub arrived. They had all been present when the college kids had walked into the pro shop. The girls had stopped the backgammon and gin games at the back table a little while earlier. It was their feeling that Lew was going to finally meet his match and they wanted to be close by to witness the sight.

Lew remained on his mission. He took dead aim at the cooler that was on one of the carts. "Where did you get that beer?" he insisted.

Again, the blonde felt that it was her job to jump into the fray. She walked over to Lew in an attempt to diffuse the situation. Experience had taught her that the quickest way to calm a man down was to use her breasts to her advantage. She rubbed them up against Lew and answered his question for the group. "We brought it along because sitting between these two studs gets me all hot and sweaty," she said in an innocent, sex-kitten voice. Her halter top revealed a sizeable cleavage and stretched to contain it.

She smiled at her friends. They all knew how persuasive she could be. Her body was a great mediator. The blonde reached into the cooler and grabbed a beer. In a convincing way she turned to Lew and pleaded. "Could you help me open this so that I won't break a nail?"

The redhead took it upon herself to enter the action. She decided to help her friend. So she walked up to Lew and rubbed her breasts against Lew in a similar manner that the blonde had. She fixed the collar on his shirt. Her breathing was directed toward Lew's ear. "I bet your bite isn't as bad as your bark. If you could smile a little, then I'll take a picture of you two. My girlfriend is a celebrity, you know," she purred.

The third college kid ran to the golf cart and fetched a camera. He handed it to the redhead and said, "Here, Raven."

Raven kept her naive spirit alive. She rubbed Lew's chest and murmured in his ear, "Now what's your name Mr. Owner?"

Lew had met his match. The two women had reduced him to a mere shadow of himself. He sheepishly replied, "Lew."

Raven kept going. Whatever she was doing was making Lew eat out of her hand. In a sultry tone she asked, "Mr. Lew, do you think that you can get Mrs. Lew to help me with this camera?"

Lew jumped at the opportunity to exert his authority. He shouted orders to Lois. "Mrs. Lew, go help her!" He knew that Lois, in her submissive state, would obey his word.

Lois, however, blew him off. She motioned her hands as if to not be bothered. She was getting a charge out of how the two coeds were manipulating her boyfriend.

The in-your-face denial to his clout enraged Lew. Lois' action was out of character for her normally compliant role. "You heard me! Do as you're told!" Lew hollered.

A brief second elapsed. Lois did not want to confront Lew. She knew how violent he could become. She acquiesced to his request, got off of the motorcycle, and walked over to Raven.

Raven was controlling the shots now. She and the blonde had Lew doing whatever they asked. She turned things up a notch. Raven brushed her hand against Lew's chest and blew some breath on his neck. With as much persuasive ability as she could muster she said, "Mr. Lew, the celebrity that you are with is named Cancun. Go introduce yourself to Cancun."

Of course, Cancun was on the other side of Lew and had been stroking his arm. She had been rubbing her breasts against him the entire time. Meekly, Lew grinned at Cancun and said, "Hi, Cancun. I'm Lew." His stating the obvious was comical to J Dub and the boys. They rolled on the ground with laughter. The two coeds had compromised the controlling nature of Lew.

The fourth college kid could see the uneasiness on Lew. "You look a little uptight and uncomfortable around those two heartthrobs." He grabbed a beer and offered it to Lew. "Here, this might loosen you up a little," he stated.

Lew seized the opportunity to return to power. He was not about to let some college kid make a suggestion to him at this juncture. "I don't drink," he said defiantly.

The first college kid felt bad for his buddy. To deflect some of Lew's momentum he confronted Lew. "You don't want Cancun to feel uncomfortable, do you?"

Lew smiled at Cancun. He enjoyed all of the affection that she was lavishing on him. With an elfish grin he said, "Cancun deserves to be comfortable." Lew saw this as an opportunity to possibly get her into his bedroom.

Cancun reacted in a manner that Lew was not counting on. She jumped with excitement. "Oh, yippee!" Cancun shouted. "I'm sooooo glad you said that Mr. Lew because it is such a hot day."

Cancun proceeded to undo her top. She slipped out of her halter top and turned to reveal a marvelous set of store-bought boobs. The boys and J Dub couldn't believe that a woman was undressing on the golf course. All of them howled with laughter.

Cancun returned her attention to Lew. She snuggled up next to him and let her breasts jiggle against his chest. He took the occasion to fondle her breasts and pinch her nipples. She played with his ear and nibbled on his neck.

As Raven looked into the camera she said, "Cancun that is going to make such a nice picture for Mr. Lew. Now everybody smile!"

She snapped the picture. Lew had a grin that wouldn't go away. Cancun's breasts were front and center in the snapshot. She continued to dote on Lew. As she rubbed her fingers through Lew's hair she said, "Mr. Lew, you don't mind if Raven gets comfortable too, do you?"

Lew was in a world of his own. The thought of two naked coeds rubbing against him practically drove him into a maniacal frenzy. That was a dream that any elderly man cherished. To have both of these women nude on the golf course was a dream come true. He could barely muster up enough strength to talk. He finally spoke in a tone so softly that it was barely audible. "It's awfully hot out here." He followed the comment with a devilish smirk.

Cancun was genuinely happy for her friend. Of course she played Lew for a stooge. In her excitement she jumped up and down and let Lew ogle at her bouncing breasts, once more. "Oh! Another yippee!" she exclaimed.

She continued to dote all over him. Her breasts made solid contact with his body. She whispered in his ear. "I'm so glad you said that," as she played up to him the best that she could. Cancun kissed Lew on the cheek.

Raven handed the camera to Lois. She then proceeded to remove her top. Raven's breasts were just as beautiful, if not more impressive, than Cancun's. Lois' mouth dropped open in awe as she eyed Raven.

"I can't wait for Mrs. Lew to take my picture with Mr. Lew," Raven exclaimed.

Lois couldn't help herself. "That's quite a matching set," she said as she focused the camera. Both women snuggled up to Lew and pressed their breasts against him. Lois snapped the picture.

"These might make good Christmas cards," Lois chided Lew.

Lew could do nothing but grin. J Dub and the boys continued their rants in the background.

As the girls put their tops back on, Lew stared at them with mouth agape. Never in his wildest imagination did he think that something like that would happen to him on the golf course. He wanted to keep the connection with the two girls. "Do you two girls need some work? I need cart girls this summer," Lew volunteered.

"I already have a job," Cancun stated matter-of-factly.

Lew's interest was piqued. "Doing what?" he asked.

Raven stepped into the conversation. "We're dancers," she said.

"At the Treasure Chest," Cancun continued.

Raven reached into her purse for some admission cards. She handed several of them to Lew. "Come by and see us, Mr. Lew."

In a sick and demented fashion Lew replied," Only if I can bring Mrs. Lew." He had a perverted grin on his face.

"Take these free passes," Raven stated. She and Cancun were ready to move along and play golf with their friends.

After being a spectator, Lois took advantage of the invitation. She was not about to let the two young women get away. "You can bet we'll be over to see you."

CHAPTER FORTY-SIX

The next day, Julie and J Dub were both in the office. On occasions like this Julie normally paid the bills. J Dub took the receipts from the prior day and counted the money. It was a good way for the two of them to catch up on the business without airing too much in front of the customers in the pro shop. Easy Earl generally filled in behind the counter a few days a week to give them a break from the cash register.

"Congratulations on the news that you got from Lew," Julie said.

"Thanks. I've had the option to buy it for quite a while. We just didn't know when he would get in the mood to sell," J Dub stated.

"You know that I'll do anything that I can to help you."

"I appreciate that Julie. Curt wanted me to get the financial statements and tax returns. He said that he could help out with the financing stuff."

Julie had been the bookkeeper for years. She knew the "ins" and the "outs" of all of the entries. "I'll copy those things for you."

"Good. Curt said that he'd like to have them as soon as possible."

"No problem, but there will come a time when I'm going to have to sit down with both of you. There's some stuff that you need to know, especially if you're thinking of buying this place," Julie hinted.

"What kind of stuff?" J Dub inquired. He stopped counting the money and looked squarely at her.

"I'd trust him about as much as a goat with two peckers," Julie blurted.

J Dub couldn't help but chuckle. "What did he do now?' he asked.

"He's been funneling money out of here faster than a hummingbird can flap its wings," Julie responded.

"He's doing what?" J Dub's interest was piqued.

"You know how he is with money," Julie continued. "He can't stand to pay taxes."

"The business has been doing okay, hasn't it?" J Dub solicited for more information.

"Of course," Julie said. "We've got plenty of cash flow."

"Then how is he doing it?"

"You've called him on it a couple of times, but you didn't know that you were hitting one of his hot buttons," Julie confided.

"You mean for raiding the checkbook when we start getting a nice nest egg built up?" J Dub's curiosity was on full tilt now.

"Yeah. If you ever noticed, that was when he came up with his little jobs out on the course," Julie rambled. It was becoming obvious to J Dub that she was getting ready to expose something about the business that he hadn't known occurred. "Most of that stuff that he does out there isn't even needed," she continued. "But that's his way of getting to the money."

"Why didn't you tell me about this before?" J Dub began rubbing his neck in aggravation.

"I'm just the bookkeeper. I do what the owner of the company and the CPA tell me to do," Julie quickly reminded him.

"I just thought . . . well, it doesn't matter now. I'm sorry, Jules."

"It's ok."

"So what does he do? How does he go about it?"

"After he gets done with the job, he'll give me a bill to pay." Julie was on a roll. "And the key thing about it is that we code that as an expense."

"How can that be?" J Dub continued to play dumb with the hopes that she would reveal more secrets.

"I don't know for sure, but I think that Walter made the original suggestion," Julie continued.

"He has stated to me several times that he can't stand to pay taxes." J Dub added.

"And keeping the books this way certainly avoids that."

J Dub pried further. "How are we getting around the taxes?"

"Basically, we have added a fictitious expense. That's an offset against income. Whatever we make, he takes for his jobs and we categorize it as an expense to show that the business isn't making any money," Julie explained.

"Huh?"

"When you and Curt look at the books you'll see that there isn't any net income. The books are done that way so that he doesn't have to pay any corporate income taxes," Julie clarified. "He might as well be taking the cash right out of the register."

"That was the main reason that he wanted me around. He wanted to make sure that whoever was working the register wasn't stealing from him," J Dub countered.

"And as it turns out, he's the biggest thief," Julie said.

"Is he paying taxes on what he takes?" J Dub wanted to get to the bottom of what was going on.

"I presume, but I don't know," Julie stated. "He'd really be taking a chance if he wasn't. And, I honestly have a hard time assuming that he does pay taxes on it."

"Get me copies of everything that I need," J Dub stressed. He knew that he and Curt would need everything for their analysis.

"Give me a few days. I don't want him to walk in on me," Julie muttered.

J Dub was still in an inquisitive mood. "What can I do about all of this?"

Julie shrugged her shoulders. "It's technically his business. He can do what he wants. I believe those three letters, s-o-l, pertains in this scenario."

J Dub thought out loud. "Just when you think you really know someone . . ."

" . . . They come back and screw you," Julie added.

"Any other ideas?"

Julie could only add something in a way that was unique to her rural upbringing. "I don't know, J Dub. If I were you, I'd be as nervous as a long-tailed cat in a roomful of rocking chairs."

J Dub forced a chuckle even though he was frustrated.

"But you do know that Coach's friend is with the IRS," she added.

J Dub jerked his head around to serve notice that he heard her.

Chapter Forty-Seven

The day had finally arrived for Maurice DiMonte to be released from prison. He had spent the better part of his term in a minimum security facility. However, make no bones about it. Prison is prison whether you are lobbying a volley or digging a ditch or chasing after a loose bar of soap.

During his stay he tried all that he could do to appeal his conviction. As a convicted felon a lot of his freedom was compromised. One of the things that Monty cherished the most was his law license. He wanted to get his conviction overturned so that he wouldn't have to give up his certification to practice law.

The appeal process did not go to his satisfaction. Time and time again he was rebuffed. It was only a formality now for the state to jerk his license. With that, his livelihood was compromised. He would have to come up with another way to make a living. Those prospects did not excite him.

Monty could go back to his old acquaintances, but his friendships were far removed. The incarceration was very costly to him. The restitution to the government alone was enough to make a grown man weep. He had lost a lot of money. He had lost almost all of his business connections. He certainly learned that crime doesn't pay.

The other obsession that he acted upon in prison was the payback to Eleanor Hackett. Her career had progressed rapidly. His, on the other hand, had plummeted. Monty could think of nothing more satisfying than bringing her down. Prison gave him time to think. He also had ample opportunity to research ways to get back at her. He was no idiot. Before he had gone to prison he ran with people that intimidated others. By nature, Monty was vindictive. In time he would pay her back. He only had to wait for the right opportunity.

Two of his most faithful supporters were Lew Zerrmann and Raymond Parsons. They were present on the day that he walked through the gates and out of prison.

Monty had lost a considerable amount of weight behind the prison walls. The food was not to his liking so his appetite decreased. The exercise time allowed him to further burn calories. In addition, he sported a short crew cut. His new look was quite a bit different than what Lew and Raymond had remembered. He actually had a refreshed, younger look when he walked out to greet them. After they shook hands, Monty said, "That fuckin' bitch." He was genuinely in a rotten mood. "I've had damn near ten years to think about how to get back at El Cerdo."

"El Cerdo?" Lew was confused.

"It's not Ellie or Eleanor with me. It's El Cerdo," he declared in an angry tone. "That's Spanish for the pig."

Lew smiled heartily. Raymond patted Monty on the back. His old friend had not changed too much. He still had that mean streak and feistiness in his personality. "What did you do in there?" Raymond inquired.

"Not a whole helluva lot except think up ways to get back at that bitch," Monty stammered. It was obvious that he would hold a grudge for the rest of his life. "You know what the saying is, 'You don't get mad, you get even'."

"El Cerdo. I like that Monty. Let's go get El Cerdo," Lew stated. He loved to have control over people. It appeared that Monty was sincere in his desire to go after her.

Monty had a determined sneer on his face. He was bitter and ornery.

"Do you have it all figured out?" Lew persisted.

"You bet I do. After I get out of the halfway house, we'll take her down," Monty stated defiantly.

"Good. Let's show her what it's like in a man's world," Raymond announced.

As they got into Lew's car, Monty proclaimed, "You can bet your ass that she's going to find out!"

Chapter Forty-Eight

A few days later J Dub walked into the office and found Julie at her desk. "Hey kiddo, how are you today?" J Dub offered as he walked in. Julie smiled and kept a nervous eye on the door. J Dub leaned back in a chair rubbing Bogey's belly with his foot as he sprawled out on the floor.

Julie nodded her head toward the corner and smiled. "The documents are in those boxes." Three boxes were stacked in the corner.

"How far back did you go?" asked J Dub.

"Ten years," Julie replied. "That copier is as slow as a wet week in April."

J Dub chuckled at her way of putting things. Rain had its way of slowing down play on the golf course.

"I would have had it done a few days earlier, but I had to keep looking over my shoulder to see if the little prick was going to pop in on me. Or should I say pop up on me?" she smirked.

"You did a good job," a thankful J Dub responded.

Later that night, under the cover of darkness, J Dub loaded the boxes into the cab of his pickup truck. Any responsible buyer of property had the right to investigate the situation. J Dub didn't want Lew to know that he was doing his homework. A deal was a deal and J Dub wanted to be prepared for any surprises that might be thrown his way. He had way too much time invested in this deal to be caught off guard.

He sped home to meet Marcia and Curt. Marcia had snacks prepared and the three of them conversed around the kitchen table. "Here's all of the stuff that you need," J Dub said to Curt. "See if you can make sense out of everything."

"Give me a few days to look over the numbers. Has he told you how much he wants for the property?" Curt probed.

"He said that he wants five million," answered J Dub.

"Okay. That gives me something to work with. I may try running the numbers backwards," Curt replied.

Marcia couldn't resist a comment. "If you want my two cents, then that price sounds ridiculous. We'll be in debt for the rest of our lives."

"It certainly doesn't sound like he is doing you any favors," Curt mentioned.

"Nor will he," Marcia said. "He could care less that J Dub has run that business for the better part of his adult life."

"See what you turn up and then I'll tell you what Julie told me," J Dub offered.

"What did she say?" Curt wondered.

"I don't want to sway your opinion. You tell me what you find," J Dub insisted.

CHAPTER FORTY-NINE

That weekend Curt played golf with Paul, Elia, and Paco. He was running a little late for their tee time and the group was waiting for him on the tee box. "Sorry I'm late guys. What's the game today?" Curt inquired.

"Same game. We're playing pig. You're third," replied Paco.

"Let's have a good one," Curt said after the guys drove their tee shots down the first fairway. As they walked off of the first green, Curt approached Paul and said, "Paul, the son of a gun is finally going to do it."

Do what?" Paul replied.

"J Dub said that Lew was finally going to sell him the place," Curt responded.

"I heard the boys talking about that in the pro shop the other day," Paul said.

"What do you think about that?" Curt asked.

Paul was held in the highest esteem by all of the members of the group. He had retired from the military and was the most respected and immaculately manicured guy that hung around the clubhouse. J Dub had taken a liking to him years previously and let him close up the pro shop several days a week. His pay was free golf. The good old barter system even worked on the golf course. Paul was like a father-figure to J Dub. He was rational, polite, and insightful.

"Don't bet on it," Paul responded. "That lousy so-and-so has something up his sleeve. It'll only happen if he can make big bucks. He'll deal from a position of strength. He screws everybody."

"Wow. Do you think that he'll take advantage of J Dub after all of these years?" Curt probed for a response.

"Don't kid yourself," replied Paul. "J Dub isn't strong enough to win a battle against Lew. He'll need someone that's a heckuva lot bigger than Lew to even have a chance of closing."

"You think so, huh? Thanks for the words of wisdom. I'll pass them on," Curt said.

Later that weekend Curt wrapped up his analysis of the financial statements. He returned to J Dub's kitchen with the results.

"What did you find out?" J Dub asked as they grabbed a seat.

Curt simply shrugged his shoulders as Marcia served him lemonade. "Was there anything of interest?" Marcia inquired.

"I have a question or two," Curt replied.

" . . . What about?" J Dub said in an inquisitive manner.

"First off, the business isn't making any money," Curt offered.

"Julie warned me about that," J Dub countered. "Is there anything else?"

"Do you lease any golf carts?" Curt asked.

J Dub shook his head. "We own the fleet."

Curt was unfazed. "That's what I suspected."

"What else did you notice?" J Dub wanted to find out if his brother had noticed what Julie had warned him about.

"What's the machinery lease expense all about?" Curt inquired.

"That's what Julie wanted to talk to me about," J Dub stated.

Curt shook his head. He looked his brother in the eye. At that time J Dub knew that Curt knew what Julie had been talking to him about. "There are three main expenses. They indicate where the money has been going," Curt explained. "Two of them are easy to figure out. The payroll expense covers everyone's salary. That's pretty self-explanatory. The interest expense is just that. It goes to the bank as an interest payment on the loan. The biggest expense is a machinery lease. What the heck is that all about?"

J Dub glanced at Marcia and back at Curt. He was afraid to hear what his brother was about ready to say. "You tell me."

"See who those checks were made out to," Curt adamantly persisted.

A disappointed look came over J Dub's face. "I think we all know."

"What does that indicate?" Marcia asked.

"The lousy son-of-a-gun has been skimming all of the profits all of these years!" Curt shouted.

"We hardly pay any taxes," J Dub conceded.

"That's no wonder. The books don't show that you make any money. He's been taking all of it," Curt declared. His anger was accelerating.

J Dub had no idea where to turn. "What should we do now?"

"Ask him some questions without tipping your hand," Curt suggested. "He'll eventually figure out that you know."

"Then what should I do?"

"I don't know off the top of my head. But you'll need some help. He's got you between a rock and a hard spot," Curt explained. "He can dictate the terms."

"Can I pay that much for the place?" J Dub wondered.

"You can, but it won't be a golf course for long," Curt answered. "If you have a rainy season or the competition steals your players or the weather burns up your greens, you'll be history."

"At least I'll be able to sell the land," J Dub countered.

"That's your exit plan, but that isn't going to keep you in the golf business. Plus it isn't going to correct what he's been doing," Curt offered.

"Then what should we do?" J Dub was anxious to come up with a game plan.

"Let's just stall for right now and see what happens. We need to gather some more information," Curt proposed. "We need to do our homework and talk to a few more people."

CHAPTER FIFTY

The Fall of 1995 . . .

J Dub watched Lew drive off toward the fourteenth hole with his bulldozer in fifth gear. He turned to Julie. "Any idea what he's up to? He said something about this tree and that tree."

"No clue," Julie responded as she carried a tray full of beers to the guys.

J Dub locked his register, ducked into the office for a moment, and saw the checkbook on Julie's desk. He opened the checkbook, noticed the balance, and saw that it was quite healthy.

Julie was making her way back to her register and put up the tray. "Did you see what's in the checkbook?"

"Yeah, I'm suddenly getting the distinct feeling that an 'expense' is going to be incurred today." J Dub sarcastically replied.

"Jeez my knees, he is as predictable as a . . ." Julie bit her lip and muttered to herself.

Meanwhile, J Dub sauntered over to the picture window and grabbed a pair of binoculars. He watched his partner as he went back and forth methodically and knocked a few trees down. Some of the smaller underbrush was crushed by the equipment. On occasion Lew would pick up a bucket of dirt and swirl the bulldozer around to dump the dirt into a pile. The downed trees were pushed into a separate heap. J Dub disgustedly put the binoculars away and returned to the counter.

After a few minutes of this, Lew picked up a large bucket of dirt. He jumped off the dozer and ran to the bucket to take a look. Inside was a human skeleton. He dug around in the dirt with his hands and quickly located the skull. One of the front teeth had a gold-capped crown. A wicked grin appeared on his face.

Lew promptly looked around and over his shoulder to see if anyone had witnessed what he was doing. Satisfied that he was alone, he hurriedly popped the crown off of the tooth and placed it in the pocket of his jeans. Seconds later he dumped the skeletal remains onto the pile of downed trees.

In a flash he grabbed a small container of gasoline and doused the trees and remains with the flammable liquid. In a matter of seconds the pile erupted into flames. Smoke billowed skyward. The intense heat forced Lew back onto the dozer.

Meanwhile, back in the clubhouse, the boys played backgammon and gin at their table in the back. Bogey napped nearby. J Dub paced behind the counter resigning himself that his partner was an idiot while Julie efficiently worked the rest of the room. The mail sat unopened on the counter top. J Dub started to go through it.

One specific piece of mail caught his eye. The return address indicated that it was from Children's Hospital. J Dub quickly opened the letter and read the contents. "Children's Hospital is going to name a conference room after Lew for his donation," J Dub declared. "Why would they be doing that?"

"They're putting a new wing on the hospital," Rollie answered from the back of the room.

"Yeah, but that was over ten years ago when we had the tournament over here," J Dub added.

"Did Mel sign that?" Rollie asked.

"His name is on it," J Dub said after he examined the letter.

"Lew's name will probably be on a plaque with a lot of others. That's a shock that they would do something like that. Mel was embarrassed that Lew ran him out of here that day," Rollie ranted.

"I think that we all were disappointed," J Dub conceded.

Rollie wasn't done with his comments. "You know, I introduced Mel to Lew and Lew sat right here in the pro shop and said that he would donate the course for one day each year to help fund the cause for the children."

"And then the no-good son-of-a-bitch denied that he said it," Easy Earl added. He was becoming more and more ornery with each passing day

"I wonder what they want from you now," Fred bellowed.

"Who knows? If the event would have stayed here, maybe they would have named the hospital after him," said J Dub.

"Wouldn't that be ironic," said Easy Earl. "He doesn't even have any kids."

"It goes to show how much of a liar he can be," Julie said as she peered out the picture window. "What in the world is he doing now?" she asked.

An abundant amount of smoke rose high into the sky above the nearby tree line. J Dub ran to the window to see the smoke. "That's over on number fourteen. I guess he was planning on clearing some trees today," J Dub shouted. The smell of smoke started to invade the pro shop.

"I bet he didn't bother to get a burn permit," Julie said. "The fire department will be over here in no time chewing our butt."

"He was just going to knock a few trees over. I didn't think that he would burn the whole woods down," J Dub stated. "I saw how much was in the checkbook, Julie." He grinned at her. Now that the cat was out of the bag they could joke with each other about what was going on.

"It's the end of the season. There's enough in the bank for all of us to have a new house," she answered. "He noticed it a few days ago."

"Let me run out there and see what's going on," J Dub yelled over his shoulder as he bolted out the door. Bogey took off behind him in quick pursuit. J Dub jumped onto the Truckster. Bogey sat next to him. They sped rapidly across the fairways. Quite a commotion was taking place on the course. Virtually all of the players had stopped playing golf and had rushed over to see the fire.

As J Dub pulled up, Lew still sat on the dozer amidst the burning trees. He was encircled in flames. "Quick! Call the fire department," Lew shouted at J Dub.

J Dub got on the two-way radio and called for help. "Get down and get out of there," J Dub yelled as the smoke intensified.

"A gust of wind came up," Lew hollered.

"Why didn't you wait for a calm day?" J Dub screamed.

"I wanted to show the boys how much better I made this hole," Lew barked.

"These woods don't even come into play," J Dub cried. "You're going to burn the whole course down!"

By this time Lew had worked the dozer around so that he had become trapped. "Turn on the sprinklers!" he yelled. "Get some water over here!"

J Dub hit the remote control device that controlled the satellite system for the sprinklers. Water started to spray onto the fairways. "They won't reach that far!" J Dub shouted.

The circumstances had become quite serious. Water sprayed yards away from the flames. Lew couldn't move the dozer. Sirens blared in the background. Golfers helplessly chuckled at the comedy of the situation. No one was in a position to help Lew. Everyone had to wait for the fire department to arrive.

"You better get down and get out of there!" J Dub yelled as he encouraged Lew to flee the bulldozer.

A hook and ladder truck and two tanker trucks raced down the fairway. They parked on the edge of the woods and sprayed several hoses of water toward the trees. Lew jumped off of the dozer and ran to safety. Voluminous amounts of smoke billowed across the golf course.

Shortly after Lew fled to safety the dozer caught on fire. As the oil burned, huge amounts of black smoke choked away the spectators. "Don't you breathe a word of this to anybody, J Dub," Lew instructed.

"What are you talking about? That dozer is sitting there for the world to see."

"Keep your mouth shut. Maybe I can get some insurance money out of it," Lew rationalized. When it came to money, nothing ever seemed to be his fault. Lew wanted to reap the rewards and didn't want to pay anything out. He would do all that he could to stage an accident and file an insurance claim. There was no way that he would eat the cost of a bulldozer.

J Dub boarded the Truckster and Lew hitched a ride by standing up on the back of it. They made the long trek back to the clubhouse. After they entered through the front door, Julie gave Lew a mild look of disgust. "Well, if it ain't Smokey the Bear," she proclaimed.

The comment further agitated Lew. He glared at her while all of the boys in the back laughed at him. Lew motioned to J Dub to keep his mouth shut.

"The whole town has been calling. Everyone wants to know if the clubhouse burned down," Julie continued.

The boys in the back really laughed it up at Lew's expense.

"Tell whoever calls that somebody had a heart attack out on the course," Lew countered.

"And we needed a hook and ladder to get them to heaven," Julie deadpanned. The boys rolled with amusement in the background.

"Go get the checkbook," Lew demanded.

"Do you want to give a donation to the fire department?" Julie questioned.

"No, for my work," Lew insisted. Lew had the audacity to bill the golf course for his clearing work. Julie retrieved the checkbook. "Write me a check for forty-five thousand. Mark it down as clearing," Lew ordered.

"How did I know that was coming?" Julie sarcastically replied.

J Dub felt the need to put in his two cents. "The only thing that you've been clearing out is our inventory. You should see the dozer, Julie."

Lew glared at J Dub. He grabbed the check from Julie and fled through the door. J Dub wasn't too pleased with the look that he received from Lew, nor was he happy about Lew going out the door with a check in his hand. He followed him to the parking lot.

J Dub wanted to ask Lew a few questions. He thought that this might make for an opportune time. Lew beat him to the punch. "Are you getting your ducks in order?" Lew asked.

"There are some things we need to talk about," J Dub offered.

"Any hints as to what?"

"Two and two aren't adding up to four," J Dub claimed.

"What are you getting at?" Lew probed.

"I need a lower price," J Dub demanded.

"Are you trying to screw me after all of these years?" Lew threw the situation back into J Dub's lap. J Dub stared back at Lew in bewilderment. "I don't negotiate!" Lew shouted.

"I want to know what you've been doing with the business," stated J Dub.

"It might be a moot point anyhow," Lew exclaimed.

"What are you getting at now?" asked J Dub.

"We've been sued. It might take a while to get it settled," Lew offered in an agitated tone.

"What is that all about?" J Dub inquired. He was not in the least bit delighted to find out that they had been sued.

"It's nothing. It's just a nuisance type of thing. I'll get it taken care of," Lew explained.

"That sort of delays things for a while," J Dub said.

"Keep working on buying the place. I want to sell it," Lew stressed.

With the news of a pending lawsuit, J Dub took on a resolved attitude. There wasn't a hurry to buy the place after all. That problem would need to be solved before he could go forward. He handed Lew a letter and changed subjects. "Here's a letter from the hospital naming a conference room after you," he stated.

Lew grabbed the letter, glanced at it, wadded it up and threw it on the ground. "I'm done being charitable! That probably cost me a million bucks out of my pocket over the years," he yelled.

He roared off on his motorcycle. He had become an obstinate old man that was near the end of the road. His life had turned to an unhappy saga.

J Dub stared into the distance. He grabbed his golf clubs, rounded up Bogey, and headed to the driving range to pound balls. He had some thinking to do and some stress to release. "Yeah, you're a regular Jerry Lewis running a telethon with your charity work," J Dub angrily muttered under his breath.

CHAPTER FIFTY-ONE

Hearing the buzzing of his alarm sounding at 4:30 am wasn't as difficult for J Dub as it was most people. He was a morning person to be sure and didn't mind starting his days this way. His new home was fairly close to the golf course. As a rule the drive would not be more than five minutes or so. Just about one hundred percent of the time he made that drive in the early morning darkness. It was his responsibility to be at the course before the crack of dawn. He needed to have things ready to go by the time the first golfers started showing up for their tee times.

The golf course superintendent and the help that operated the greens mower usually arrived well before J Dub. The first greens had to be cut in the darkness. It took a special person to arrive in the wee hours of the morning to get the place set up for play. The payback for those employees was that their work day was generally over by lunchtime.

When J Dub pulled into the parking lot on this specific morning he expected things to be the same as every morning. After parking his pickup truck his habit was to continue to the cart barn and greet Bogey. The dog would jump into his arms and lap at his face. J Dub would make sure that Bogey's food bowl and water bowl were replenished. Then the two of them would pull golf carts out of the barn and park them in front of the clubhouse.

Nevertheless, this morning was a little different. Shortly after parking his pickup truck another set of headlights entered the parking lot. J Dub thought nothing of it. He guessed that some golfers couldn't sleep and wanted to get an early start. Once in awhile a couple of golfers would show up and want to shoot the breeze in the pro shop rather than a coffee shop somewhere.

The car continued across the parking lot and parked next to his pickup. Two men got out and approached J Dub. One of the men was black. He wore a shirt and tie. His size suggested that at one time he was involved in athletics. The other man was considerably smaller and white. He wore glasses, but also had on a shirt and tie. His look suggested that he had spent the greater part of his life reading books. His frail appearance was quite a contrast to the driver of the car. J Dub immediately thought that something was amiss. Golfers normally would not show up to play a round of golf dressed in a shirt and tie.

"Are you J. W. Schroeder?" the black man asked in a voice that bellowed across the parking lot.

"Sure am. I go by J Dub."

"My name is Thomas Jefferson Booker. I'm with the U. S. Department of the Treasury. I work for the Criminal Investigation Division of the Internal Revenue Service," the black man replied as he offered his hand.

J Dub was caught off guard. He was apprehensive as he shook Booker's hand.

"This is my assistant, Daniel Hayden," continued Booker. Hayden nodded and extended his hand.

"We think that you might have some information that can throw some light onto some improprieties we've noticed," Hayden said.

"I'm not in trouble, am I?" J Dub probed. He was visibly shaken and nervous. His concern was understandable. Not every person is approached by the IRS in a dark parking lot.

"No, not at all," Booker replied. "We'd like for you to come in and answer a few questions for us."

"You don't beat around the bush, do you?" J Dub quipped.

Booker smiled. "We did sound a little forward I suppose. It's just that we're in a little hurry. We'd like to get off of the parking lot before your partner shows up."

"He's the person that we'd like to ask you questions about," Hayden admitted.

"You mean Lew?" J Dub asked.

Both men nodded their heads.

"Do I need a lawyer?" J Dub asked.

"You are certainly entitled to one," Booker stated.

"At this stage of the investigation it probably isn't necessary," Hayden said. "We just want to ask you some basic questions."

"Can you be in our office sometime this week?" Booker asked.

"I don't see why not."

Booker reached into his pocket and handed J Dub a business card. "We'll see you soon."

He and Hayden shook J Dub's hand and turned to get into their vehicle. "And by the way, keep this in strictest confidence," Booker concluded.

J Dub watched the men drive off and made his only comment to himself. "Shit."

Chapter Fifty-Two

J Dub was not too excited about how the day had started out. He immediately picked up the phone and called Curt. They agreed to a kitchen table meeting later that evening with Marcia in J Dub's home.

"I'm not real thrilled about all the nonsense that has been going on around here lately," J Dub started.

"He's nothing but trouble," Marcia warned.

"Fill me in on the details," Curt prodded.

"It's a series of things," J Dub stated. His life had been going along in cruise control the last several years. He had learned to deal with Lew on a certain level. Now their relationship was being changed and a lot of uncertainties were being pushed to the forefront. "First I find out that he has been skimming all of our profits. Then he told me that we were being sued . . . ."

"Whoa, what's that all about?" Curt interrupted. That was news that he didn't know about.

"Lord if I know. He was real vague about it," J Dub answered.

"Did he say what it was about?" Curt probed.

"No. Not really. Other to say that is was a misunderstanding. He thought that he could get it all taken care of, but it would have to be dealt with before I could buy the place," J Dub admitted.

"We need to find out what is going on with that," Curt suggested.

"Honestly, J Dub. I've been asking you for years now, just get away from the guy," Marcia interjected.

"We're trying," J Dub cried in a frustrated manner. "I can't get up and walk away. We've got too much time invested in this deal."

"Sometimes I wonder if it's all worth it," Marcia muttered.

"I can't turn my back on darn near fifteen years. That's too much time to walk away from something empty-handed," J Dub pleaded. "And now I have this IRS stuff to deal with."

"What's with that?" Curt wondered.

"They want me to answer some questions."

"Did they say what about?"

J Dub was exasperated. Too much negativity had surrounded him. "I don't know. They said basic stuff."

"Somebody had to tip them off to something," Curt surmised.

"Who would have done that?" J Dub asked.

"The likely candidates would be one of us," Curt suggested.

"Or, maybe Julie," J Dub offered.

"I said something to Paul," Curt added.

"What difference does it make?" Marcia exploded. "It might have been a simple thing that a computer could have kicked out!"

"That's true, too," Curt conceded.

"It really doesn't matter," J Dub rationalized. "The bottom line is that they want me to come in."

"Do you want a lawyer?" asked Curt.

"They said it wasn't to that point yet. It isn't about me, supposedly," J Dub said in a tone that indicated that he had calmed down a little.

"Remember, if they start asking stuff that you don't want to talk about, tell them that you want your lawyer with you," Curt advised.

"But I don't even have a lawyer!" J Dub yelled as his emotions got wound up again.

"Let me work on getting one for you," Curt offered.

Marcia's ire was raised. "You know how lawyers are. I don't want to start paying for one unless I have to. They charge you for every mille-second!"

"I'm getting into this mess way over my head. Maybe it is getting to be the time where I need one," J Dub admitted, ignoring Marcia.

"They are a necessary evil," Curt said. "A good one can be worth his weight in gold."

"Let me go in and see what they want," J Dub stated.

"And then we'll have to finish our homework," Curt added. "We'll have to find out about the lawsuit, and the appraisal, and run title on the property, and talk to the banker, and deal with the IRS, and check with planning and zoning, and . . . ."

"Stop! That's enough! I don't want to deal with any more right now!" J Dub was clearly annoyed. "Curt, I can only deal with one thing at a time."

Curt and Marcia exchanged glances. "That's enough for one night," Marcia concluded.

CHAPTER FIFTY-THREE

On his next day off, J Dub pulled up in front of a building that had INTERNAL REVENUE SERVICE in large, bold letters across the front. If there is one thing that scares half of the people in America, it is the IRS. J Dub was no exception, he was petrified.

The environment that surrounds the IRS is impersonal. Long waits and slow responses drive the frustration level of dealing with the IRS to an all-time high. Once in the system, it is hard to get out. Those people who are unfortunate enough to deal with the IRS usually communicate with a computer halfway across the country. It is tough to get a straight answer or one you trust to be correct.

The minute that J Dub walked through the door he felt the distant mood that permeated the walls. After going past a metal detector, he was led to a conference room where he was told to wait. The room itself was tiny and contained only a small conference table and chairs in the center.

There were no windows, no pictures and nothing to read. The room looked and felt as if it was bugged. The walls were painted a stale color and the chairs were uncomfortable and in need of re-upholstery. He was told to wait and that someone would be in to get him shortly.

Finally, after what seemed like an eternity, the door cracked open and Booker poked his head through the opening. He had a smile on his face from ear to ear. "Don't let this place scare you," Booker joked.

"That was an introduction that I wasn't counting on," J Dub said. Booker's congeniality made him relax.

"Come on into my office . . . Coffee?" Booker offered.

" . . . Why not? If I was at the course I would have had a cup by now," J Dub said.

Booker led J Dub into his office. It seemed as personable as any office he had ever visited. Plaques commemorating Booker's accomplishments decorated the walls. Diplomas indicating his schooling were posted. Pictures of his wife and children were in abundance. The overall impression that J Dub felt was that Booker was a normal guy.

Sitting in a chair across from Booker's desk was Daniel Hayden. He looked much more frail and timid in the light of the room than he did on the dimly lit parking lot. His nerdy-looking glasses made him appear to be barely out of college. It almost seemed like he had taken an entry level position with the IRS. J Dub wondered what was going to happen.

"You remember Daniel Hayden from the other morning, don't you?" Booker asked. J Dub nodded as Hayden rose to shake his hand. "He and I have been partners for almost eleven years now," Booker continued.

That seemed hard for J Dub to fathom. Booker looked to be in his thirties. Hayden appeared to be much younger. Yet if they had been together for that length of time then they must have been about the same age.

"Have a seat," Booker encouraged.

"I'm not in trouble, am I?" That was a question that J Dub repeated from the parking lot. He hoped that the answer would be the same.

Booker shook his head. "No," he said.

"I hate to keep looking at you," J Dub clamored, "but you look familiar."

Booker smiled. J Dub didn't get a good look at him in the parking lot. It was too dark out that morning. It didn't surprise Booker that J Dub started to figure out where they had met.

"The brownies," Booker said as his smile lit up the room. He beamed from ear to ear. "That was how we met and Lew is one of the reasons you're here."

J Dub felt awful. He shook his head in disbelief. " . . . With Coach!" J Dub exclaimed.

"You got it."

"I had no idea," J Dub said in total surprise. He had entirely forgotten that Julie had mentioned that Coach played golf with a guy that worked for the IRS. "It's a small world, isn't it?"

"Are you starting to feel a little more comfortable?" Booker asked as he continued to kid J Dub.

"Now I feel like it is old home week," J Dub joshed. "How did you two meet?"

"We played college ball together. Coach was our scoring forward and I was our point man."

"You guys had a good team."

"Oh, yeah. I think we were like eighty-eight and ten the three years that we played together," Booker grinned with excitement.

"Coach sure has developed some good high school squads," J Dub said. He felt like he was in the pro shop talking sports with the guys. That was something he truly loved to do.

"He knows what he's doing. But more importantly, he's a good man," Booker explained. "If there is anything that those kids will learn from him, then it will be how to live life. Coach will teach them how to grow up and be productive members of society. He will show them how to become men."

"I felt so bad for you guys that day," J Dub stated apologetically.

Booker shrugged as if to let bygones be bygones. "You didn't have anything to do with it. In fact, Coach had nothing but praise for you. He was very appreciative of the fact that you allowed teachers to have school passes. The reduced rates helped him out."

"Yeah, but that is some of the nonsense I've had to deal with. You know, from a rude partner," J Dub continued. "You guys don't come out that much any more."

"Can you blame us?" Booker muttered. "You have to go where you feel welcome. He didn't seem to want us over at his place."

"If I have anything to say about it, then you guys can come over whenever you feel like it. Next one is on me," J Dub offered.

"Thanks. I'll mention it to Coach. He always had liked playing over there."

The tension in the room had subsided immensely. The conversation was about to continue in a different direction. "What else can I do for you fellas?" J Dub had gotten into a cooperative mood.

Hayden was about to take a more active role in the conversation. He was going to go from a spectator to a participant. "We set up different models of different businesses around the country. That way we can program our computers to look for things,"

Hayden started. "The golf business is so unlike any other business out there. We wanted to talk with you to get a better understanding of how the business side of golf works."

That was nothing for J Dub. He would be able to tell them exactly what they needed to know. He would be able to fall back on over fifteen years worth of experience. "That's no problem."

Booker reinforced what Hayden said. "We noticed that you had the longest tenure of any golf-professional in town, especially at one place, and the fact that I knew you . . ."

" . . . It made sense for us to contact you and have you come in," Hayden finished.

"That's nothing guys. I'd be more than happy to help." J Dub didn't really know if he would be helpful or if they were going to pump him for information about Prairie Winds, but at that point he didn't care. His frustrations with Lew were hitting their peak.

"How does the golf business work?" Hayden pried.

"Truthfully, it's a lot like a daytime bar," J Dub said matter-of-factly. "You need to have your regular players during the week to cover expenses. The weekends take care of themselves. Instead of selling beer and other beverages, we're selling people the right to walk over our property."

"How do you watch the cash?" Hayden's interest was piqued.

"Usually, it's either Julie or I that is on the register. That was the main reason that Lew wanted me as his partner. He wanted to make sure that he had someone he could trust with the money, you know, someone that wasn't going to steal from him," J Dub rambled.

Hayden continued his line of questioning. "What happens with the money?"

"It gets counted and either Julie or I make the deposit into the bank," J Dub answered.

"We've noticed some improprieties with the money," Hayden explained.

"We'd like for you to fill in some of the blanks," Booker added.

Booker got up from behind the desk and walked to the door. "We've got a gal around here with brass kahunas."

Booker grabbed his crotch. "You've been in a locker room. You know what I mean."

Booker smiled from ear to ear once again. His grin was deviously contagious. "The U. S. Attorney would like to hear what you have to say."

Booker opened the door. Ellie Hackett and Peter Dooley entered. Hackett had been appointed the U. S. Attorney recently and her number one assistant was Peter. Peter appeared to be very clean cut. He looked to be in his mid-thirties. He was well-groomed, meticulous, and polite. "I'd like for you to meet Ellie Hackett and Peter Dooley," Booker stated.

J Dub wasn't ready for this surprise. His eyes opened wide. He got the jitters. "Are you sure I'm not in any trouble?" J Dub looked squarely at Booker.

"It's okay," Booker replied.

"Anyway I'd like to continue with what we were talking about," Hayden interjected. "The cash always went into the bank, right?"

J Dub nodded. "That's correct."

"Lew never took any money and put it in his pocket, did he?" Hayden wasn't going to let go of the cash angle of questioning.

"No, he never did that. I take that back, I saw him put twenty bucks in his pocket once when he couldn't figure out how to use the register," J Dub reflected.

"Where does all of your money go?" Hayden asked.

"That's a good question. In fact, that has been a topic in recent weeks. I carry the option to buy the business and we've been going through the books."

" . . . And?" Booker wondered out loud. "Was anything out of the ordinary?"

"We discovered that one of the expenses was made up," J Dub said.

"That is one of the blanks that we needed you to fill in," Hayden admitted. "It seems that your business has expenses that are running twelve to fifteen percent above what a normal golf course company operates within."

"Is it that much?" J Dub asked naively.

Booker nodded his head. Hayden nodded his head. Both felt the disappointment that poured from J Dub's body.

"We'd like for you to continue to help us. We'd like for you to provide more information," Ellie stated in an attempt to break the silence in the room.

"I definitely would want assurances that I am safe from any wrongdoing," J Dub offered.

"That can be agreed to. We don't want you," Peter pledged.

J Dub eyed Booker. He turned to Ellie and commented, "My focus is buying the golf course. That is my livelihood to support my family. If I help you and Lew finds out, then I can kiss the golf course goodbye."

"Swell guy, isn't he?" Ellie said. She had not been too fond of the guy since her previous investigation of him.

CHAPTER FIFTY-FOUR

Curt and Marcia were ready to question J Dub later that evening. They met around the kitchen table as they had in the past. "What are they after?" Curt asked right off the bat.

"They just wanted a more clear understanding of how the golf course business worked," J Dub explained. He wanted to downplay the meeting. "They told me that they wanted me to provide information to help them develop a model for golf course operations around the country."

Curt was skeptical. "That sounds like a set up."

" . . . Maybe. Maybe not," J Dub shrugged.

"Could you help?" Curt persisted.

"I think so."

"Are you?" Curt continued to pry. There was a momentary pause. Curt and J Dub looked at each other. "That was a stupid question, wasn't it?" Curt said. "You really don't have a choice, do you?"

J Dub raised his eyebrows. "It's the federal government, you know." Curt realized that J Dub had no choice. He had to cooperate. "They don't want me. I haven't done anything wrong," J Dub added.

"Will you need a lawyer?"

"Not right away. Will you be able to get one for me if I need one?" J Dub turned the tables and asked a question.

"It's going to be tough to get a good one. Everybody around here knows the guy," Curt suggested.

"What does that mean?"

"They might have a conflict of interest. But we'll worry about that when the time comes," Curt explained.

"What should we do now?" J Dub inquired.

"The only thing that I can think of is for you to continue to live your life. Let's continue to do our due diligence and monitor the lawsuit that is filed against the business," Curt replied. "Did you ever find out who filed the suit?"

"Go ahead and tell him, Honey," Marcia urged.

J Dub paused and looked at Curt. "It's the heirs to the Morton Estate."

CHAPTER FIFTY-FIVE

"Dammit!" Walter yelled. "I don't want to deal with all of this crap." It didn't matter how nice the weather was or how well things had been going for Walter. When Lewferd E. Zerrmann walked through the door to his office, turmoil seemed to enter with him.

"Hey, they were your account," countered Lew. He always wanted to deflect the blame off of himself and onto someone else.

Lew had showed up once again in Walter's office. The two of them had some issues that had been pushed to the forefront. The topic of the meeting was the lawsuit that the Morton heirs had filed against both of them. Not only had a possible gray area of the past been challenged but Walter was going to have to incur the expense of a defense lawyer.

Walter got up from his desk. He was severely agitated. He started to pace back and forth across the room. It was something that he only did when he felt the walls closing in on him. His fidgety nature had been pushing him to the brink of panic. "And it was your lousy driving!" Walter could not let go of the fact that a hooker had been run over.

"What does that have to do with this damned lawsuit? Forget about that," Lew insisted.

"How can you just forget about something like that?" Walter cried.

"She was a 'nobody.' No family. No home. No nothing. Forget about the rotten wench!" Lew demanded. He was clearly frustrated with Walter's obsession over a person that no one missed. "Forget about that slutty, black streetwalker!"

"It's on my mind every day," Walter whined. "I can't let it go. We ran over an innocent person."

Lew reached into his pocket and pulled out a gold-capped crown. He held it up in the light and admired it. It glittered brightly after Lew polished it. "Does this make you feel better?"

"What's that?"

"She had a gold-capped front tooth, remember?" Lew tried to explain.

"Oh gosh, where did that come from?" Walter was visibly shaken.

"I had a barbecue a few weeks ago," Lew explained. "I just went to where the body was buried, dug up the bones, doused the pile with gasoline, and started a fire. It just so happened that a sack of bones went up in smoke with the trees. The master would have been proud." Lew crowed. The ice cold, methodical way that Lew described the incident sent chills up Walter's spine.

"You are sick!" Walter shouted. "Not to mention disgusting. And what do you mean by 'the master'?"

"Hitler, of course. But, never mind that! Over and done with! Forget about it! Let's move on!" Lew yelled back at Walter.

Walter stared out the window. The daylight had a calming effect on him. He started to regain his composure and settle down. "Okay, okay. You win."

"I doubt if there was even a missing person's report filed. Just let it go. She was *a **nobody**,*" Lew emphasized in a voice that reassured Walter further.

" . . . Very well. What are we going to do about this other mess?" Walter was worried about the lawsuit that the heirs had filed.

"I have no idea what you did," Lew said as he threw the issue back into Walter's lap.

"I got involved with you," Walter lamented.

Lew forced a grin. "It hasn't been such a bad run for you, has it?"

"Yeah, right. Dead bodies, lawsuits, red flags, barbecues, and your morbid fascination with Hitler crap," Walter ranted. "It's all too much for me to handle. I don't know how you deal with all of it."

"It's a dog-eat-dog world out there. It's tough to make a buck. You have to stay one step ahead of them," Lew rationalized. The impersonal, matter-of-fact manner in which Lew compartmentalized things drove Walter crazy.

"And be half of a crook too," Walter conceded.

"That's the way it is. Deal with it," Lew said. He was comfortable with the cards that he had been dealt. His next goal was to deflect the problem at hand. "Now what did you do to the estate?"

"Lord if I know. I haven't read the complaint yet."

"Do you need a lawyer?" Lew asked. "I know some good ones."

"I bet you do," Walter laughed.

"No. Seriously."

"I think that we'd be better off with our own lawyers. I don't want to be tied to you any more than I am," Walter maintained. "What do you think?"

"I think that I'm going to try to get this frivolous lawsuit dismissed," Lew stated adamantly.

" . . . On what grounds?"

"First off, Statute of Limitation concerns. Secondly, I didn't have a thing to do with the heirs of Margaret Morton's estate," Lew said defiantly. His ire was raised as he spoke. "They were your clients, dammit! Didn't you take care of them?"

Walter was incredulous to Lew's reaction. "And how do you plan on getting all of that done?" Walter probed.

"It pays to have connections," Lew exclaimed deviously. Walter forced a smug grin. "Do you know Judge Rowland?" Lew asked.

"Troy Rowland?" Walter countered.

Lew nodded his head. "We need to get the case transferred over to his court," Lew explained.

"And how do you plan on getting that accomplished?" Walter inquired.

" . . . With a little legal maneuvering. You get your attorney and I'll get mine," Lew continued. "Let's put this estate stuff behind us."

"For a piece of crap, you sure have a healthy mind," Walter grinned when he spoke the words.

"Business is business," Lew stated.

"Who is this Sneed guy, anyway?" Walter wanted to try to find out about the lawyer that represented the Morton heirs.

" . . . Never heard of him. Just a young kid that chases ambulances," Lew sighed. "We all know about that kind."

"Yeah, well, let's rattle his cage a little. I don't want him influencing my client," Walter suggested.

"You never did tell me what you did," Lew revisited a topic that Walter did not want to talk about.

" . . . Nothing. Just like you," Walter said. He clearly wanted to avoid discussion about his role with the Morton heirs. "You get your attorney. I'll get mine. Let's get the suit thrown out of court or at least in a court where the decisions will be favorable to us."

CHAPTER FIFTY-SIX

The lounge at LUCKY LADY LANES was a spot that made J Dub feel more comfortable. It was difficult enough for him to provide information on Prairie Winds Golf Course to the government. A neutral meeting spot was agreed upon so that he didn't have to drive over to the IRS building and park his pickup outside a sign that screamed INTERNAL REVENUE SERVICE.

He and Booker had several conversations about where to meet. Both were bowlers and sports fans. The bowling alley was convenient and they agreed that being seen together in its lounge would not raise any suspicions. An added bonus was that it was a dark environment in which they could hide better.

"Maybe I would blend in better at the ice skating rink," Booker commented as J Dub approached the corner table. Booker had a subtle way about him.

"You didn't ride a motorcycle over, did you?" J Dub grinned as he grabbed a chair.

They both chuckled at their time in history. J Dub handed him a folder. "Here's some more stuff that should help you."

"We've been onto him for quite a while," Booker revealed. He wanted to give assurances to J Dub that it was Lew that the IRS wanted to investigate.

"He'll do all that he can to beat you," J Dub hinted.

"We expect that he'll use all of his standard tricks. The madam's been down that road with him before," Booker mentioned.

"Huh?"

Booker shrugged nonchalantly. He had been in the investigation business a long time. He realized that it was tough to catch all of the crooks. "She was a rookie prosecutor back then. He got off," Booker continued.

"I never knew anything about that," J Dub confessed.

"He beat her on a technicality. He and his lawyers are good at that," Booker carried on.

"What happened?" J Dub asked.

"Nobody talked, but one of his associates had the noose wrapped pretty tightly around his neck," Booker rambled. "That guy took the fall for Lew and the others."

"He can't stand to lose an argument," J Dub offered. "He has to win at everything and he'll spend any amount of money to vindicate himself."

"Time has a way of settling scores," Booker said. "We've been keeping your business under a watchful eye for quite a while."

"Then it wasn't our imagination when we couldn't make the numbers work," J Dub sighed.

Booker shook his head. "I don't know what you figured out. All I know is that it looks like you should be claiming more income than you have been," Booker said. "The returns show that you make a few thousand dollars a year. That's pushing things a little too far."

"We'll make that in a weekend," J Dub confessed.

" . . . Exactly! Does he think that we don't notice stuff like that?" Booker offered.

"I had nothing to do with the way he kept the books. He had Walter set everything up," J Dub pleaded.

"We know that," Booker stressed. "The accountant isn't new to us either."

"Oh, man," J Dub whined. "What kind of a mess am I involved in?"

Booker raised his eyebrows and shrugged his shoulders to indicate that the answer to that was anybody's guess. "We're just on to Plan B now with the guy," Booker said.

"What's that?"

"Tax evasion," Booker stated bluntly.

"Winning is one thing that he loves more than himself," J Dub confided.

"We know that he's an adversary that will put up a fight," Booker admitted.

"I'm in this deep enough. If I have to pick sides then I might as well be on your side. Your pockets are deeper than his," J Dub rationalized.

Booker's smile lit up the dank room. "If there is one guy that the two of them don't want to tick off, it's me."

"You mean Lew and Walter?" J Dub asked.

Booker nodded his head. "I can make life miserable for the two of them for a long time running," Booker disclosed. "We're not going anywhere. If things don't happen this year, then there is always a later date."

"How can I help you?" J Dub volunteered.

"I work for the government. Just cooperate and do as you're told," Booker stated. "I've already said more than I should have."

"What happens if he finds out?" J Dub pried.

Booker raised his eyebrows and grinned. "He'll have enough to worry about from us. I'm pretty good at keeping the pressure on and demanding specific answers. Just remember I won't be able to talk about the investigation. Don't ask me any questions about it."

"So I'll be in the dark as to what you're doing?" J Dub solicited a response.

Once again Booker nodded as the two men got up and walked away from their corner table. They opened the door from the lounge to the bowling alley. The sound of pins rattling was heard in the background. "It will be a private matter between the IRS and a taxpayer. Remember not to ask me any questions about it," Booker reiterated. The shook hands and headed for the exit.

CHAPTER FIFTY-SEVEN

A few days later . . .

Booker and Hayden from the Criminal Investigative Division of the IRS as well as Ellie Hackett and Peter Dooley from the U.S. Attorney's Office met in a conference room adjacent to Ellie's office. Hayden had been assigned to do the forensic accounting on the books for Prairie Winds Golf Course.

"My pleasure," mumbled Hayden as he shook outstretched hands.

"You'll find Daniel here to be a top-notch tax accounting expert, folks. He's handled everything from small business to corporations to mid-level drug dealers. If there is a scam, he'll find it," boasted Booker.

Ellie leaned over to Dooley and whispered, "I'm surprised he's not wearing a pocket protector. Good Lord, did he say his name was Poindexter?" Dooley smirked, but knew they were in good hands with their tax expert.

"Okay, gentlemen, shall we get down to brass tacks as they say?" Peter Dooley was the typical All-American boy that played his cards right and landed a job in the U.S. Attorney's Office. He was bright, articulate, meticulous, and perfectly groomed. As a prosecutor he had it all going for him in the courtroom and even earned the nickname of 'Bulldog' for his tenacity.

Most Americans have contact with the IRS through their annual filing on April 15th. Taxes are paid and another fiscal year starts. A select few are audited and have to deal with any errors and omissions that may have occurred with their filing.

Each year approximately three thousand taxpayers in the United States come under investigation by the Criminal Investigative Division of the IRS. The CID goes after those taxpayers that may have committed much more serious crimes involving violations of the Internal Revenue Code. In other words, they go after the taxpayers that they suspect are intentionally cheating the government out of taxes through tax fraud.

The CID investigates the various taxpayers and determines if there is enough evidence to recommend prosecution. They work closely with the U. S. Attorney's office which is responsible for the actual prosecution of the criminal. It was no surprise that these four people met early on to talk about the preliminary findings in this investigation.

"What did your analysis show?" Ellie asked Hayden.

"Zerrmann took a little more than two million over the years," Hayden confirmed. He had meticulously gone through each item on the financial statements and had reviewed the tax returns.

"My breakdown shows that with penalties, fines, interest, and back taxes he owes us at least four million dollars," Booker added.

"That's certainly a significant amount of money to go after," Ellie conceded. "Are we sure how he did it?"

"In talking to his partner it looks as if he created an expense account to offset income. That was the machinery lease account that he talked about the other day," Booker clarified. "In the process he did not pay self-employment taxes, corporate income tax, taxes on dividends, and social security taxes."

"So he effectively defrauded the Social Security Administration too," Ellie suggested.

Booker nodded his head. "It appears that way."

"Who is Zerrmann's accountant?" Peter asked.

"A guy by the name of Walter Hancock," Hayden replied.

"Do we know how long he has been doing the books?" Peter inquired.

"Since the corporation was formed," Hayden said.

Ellie looked at the massive amount of paperwork that was spread across the conference table. She stared out the window at the birds that were perched on a nearby power line. Their bloated breasts signified the November chill that was in the air. "Four million dollars is a lot of money to go after. It certainly is worth the time and effort."

"Are you kidding?" Booker asked incredulously. "I've gone after people before for less than a thousand dollars!"

"What I was getting at, is that we know how much an investigation of this magnitude is going to cost. I want to be able to justify whatever expense we might incur against the possible monetary decision that we might stand to gain," Ellie said as she backpedaled a little.

"It all depends on if he folds his tent," Booker interjected. "We need to get one of them to talk and admit to what they've done."

"The odds are not good that Zerrmann will cooperate," Ellie suggested before raising a question. "What about the accountant?"

"He's the weakest link of the two. Your guess is as good as mine as to whether or not he will assist us," Booker rationalized.

"We don't stand to get anything from him. If it comes down to it we can offer him some immunity," Ellie thought out loud.

"Let's see how the events play out before we get to that stage," Booker stated.

Ellie posed a question to Peter. "Do we stand a chance of winning this case in court?"

"Maybe. We'll have to wait until all of the evidence comes in," Peter deadpanned.

"Our hands are tied. It's up to you," Booker said to Ellie. "We can't go forward until you decide to pull the strings."

She was unmistakably at a crossroads. She wanted Zerrmann badly. Yet, she also knew that the investigation would be costly. Tax evasion was a tough crime to prove. The evidence would have to show that the two targets of the investigation had conspired to evade taxes. Her past experience with Zerrmann had indicated that he was going to hire the best criminal defense tax attorney that money could afford. She knew that he would say nothing. In the end it was going to come down to whether or not one of them squealed on the other. The government's chance of victory on a circumstantial case was not going to be nearly as great. Ellie knew that she was going to eventually need one of them to talk.

Booker and Hayden awaited her decision. They couldn't do anything until she started the process.

"If we go on this, then the case will be assigned over to Peter. The three of you will have to work together to make this case stick."

Booker nodded. Hayden and Dooley looked at each other.

"You guys have worked together before. I don't want this guy to spit out the hook like he did last time. If we're going after him, then I want to succeed." Ellie lowered the boom. "Do you guys understand?"

The silence was deafening. "I'll authorize the necessary paperwork," she stated.

A big grin came over Booker's face. He wanted to get Zerrmann for his wrongdoing, but he also wanted to indirectly aid J Dub. Not only had Zerrmann defrauded the IRS and the government, but, in the process, he had pulled a fast one on an unassuming victim that didn't stand a chance.

"I want to work closely with you guys. Keep me informed. Get the survey out and start the interview process," Ellie concluded. She made reference to the first couple of tasks that Booker and Hayden had before them.

"Let's get this guy! Make this one stick!" Ellie was fired up to settle a grudge.

CHAPTER FIFTY-EIGHT

It was hard to believe, but Monty had spent nearly a decade in prison. The last six months were spent in a halfway house just around the corner from his old stomping grounds. His law license had been stripped by the State of Illinois. He needed to find new employment. The halfway house served as a temporary stop to reacclimatize him to society and prepare him for his next means of contribution to the public.

Lew thought that it would be appropriate to have a small gathering of old friends. He felt that it was the least that he could do since Monty had more-or-less taken the fall for him. Lew made a call to Raymond Parsons and arranged for him to pick up Monty and drive over to the Big Z.

When Lew mentioned that he wanted a small gathering, he meant it. He wasn't a very social person. In fact, he was anti-social. He shied away from large get-togethers. In reality, the party that he was going to throw for Monty ended up being a very small congregation.

Raymond pulled the car up to the gate, received permission to enter, and drove down Lew's winding driveway. As was customary, Lew was outside awaiting their arrival. Upon exiting the car, Lew took a hard look at Monty. It was obvious that his old look was returning. He had put on a few pounds at the halfway house. His ponytail showed signs of returning.

After shaking hands, Lew led the men into the barn. It was just like old times sake. Monty and Raymond grabbed shotguns out of the barn and Lew grabbed an assault rifle. They proceeded to the back of the barn and blasted away at clay pigeons as the gloom of winter hovered overhead. The conversation was peripheral, almost non-existent, as the men mainly shot the guns and enjoyed themselves.

As they returned the rifles to the barn the conversation heated up a bit. Monty was not too happy that he had given up a large chunk of his life for Lew. "I wasted nearly ten years of my life for you," Monty said.

Obviously Lew could only think of himself. "Hey we won!" he exclaimed.

"You won!" Monty hollered back, his bitterness evident.

Lew led the men inside demanding they take off their shoes to protect the carpet from wear and tear and guard against dirt. Lew hated to vacuum. As they went down the steps to the lower level Lew said, "You did what you had to do. Raymond and I appreciate it."

"Yeah, well, you two guys don't have to start life all over again. I've lost everything. The restitution alone to the government cleaned me out. Then the state yanked my license to practice law. I've lost my livelihood," Monty complained.

"We'll come up with something to help you out," Raymond conceded.

"It can't come soon enough," Monty reiterated.

" . . . Beer?" Lew offered as he reached into the refrigerator that was behind the bar in the lower level. Both men nodded. "We do have good reason to celebrate," Lew continued.

"Why? Because I didn't rat on you?" Monty persisted.

"No. You're out of prison. Now you're a free man again," Lew said.

"He did us both a favor," Raymond admitted to Lew.

"If I had it to do all over again I'm not so sure that I would make the same choices," Monty complained.

"It's over and done with. Let's move on," Lew urged.

"Then help me out. Times are tough right now," Monty begged.

"That's what I intend to do," Lew said. "Come on."

A wry grin encompassed Monty's face. "What are friends for, right?"

"Let me give you a little tour," Lew said as he motioned for them to follow him down the hallway. The two men grabbed their beer and trailed Lew by a few steps. The lower level was gloomy. Dark walnut paneling soaked up any inkling of daylight and the low ceiling sapped all of the air out of the room.

Lew stopped at a doorway. Next to the opening was an Uncle Sam yard jockey. It was complete with red-and-white striped trousers and a blue shirt with white stars. The top hat gleamed red, white, and blue. Lew grabbed a set of keys that hung from an ear and unlocked the door.

"This is my bomb shelter," he declared. Monty and Raymond exchanged mystified glances. Lew entered the bomb shelter and yelled over his shoulder. "It's complete with twelve-inch thick concrete walls, a years' supply of food, and separate ventilation and utilities. Of course, it's radiation proof in case we get a nuclear attack."

The inside of the shelter was like a fortress. Bundles and bundles of cash were neatly stacked next to piles of old newspapers. Enormous supplies of pork and beans, bottled water, tomato juice, and chicken noodle soup crowded the space. Light porno from cheap detective magazines adorned the walls and Lew's Tupperware collection was neatly stacked in one corner, each containing a pair of women's panties and labeled with a name and date. A Nazi uniform and a Ku Klux Klan robe hung from hangars.

Littered around the bomb shelter were copies of *Mein Kampf* and *The Rise and Fall of the Third Reich*. It was true that Lew was a disciple of Adolph Hitler and a worshipper of his principles. It was his opinion that Jews deserved discrimination. In fact, Lew idolized the most notorious dictator the world has ever known. He adopted "The Fuhrer's" doctrine and applied it to life around him.

Strewn around the shelter were pamphlets from the Aryan Nations. Lew's take on this ideology was that for a group of people to survive they must have their own land so that their own ways could be adopted. He believed that the system had to be broken down so that the oppressed people could prosper.

Leaflets from the Ku Klux Klan were scattered throughout the shelter. Lew's views about white supremacy were vindicated in these writings. The literature called for a one-race society and an anti-gay movement. The writings supported his belief that blacks were an inferior race and needed to be extinguished.

It was as if Lew had created a shrine to himself inside the bomb shelter. The text in these books and pamphlets would most certainly provide insight into the principles of Lewford E. Zerrmann. He was dangerously close to making that knowledge available to Monty and Raymond.

Standing in the room made Lew's excitement level rise. He started to hyperventilate. His breathing increased rapidly. He hurriedly grabbed two bundles of cash and wrapped them in newspapers. He exited the bomb shelter and handed a separate package to Monty and Raymond. Perspiration dripped from his brow and soaked his clothing.

"You're my guests tonight. This should show you my appreciation," Lew stated. His tone was formal, as if he was conducting a funeral.

Lew was dripping with sweat. "What the hell happened to you?" Monty asked inquisitively.

"Oh, nothing," Lew stammered weakly. The adrenalin rush caused him to be light-headed. "Sometimes I get claustrophobic in there." Monty and Ray opened the bundles and saw a huge quantity of cash. They both forced a grin, but were confused by the odd circumstances. "That should help both of you. I appreciate how you have protected me."

Monty and Raymond were dumbfounded. Both of them thought that they knew Lew pretty well. The last several minutes completely caught both of them by surprise. They were speechless.

With a jerk of his head Lew motioned for both of them to follow him further down the hall. He led them to another door. "This is my favorite room," he said mischievously. "I've prepared it especially for you."

Lew threw open the door and led them into an elaborate sex dungeon. He and Lois had made it especially appealing to any guests. A six by six foot flag bearing a Swastika hung on the dark paneled wall. A cache of guns filled the far corner of the room. Sophisticated bondage equipment was centered in the dungeon. A table covered with sex toys sat nearby.

Whips and chains, ropes, and dog collars were scattered throughout the room. A stained pair of women's panties was wadded up on the floor. Spread out around the dungeon was a slave collar, ball gag, muzzle, mask, hood, paddle, nipple clamp, and harness. Lew had even erected a sex swing in one corner.

Monty and Raymond stood with gaping mouths at what was before them. For years they had both known that Lew was a little unorthodox in his approach to things, yet, seeing all of this shocked them. Monty immediately thought about his ex-wife and what she must have been exposed to under Lew's domination.

A very shapely and beautiful Cancun and Raven entered from a side door. Cancun wore a black choker. She was dressed in black leather thigh-high ballet boots with a red garter belt and crotch-less panties. Her eyes were covered by a black blindfold. She had a red ball gag in her mouth. Her long, exquisite blond hair provided sizzling contrast to the black shining leather. She was hooked up to a leash and was led into the room by Raven.

Raven carried a whip and handcuffs. She wore white-lace, thigh-high stockings and as if to compliment her auburn hair, she wore a forest green thong. A white open breast bra highlighted her tremendous attributes. Monty and Raymond had no idea what to expect.

"This room is complete with live entertainment for my good friends. Enjoy!" Lew said as he turned and exited the room.

Raven led Cancun to Raymond and handed him the leash. Cancun purred like a kitten and crawled up and down Raymond's body. She rubbed and stroked every inch of him while bringing out various toys, lotions and lubricants. The night had just begun.

Monty was handcuffed by Raven. She proceeded to strip him of his clothes and whip him unmercifully. In time, he too, would have his way with Raven. The pair of twosomes eventually became a foursome. The party was in full swing.

After what seemed like an eternal blissful moment for Monty and Raymond, the door to the dungeon cracked open. In the doorway Lew Zerrmann stood dressed in a full Nazi uniform. He looked like an exact clone of Adolph Hitler, complete with a fake moustache.

The four participants in the room were momentarily startled and looked up from their various sexual escapades. Just when Monty and Raymond thought they had seen it all and done it all, Lew gave the Nazi salute. He stood before them at attention and witnessed their every move just like the concealed and undetected video camera in a high corner of the room.

CHAPTER FIFTY-NINE

Walter was still miffed and a little uptight from the lawsuit when a knock on his door came from Booker and Hayden. He answered the door and quickly found out that the IRS meant business.

Booker was the special agent assigned to the case and spoke immediately. "In connection with our investigation of Lewferd E. Zerrmann, I would like to ask you some questions. However, first I must advise you that under the Fifth Amendment to the Constitution of the United States, I cannot force you to answer any questions or to submit any information if such answers or information might tend to incriminate you in any way. Anything that you might say or submit might be used against you in any criminal proceeding. If you wish, you can seek the assistance of an attorney before responding."

Walter shifted his weight from one foot to the other. If the coffee hadn't gotten his attention by now, Booker certainly did. His eyes were about to pop out of their sockets. Walter's worst nightmare was unfolding right before him. He was certain that his association with Lew Zerrmann had led to this predicament. However, what stood before him did not come unexpectedly. He had lived on the edge during his tax consulting career. He anticipated that this day would happen at some time.

"This matter should be easily resolved if you cooperate and tell your side of the story," Booker continued. Walter stood in stunned silence in the middle of the doorway. "Will you waive your rights?" Booker asked.

"No. I want you to contact my attorney," Walter wisely blurted.

"That is a right that you are entitled to," Booker stated. "Who is your attorney?"

"Donald Farrell," Walter revealed.

" . . . Very well. We will be in touch," Booker concluded. He and Hayden turned and left.

Walter stood in astonished distress with mouth agape as they drove off. His first thought was that the red flags that he had cautioned Lew about had finally gotten the attention of the IRS. He was going to have to wait until the conference with the IRS agents to find out what they were after.

Walter had been successfully filing tax returns for clients for years. His accounting methods had been aggressive. This was the first time that the IRS had actually knocked on his door. After thinking rationally for a second, he picked up the phone and called his attorney.

Walter felt confident that Farrell would help him out of this mess. He most certainly would accompany him to the conference he thought. During their brief conversation, Farrell advised Walter to not have any contact with Lew Zerrmann. It became clear that it was going to be "an-every-man-for-himself" situation.

It didn't come as much of a surprise when the phone rang later in the day in Walter's office and Lew was on the other end of the line. "Were they over at your place, too?" Lew demanded.

"My attorney has instructed me to cut all my communication with you," Walter advised Lew.

"You didn't say anything, did you?" Lew inquired.

"It's better if we don't talk," Walter stressed.

"You're my accountant!" Lew yelled.

"And in this matter we might have conflicting positions."

"Look, dammit! If you keep your damn mouth shut the burden of proof is on them," Lew shouted. The earpiece to the phone was about a foot away from Walter's head. "We didn't do anything wrong!"

"That is all we should probably say to each other right now. Have a nice night," Walter said as he quickly wrapped up the conversation.

An IRS investigation was an event that Walter always thought could happen in his business. It could be nothing or it could turn into the biggest headache that anyone could imagine. Upon ending the conversation he immediately started doing research. He wanted to find out the severity of the probable yet undisclosed and declared situation and what penalties might be involved.

Walter quickly found that if he was to be found guilty of tax evasion it would be a felony offense. The maximum fine would not be more than one hundred thousand dollars. The longest prison time he could serve would be five years. Plus he would be liable for the costs of prosecution. This was information that he already knew but re-reading the statute reminded him of the severity of the crime that he might be accused of.

Walter also discovered that if he admitted to filing a fraudulent tax return the maximum fine was only ten thousand dollars and a maximum of one year in prison.

After digesting that information it became clear that he was in a little bit of a quandary. Yet, Lew was right. The government had to prove that he had knowledge that he was filing a false return. It was true what Lew had said. If they both shut up, then it would make the government's task that much more difficult.

He was going to have to wait and see how the investigation unfolded. It was going to be a long and tedious process. He quickly deduced that his interests would best be served by cooperating with the government to some degree. However, when push came to shove he would be better off saying nothing.

Walter had a tough few nights of sleep ahead of him. The knock on the door had worried him a little. What he was truly concerned about was what Nora was going to say when she found out. "I told you not to get mixed up with that guy!" Nora screamed that night at dinner.

"It's just a misunderstanding. I'm sure that it is something that we can explain out," Walter said as he tried his best to soothe his wife.

"They don't come knocking unless they have a pretty damn good idea what they are looking for," Nora shouted at a decibel level close to climbing off the chart.

"We'll have to see how the investigation unfolds," Walter explained as calmly as he could.

"If you're mixed up with that idiot I can't imagine anything good coming out of it." Nora was not going to let the topic die.

"You're innocent until proven guilty, remember?" Walter said meekly.

"You better damn well make sure that you are innocent or you'll be hearing from my lawyer, too," Nora shouted.

"Where's the support that I was hoping to hear?"

"I told you several years ago to get away from that guy. You didn't want to listen then. Now look at the mess he's gotten you in," Nora ranted.

"Farrell told me not to talk with Lew," Walter stated.

"And you'll listen to your lawyer and not your wife?" Nora crowed. "What kind of fool are you?"

Walter did all that he could do. He had to sit at the dinner table and take it. His wife was right. He should have listened to her years before. "Let's focus on getting out of this mess," he conceded. "I'm going to need your support."

Nora glared across the table at her husband. "Get away from the guy and stay away from the guy! Hopefully we won't lose our house and you won't have to go to prison!"

CHAPTER SIXTY

The Morton heirs were having a tough time in court keeping their civil claim alive. They had sued Lew, Walter, and the golf course corporation. So, in effect, J Dub, as a minority partner, was being sued. He didn't know about the specifics of the lawsuit because all notices had gone to the managing general partner. He only was aware of what Lew had told him . . . that it was some sort of misunderstanding. Lew had hired Grady Patterson to represent the golf course and be his personal defense attorney in that matter.

Grady Patterson was connected into the good 'ole boy network around town. He was in his mid-sixties and had shared cocktails with nearly everyone in the state. He had been introduced to Lew several years earlier by Raymond Parsons. In fact, Grady had been over to Lew's house once for an afternoon of target practice and drinks.

The heirs had claimed in their suit that the property had been fraudulently transferred. However, the transfer of the property had taken place before Margaret Morton's death. To combat the heirs and their claim, Grady needed to get the case moved to a more favorable venue and doing so was the first item on his agenda.

"Good morning! May I speak to the Honorable Judge Rowland please?" Grady smiled smugly into the phone and waited for the legal secretary to connect her boss.

"Judge Troy Rowland."

"Well, good mornin' Troy! How the heck are you?" Grady leaned back in his comfortable but squeaky leather chair and chit-chatted with his good friend. After exchanging cordial greetings Grady got right down to business. "You know that plot of land where we always go duck hunting together?"

"Sure, we've gone there for years."

"Anyway, that property is owned by Lew Zerrmann and he's got himself in a little bit of a jam," Grady continued to explain.

"Yeah, well, it happens," Judge Rowland replied.

"He's being sued and we're not particularly fond of the court and judge where the case has been assigned. I'm going to file a motion to recuse the presiding judge," Grady put into plain words.

"That's the proper thing to do," Judge Rowland acknowledged.

"But I was wondering, since he's a friend and a client, if your court wouldn't want to get involved in this little civil misunderstanding," Grady suggested.

"Ha, ha, ha, ha," Judge Rowland chuckled. "You know the way the system works, Grady. It'll be assigned after your motion is granted."

"But you know what I'm talking about," Grady implied. "If that motion is granted Troy, then I just want you to git 'er done!"

"I'll see if I can help you," Judge Rowland laughed. Grady hung up the phone and checked his first to-do off his list.

With a lot of confidence a few weeks later, Grady sauntered into Judge Rowland's court to argue that the Statute of Limitations for the Morton heirs had expired. Denny Sneed argued that the heirs were an extension of Margaret Morton based on the last predicate act, but Judge Rowland saw it differently. The case was thrown out of court on a technicality and Lewferd E. Zerrmann felt the winds blow a dark cloud away. The civil case against him and Prairie Winds Golf Course was dismissed.

Denny Sneed and the Morton heirs could see the politics in action when the motion was requested and granted. Even though he and the heirs were greatly disappointed, they still had the suit filed against Walter Hancock alive and well in a different jurisdiction. Denny had filed a separate lawsuit against Walter Hancock for accounting malpractice. Even though Lew and the golf course corporation escaped round one unscathed, Denny was going to try with all of his might to go after Walter Hancock.

Walter had done work for Vern Morton prior to his death. He also had done work for Margaret Morton before she succumbed to old age. In addition, Walter had done work for the Morton Estate which included Lucille Morton and her son, Matt. It was going to be a lot tougher for Walter to get the lawsuit against him thrown out of court on a technicality, despite the number of years that had passed.

Denny stayed with it. He was tenacious. He had filed the malpractice lawsuit against Walter in a different court in a different county. After months and months of filings and motions Denny finally received a favorable ruling. Walter and his attorney, Donald Farrell, weren't as successful as Lew Zerrmann. In 1996, the time had finally come for Walter Hancock to be deposed.

~ ~ ~

Spring of 1996 . . .

Walter, and his attorney Donald Farrell, had some important decisions to make. They were at a crossroads. It was one thing to plead the Fifth Amendment in criminal proceedings when the IRS came knocking. It was a far different scenario in civil proceedings. Since there was no criminal charge in a civil action, pleading the Fifth was not an option.

Denny started the questioning for the deposition. "In looking at the balance sheet for the estate could you show me where the entry is for the funds that were received from the sale of the golf course property?"

"No," Walter replied.

"Can you show me what capital gains taxes were paid on the sale of that property?"

"No."

"Can you tell me why the land is no longer listed as an asset?"

"No."

"Since the land is no longer an asset, can you tell me why the cash assets didn't increase accordingly?"

"No."

"Is it because you didn't receive any cash for the transfer of that asset?" Denny asked.

"No, no, that wouldn't be the case," Walter stammered.

"Can you produce a copy of the check to show that the estate received payment for that property?"

"I'm sure that it is around here somewhere."

"Where is it?"

"I don't know. The sale of that property took place at a busy time of the year for me. I must have misplaced it."

"Yet, in looking at the balance sheet for the estate the cash position of the estate remained the same, is that correct?"

Walter was clearly getting backed into a corner. "I don't know why that would be."

Denny had gotten what he was after. It was obvious that Walter had not received any money for the sale of the golf course land. "If the money didn't go to the estate, did you keep the funds?" Denny probed.

"No! Absolutely not!" Walter shouted.

"Then where did the money go?"

"I don't know. There has to be an oversight somewhere."

"Is it normal for you to misplace several million dollars?"

"No, I wouldn't do that."

"That is what it looks like the balance sheet is suggesting, don't you agree?"

"I'm going to need some time to review the documents," Walter mumbled. He plainly wanted to stall.

Denny thought that it might be appropriate to shift gears. "Can you produce a copy of the contract?"

"I'm sure that it is around somewhere."

"Why did you not give a copy of the contract to the heirs of the estate?"

"I'm sure that they received one."

"Who was the purchaser of the property?

"Lew Zerrmann."

"What title company closed the transaction?"

"FARMBELT ABSTRACT AND TITLE COMPANY."

"Who was the principal owner of the title company?"

"The Pierce brothers. Mainly George Pierce," Walter whimpered.

"Where is George Pierce today?"

"I don't know. He left town."

"Can you produce a copy of the cashier's check from FARMBELT ABSTRACT AND TITLE COMPANY?"

"Yes, I am sure that I can."

Can you produce a copy of the contract between the estate and Lew Zerrmann?"

"Yes, I am sure that it is available."

"You were the executor of the estate, weren't you?

"Yes."

"I would very much like for you to submit those documents into evidence. Do you agree to do so?"

"Yes, I will," Walter said.

Denny had scored some points on behalf of the estate.

CHAPTER SIXTY-ONE

Later During the 1996 Summer Golf Season . . .

The time had come for J Dub to have another meeting with Booker. It seemed as if the IRS investigators wanted information from him every other day. Some of the data that they wanted were copies of documents that J Dub could easily obtain.

The lounge at LUCKY LADY LANES seemed like the perfect spot for a clandestine meeting between Booker and J Dub. It had worked before and it would probably work again. There was something about the smell of stale beer and a smoky haze in a dark corner that excited J Dub. It made him feel like he was instrumental in catching a crook.

"How's the investigation going?" J Dub inquired as he placed a folder of documents on the table in front of Booker.

Booker shrugged. "We need more information."

J Dub produced a sawed off golf club and presented it to Booker. "Here. This will help you teach your eight-year old the basics. It's never too early to learn how to swing."

Booker's glowing smile lit up the corner. "He's already asking me when I'm going to take him to the driving range."

"This little club will help his eye-hand coordination."

"Just the excitement of hitting real balls off of real grass is better than the plastic balls and plastic clubs off of carpet," Booker explained.

"We all have to start somewhere."

"It's the same with us when we start one of these investigations," Booker offered. "The information that you're giving us will lead us in the right direction. Some of it is exactly what we are looking for. Some of it opens up other areas that need to be looked at more closely."

"I'm glad that I can help."

Booker pried, "How could you not know what was going on?"

"You mean with the business?" J Dub asked. Booker nodded. "First off, I was probably too trusting. Secondly, he told me to work the pro shop from dawn to dusk and keep my nose out of the checkbook," J Dub put into plain words.

"So he could rob you blind?" Booker asked.

"Hey, he fooled you too," J Dub countered.

Booker raised his eyebrows and conceded the obvious.

"You know, I'm a licensed golf pro," J Dub continued. "I'm not an accounting whiz. My job is to serve the public. I need to keep the complaints down on the golf course and keep the pace of play flowing smoothly."

"Didn't you wonder why you never got a year-end bonus?"

"I've always wondered where the money went. But at the end of the year we never seemed to have any," J Dub clarified.

"That may have been in part to some creative accounting," Booker said.

"I'm beginning to realize that," J Dub admitted. "Can you help me with some other stuff?"

"It depends. If it is about the investigation, I won't be able to comment," Booker stated.

"No, it's about IRS stuff," J Dub acknowledged.

"Try me."

"You know that I'm trying to buy the place," J Dub admitted. Booker nodded. "We're being sued, so he indicated that nothing can happen until that is settled," J Dub disclosed.

"That's understandable."

"Look, I've got twenty percent of the stock in the corporation. The last time that we talked Lew told me that he might want to spin off or spin up or split up the stock of the corporation," J Dub rambled. "What's he referring to?"

"It's a move that he probably wants to make to lower his tax liability," Booker explained.

"What's the process?" J Dub inquired.

"The first thing that he'll probably do is contact us to get what is called a private letter ruling," Booker divulged.

"What is that?"

"Basically, he requests that we make a ruling on his tax liability before he makes the transaction," Booker revealed. "Depending on what we tell him, he will decide whether or not he will spin off assets or split up the stock."

"Knowing him he will do whatever it takes to pay the least amount of taxes," J Dub declared.

"You may not have to worry about it."

"Why is that?"

"He's dealing with us right now. The time might not be good for him to ask us for a ruling on his tax liability," Booker disclosed.

"It's another thing that I have to deal with," J Dub lamented. "I need for you to help me."

"If you want me to help you, then you'll have to help yourself," Booker purposely let slip.

"I'm doing all that I can," J Dub confessed. "What do you mean?"

"If we can't get either one of them to talk, then we're going to have problems," Booker declared.

"What sort of problems?"

"All the evidence will be circumstantial. That makes intent tough to prove."

"What does that have to do with me helping myself?"

"We need for you to get either Lew or Walter to talk," Booker blurted.

Chapter Sixty-Two

J Dub and Marcia had work to do for an important catering job. They knew that they would have to work in the kitchen preparing food. So they took the opportunity to invite Curt over for a question and answer session to try to kill two birds with one stone.

Marcia sliced up assorted vegetables for a tray that she intended to put on display and rationed limited tasks to J Dub and Curt. Several baskets needed to be prepared and Marcia figured the guys could load them with bananas, apples, oranges, grapes, and cherries.

"Could you get him to put his offer to you in writing?" Curt asked.

"That's not the way he does business, Curt. You know that," J Dub answered.

"Then I don't think that he is too serious about selling you the course," Curt replied.

"He'll never sell it to J Dub," Marcia interjected.

Whenever Marcia started talking negatively about the golf course, J Dub would get perturbed. " . . . Why not? I've got the option to buy it," J Dub said.

"He doesn't care about you, Honey," Marcia stated emphatically dampening J Dub's hopes with her dose of reality.

"If he won't let me exercise my option, then at least I have the right of first refusal to match any offer that he gets," J Dub stressed.

"By looking at the numbers, I can't imagine any other fool paying that kind of price for it," Curt offered. "If they do, then it won't be a golf course anymore. The next guy will be paying everything to the bank and is liable to go broke."

J Dub voiced his opinion. "If I can't operate it as a golf course, then I don't know if I even want it."

"You can always take the land and sell it to a developer for a subdivision," Curt suggested.

"There's too much of me in the place for that," J Dub conceded. "It looks like whatever he decides to do will most likely be whatever costs him the least in taxes."

"Then don't count on him selling it to you," Marcia repeated. "I know that isn't what you wanted to hear, but that is what my instincts are telling me. C'mon, J Dub, I know you're a bit naive about all of this but you need to listen to reason."

"J Dub still has rights that are spelled out in the buy/sell agreement," Curt stated. He didn't want Marcia to rain on J Dub's parade too much.

"Nothing is going to happen until some sort of resolution comes out of the lawsuit," J Dub declared.

"Which reminds me," Curt advised, "if he was dishonest with you concerning the financial statements then I wonder what else he was untruthful about."

J Dub's attention was aroused. "What else could there be?"

"A lot of things," Curt responded. "The appraisal could be skewed, the title work might be messed up, or the survey may well be inaccurate. The buy/sell agreement could have a loophole in it. We need to talk to some people and try to find out a little about who this guy is."

"I think that it's time to get an attorney," Marcia recommended.

"I don't want to spend a lot of money on one," J Dub said.

"I've told you before that a lot of times they are worth their weight in gold," Curt stated. "We should at least get one so that we can ask some basic questions."

"You can talk to Hank Lowery," Marcia suggested. "We go to church with him and I'm good friends with his wife."

"Lew owes you a fiduciary duty," Curt interrupted. "He has to be truthful with you."

Marcia's suggestion about talking to Hank Lowery suited J Dub just fine. He knew Hank and liked the guy. "It doesn't hurt to get some opinions," J Dub conceded.

"Now you two put that stuff behind you," Marcia declared as she started putting vegetables on a tray. "Help me finish this. We can't mess this up tomorrow."

J Dub smiled and said, "It'll go fine."

"I hope so. Every big shot in town will be there."

"Do you want me to borrow the "Big Shot" music from the course?" J Dub offered.

"No!" Marcia exclaimed. "Don't even think about that!"

J Dub leaned over and gave his wife a peck on the lips. He wanted to assure her that things would go as planned. More importantly he wanted to give her assurances that the purchase of the golf course would happen.

CHAPTER SIXTY-THREE

The next day, J Dub left the golf course in the middle of the afternoon. He drove home and helped Marcia load the food and all of the accessories into the car. She was noticeably nervous. Everyone on the local "Who's Who" list was to be at the banquet. Marcia wanted to make sure that every little detail was carried out to perfection.

They drove to the hotel and carried everything into the ballroom. J Dub lit the Sterno burners while Marcia arranged the place settings. She had planned the menu, prepared the food, color coordinated the presentation, picked out the appropriate flowers and trimmings, and made sure that plenty of her business cards were available. She had thought of everything to make her presentation come off perfectly.

The only thing left was to wait for the people to show up.

At long last, throngs of people started to file through the door. The women were dressed in evening gowns. The men wore business suits mostly and Marcia even spotted a few tuxedos in the crowd.

Marcia had on a uniform that exemplified her professionalism. She put on a great performance and turned on the charm. J Dub, on the other hand, stayed in the background and assisted her when needed. It was his job to make sure that the stock was replenished.

The initial rush was hectic. Both J Dub and Marcia moved at a frantic pace. After the crowd got food the tempo slowed down. That allowed J Dub to take a short break. He moved to the cooler and reached for a soft drink. While he enjoyed a sip he felt a tap on his shoulder.

"Long time, no see," Mel Parker bellowed.

J Dub was elated. "I thought that you might be here!" he howled. "I figured somebody would be representing the hospital."

"You know how these functions are for me," Mel said as he smiled and raised his drink in the air.

J Dub reached into the cooler and grabbed a Peach Snapple. "My wife made sure that we were prepared."

"Oh my, those get me in trouble!" Mel shouted as he laughed heartily.

J Dub handed the Peach Snapple to an invigorated Mel. "One won't hurt you."

"How's life been treating you?" Mel inquired. "Did you ever buy the golf course?"

"I'm working on it. What a long drawn out process that is," J Dub responded. "What was all that about you naming a room after Lew?"

"We're adding a wing on to the hospital. All the people that have donated over the years will get their name on a plaque," Mel explained. "It's nothing."

"He'll be grouped with all the others?" J Dub fished for a response.

Mel nodded. "Speaking of which, I see that your partner is over with the number one power broker in town," Mel offered.

J Dub had a confused look. He didn't know what Mel meant. Mel motioned his head in the direction of the podium. A small gathering of people could be seen talking.

Near the stage was a banner that read: PARSONS FOR CONGRESS

Standing underneath the banner was Raymond Parsons and an unattractive gentleman with a short ponytail dressed in a frumpy suit and a necktie that reached about four inches above his belt. Lew and Lois stood to the left of the man with the ponytail. Lew looked very uncomfortable and out of place in his mechanics' uniform. Lois tried to look her best in a wrinkled suit but had the ragged look of a middle-aged woman that was going downhill rapidly.

"I can remember back to the very first one of these, Monty. At that time one term would have been nice," Raymond said.

Monty smiled. "You've done a great job of taking care of your constituents."

"I would have never thought that my power base would have expanded this much."

"You've got everybody in this room from the civic leaders to the bankers to the attorneys," Monty declared. Raymond had a satisfied demeanor.

"Congratulations, Ray," Lew proclaimed as he extended his hand.

"I can't thank you enough for all of your support, Lew. As the largest single property owner in my Congressional district you have certainly been a positive influence in my personal and professional life," Raymond gushed.

Lew nodded toward Monty. "You've got a good man in your corner, Ray."

Raymond smiled at Monty. "Yes, I do. It is invaluable to have long time relationships based on trust."

Monty and Lew could feel the positive vibrations thrown in their direction. The accolades from Raymond caused each to wear a smug grin.

Raymond looked Lew squarely in the eyes. "With all that you have done for us, you make sure that you let us know if we can ever be of any assistance to you at any time or at any place."

From the other side of the room J Dub witnessed the exchange between the parties. It was obvious that Lew had enjoyed a fruitful liaison with Raymond Parsons. His first thought was that maybe the time was right to look at their relationship a little more closely. Perhaps Curt was onto something.

A voice blared through the public address system. "And it's my pleasure to announce, running for his eleventh term as a United States Congressman . . . Raymond Parsons!"

Raymond advanced to the podium under a thunderous ovation. J Dub shook his head in disbelief. Marcia, after noticing Lew and Lois near the stage, glared at her husband and said, "That's just great! He controls the politicians . . . and probably the judges and lawyers, too! Get away from the guy!"

Chapter Sixty-Four

Despite the bits and pieces that were occurring behind the scenes, life on the golf course continued on a daily basis. On a Sunday morning, nearly nine months after the fire on the golf course, Paul, Curt, Elia and Paco enjoyed a round of golf. Bogey joined the guys for an early morning eighteen.

It was an uneventful morning. The sun was shining brightly. The guys were playing at a steady pace. Bogey was chasing the ducks and watching them fly away into the lakes. The trees were in full bloom and the temperature was perfect. The foursome had just visited with "Easy Earl" who had been out on the course tending to his marshaling duties. Typically on Sunday mornings, he would empty the trash containers, make sure that the play was steady, and cast his fishing line into one of the lakes on the course with the hope of landing a few bluegills and an occasional bass.

The guys putted out on the thirteenth green and headed for the fourteenth tee box. They pulled their golf carts to a stop by the tee box. "I wonder where that idiot is today," Paco said. "He normally pulls up to bother us before now."

"He won't be around to pester us on this hole," Curt replied. "We've reached the spot of His Majesty's creation."

The trees to the right of the tee box were charred beyond belief. A burnt bulldozer still sat in the woods completely destroyed. The guys stood and stared at the damage. "Oh, my," Elia exclaimed. In a sarcastic tone he added, "You know, he does such good work. I wonder if Lew is ever going to move that."

Muffler sounds broke the peace and quiet of the golf course. Lew could be seen in the distance racing toward them. He cut in front of a foursome that was hitting and revved the motor toward the boys.

"It looks like you spoke too soon," Paul said. "Here he comes."

"I wish that he would have thrown that noisy piece of crap in the fire too," Paco blurted. "Do you think it's too late?"

Lew pulled up to a stop next to the guys and asked, "What do you think?"

" . . . About your artwork," Elia kidded "or your clean-up job?"

"You know, that new look," Lew blurted. He wanted to hear that what he had done was acceptable to some of the regulars.

"You should have kept your seat belt on," Paco offered.

Elia couldn't resist the opportunity to add, "I bet you felt right at home in that heat."

"Hey look at it this way Elia, at least we don't have to worry about the birds shittin' all over us on number fourteen," Paco joked. The branches and foliage had disappeared from the tree trunks.

"Yeah, there ain't no birds in those trees now," Elia replied.

The guys laughed heartily at Lew's expense. "Say, Lew, when we have the Boy Scout scramble you can throw in a wienie roast," Paul yelled.

"And you can roast your buns in the drivers' seat," Elia added. The guys howled. They thought that the situation was hilarious. Bogey barked at Lew.

"What in the world were you thinking?" Paul inquired.

Lew's temper boiled over. He couldn't stand being the butt of the joke. He gave the guys a defiant stare. Without saying a word, he raced the engine on his motorcycle. In a split second he popped a wheelie and squealed off. The sounds of the muffler echoed across the golf course. He could be seen cutting in front of agitated players on the course.

Sunday mornings at Prairie Winds Golf Course were notorious for patterned behavior. The same golfers had the identical tee times week after week. The part-time help fell into a routine also. Easy Earl would always get up early and fish in one of the lakes while tending to his chores. After he killed a few hours he would take a circuitous route back to the clubhouse. During that time he would reach into all of the trash cans and grab the empty aluminum cans.

This Sunday morning was no different, except that Lew, in a rotten mood, pulled up to Earl as he reached into a trash container. "What are you doing out here this morning?" Lew asked.

"What does it look like I'm doing?" Easy Earl countered.

Lew shrugged his shoulders. " . . . Nothing. Whatever we pay you is way too much. You're about as worthless as they come."

"I'm doing the same thing that I do every Sunday morning you idiot. I just got done fishing and now I'm picking up some trash," Earl replied. "And, by the way, I'm not on your payroll this morning."

Earl threw several cans on the ground and proceeded to step on them. Lew looked at him with amazement. "Why are you throwing the cans on the ground?" a bewildered Lew asked.

Earl picked the crushed cans up and placed them in a trash bag. "I recycle these," he said.

"Why bother with that garbage? You look like some bum off the street going through trash," Lew declared.

Easy Earl had been retired for a number of years. He had been living on a fixed income for quite a while and every little penny that he made helped him make ends meet. "I get three-thirty five a bag."

Lew was baffled. He asked, "Three hundred and thirty-five dollars?"

"No!" Earl shouted. He then continued to laugh at Lew. "Three dollars and thirty-five cents, you dummy. If I turn in three bags to the recycle center then they will pay me ten bucks."

When it came to money, Lew could never let an opportunity pass. With an ornery spirit he bluntly declared, "That's golf course money."

The statement caught Easy Earl by surprise. "What?" he proclaimed in an astonished tone. He glared at Lew. The thought of Lew ordering him to do something in a condescending way irked him. After all, Easy Earl was at least fifteen years older than Lew. He didn't need to be told what to do.

"You heard me! From now on you turn that money into Julie. That adds to our bottom line," Lew shouted.

The whole idea incensed Earl. In his opinion he was spending some of his own time to help clean up the golf course. If nothing else, he felt as if Lew should be thanking him. "I'll tell you what," Earl yelled. "Do it your fucking self!" He threw a trash bag at Lew. Earl then reached into the trash barrel and tossed cans all over the tee box. "I'm way too old for this shit!" Earl was miffed. His boiling point had reached its' limit. He jumped into a golf cart and sped away.

Lew was left holding an empty trash bag. He stood in the middle of the litter and watched Earl disappear in the distance.

Easy Earl was livid. He started to hyperventilate. As his breath labored he clutched his heart. His body slumped at the wheel. The speeding golf cart moved erratically until it ran into a sand trap and stopped abruptly.

CHAPTER SIXTY-FIVE

The passing of Easy Earl was upsetting to J Dub. Earl had been a "golf rat" the entire time that J Dub had been at Prairie Winds. He had retired years before and wanted to enjoy his golden years by doing something that he loved.

His passion had been golf. He loved to tee it up with the guys on a daily basis and hang around the clubhouse. The camaraderie with the rest of the fellows was what he really enjoyed. He had ample opportunity to play cards, backgammon, or roll the dice with the guys every afternoon. All he had to do was show up.

Earl was in the clubhouse every day in the early years. He became a trusted friend of J Dub to the extent that J Dub would let him run the register frequently. Since Earl was on a limited retirement stipend he wanted free golf. So J Dub put him on the payroll to help out around the golf course and play for free.

If he didn't fill-in on the register, patrons would see Earl as a starter on the first tee box or as a marshal on the course. He would run odd jobs for the maintenance crew or simply take some kids out to fish in the lakes. If he was needed to fix a flat tire on a golf cart, then J Dub could count on him.

Earl was up every morning at four and was normally the first guy to show up right after dawn. J Dub could depend on Earl to be there early every day for a cup of coffee and some sunrise banter. If J Dub wanted Easy Earl to open up with him a few minutes before daybreak, then he could depend on Easy Earl to be there. Now it was over.

Everyone handles the death of a personal friend in a personal and private way. J Dub's way of handling the death of Earl was to drive around the course that Earl loved to play. He remembered the stories that were shared in the clubhouse after the rounds of golf. J Dub was going to miss Earl. He lost a good friend, a trusted confidant, and an all-around good guy. He got on the Truckster, drove onto the course, and had an emotional cry on the lake bank where Earl normally liked to sit. He had a chance to privately share a tear for his old friend.

Word of Earl's death traveled quickly to the close-knit family of regular golfers that played at Prairie Winds. The next order of business was to hold a simple gathering in Earl's honor. Earl had gotten four hole-in-ones on the same par-three at Prairie Winds. J Dub knew exactly what he wanted to do.

Rollie, BT, Fred, Paul, Curt, Paco, Elia, Julie, and Bogey joined J Dub a few mornings later on the tee box of the par-three where Earl had gotten his glory. Conspicuous by his absence was Lew who was intent on snubbing Earl's private memorial service. The boys had learned that another group of golfers had reported seeing a confrontation between Lew and Earl just prior to Earl's heart attack.

J Dub conducted a short sermon. "This was Earl's favorite spot out here. He had several enjoyable moments here watching his tee shot go into the hole. This tree will be in his remembrance." He took a tree out of the Truckster and placed it into a hole that Rollie had dug.

"Each and every one of us has a story by which we'll remember Earl. To some he was an old coot, to some he was a dad and a grandpa, but to us he was a good old friend," J Dub said as the tears started to flow, "as good of a friend as a guy could ever hope for."

Rollie threw dirt back into the hole so that the tree was anchored. One by one all of the guys in attendance stooped and placed a flower at the base of the tree. Julie had taken an old scorecard, on which Earl had broken seventy, encased it in a plastic covering, and mounted it on a stand by the tree. J Dub reached into the Truckster and grabbed a plaque that dedicated the tree to Easy Earl. He placed it at the base of the tree.

The guys had lost a good buddy. There wasn't a dry eye in the group.

CHAPTER SIXTY-SIX

Marcia was getting more and more impatient by the day. She wanted to get her husband away from Lew. Easy Earl wasn't actually killed by Lew, but in Marcia's mind Lew was the one that was responsible for bringing on the anxiety that triggered the heart attack. She didn't want that same stress level to rise in her husband.

There was a part of Marcia that wanted J Dub to get the golf course. It would offer a tremendous business opportunity for them. Their financial security would be well established for the remainder of their lives in all likelihood if that was to happen.

Yet, there was another part of Marcia that wanted to get her husband out from underneath the shadow of Lew Zerrmann. She didn't like him or trust him. She didn't think that he was going to deliver on his contractual obligation to sell the business to J Dub. Marcia hated to see her husband used and controlled by such a contemptible person.

The delays and the lawsuit and the IRS investigation and the due diligence period that Curt and J Dub felt was necessary were all factors that contributed to her uneasiness. Little did Marcia know that all of those things played right into Lew's hand. Lew wanted Marcia to feel impatient. He wanted to get J Dub to leave. The sooner that he could get rid of J Dub, the quicker he could make a better deal for himself.

Emotions seemed to boil over soon after Earl's death. J Dub and Marcia were doing some minor landscaping in front of their home. A few of the bushes needed to be replaced. In addition, Marcia wanted to plant some flowers to add a colorful, vibrant look to the scenery.

Marcia worked on her hands and knees and was busy digging a hole when she looked over her shoulder toward J Dub and said, "You never know, but this might be your calling in life."

She was upset with the delays on the purchase of the golf course. The comment was her way of trying to plant a seed in J Dub's mind. J Dub had no idea what she was referring to so he just looked in her direction and continued to plant flowers and back fill dirt into the holes that had been dug.

"You're not the next one that gets put in the ground, are you?" Marcia continued.

"If I am, then make mine an oak tree, too." J Dub made reference to the type of tree that was planted in Earl's honor. He wanted to make light of the conversation.

Marcia's impatience and irritability had been on the rise the last few weeks. J Dub's comment struck a nerve with her. "J Dub, I'm serious." She held her gaze at J Dub to emphasize her point and then continued digging.

Marcia's digging became more rapid. She was frantically throwing dirt away from the hole. Her temper was starting to get the best of her. With the next thrust into the ground she hit a rock with the hand shovel. She grimaced and shook her hand.

"Dammit! Get away from that creep!" she yelled.

J Dub wanted to stay calm, cool, and collected. He knew that they had started a plan of action with the due diligence and he had no intention of abandoning it. "We need to gather more information."

"Then get a move on it! This family can't lose you. I'm scared he's going to drive you to an early grave, dammit!"

J Dub went to her side and examined her hand. "It's a slow process."

"At some point you need to crawl out of that divot and stand up to the guy!" Marcia shouted. She made reference to the day that his shot landed in the divot and his life changed.

"This fight is not just for me. It's for all of us," J Dub explained.

Marcia's eyes stung with tears. She was angry, aggravated and scared.

"Then cover your tracks before I have to dig a bigger hole! The last thing I want to do right now is have to bury you!"

CHAPTER SIXTY-SEVEN

Later During the Summer of 1996 . . .

The government had reached the critical stage of the investigation into tax evasion against Lew Zerrmann and Walter Hancock. The initial interview had taken place and both Lew and Walter decided not to talk unless an attorney was present. Ellie Hackett, Peter Dooley, Thomas Booker and Daniel Hayden all knew that the timing of the next move was important. They sat around a conference table at the U.S. Attorney's office and discussed various strategies. It was agreed that they would act in a matter of days.

Enough preliminary information had been gathered to indicate that serious crimes may have been committed. The government needed original documents and hoped to turn up more information that would solidify their case. "I've authorized the search warrants," Ellie declared.

"We'll coordinate the raid with the FBI, the ATF, and the IRS," Peter announced.

"Peter, make sure that everyone involved knows that we want accounting documents to substantiate tax evasion and fraud," Ellie stressed.

Peter nodded and gave her assurances that that would be the case. Ellie looked at Booker. She stared at Hayden. The look in Ellie's eye indicated the adrenalin rush that was flowing through her veins. She had been close to catching Zerrmann many years prior to this, but she could only get one of his associates. "I want to get his ass this time! No screw-ups. Do you understand?" she stressed. The men in the room realized the seriousness of what needed to be done. They nodded in agreement.

The sunrise was very much like many others that had preceded it. Darkness turned to a gentle haze. Ground fog blanketed the low lying areas. A bright orange ball began to peek out from the eastern sky. This particular morning was similar to many others in the past.

J Dub pulled his pickup onto the parking lot. He was greeted by Bogey. The dog jumped up his leg with tail wagging. He lapped at J Dub's face. The boys started to roll in one by one for their cup of coffee and early round of golf.

Lew slept in, which was customary. The rising sun cast long shadows as it shined on the grain bins and barn. There was no need for him to be at the pro shop at daybreak. He knew that J Dub had things under control.

Walter had just parked his car and stopped on the sidewalk to take in a nice breath of fresh air. The birds were chirping. Rabbits and squirrels scurried in and around the bushes. He stooped to pick the morning paper up off of the porch and entered his office.

The tranquility was soon disrupted. All hell broke loose at the three locations.

The raid had been very well coordinated. Two FBI agents, two ATF agents, and two IRS agents were present at all three locations. Getting raided is not a pleasant experience. It is a way for the federal government to show its force in addition to legally seizing documents.

The agents offered a fruit basket at two of the sites. To get into the locations they posed as delivery men. That wasn't needed at the pro shop. That business was up and running and several golfers were present. However, it was an effective way to get onto the premises at Lew's home and Walter's accounting office.

One of the first things that they established was whether or not there were any weapons that were readily available. The last thing that the feds wanted was an early morning shootout over some accounting files.

J Dub was told to place his hands on the wall and he was frisked. The boys were in and out of the pro shop. They had gathered to play golf and once it became obvious that they had nothing to do with the business, the agents let them tee off.

The agents wanted accounting documents for the past ten years. J Dub easily accommodated them. He took them into the office and showed them what file cabinets stored the records. They confiscated the originals and after about an hour and a half wrapped up their business and left the premises.

It was a little different situation at the other two locales. Walter, who by nature was a nervous person, just about had a breakdown. After the agents entered the accounting office they had Walter place his hands on the wall. He was then patted down for weapons. Once it was determined that he was clean, they asked him to lead them to the tax records for Prairie Winds Golf Course and Lewferd E. Zerrmann.

He was very hesitant to be helpful. In fact, Walter resorted to pacing back and forth down the hallway. He kept whining about his wife and needed to be watched each and every second. It looked like he was exploring ways to bolt out the door at any moment.

Walter was clearly in an uncompromising position. He had been receiving monthly reports from the golf course for years and had been compiling twelve financial statements a year for well over a decade. It was clear that the feds were going to get everything that he had logged into his system. He let them have a free run of the place and told them to take whatever they needed with the hopes that they might miss something.

There was no way that the agents would miss anything. With that sort of freedom, the agents took everything that they could legally get their hands on. They spent the entire morning at Walter's accounting office and confiscated everything that vaguely resembled Prairie Winds Golf Course and Lewferd E. Zerrmann.

Agents Booker and Hayden accompanied the FBI and ATF to Lew's residence. Booker especially wanted to intimidate Lew on his own turf. He had the search warrants from the U.S. Attorney's Office and wanted to demonstrate to Lew what sort of might he possessed. To do it within the boundaries of Lew's fortress with guns trained on him would make an even greater impression he thought.

The agents got through the gate under the guise of UPS delivery men. Lew came to the door in his underwear and was served the search warrants by Booker and Hayden. Shortly thereafter, Lew had his arms up against the wall and his legs spread-eagled. One ATF agent patted him down while the other had a rifle trained on him. Lew stood in his underwear and faced the wall. An FBI agent asked, "Any weapons?"

The agents had done their homework. They were well aware that Lew had a stockpile of guns at his residence. It was fairly obvious to all parties that Lew was going to stay in that position against the wall for the better part of the day.

Lew nodded his head. He was disgusted that he was forced to stand in his underwear in his own home with his hands on the wall. The mere order belittled him. His mind had already been working overtime. He immediately tried to figure out who was behind the raid. He made a pledge to himself to get even with whoever was responsible.

"What firearms do you have?" the FBI agent asked a second time.

"They're everywhere," Lew replied. He was not lying. He had a cache of guns in the dungeon. Several rifles were out in the barn. It was hard to guess where else Lew had weapons in his home. They were probably stashed in his office or bedroom. That was not taking into consideration the likelihood of a gun or two being in his pickup truck or motorcycle, both of which sat nearby.

Lew shifted his weight and let his arms drop to his side. "Keep your hands against the wall," the FBI agent ordered. The ATF agent raised the rifle and took aim at Lew. One look down the muzzle of the rifle was a clear indication to Lew that they meant business.

Booker and Hayden entered Lew's home office. They looked around and started going through desk drawers and file cabinets. Lew turned his head to look over his shoulder at Booker. A look of spite and hatred enveloped his face.

Booker had a personal feeling of satisfaction. Years earlier Lew had run him off of the golf course because he was black. At that time, Booker had to bite his tongue and take every bit of discrimination that was directed his way. Now he could extract his revenge . . . on Lew's own turf. He stared back at Lew.

The two IRS agents continued down the steps to the lower level of the residence. They noticed the bar but walked right past it. Booker went straight to the Uncle Sam yard jockey. He and Hayden both forced a chuckle. They couldn't keep a straight face. The irony of the attempted patriotism was more than they could handle.

That all changed a few seconds later when Booker took the set of keys off of the yard jockey and opened the bomb shelter. He and Hayden were shocked to see the stacks of bundled cash. The other items were equally as numbing. The piles of newspapers along with the chicken noodle soup, bottled water, tomato juice, and pork and beans were clear-cut indications that they were dealing with someone who did not think along the same lines as the vast amount of American citizens.

The cheap detective magazine photos and Tupperware collection inside the bunker were disturbing to Hayden. The Nazi uniform and KKK robe sent shivers up Booker's spine. "What the hell is this guy into?" Booker questioned.

"It explains why he tried to intimidate you," Hayden commented.

Booker picked up *Mein Kampf.* "He must think that he's a little Hitler."

"And by the looks of this fortress he might be . . . at least in his own small way," Hayden added.

Booker picked up a bundle of fresh one hundred dollars bills. "How much cash would you say is there?" Booker asked.

"At least a million, maybe two," Hayden guessed.

"Ellie is certainly going to be interested in this," Booker declared.

"More than you can ever think," Hayden replied.

"Why do you put it like that?" Booker inquired.

"She's Jewish."

The mere mention of that caused Booker to bury his face into his hands. "We sure are getting more than what we bargained for this morning. Come on. Let's see what else is down here."

The two men exited the bomb shelter and continued down the hall. They stopped outside the door to the dungeon. Booker jiggled the knob only to find that the door to this room was also locked. He tried several keys until one finally unlocked the door.

What was in the dungeon shocked them more than what they had just seen in the bomb shelter. They took one step into the dungeon, stopped in their tracks, and peered at each other.

Tied to the bondage apparatus was Lois. She had a gag in her mouth and had been beaten until her eyes were swollen shut. Her face was black and blue. She was dressed in black leather boots, crotch-less panties, a garter belt and wore a bra that allowed her nipples to show. "Who is this guy?" Booker whispered to Hayden.

"Man. This opens up a ton of questions."

"But a lot of what we've just seen is out of our jurisdiction," Booker conceded.

Lois could feel the presence of people in the room. Her back had been facing the door. Due to the swollen condition of her eyes and the position that she was in she could not identify who was there. "Lew, is that you?" she meekly mumbled. Her voice choked on the gag.

"No. This is special agent Thomas Booker and special agent Daniel Hayden of the IRS," Booker stated.

Lois squirmed. She was embarrassed to be caught in such a demeaning fashion. "Do you want to be released?" Booker asked.

Lois shook her head in a negative fashion. She clearly was strangling on the gag. "I've been a bad girl," she mumbled in a muffled tone.

Booker and Hayden shook their heads at the pathetic site. They panned the room to see the Swastika, the cache of guns on the floor, and the large collection of sex toys. All they could do was turn and head toward the upper level.

Hayden went through the desk and cabinets and catalogued everything that was related to Prairie Winds Golf Course. He rapidly boxed up the pertinent information and attempted to finish his portion of the job as quickly as possible. What he had seen in the lower level alarmed him. He felt as if he needed to get out of there so that Lew could return to the basement and release Lois.

Booker snooped around in the office for more incriminating documentation. After over four hours Booker was satisfied that they had gotten everything that they needed to get. He moved toward the door. In so doing he passed dangerously close to Lew who was still standing spread-eagled in his underwear with his hands against the wall. "You're disgusting," he whispered in Lew's ear. He was so close to Lew that Lew could feel the breath on the back of his neck.

Lew cocked his head and peered out of the corner of his eye. "You get your black, monkey-ass out of my home. I don't like your kind in here," Lew said defiantly, "it smells up the place."

Booker turned and laughed out loud in his face.

CHAPTER SIXTY-EIGHT

Lew was miffed and sulked, but he was wise enough to know that he needed to get a lawyer right away to get the misunderstanding with the IRS settled as quickly as possible. He contacted Grady Patterson who had helped him out of the lawsuit with the Morton heirs.

After hearing that Lew had problems with the IRS and taxes, Grady referred him to Garrett O'Connor, an high profile attorney who specialized in tax matters. Garrett looked imposing and distinguished. With touches of gray at his temples, he commanded attention when he entered a room. His voice was strong and clear, like that of a radio announcer and he used it to his advantage frequently booming to intimidate an overzealous foe.

Lew set up an appointment and immediately got in to see Garrett. After hearing Lew's version of the raid Garrett wasted no time placing a call to the U.S. Attorney's office. The call that he placed got right through to the U. S. Attorney.

"Ellie Hackett."

"My name is Garrett O'Connor. I have been hired by Lew Zerrmann. He wants to know what is going on."

"His home and business were searched yesterday."

"What does it involve?"

"Lewferd E. Zerrmann is under investigation for fraud and tax evasion."

"Please have no further contact with my client. Send any correspondence to my office. He feels as if his rights were violated during yesterday's raid."

"He was served with search warrants."

"I want you to have no further contact with my client," Garrett said emphatically. The tone of his voice signaled that he was mad and meant business.

Garrett ended the conversation right then and there by hanging up the phone. He turned to Lew who was sitting across the desk. "Now keep your mouth shut and don't talk to your accountant either."

Chapter Sixty-Nine

Life continued at the golf course as if nothing had happened. The boys joked with J Dub a little about how cute he looked with his hands up against the wall and his legs spread wide open. They got to go out on the course and play golf during the raid. Their lives were not impacted in any way, shape, or form by the actions of the government. So, to them, it was business as usual at the course.

One morning as the '96 golf season was winding down, Paul, BT, Rollie, Fred, Curt, Paco, and Elia were at the back table settling their bets. Bogey parked himself in his usual spot to take a nap. J Dub and Julie worked the counter. Paul yelled from the back of the room. "J Dub, you should have been out there today! We get to number six and BT stripes one right at the stick."

"It takes two bounces and goes in!" Rollie shouted.

J Dub was well aware that BT had made several holes-in-one. "How many is that, BT?"

BT had a smile from ear to ear. Getting a hole-in-one was every golfer's dream. Many can play all of their life and not get one. Yet, if a person takes enough swings, then sooner or later the odds start to improve.

There were countless stories about how guys had made aces by hitting the ball off of a tree, or off of a golf cart, or off of a rock, or rolling one all the way to the green and seeing the ball disappear. Those are only a few of the untraditional ways to score a hole-in-one.

However, with BT it normally meant that he had hit a perfect shot. BT had the lean, lanky physique that allowed him to have a gorgeous golf swing. So his answer was not surprising. "That was my ninth one." Many had come at one of the par three's at Prairie Winds Golf Course.

Fred thought that he would continue the story. "Bogey was down by the green when the ball went in the cup. He started going crazy."

Bogey heard his name and raised his head from the snooze that he was taking. He muzzled a soft bark. "Bogey, show J Dub what you gave BT for his hole-in-one," Elia coaxed. Bogey, jumped up, ran to the corner of the pro shop, and fetched a pair of panties. He sprinted to the center of the pro shop. All the guys burst into laughter.

"This was what had been lying next to the panties," Fred hollered as he held up a plastic six-pack holder.

"It must have been quite a night for some high-school kid down by that green," Paul suggested.

The afternoon amusement persisted until "Big Shot" boomed through the speakers. Julie looked at J Dub and rolled her eyes. She knew that the festive atmosphere was about to come to an end. "Oh crap. Here he comes again. You know, one day, I wouldn't be surprised if Billy Joel sued us for associating his song with Lew."

Lew marched through the door. The laughter ceased. The energy level disappeared. Lew appeared ecstatic in front of all the occupants of the pro shop. "I fixed the first tee box!" Lew exclaimed.

The first tee box had been a sore spot for J Dub since the first day that they walked onto the site. "That only took fifteen years," he said facetiously turning to Lew. "What did you do?"

"Look for yourself."

J Dub twirled around to look out the window to see what Lew had done. He hadn't noticed that Lew had been working in that area, so he was curious to see what sort of work Lew had accomplished. A new four foot by four foot piece of Astroturf was lying on the first tee box. "Does it play a song when they tee off?" J Dub asked Lew. He made reference to the Astroturf in Lew's parking spot that played music.

"Feel fortunate that it is fixed," Lew replied. He had only replaced the old Astroturf.

"We're trying to run a golf course around here that has grass for a playing surface," J Dub commented. "That looks so tacky."

Lew gave J Dub a fierce look and then headed into the office. "Julie, come here." Julie ran after him. She could tell that he was in a hurry. "Grab the checkbook," he ordered.

"You haven't had any jobs on the course lately," Julie stated.

"I took the dump truck in for some brake work and a new transmission," Lew declared. With mounting legal bills Lew had to come up with some excuse to raid the course's bank account.

Reluctantly, Julie grabbed the checkbook. She was resolved to fate. He was going to raid the checking account again, despite all of the heat that the government was putting on him. "How much and to whom?" she asked.

"Make it to Lew's Repair Service," Lew said with a smirk. Julie stopped writing and glared at him. "The total bill was seventy-nine thousand, four hundred and thirty-six dollars," his voice trailed.

Julie put the pen down and placed her hands on her hips. Lew didn't know when to quit. "And eighty-two cents."

Julie sat motionless in the chair. Lew walked over and positioned himself behind her. He rubbed his crotch against her back. Julie cringed and pulled away. "That dump truck is over thirty years old and worth about four thousand bucks."

"It needed some work," Lew said as he forced a grin.

"There is no way that will fly with the accountant," Julie said adamantly.

"That's taken care of, Sweet Cakes. Just write out the check." Lew walked around to the front side of the desk. He stared at Julie's breasts. "And if you're a good girl, maybe I'll buy you some boobs," he suggested. His forwardness toward her was taking new heights.

"Cut it out!" Julie yelled. She was nearly in tears.

"That would be a good business move for both of us. Plus I can expense it out. The bigger your boobs are the more guys we'll be able to pack into the pro shop. We'll sell more drinks and you'll make more tips."

"You're disgusting!" Julie wrote the check unwillingly and handed it to Lew. "If you don't shut your trap, I'll get my rifle and change you from a rooster to a hen with one shot!" she said defiantly. "And don't think I can't."

Lew grabbed the check and exited the office. Julie momentarily contemplated whether or not she should pursue pressing sexual harassment charges against him. After a second, she gathered her bearings and walked into the pro shop. "J Dub, the little prick just took over seventy-nine thousand dollars to fix the dump truck."

They both peered out the window. J Dub saw that Lew was headed for his motorcycle. He bolted out the door with Bogey at his heels. J Dub was incensed. He stormed up to Lew. Bogey started barking at Lew. "Where do you think you're going? We need that cash for winter!" he yelled.

"I'll do what I want!" Bogey started growling at Lew when Lew raised his voice to J Dub. "If you don't play your cards better, you're going to lose this place," Lew continued.

"That won't happen! I'm protected in the buy/sell agreement. Besides, you need to give me a contract before I can go any further."

"Let me tell you something!" Lew shouted as he revved the engine on his motorcycle. Bogey's barking increased. The noise that was being generated was not normal for a golf course environment. "If you lose it, then it's your own fault. You've lost out!" Lew hollered.

He reached into the storage pack on his motorcycle and pulled out the black velvet pill box that he had privately nicknamed "Nirvana." He took a capsule out of the pill box and shook it in J Dub's face. Bogey's barking continued. "Hitler made sure he never lost!"

Lew threw the motorcycle in gear. The cycle lurched toward Bogey and ran over his hind quarters. One of Bogey's rear legs took a direct hit. Lew gunned the engine and raced off of the lot. Bogey whimpered and limped away.

J Dub watched as Lew sped off of the lot. He hurried after Bogey only to see that the right rear hind leg was so badly mangled that it was beyond repair. J Dub grabbed Bogey and consoled him. "Oh, Bogey, I'm so sorry that you came out here with me. He's too much for me and I know that he's too much for you. Let's get you fixed up the best we can."

J Dub ran to his pickup and rushed Bogey to the animal hospital. It appeared that Bogey lapsed into shock on the way to the veterinarian. His energy level decreased. He lost a great deal of blood. Later that evening the vet worked feverishly on Bogey's lower extremities. He did all that he could do. After consulting with J Dub, the vet amputated Bogey's leg.

CHAPTER SEVENTY

Special agents Booker and Hayden interviewed several witnesses that might have had knowledge of what had been taking place at Prairie Winds. They conducted the taxpayer interrogations with attorneys present for both Lew and Walter. Formal affidavits were written, signed and filed. Testimony had been provided under oath.

Booker and Hayden were knowledgeable, efficient, and experienced. They knew exactly how to gather evidence and develop it. They then evaluated the evidence and analyzed it. The next step was to decide whether or not the allegation was, in fact, a criminal violation.

One more step was needed. They felt compelled to call J Dub back in for some more questioning. After he arrived at the Internal Revenue Service offices he was escorted to a conference room.

Seated at the table were Peter, Booker, Hayden, and Ellie. The entire atmosphere gave him mixed signals. The cold, impersonal impression of the room itself was depressing. There were no windows to allow sunlight to enter the room. No wall coverings were visible. The pale green paint on the walls was enough to cause his stomach to rumble.

Papers and files were strewn around the room. It was obvious that they had gathered a lot of evidence and had assembled it. He was anxious to find out what more they wanted. Before J Dub's butt hit the seat, Peter blurted, "You're holding out information!"

J Dub thought that it was rude to be approached like that before any cordial greetings had taken place. He was there to help. He really didn't expect to be antagonized after all that he had done to assist with the investigation. Once he had been contacted he had fully cooperated with the investigation and had been truthful in answering any questions and forthright in providing information.

"What are you talking about? You've got the tax returns and the financial statements," J Dub barked at Peter. At that point he didn't care if he was somewhat disrespectful toward the assistant U.S. Attorney. "That's what you asked for."

"Where's he funneling the money?" Peter demanded.

Booker came to J Dub's defense. It was the classic "good cop, bad cop" routine. Booker chastised Peter. "Lay off him. He was paid to run the business."

Peter turned to Booker. "How can he be that stupid? He's got to know where all of the money went."

Booker had shared many conversations with J Dub. He felt comfortable with his answer. "He ran the day to day stuff. Lew controlled the money."

"He told me way back when to show up for work and be responsible for bringing money through the door. I treated the golfers with as much respect as I could and thanked them for their business," J Dub emphasized. "He told me that he would take care of the financial end of things."

Two days prior to the meeting, Booker and Hayden made a recommendation to the U.S. Attorney's office to prosecute. After examining all of the evidence the U.S. Attorney's office wasn't as sure of getting a conviction as the two special agents. Garrett O'Connor, Lew's tax defense attorney, had shut Lew up and had argued against intent. He claimed that what had been done with the books was an unintentional oversight.

Booker knew that the heat had been turned up a notch. He turned to J Dub. "Are you concerned for your safety?"

"Thieves don't kill, do they?" J Dub answered.

"Our profiles don't indicate that," Booker replied. "Loose cannons might though."

"If you're concerned for your safety, then we can protect you if you'd like," Ellie offered.

"Have you heard something that I don't know about?" J Dub asked.

" . . . No, not at all. We were only wondering if you felt threatened," Ellie responded.

"I've run the business for him for quite a while. He won't cause any physical harm to me," J Dub responded in a naïve way.

Booker felt compelled to go into another direction. They had decided prior to J Dub's arrival that Booker would make the suggestion since he had established the strongest relationship with J Dub. "Look, we've got some problems securing a conviction," he went on to explain. "For this thing to really get some meat on it, we need to get Lew and the accountant on tape," Booker put into plain words.

"Are you willing to wear a wire?" Ellie offered.

"I have a wife and kids to care for!" J Dub shrieked.

"The investigation has produced mixed results. All of the evidence is circumstantial," Booker clarified. Hayden started to put a wire around J Dub. Booker moved to assist him.

"What are you doing?" J Dub asked.

"I'm just taking some quick measurements," Hayden deadpanned.

"Think about it," Booker reasoned. "When the time comes we'll be in a van across the street. Your safety will be the utmost priority."

"It may be the only thing that we'll be able to hang our hat on," Ellie concluded.

CHAPTER SEVENTY-ONE

Early February 1997 . . .

The winter of late '96 and early '97 was especially cold and icy, and not conducive to many rounds of golf at Prairie Winds. J Dub couldn't do much about the resulting financial state of the business so he took the winter to think through the limited alternatives that were available to him. He finally decided to heed Marcia's advice and call a lawyer.

J Dub needed to bounce some legal matters off of someone. He was in need of advice and opinions that might shed some light on what was going on. Lew was getting more and more hostile by the day due to the pressure caused by the ongoing IRS investigation. And, to compound matters for J Dub, he had just learned that the lawsuit by the Morton heirs had recently been thrown out of court.

The funds that J Dub had available to pay for legal counsel were limited, so he sought out an acquaintance based on his wife's referral that would be happy to help him at a reasonable rate. Hank Lowery, Esq. handled small-time domestic affairs. He and his wife, Joyce, were members of the same church that J Dub and Marcia attended. In fact, Marcia and Joyce shared babysitting duties at one time for a group of pre-schoolers. Hence, a meeting with Hank Lowery was scheduled. Curt had agreed to go with him.

Hank had an affable personality. He greeted J Dub and Curt hospitably and immediately made them feel welcome. Hank operated his practice out of a modest business condo in a progressive part of town. It was easy to notice that he was not a corporate lawyer with a lot of connections. "I understand that you're having some partnership problems," Hank began.

J Dub nodded. "I got involved in business with my partner around fifteen years ago and now it's time to act on the provisions of the buy/sell agreement."

"What have you done?"

"Basically, my partner has agreed to sell the business to me. He got the property appraised."

Hank wanted to pump J Dub for as much information as possible before answering questions specifically. "You have the rights to buy it?"

"Yes, I carry the option to buy the business and the first right of refusal," J Dub explained. "That's all spelled out in the buy/sell agreement that we have."

"J Dub's partner is Lew Zerrmann. He won't give J Dub a contract to purchase the property," Curt interjected.

"He doesn't have to, does he?" Hank interrupted.

J Dub was shocked by that revelation. "What are you talking about?"

"You're a minority partner. Correct?" Hank probed.

"Sure. My minority interest is twenty percent."

"You don't have any rights," Hank declared.

"But I own twenty percent of the business," J Dub stressed.

"It's not worth anything," Hank said matter-of-factly.

"It's probably worth well over a million dollars," J Dub countered.

"Not really. You can't go out on the open market and sell it to anyone. Therefore it has no value. No one else would want to pay that kind of money to be in a minority position," Hank put the bad news into plain words.

"Nothing makes any sense," Curt butted in.

Hank's interest was piqued. "What do you mean?"

"The financial statements are bogus," J Dub blurted.

"Do you know that for a fact?" Hank insinuated.

"The IRS has put him under investigation," J Dub admitted. "I'm sure that they are headed in that direction. Normally where there's smoke, there's fire."

"In that case, that changes things a little," Hank conceded. "He owes you a fiduciary duty. He has to be honest with you."

J Dub's ears perked up. "What if he's not?"

"Then you might have a civil claim against him," Hank offered. "But we're a long way from that."

"What's involved?" Curt asked.

"First off, a civil action is a road that you probably don't want to go down. I'd avoid it at all costs," Hank said.

J Dub had traveled a long, bumpy ride with Lew. He was all ears. "Why?"

"Any civil action is costly. Plus it could take ten to twelve years to get through the justice system," Hank explained, "with no reasonable expectations that you can win."

"That would eat up the prime years of my adult life," J Dub shrieked.

"Exactly," Hank affirmed. "I don't have the resources or experience to help you with something like that anyway."

"What would I need to do if that were to occur?" J Dub requested.

"Probably get a heavy duty law firm to take the case on a contingency basis."

J Dub sighed and looked at Curt. "For crying out loud," J Dub uttered. "You know, I'm just an average guy that gets up and goes to work every day. I have sincerely wanted to buy the business that I have run for the last fifteen years. It's spelled out in our agreement that that opportunity is available to me. I don't want to sue for something that I feel that I'm entitled to."

"That's why it would be best to get the issue settled," Hank advised.

"Now we're back to where we were when we walked in," Curt proclaimed.

"You've got problems," Hank admitted. "He controls the business and doesn't need to sell it to you."

"Dammit!" J Dub screamed. "I'm not going to give up fifteen years!"

"If he's being a horse's rear end, then maybe you'll have to prove that the business was run fraudulently. It may come down to that if he's not cooperating with you," Hank said.

"Now you're talking lawsuit again," J Dub pointed out. "I don't want to go in that direction."

"Good. I wouldn't recommend going that route. It's too tough to prove."

J Dub was fraught with stress. What once appeared to be a wonderful business opportunity was crumbling right in front of his eyes. Curt felt like he needed to console J Dub a little. "It looks like it was run fraudulently. At least that is what the financials indicate."

"Then the burden of proof is yours. You'll have to build your case, have a trial in front of a jury, and hope for the best. It's very high risk." Hank wanted to hammer home his point. "That's not to mention that that sort of process is expensive and time consuming."

J Dub felt himself getting sick to his stomach. He was getting lightheaded. The temperature in the room seemed warm. He felt as if he was going to pass out. "What's my next move?" he muttered.

"The ball is in his court. Wait to see what he does. Don't be surprised if he doesn't give you what you think he should," Hank reiterated.

"If he doesn't, then I'll have no other choice but sue him for non-performance on the partnership agreement," J Dub stressed.

"What you have to guard against is if he wants to get rid of you," Hank warned.

"What then?"

"Essentially what will happen is that you will say that your twenty percent is worth x number of dollars. Lew will say that it is worth nothing. If it goes in front of a judge, then the judge will say to split it down the middle. But you'll have to pay an attorney. In the end you'll get whatever the median value is minus attorney's fees," Hank clarified.

"What will that amount to?" J Dub pried.

"In the cases that I've seen you're talking about maybe thirty to thirty-five cents on the dollar, if you're lucky," Hank stated. "That's if the majority partner wants to be cordial."

"Cordial? That's disgusting after all these years of hard work," J Dub whined.

Hank truly felt sorry for J Dub's plight. "Sometimes life isn't fair." He looked squarely at J Dub. "Feel free to call me whenever you'd like. I'll be here to help you," Hank said. "You might be screwed though." Hank escorted the two to the door.

"Are there any other things I should be aware of?" J Dub asked.

"Just remember that business is business," Hank warned.

J Dub looked livid. He was not angry with Hank but was disappointed that he had to deal with all of the negative news. Lew had always portrayed himself as a victim through the years. He always claimed that everyone was out to get him. Yet now, J Dub started to realize that Lew may have been taking advantage of him and taken the best years of his life away from him. He muttered, "Business is business, huh? That's the same thing that Lew has said over and over and over again."

~ ~ ~

Several days later . . .

Marcia got another catering job for which she had to prepare food. She and J Dub felt like it would be another chance to talk to Curt. They gathered around the breakfast island in the kitchen to slice fruits and vegetables. "You heard what he had to say," Curt said to J Dub.

"It doesn't look good, Marcia," J Dub mumbled.

"I can't say that it comes as a surprise," Marcia said.

"He's been skimming so much that I can't buy the place in the financial condition that it is in," J Dub rationalized.

"Take your cut and get out of it," Marcia urged.

"That might pose a whole other set of problems," Curt cautioned. He turned to J Dub. "Have you told her?"

J Dub shook his head. He had postponed delivering the not-so-good news to his wife.

"What do I need to know?" Marcia asked.

J Dub's frame of mind had been altered by the words of Hank Lowery. He had not had his wits about him since leaving the law office. "Basically, we are a minority shareholder. We don't have any rights. He can legally give us thirty cents on the dollar and get away with it if he wants to. Technically, he could give me nothing," J Dub explained.

"That's not right!' Marcia screamed.

"I didn't think so either," J Dub agreed. "But that is the way our system works. And it's perfectly legal. The only way that I can recover what I feel is mine is to sue him."

"I still think that we need to do our homework and gather as many dirty pictures as we can on the guy," Curt offered.

"What good would that do?" Marcia complained.

"At least it would offer us an insurance policy for whatever might happen down the road," Curt proposed. "Lew still owes J Dub a fiduciary duty."

"What is that?" questioned Marcia.

"He has to be truthful with J Dub," Curt clarified. "That hasn't exactly been the case based on what J Dub has been told and the documents that he's been given."

Marcia disagreed. "I don't know! I'm leaning toward J Dub taking his cut and moving on. I'm done fiddling around with this guy."

"That's letting him win!" J Dub butted in.

Marcia didn't care who the perceived winner was going to be. "I want you away from that disgusting excuse for . . . ."

"I'm not giving up that easy!" J Dub interrupted.

"Everybody calm down. We're not to that point yet," Curt cut in.

"My patience is over with all of this nonsense," Marcia howled. "I may not be around to see the end."

J Dub felt the need to take charge of the conversation. "Everybody hold on. We're not forced to make any kind of a decision tonight. We just asked Hank a few questions and got some answers that we weren't necessarily prepared for. Besides, there are still a few more holes left in this round."

"Why do you have to put everything into a golf analogy?" Marcia whined.

"Golf is like life," J Dub reasoned. "Just because we're stringing up a few bogeys right now doesn't mean that we don't have a lot of birdies left in our bag."

CHAPTER SEVENTY-TWO

The Summer of 1997 . . .

Lew couldn't help but chuckle to himself. A lot of things were starting to happen in his favor. If he continued to play his cards right he could make one last big score. Manipulating J Dub was simple. However, he needed to get the U.S. Attorney off of his back. In his mind Ellie Hackett presented a much more formidable obstacle to him than his partner.

Whenever Lew wanted to talk about things his experience told him to contact Monty and Raymond. They were trusted friends that he could count on. The favors had lasted a lifetime and had been extended both ways. He placed a couple of calls and invited them out for some target practice.

The guys liked to assemble late in the afternoon, usually an hour or so before the sun went down. Typically, the wind would die down at that time of day. They would go behind Lew's barn, set up the skeet machine and then fire away at the clay pigeons as the sun vanished beneath the horizon. The targets burst against a colorful and majestic sky.

As the oranges and yellows turned to dusk a sinister tone was cast upon the group. Monty and Raymond knew the routine. The rifles and skeet machine were returned to the barn. As the three men strolled out of the barn and across the driveway, Lew posed a question to his pseudo legal advisor. "Have you got anything in the works, Monty?"

Monty smiled. The strong-armed tactics that he learned while negotiating for the union leaders in the early days of his career had prepared him well.

"I've got a few more things that I need to have done," Lew hinted.

"You've always been good to us," Raymond said.

"Just keep those packets coming," Monty stated with a grin.

Lew stopped in mid-stride and looked at the two men straight on. He was sick and tired of the hassles that the government had been putting him through. "You need to find out what she's up to, Raymond."

Over the years Lew had angered quite a few women. Raymond was a tad bit confused. "Which one are you referring to?"

"Hackett," Lew responded.

Raymond acted like he thought that the tax matter had been resolved. "Is she still causing problems?"

"She won't get off my ass!" Lew exploded. The pressure of the investigation seemed to be causing him to have a few sleepless nights. He turned to Monty. "Have you come up with anything for El Cerdo?"

"Yeah, a couple of things have turned up," Monty replied.

Lew was all ears. "What kind of things?"

"Technical stuff," Monty replied. "She might not live in her district."

"Can you get to the bottom of it?"

Monty nodded. "That one is easy. I'll have to put a tail on her to get the answers on the other one," Monty offered.

Lew was very interested in what Monty was talking about. "Need some help?"

Monty nodded. "I'll have to hire some guys. That takes money."

"You two sit tight. I'll be right back," Lew said. He headed into his home.

In Lew's absence Raymond turned to Monty. "What have you found out?" Raymond asked.

"She has a house in her district, but she's not living in it," Monty alleged. "She's got some broad that she's renting it to."

"How long has she been doing that?"

"Six months. She's got her kid in a private school across the river," Monty explained. "She moved over there so that he'd be close to it. That way he wouldn't have to drive too far to class."

"That's in a different state!" Raymond exclaimed.

"Exactly," Monty said with a grin. "We'll get her."

"She can't be doing that," Raymond maintained. "What other stuff do you have on her?"

Lew appeared at the door. "I'll tell you about it later," Monty whispered.

Lew walked up to the men and handed them several packets wrapped in newspaper. "Here this should help both you guys out a little."

Large amounts of cash had been wrapped in the newspapers. "Get done what needs to be done," Lew ranted. "And make sure that you-know-who is taken care of."

Monty nodded.

"She thinks she has me this time, Raymond. Get her off of my ass. Talk to your friends in Washington!" Lew pleaded with the Congressman to use his authority to sway opinions.

Raymond was the quintessential politician. He knew how the game was played. However, tinkering with the Justice Department put him in tenuous territory. "That might be too tough even for me to pull off. She's putting people away, Lew."

"And I don't want to be one of them! I've paid you a ton to protect me! Use your influence!" Lew yelled.

224

"That's easier said than done," Raymond responded. "I'll do my best."

An evil grin spread over Lew's face. Everyone was a mark for him, even Monty and Raymond. Lew had learned early in life to try to get the other guy before the other guy got him. "You better give me more than your best. You remember one thing and keep it straight. If I go down, then you guys go with me."

Monty was petrified of going back to prison. "What do you mean?"

Lew had a smirk on his face that Monty wanted to slap. "Remember the party when you got out?"

Both men nodded in agreement. How could they ever forget that night? Cancun and Raven did anything that the two of them had requested. Lew paused and his grin reappeared. "I've still got the tape."

Raymond considered himself a family man. Lew's threat could put his political career in jeopardy. He glared at Lew and under his breath whispered, "You mother-fucker."

CHAPTER SEVENTY-THREE

A few weeks after that . . .

Monty and Raymond had some work to do. They both knew that their interests would best be served if they didn't waste any time. Lew had a mean, evil streak. When he coughed up the cash, they understood that he wanted immediate results. There was to be no delay.

There wasn't a whole lot for Monty to do during the day. He had served his sentence. The time that he spent at the halfway house got him ready to re-enter society. However, that wasn't as simple as it appeared. He had lost his livelihood and spent the better part of each day trying to reach out to his old contacts.

His day started out like most of the others, hanging out at his old law office and making a few phone calls. He shared a couple of cups of coffee and shot the breeze with whoever poked their head in the lunchroom. Then, just before lunch, Monty got into his car and made a drive that he hadn't made in a few years.

After negotiating several stoplights he wound up on the outskirts of town. As he pulled onto a state highway memories of his life before prison flashed through his mind. He had made this drive many times in the past. Nothing really had changed.

The farm fields were still sprouting wheat, corn, or soybeans. Storage bins that stockpiled grain dotted the countryside. A new Butler building or two was sprinkled across the landscape. The road crew had one lane shut down for asphalt patching. All in all, the more things changed, the more things stayed the same.

His pot-belly showed signs of reappearing. Monty felt good about putting some weight back on. The ponytail started to acquire some length. Now, when Monty put a rubber band around it, some hair actually dangled. The REDMAN chewing tobacco would slide across the dashboard on every right turn. Monty grinned. In his mind things were returning to normal.

He approached a flat stretch of the highway. He was on the part of the road that traversed the river bottom. Signs of civilization started to appear. He neared his old stomping grounds.

Monty couldn't help but notice the familiar surroundings. He drove past a used car lot located behind a chain link fence, a temporary church that operated out of a metal building, and a modular home sales trailer.

Two near-vacant strip malls came into view. Both were in need of repair. A pawn shop anchored one and the other had signs posted on it that read: GUNS / AMMO and CHECKS CASHED HERE.

An over-the-road truck dealership sat next to a dilapidated motor motel. CINDY's MOTEL always had one or two cars parked outside during the day. If it wasn't a traveling salesman, then it was someone that scored with a hooker or perhaps a married guy that had sneaked off for a "nooner" with some other guys' wife.

The truck stop toted diesel fuel and truck washes. A drag strip and dirt track were located on the river side of the road. Monty could see the hangars that housed single engine aircraft at the adjacent landing strip.

THE TREASURE CHEST was housed in an old Butler building. Just down from that was an area known as "The Promenade." During the night time hours the ladies would parade up and down the road in their skin tight jeans, shaking their money makers. Close by was PEDRO'S PORNO PARLOR where he and Lew frequented as young adults to visit the glory hole booths for a buck or two. Monty at one time had a huge client base located on that piece of the highway. He had spent a memorable foggy night there at one time.

SMOKEY's was the roadside tavern known for ice-cold longnecks. A winning lottery ticket was once purchased there and the portable sign in the parking lot served as a constant reminder that the place was luckier than most. Next to that was a heavy-equipment operator. Bulldozers, scrapers, and a backhoe could be seen beyond the barbed wire.

The hodge-podge of assorted businesses suggested a scattered zoning category. There were light industrial applications mixed in with warehouse storage facilities. Retail businesses stuck out like sore thumbs. It seemed like whoever had money and an idea could go into business on the river bottom. Anything was possible just so the township could collect tax dollars.

After he passed the offices of a heating and cooling contractor Monty turned his car into Fricke's Salvage Yard. Wrecked cars were stacked on top of each other. Several tow trucks could be seen on the fenced lot. The locked gate supported a "NO TRESPASSING" sign.

Two men approached Monty before he could get out of the car. Monty reached for the bundle of newspapers that he had placed on the passenger seat and jumped out to greet them.

"Long time, no see," Fricke said. Gary Fricke was a rough looking man in his early forties. He had gotten control of his father's business after his dad dropped over from a heart attack. That was back when he was in his twenties. The life of a junk peddler was tough and Gary showed the years.

His younger brother, by two years, was Larry Fricke. He had gotten the short end of the hereditary stick and lived with the nickname of Frack. He was the tougher of the two and had the face to vouch for it. Between the brawls, petty thefts, and Magnum escapades, Frack was lucky that he had made it this far in life.

The two of them together were street smart and fearless. They had the ability to tow away broken-down, semi-tractor trailers or swindle someone on a set of hot hubcaps. There wasn't anything that these two wouldn't do for a buck. Monty had been acquaintances with them for a number of years. He especially needed them to do his dirty work.

"You made it," Frack acknowledged.

"The halfway house was the toughest," Monty admitted. "You can see the light of freedom but can't quite reach it."

"Whatcha got for us?" Fricke blurted.

"A couple of jobs," Monty volunteered.

"Need anybody rubbed out?" Frack inquired. He was never one to mince any words.

Monty smiled. Frack hadn't changed a bit. He was always the one that begged for the dirty work. " . . . No, nothing like that."

"Easy stuff then," Frack uttered.

"For you it might be boring," Monty countered.

"Whatcha you need?" Fricke asked again. He could see the bundle of cash that Monty had in his hands and his eyes were feasting on it.

"Let's go inside and settle up and I'll tell you what I need to have done," Monty proposed.

"We've never been known for our smarts," Frack admitted.

The three men headed into the office of the world headquarters for Fricke's Salvage Yard. To enter the office the men had to climb up an outside set of stairs that led to the second floor office located above the garage of an older two-story home. Fricke's desk was cluttered with carburetors, hubcaps, and a steering wheel. The filing system for any paperwork appeared to be on the floor. Monty took a seat on a worn out leather couch that had foam busting from its seams. Monty proceeded to spell out his plans and then paid handsomely to have them carried out.

~ ~ ~

Raymond, on the other hand, had a totally different journey to make. His method of operation was a little more upscale than Monty's. Raymond put on a suit and bought a new tie. He then headed off to the U.S. Attorney's office to try to broker a deal. Politics were his business and he wanted to exert a little power.

It had been quite a while since he had spoken to Ellie Hackett. Politically, they were on opposite sides of the fence. Her appointment had been confirmed by the opposing party. Even though they had been invited to several of the same social gatherings, the two of them didn't have a lot of reason to speak with each other.

Yet, both of them were in positions of authority. They were powerful people in their own right. It wasn't such a bad idea for them to meet to air a little dirty laundry. Posturing was posturing. It was hard to tell when someone might need a favor.

Raymond felt uneasy the minute he walked into Ellie's office and sat down. He was used to being catered to and he could tell that she was doing everything in her might to intimidate him. For a power broker and deal maker that gave him an uncomfortable feeling. He was on her turf and wasn't real sure whether or not he was being recorded.

Ellie was cordial, yet cold. She was friendly on the surface, but businesslike in her approach. As Raymond sat, she stood and walked to the window quietly. Her back gave Raymond the impression that she was being standoffish. He was almost scared to speak.

After what seemed like hours of silence Raymond thought that he would pay Ellie a small compliment. "You should be congratulated for the excellent job you've been doing against white-collar crime in my district."

"That's a bunch of bull," Ellie said turning to him. They both knew that she almost put him away a decade earlier. Raymond lived in the gray areas of business. However, he always seemed to stay lily-white with his reputation. Her expertise in the white-collar crime activities had been hitting close to home for Raymond.

Raymond was surprised a tad by her reaction. "The party has noticed."

Ellie knew how Raymond could manipulate. She wanted to find out exactly what his motives were. "What are you here for?"

"You never know when we can help each other out."

"Like I said a minute ago, that's a bunch of bull." Ellie always felt as if she could see right through the façade that Raymond carried on the outside.

"It's not a good idea to be adversaries," Raymond cried.

"What are you fishing for . . . an update on the Zerrmann investigation?" She correctly surmised that Lew had gotten Raymond to do his dirty work for him.

Raymond shrugged. His eyes carefully followed Ellie as she walked back to her desk. She turned again and glared at him. Ellie knew that Raymond and Zerrmann were close associates. "You put the word out that I have his ass. And that's in spite of the fact that nobody is talking."

Raymond licked his lips. They were starting to dry at the corners. When that didn't work he reached for his chap stick and slowly worked it around his oral cavity. He took a big gulp and tried not to give her the impression that what she was talking about was hitting right to the core.

Ellie, still standing, placed both hands on her desk and leaned forward. "Look. Zerrmann has a paper trail that lasts a lifetime, Ray. And I'm not concerned about what politics you bring into this office."

Her eyes pierced through him. He could do nothing but receive her fury. "I was hoping that we could have had a more enlightening conversation." In fact, a conversation didn't really exist. Raymond had pretty much done nothing but listen.

Ellie was still peeved at what had happened years earlier. "I intend to do the same thing to Zerrmann that I did with your other associate. With my recommendation he'll never see daylight again."

Raymond had gone in with the full intention of wielding his clout. Instead, he wanted to crawl under the desk.

Ellie knew where Raymond's next stop was. "Make sure that you pass that word on."

CHAPTER SEVENTY-FOUR

September 1997 . . .

Lew had his buddies to thank for referring him to the best tax litigator in the area. Garrett O'Connor was a well-established tax authority and worked diligently behind the scenes. He was a licensed certified public accountant and an attorney that specialized in civil and criminal tax controversies. He served on numerous committees and was well connected in the community. His expertise was recognized statewide and, to a small extent, on the national level.

O'Connor had Ellie in somewhat of a pickle. Tax evasion is a crime only if intent can be proven. If intent can't be proven, then the matter becomes tax avoidance. From a criminal perspective that is a major difference.

Tax avoidance can become a civil issue with the Internal Revenue Service. Tax evasion is a criminal matter with the U. S. Attorney's office. The major disparity is that with the crime of tax evasion, felony offenses can be charged. A guilty verdict calls for prison time and restitution to the victim, which is the United States government, along with fines and penalties. With tax avoidance the IRS must decide if it wants to sue a taxpayer in civil court.

So, O'Connor used that knowledge and forced Ellie's hand. His argument was that Lew had not intentionally evaded taxes. Since Lew and Walter kept their mouths shut and didn't talk, there was no admission of guilt. The two of them stuck together and didn't allow the government to intimidate them. Therefore, the government had a weaker case against them. Garrett also found out through his connections that Ellie and Peter had a meeting scheduled with attorneys for the government to discuss the viability of the case.

Monty had been working the streets. He kept his ears open. The scuttlebutt was that Ellie was having an affair with a married man. The likely liaison was with a fellow that worked in the U. S. Attorneys office by the name of Peter Dooley.

The role for Gary Fricke and Larry Fricke was well defined. When Monty handed over the money in the world headquarters of Fricke's Salvage Yard he also gave the two thugs a digital camera. The instructions to Fricke and Frack were to follow Ellie and Peter on their way to meet the attorneys for the government.

On the morning of the mission Fricke and Frack sat a couple of blocks away from the U. S. Attorney's office and waited for a white Taurus to leave the secured parking lot. The vehicle would have official government license plates and be driven by Ellie. Peter was to accompany her.

The information that they had received was right on the money. Ellie exited the lot just after eight in the morning and Peter sat beside her in the front seat. Fricke and Frack pulled their SUV out behind them.

Tailing someone isn't the easiest thing in the world to do. However, in this particular instance, access to the interstate system was elementary. It was easy on and easy off. The two thugs just had to make sure that they had enough gas and were coy enough to not get noticed. Within a couple of minutes they could tell that they were home free. Ellie and Peter frolicked in the front seat and were oblivious to anything that happened around them.

Frack got a charge out of snapping the pictures. While Fricke drove, Frack busied himself with the camera. He took several shots of Ellie and Peter in an animated conversation. A few more shots captured Peter leaning over and giving Ellie a kiss on the cheek and a tongue in her ear. As time went on Frack captured Peter's head disappearing into Ellie's lap.

The beauty of their work was that all of the pictures had a date stamp. Plus, Frack made sure that he got the license plate in the frame. He was confident that the shots would look even better when blown up.

Aside from the picture-taking episodes, the trip was non eventful. Acres and acres of Midwestern corn fields passed through the rear view mirror. Halfway through the trip the lovebirds exited I-55 to fill up with gasoline. Fricke followed and maneuvered the SUV to the side lot of a convenience mart.

Frack took several pictures of Ellie, in casual clothes, pumping gas into the car and paying with a credit card at the pump. Peter cleaned the windshield. They embraced and kissed again. Peter grabbed the keys and took the wheel for the drive into Chicago. Fricke pulled out of the lot and quickly settled in comfortably behind them.

"Damn, he's got a lead foot," Fricke exclaimed.

"You don't think that he thinks he's being tailed do you?"

"Hell, no. Look at them. Get the camera!"

Frack positioned the camera to shoot more pictures. Ellie had scooted closer to Peter and her head disappeared from view. "Did ya get it? Did ya get it?" Fricke yelled.

"Oh, yeah . . . the whole move!"

The men reveled in their success. Their mission had turned into an incredible display of good fortune. Frack got a great shot of the Taurus moving past the Chicago City Limits sign. Ellie had moved over next to Peter for that one.

The two followed them to the downtown Westin Hotel and continued to snare snapshot after snapshot. Peter and Ellie were caught holding hands and checking into the hotel together. Fricke and Frack knew that Monty was going to be very pleased.

~ ~ ~

Two Days Later . . .

Monty had gotten a call and couldn't wait to pull into the lot of Fricke's Salvage Yard. Fricke and Frack scurried out to meet him. "Hey boss, we're due for a bonus," Fricke gushed.

"What was she up to?" Monty inquired.

Frack handed over the camera. He was quite proud of the work that he accomplished. "She's quite a little lovebird!"

"Yeah, about the only thing that we don't have is the audio," said Fricke. The brothers laughed.

Monty flipped through the memory command on the digital camera. Picture after picture showed Ellie and Peter in some sort of affectionate position. He was shocked that the quality and quantity came out as well as it did. "You two deserve a bonus! This is great stuff," Monty called out. "Did they have any idea that they were being followed?"

"If they did, it didn't seem to bother them," Fricke said with a chuckle. "Look at the two of them . . . over and over, on every pic."

He was right. Ellie and Peter put on quite a public display of affection. Monty knew exactly what to do. He seized the camera and headed straight for his car. "I owe you guys one."

"We know you're good for it."

"That's one job down and one to go."

Fricke knew that Monty would come through with a nice present after the second job was wrapped up. "We'll take care of that when the time is right, boss."

"Good job, guys." Monty raced the car off of the lot. He had to meet someone.

It was a gorgeous autumn day. The beautiful blue sky was cloudless. A cold front had moved through a few days earlier and had knocked all of the humidity out of the air. Monty went to the local park. That was a favorite spot for him and Raymond. They could walk around the thirty acre lake in anonymity.

The duck population had invaded the area. It was always a challenge to avoid the droppings on the asphalt jogging path. A wind surfer tried to negotiate a two foot wave. That was a tough task on a calm day. A local rowing team practiced their rhythmic strokes in tandem.

Raymond was all too anxious to meet Monty for an extended lunch. "Did anything turn up?' he asked.

"Are you kidding me?" Monty fired back. He handed the camera to Ray. "Here are your meat and potatoes."

"What was she up to?"

Monty was quite proud of the hires that he had made. "Flip through the memory. She and Peter were having quite the little fling," Monty exulted.

Ray viewed shot after shot. A wide grin encompassed his face. "This is what the doctor ordered."

"Looks like El Cerdo met her match," Monty exclaimed proudly.

"You don't suppose that this was on government money, do you?" Ray queried. He was well aware that the dates could be properly documented.

"With those government plates on the car and the date stamps on the pictures I'm sure that someone can easily look at her day timer and figure out what was going on." Monty relished the thought.

Ray said with a sly smile, "You don't suppose that these pictures would be enough evidence to open up an investigation for inappropriate behavior, do you?" Raymond was tickled by his own sarcasm.

Monty looked and Ray and laughed. " . . . Nah. You don't think that any of this occurred on taxpayer money, do you?" Monty had thought up that payback during his days in prison.

Water spouted out of a spring and cascaded down a hill. It formed a short, but robust waterfall. Raymond stopped and looked at the flowing water. He was buried in thought.

"Screw her!" Monty said viciously. "That bitch got me for one helluva long time!"

"Thanks for the camera, Monty. I know just where do go with this," Ray chuckled. "El Cerdo. That is a good one, Monty." He laughed over and over. "Where did you pick that nickname up anyway?"

"Prison gave me quite an education." Monty couldn't contain his devilish grin. "I taught myself Spanish."

CHAPTER SEVENTY-FIVE

November 1997 . . .

The day was gray and overcast. It was one of those late fall days in the Midwest where the sky sort of blends into the trees. Most of the leaves were on the ground. The wind was blowing and the temperature was raw. There were no golfers to be seen. Even the boys stayed at home. It was a nice day to stay inside, warm up a pot of chili, wrap up in a quilt, and read a book in front of the fireplace.

Yet, Lew was bored. His circle of friends was limited and he had nothing to do. Sitting at home didn't give him the action that he desired and being around the pro shop never made him feel comfortable. He retreated to the objects with which he could relate. After adorning his insulated coveralls he hopped onto his motorcycle and raced over to the golf course.

Lew didn't bother stopping in the pro shop. He could tell by the looks of the parking lot that only J Dub and Julie were in the building. The weather appeared to discourage even the most optimistic and hearty golfers, no one was playing.

J Dub and Julie were the sole occupants of the clubhouse, aside from Bogey, who was limping around on three legs now. Bogey had managed the best that he could after the accident, but the last year had taken its toll on him. Even though the bandages had long disappeared, the scar from the accident still remained. His days of going eighteen holes with the boys were probably over, but he had managed nine holes as recently as two days before. Bogey had hobbled around on three legs all summer and the extra work had taken a little endurance away from him. His aging body was missing that extra oomph.

J Dub and Julie were taking the break in the weather, stringing up Christmas lights and enjoying the warmth of the clubhouse when the noise of a motorcycle raced by. Julie glanced out the window and saw Lew going full throttle onto the golf course. "What's he up to today?" she asked J Dub.

"Your guess is as good as mine."

"Let's hope that he stays out there and doesn't come in here to bother us."

"Do you really think that he would bother to get into the Christmas spirit?" J Dub quipped.

"Are you kidding?" Julie cried out. "He might as well be Scrooge."

Out on the golf course Lew pulled up to a new bulldozer that the course had acquired from insurance proceeds. He had played on it a few weeks earlier and had left it parked on the side of the eighth fairway. For lack of anything better to do he started the bulldozer up and began moving dirt from one side of the fairway to the other.

It appeared that he was shaving dirt down from the left side of the fairway and carrying it over to the right side of the fairway. Then he would shape some mounds with the dirt that he had dumped. It made no sense to carry out this work on such a damp, chilly day unless, of course, he wanted to raid the checkbook again.

After going back and forth for a while it appeared that he got disoriented. While stopping and starting and pulling forward and backwards, Lew had lost sight of his motorcycle. *Kaboom!* A collision ensued. He had backed over his Harley.

The impact startled Lew. He stopped the dozer and foolishly looked around to see if anyone had seen him. Then he jumped off, walked to the rear to survey the damaged bike, and added insult to injury by kicking the dozer.

The boot didn't stand a chance against the hard steel of the earthmover. Lew injured his foot. "Dammit!" he yelled. He grabbed his foot and limped away.

J Dub and Julie were putting the finishing touches on the Christmas decorations. The tree was decorated with ornaments. The multi-colored lights blinked on and off around the pro shop. Bogey had curled up in the bunting under the tree and was napping. Lew hobbled through the door and headed behind the counter. "You're back early," Julie stated. "I saw you fly by here a little while ago."

"Needed some water," Lew meekly replied. He wasn't about to admit that he hurt his foot and wrecked his motorcycle.

"There's a water jug on number four," J Dub volunteered.

Lew snapped at J Dub. "I didn't want to drink water out of a water jug!"

He shuffled over to the cooler and reached for a bottle of water. Julie noticed that he was moving slowly. She asked, "What did you do to your leg?"

"My leg is fine!" Lew shouted. "It's a little cold outside." The racket that Lew made when he raised his voice startled Bogey. He started to growl.

Julie continued the interrogation. No music blared out upon Lew's arrival. "Then where is your cycle? I didn't hear you pull up."

Lew was agitated. He was short with Julie. "Are there any more questions today that you'd like the answers to?"

"Well, I was going to ask about the meaning of life, but I'll take a rain check," Julie smiled sarcastically.

Lew looked toward J Dub. "I need a ride."

J Dub looked perplexed. *Why would he be asking me for a ride if he has his cycle?* "Where do you want to go?" J Dub asked.

"I need to go home to get my pickup." He stared at J Dub. "Are you full of questions today too?"

J Dub looked at Julie. Nothing seemed to be making any sense. "Where's your cycle?" he pried. "We saw you go out on the course on it."

Lew became unglued. He went totally berserk. He grabbed a towel off of the counter and flung it to the floor followed by a stack of magazines. He bounced the water bottle off of the wall. "Screw both of you! I'm sick of all the questions. I'll do what I want! Is that good enough for you two?"

J Dub and Julie started to giggle at the temper tantrum that Lew was throwing. Bogey started to bark repeatedly.

"Tell that lousy mutt to shut up, J Dub!" Lew ordered. "Listen, since both of you are in here, I'm going to tell you something that I have wanted to say for years." He reached up and ripped down the Christmas lights. "There! We needed to short these out years ago for an insurance claim! Who needs all of this Christmas crap on a golf course anyway?"

After witnessing the lights being ripped down, J Dub had just about had enough. "What are you talking about?"

"You heard me!" Lew got right up into J Dub's face in spite of the fact that J Dub towered above him. "And secondly, I'm tired of the groups that you're letting tee off on Sundays. If you allow one of them out here, then the next thing you know we'll have twenty of them out here. Then our business will start going down the crapper!"

"You mean what's left of it," J Dub countered.

" . . . Yeah! And that's in spite of how hard I work around here!" Lew ranted. Bogey's bark turned into a constant growl. The tone of Lew's voice toward J Dub had upset the dog.

"If you're talking about Coach and his buddies, then they haven't been around for years. Not since you ran them out of here," J Dub argued.

"Yeah, I'm talking about Coach and his tar-baby buddies! Pretty soon they'll be over here eating watermelon and fishing out of our lakes. Then the black g-men will investigate us for tax evasion!" Lew was clearly on a roll. Bogey tottered over and nipped at Lew's pants. Lew kicked his leg toward Bogey and landed a blow to the side of the dog.

J Dub took a quick glance at Julie. She had privately expressed to J Dub her dilemma with the sexual advances that Lew had made toward her.

"You two keep your damn mouths shut!" Lew screamed. The pressure of the IRS investigation had visibly shaken him.

Julie had reached her limit with Lew. "Go screw yourself . . . you lousy piece of shit!" She raced behind the counter and grabbed a video cassette. "If they don't get you on tax evasion, then I'll get you on sexual harassment!"

Julie grabbed her coat, flung it over her shoulder, and bolted out the door with the video cassette. She slammed the door so hard that the building vibrated.

J Dub glared at Lew. For years he had been a wonderful servant for Lew, but he too had reached his boiling point and now he measured his words carefully. "What's wrong? Are you afraid you might not win against the tax man?"

Lew stared at J Dub, but J Dub continued. "Are they a little bigger than you and you don't like it?"

Lew remained silent. J Dub was ready to release years' worth of frustration. He kept going. "Or do you think that those black guys put up stiffer competition for your women?"

The anger was rising in Lew. His face started to redden. He bit down on his teeth so hard that his jaws seemed to pop out of the sides of his face.

J Dub kept pushing. "You're no man! In fact if they dropped it off your name, do you know what you'd be?"

Lew started to clench his jaws harder.

"You'd be Lew Zerr! Which is exactly what you are . . . a loser! . . . A lifetime loser!"

Lew, shaking with anger, reached for the checkbook and wrote a check to himself.

"Go to hell!" J Dub shouted.

Lew ripped a check out of the checkbook and in an effort to mask his misery, glared at J Dub.

"Now get out of here!" J Dub hollered.

Bogey started barking as Lew headed for the door. Lew stomped out into the cold with Bogey chasing after him on three legs and barking incessantly. Once outside, Lew realized he was completely without transportation and frantically jumped on J Dub's Truckster.

Lew was not at all familiar with operating the Truckster. As he turned the key and floored the pedal, the front tires unexpectedly raised off the ground, then lurched the vehicle forward to where Bogey stood barking. Lew heard the yelp and felt the thump as the wheels rolled over Bogey. "That's what you get, you no-good mutt," Lew hollered. "Next time maybe you'll get out of the way," he yelled as he delivered a kick to the dog. In seconds he sped off of the parking lot.

J Dub sprinted out of the clubhouse to where Bogey lay whimpering. Already his breathing was labored and a slow trickle of blood came from his nose. J Dub was on the ground cradling the dog's head and whispering to him. "Bogey, you didn't need to help me do the dirty work."

On that dreary day in the howling wind, J Dub gathered Bogey's broken body into his lap. There would be no need for a vet. He raised his knees, slumping forward and encircling the dog, bringing him close to his chest. J Dub felt his heart beat solidly against Bogey's side. He rocked him tenderly, comforting him and talking to him. Bogey raised his head and looked into J Dub's eyes. And there they stayed, connected as best friends in wordless understanding, until Bogey's eyes fluttered to a close and his breath came no more.

CHAPTER SEVENTY-SIX

The Next Day . . .

The cold front passed through. The weather was a little warmer and the sun a tad brighter the next day. J Dub shared his grief with Marcia at home the night before. After a sleepless night he came to a decision on where to bury Bogey. BT, Paul, Rollie, Paco, Elia, and Fred had finished their round of golf and had gathered at their table in the rear of the pro shop.

"I can't believe the little guy isn't around to go a few holes with us any more," Elia said sorrowfully.

"It happened so fast," J Dub replied tearfully. "At least he didn't suffer."

"That damn Lew," Fred cried out. "Somebody needs to slap him into tomorrow."

"It's over and done with," J Dub blurted through sniffles. "Bogey was a good one." J Dub took his handkerchief out of his pocket and blew his nose. "Say guys, you don't mind if I tend to a little personal business by myself, do you?" All the heads at the back table shook from side to side. "Can you watch things for a while, Julie?"

She nodded. "Of course I can."

"I'll be back in a few minutes," J Dub said as he went out the door.

"What was he in such a hurry about?" Paco inquired.

"I think that he wanted to spend one last minute with Bogey," Julie replied with tears in her eyes.

"Ole Bogey was getting around pretty well on three legs," Rollie said. "We're all going to miss that little guy."

"Not as much as J Dub," Julie cried.

"That little guy was a friend to all of us," Paul stated. "J Dub will never be the same."

"They did everything together around here," Fred said.

"Bogey nearly made the coffee in the morning when we rolled into the pro shop," Rollie stated.

"It's such a sad day," Julie said as she began to weep. "He was part of our family," she sobbed as tears rolled down her cheeks. BT walked over and placed his arm around Julie. She reached for a tissue and wiped her runny nose. The sniffles wouldn't cease. "I don't think that J Dub wanted you guys to see a grown man cry."

After the incident the day before J Dub had wrapped Bogey in his windbreaker that was soaked in blood. He had placed Bogey's body in his bed and had covered it with a blanket. As he went to retrieve the body he grabbed a crate out of the cart barn and fashioned a makeshift coffin. J Dub loaded the remains onto the seat next to him and threw a shovel into a golf cart. He headed for the driving range.

J Dub finished digging the grave down by the driving range. He had shared so many moments with Bogey on the range that he thought that that would be the best place for his final resting spot. They would normally go over to the edge of the range. J Dub felt that it would be appropriate to put Bogey in the same spot where they had shared so much time.

In the past, Bogey had sat on the driving range on many days, cocked his head, and listened to J Dub vent his emotions. He would watch J Dub pound ball after ball to improve his game. When J Dub would take a break Bogey would roll over on his back and insist that his stomach be scratched. There was no doubt that this was where he belonged.

J Dub paused for a second and stared at the coffin that he had placed on the seat next to him. He grabbed the box that contained Bogey's remains and slowly lowered it into the grave. After a brief moment J Dub did what he dreaded to do. With tears forming in his eyes, J Dub took the shovel and threw some dirt into the hole until the entire grave was full. J Dub angrily threw the shovel back into the golf cart.

Then he stepped back and sobbed.

It was over in a few minutes. J Dub gained his composure, got back into the golf cart, and began the journey back to the clubhouse. As J Dub pulled into the parking lot, Lew was parking the Truckster in his spot by the door. Dried blood was still on the front of the Truckster. "Big Shot" began to play. Lew bounced off of the Truckster and hurried over to J Dub.

"You can forget about buying this place now. It's too late," Lew announced as if it was punishment for the argument in the pro shop. He was oblivious to what J Dub had just done.

"What are you trying to do, kill me, just like all the others?"

"A deal is a deal."

J Dub stood his ground. "And you've had home field advantage the entire time, haven't you?"

"For a guy like me that's worked all of his life, isn't that the way the game's supposed to be played?" Lew's narcissistic behavior had reached a new level.

"Over my dead body," J Dub blurted.

Lew reached into his pants pocket and pulled out a black velvet pill box. "Did you finally decide that you want a little Nirvana?" Lew made reference to the cyanide tablets that he always carried, just like Hitler. "This will help serve the purpose."

J Dub looked fiercely into the eyes of his partner. After biting his lip he turned and walked away. Lew had a pleased smirk on his face.

CHAPTER SEVENTY-SEVEN

Thanksgiving 1997 . . .

J Dub lamented the fact that he lost his temper in the pro shop. He was aware that the blowup may have bruised Lew's fragile ego so severely that fifteen years of hard work had been destroyed. True to form, Lew didn't have the guts to walk into the pro shop to speak to J Dub. Instead, he sent a letter to J Dub addressed to the pro shop via registered mail. The notice informed J Dub to be at Walter Hancock's office at three o'clock in the afternoon a few days before Christmas.

J Dub had a small number of days to prepare for what might happen. Another meeting was scheduled with Marcia, Curt, and Hank Lowery. "He told me that it was too late for me to buy the place," J Dub admitted moments after sitting down in Hank's office.

"That's his prerogative," Hank conceded. "It looks to me like it is the classic minority partner freeze out," Hank offered.

"What is that?" J Dub asked.

"It sounds like he has already employed one of them," Hank started. "In setting up the lease payments to himself he siphoned profits out of the corporation."

"Is that illegal?"

"Not really. He controls the decisions made by the corporation."

Curt butted in. "It sure sounds unethical."

"It's extremely unethical!" Hank stressed. J Dub was sick to his stomach. The possibility of throwing fifteen years down the drain was becoming a very real situation. "Can I get you something to drink?" Hank offered.

J Dub nodded. "Anything wet."

Hank's assistant brought sodas in for all of them.

"He's a real clever guy. You're up against a pretty shrewd adversary," Hank ventured. "He doesn't sound like much of a partner."

J Dub was clearly worried about his future. "What move is he going to make next?"

Hank got up, walked over to the mini-refrigerator that was in his office, and grabbed more ice. His mind was buried in thought. "You won't like what I have to say," he started.

J Dub turned to Marcia and had a resolved look on his face. "My wife has prepared me for the worst."

"It's highly unlikely that he will sell you the business." Hank paused a second to let the news sink in. "What he'll probably do is one of several things. He could either sell off assets . . ."

"Is that legal?"

Hank nodded. " . . . or he could transfer the assets to another corporation that he controls one hundred percent and dissolve the old corporation."

"I suppose that is legal too."

Once again Hank nodded. " . . . or he may decide to merge or consolidate the company under a plan that is unfair to you."

J Dub placed his hand to his brow and applied pressure. "It sounds like my butt will be sore by the time he gets done with me," J Dub deadpanned, "despite the partnership agreement."

Hank agreed. "He can do what he wants to you. He's probably figuring that you don't have the financial resources to fight him."

"If it boils down to all of this, can you help me?" J Dub asked.

"Possibly from a consulting standpoint," Hank answered. "You'd probably be better off taking some referrals from me and getting a top notch firm to help you. It's more work than my practice can handle."

"Thanks for enlightening me," J Dub announced. "It sounds like I'm going to get an expensive lesson on what it's like to live in the real world of business."

Hank nodded. " . . . From someone that will put up the fight of his life," he said.

~ ~ ~

The investigation of Lew and Walter by special agents Booker and Hayden of the Criminal Investigation Division of the IRS had run its course. The evidence had been gathered, compiled, and presented. What remained was in the hands of the U.S. Attorney's office.

Ellie and Peter had been working overtime on the case. Ellie's tenacity had made her a very effective prosecutor. Her experience in the white-collar crime area was unmatched. After looking at all of the evidence and presenting it to the attorneys for the government in Chicago, she and Peter realized that the legal nuances involved did not make a slam dunk case. Yet Ellie was willing to personally put her efforts behind the scenes just so she could get Lew Zerrmann.

The two of them had many discussions concerning the complexities of the case. They thought that it would be wise to invite Booker and Hayden over for a brain storming session to see if everything was covered or some minute detail had been omitted.

Nothing glamorous can be stated about a business-like meeting in a conference room. There were no windows to shed daylight on the gathering. A pot of coffee and a pitcher of water sat on a tray at one end of the table. Booker and Hayden came prepared with their evidence. Booker had meticulously prepared a time line and documented every little detail in building a circumstantial argument.

"Have we uncovered every loose stone?" Ellie started.

"We know that it's a complex case," Peter added.

Booker was proud of the work that he and Hayden had done on the investigation. They had methodically gathered information and cross-referenced their sources. "Nothing has changed from our first analysis," Booker said. "Except now we are more prepared with accurate and original documents."

"He evaded taxes and we know how he did it," Hayden included.

"It's all right here," Booker stated as he stretched his arms to show all of the evidence that had been spread out across the table.

"We have a few problems to deal with," Ellie explained.

"It's all circumstantial," Peter clarified. "You know that we don't have as great of a chance for success when we go that route."

"We've got a ten-year history all written down," Booker whined. "Between what the partner gave us, and the evidence taken in the raid, and the interviews, everything points to the obvious."

"It doesn't solve out basic dilemma though," Peter stressed.

"Zerrmann hired Garrett O'Connor," Ellie offered. "You know that. He's the best in the business. He told his client to shut up."

"Everything that we have is circumstantial," Peter reiterated. "We have to get around that. It becomes too confusing for a jury to follow. We might not get a conviction."

Booker and Hayden glanced at each other and shook their heads. They had gone above and beyond the call of duty in putting the case together. The last thing that they wanted to hear was that their efforts were not good enough. "We've tried everything that we know," Booker conceded.

"Including a wire?" Peter suggested.

"You know about the fine line between avoid and evade," Ellie put forth.

"All too well," Booker said as he reluctantly nodded his head. His many years of experience had seen several targets go scot-free on technicalities.

"Garrett O'Connor is maintaining that it was an innocent mistake that his client made. It went unnoticed for a long time by the IRS, therefore the client thought that he was doing everything properly," Ellie explained.

"He's suggesting that his client avoided taxes rather than evaded them," Peter chimed in.

"That's a bunch of BS," Booker lamented.

"Both of you know that and Peter and I know that," Ellie agreed.

"But he can make a convincing argument to a jury," Peter continued.

"So much so, that it puts the case in peril. You know how skittish our guys get on a fifty-fifty deal," Ellie stated.

"With the taxes that he avoided added to penalties and fines he owes us nearly four million," Hayden interjected. "That's easy to determine. We had that figured out in the first forty-eight hours of this thing."

"And we've got nearly a half million invested in the investigation," Ellie added.

"The case is written down in black and white," Hayden cried. "It's not going to change."

"And it's all signed by the two of them," Booker added.

"But we can't prove intent if nobody talks," Ellie conceded. "We need a taped confession. Look, I'm ready to take a chance on this case. I want his ass worse than anybody. But without a confession, everything's down the drain. The thought of that disgusting racist spitting out the hook a second time absolutely nauseates me."

~ ~ ~

J Dub notified Hank to meet him at Walter Hancock's office a few days before Christmas. Julie was instructed to take care of things at the golf course. As much as he didn't want to admit it, he felt that his last days at Prairie Winds Golf Course might be numbered. For some reason it hadn't seemed the same around there. Easy Earl was no longer around. Bogey was gone. The struggle to hang on had affected his attitude about life in general. That, coupled with the gloomy winter weather, brought about a mood of despair.

There was one thing left for J Dub to do prior to the meeting. He picked up the phone and telephoned a confidant.

"I might be ready to take out that insurance policy," J Dub started.

"What do you mean?"

"It looks like in order to help myself . . . I have the opportunity to help you too."

"What did you decide?"

"Where do you want me to be fitted?"

"Glory be! This will give all of us a better chance," Booker exclaimed.

J Dub headed over to the Internal Revenue Service building and allowed Booker and Hayden to get the proper measurements for him to wear a wire. Even though the technology was quite sophisticated, the bug was actually simple and easily hidden. The quality of the sound was outstanding, too.

It was now up to Booker and Hayden to do what they did best. They assured him that they would be close by in a van and that plenty of reinforcements would be around the corner in the event that anything went wrong. J Dub wasn't too excited about having his fate in the hands of investigators, but he had come to the conclusion that he needed to gather some evidence on his own in the event a civil suit was to occur at a later date.

The day arrived for the meeting in Walter's office. The weather was sunny, but crisp. There was a little nip in the air which had been expected around the holidays. J Dub parked his pickup and strolled down the sidewalk. He was still optimistic that something favorable could be worked out between the partners. His desire was to buy the golf course. Outside of playing on the professional tour, purchasing the golf course had become his major goal in life.

He peeked in a couple of directions to see if there was any sight of the van that Booker said that he would occupy. Booker didn't disappoint him. A white panel van was parked a half of a block away. The lettering on the outside of the van read: WATER POLLUTION CONTROL VIDEO INSPECTION UNIT.

Booker and Hayden sat inside the van amidst all of the surveillance equipment. Booker had seen J Dub's pickup drive up and park. Hayden waited for the moment when J Dub would speak. He was instructed to do that prior to entering Walter's office.

"Testing one, two, three," J Dub announced as he walked down the sidewalk. The sound was wonderful. Booker flashed the lights on and off to give a signal to J Dub that everything was in perfect working order.

The only item that remained was for J Dub to get Walter and Lew to talk. He entered the door and was greeted by Hank who had arrived about five minutes ahead of J Dub. Walter's assistant lavished a few formalities on them and escorted them to the conference room.

Seated around the conference table were Lew, Walter, and Monty. No one had a smile on their face. No pleasantries were exchanged. That was not a good sign. J Dub immediately felt the negative energy that permeated the room. What was just as scary was the lack of eye contact between the parties. It seemed as if everyone had their vision glued to the top of the table.

Monty spoke up first. He was very straightforward and rambled in monotone. "J Dub, we have never met. My name is Maurice DiMonte. Lew has asked us to gather at this meeting to help facilitate a transaction that he is trying to make. He has expressed a desire to sell the golf course to you, but you have no motivation in completing the transaction."

"That's not true. I've asked questions about the business and can't seem to get any answers to my satisfaction."

Monty was terse. "My client, Lew Zerrmann, has informed me of the buy/sell agreement that the two of you have in place. He feels that he has performed admirably under the terms of that agreement," Monty continued.

"And so have I."

Meanwhile, Booker and Hayden used hand gestures in the van. They tried their best to egg J Dub on. Both sat with headphones on and waited for any bit of incriminating evidence that they could record. "Come on J Dub," Booker urged.

Hank spoke up. "My client has indicated that he would like to buy the golf course under the terms of the partnership agreement."

Monty countered. "My client has instructed me to inform you that he has found another purchaser for the golf course."

"I want to buy it!" J Dub shouted. "No one has told me how a business with six thousand dollars worth of income can justify a five million dollar sales price. Do you know, Walter?"

Walter fidgeted with his hands. He looked down at the table and away from J Dub. It was apparent that Walter had been told to keep quiet.

J Dub turned his focus to Lew. " . . . How about you, Lew? Where is the money going?"

Lew sat silently at the table. He would have nothing to say. J Dub glared at his spineless partner with the hopes that Lew could feel the wrath of J Dub's anger. Lew cast his eyes downward and didn't blink.

After thirty seconds of silence Monty spoke. "I am here to complete the transaction."

"I have the option and right of first refusal to buy the business," J Dub declared.

"That is not in Mr. Zerrmann's best interest. It is his feeling that as a minority shareholder you have no rights."

"Then I'll take my twenty percent cut. Things could be worse."

"And they may be," Monty expounded, "since you have no rights as a minority shareholder. Mr. Zerrmann does not feel that your twenty percent stake is worth anything."

J Dub glanced at Hank. He had been prepared for that answer but still hated to hear it. "Sure it is," he replied.

"It is my client's feeling that on paper it may appear that way. However, if you were to take this in front of a judge, then Mr. Zerrmann would state that he feels your interest in the business has zero value," Monty announced.

J Dub looked directly at Lew. Lew sat motionless. His eyes had shifted to the wall. They were fixed on a spot and Lew didn't flinch. J Dub was furious that Lew wouldn't even look at him. "Is that what you would say, Lew? After fifteen years?"

Lew was stoic.

Booker and Hayden were discouraged. "They're not going to say anything," Booker said with a disappointed tone.

"Have your lawyer contact us," Monty offered.

"He's right here."

"We have a lot of work to do in a short period of time. Mr. Zerrmann wants to close on the sale of this property in sixty days," Monty rambled. "If you don't like that, then Mr. Zerrmann has instructed me to tell you that you can sue him."

"I can't do that. All of my money is in the business," J Dub begged.

J Dub looked again at Walter. "Where's the money, Walter?" Walter was frozen in time. "Are you going to sit there and stay quiet too?"

Walter's eyes were focused down on the table. He nervously tapped his pen against a stack of papers.

Hank looked at J Dub. He could feel his pain. Lew and Walter were not going to say anything. The meeting was being conducted exactly as he had imagined.

J Dub glared again at Lew. "Winning on this deal is more important to you than putting me on the sidewalk with a wife and three kids, isn't it Lew?"

Lew's eyes stayed focused on the wall. He didn't move a muscle.

J Dub was irate. To be treated like this by a greedy old man was demeaning. "After fifteen years, is that what you plan to do, Lew?"

245

The silence was numbing.

The more silent the room became, the more incensed J Dub got. "Dawn to dusk? Seven days a week? Is this what I get, Lew?"

Lew sat like a statue.

J Dub exploded out of the chair. He wanted to grab Lew and Walter by the shoulders and shake them down. "You three deserve each other! This is nothing but a crock of crap!"

J Dub threw a stack of papers off of the conference table. "You guys haven't heard the end of this!" J Dub glanced over to his lawyer. "Let's go Hank."

They exited the room and got outside as quickly as they could. Booker and Hayden slowly peeled off the headphones. "That guy is an asshole," Booker stated to Hayden. "We need to bear down on that scumbag."

J Dub and Hank ambled down the sidewalk. "I can't say that I didn't see it coming," Hank declared.

"If that's the way he wants to be, then let's hunker down and get ready for a fight."

J Dub got into his pickup truck. All of the pressures of the last fifteen years had reached an emotional crescendo. He didn't know what to say to Marcia. She had been right all along. He certainly hoped that she didn't throw it back into his face. Virtually everything that he had worked for all of his life had gone down the drain. He gripped the steering wheel as tightly as he could and privately bawled all the way home. He vowed to get even.

CHAPTER SEVENTY-EIGHT

The Next Day . . .

Lew moved forward with his plan. He had entered into the buy/sell arrangement with J Dub years earlier and had no intention of honoring it. Lew returned to Grady Patterson who had been his attorney when the lawsuit from the Morton heirs had been dismissed. Now he needed advice from Grady Patterson on a different matter.

Grady was at the point in his career where the cocktail hour was a lot more important than wrangling around with other people's problems. He had taken care of various things for Lewferd E. Zerrmann off-and-on for the past thirty years and was slightly perturbed that Lew needed to meet so abruptly. "What is so important that it can't wait until after the holidays?" Grady asked as he motioned for Lew to take a seat. "It's only a couple of days before Christmas."

"I need a little help," Lew replied.

"More free advice is a better way to put it," Grady paraphrased. He was used to the way Lew operated.

"I want to legally make sure that I can do what I want to do."

"If you would hire a good lawyer, then you can probably do anything you damn well please," Grady retaliated. Lew's penchant for whittling the legal fees down had been widely acknowledged. His way of paying lawyers was to trade something for their services. If he could find one that golfed, then he would trade greens fees for legal services rendered.

"As you well know, I want to get the golf course sold."

"Considering the other messes you are in that should be the least of your problems," Grady deadpanned.

"But it's my partner."

Grady knew J Dub. He personally liked the kid and knew that Lew had taken advantage of him from the very first day of their liaison. J Dub had been helpful to Grady's wife when she had struggled with her golf game. He had given her several lessons and straightened her swing out. Now she wasn't such a bitch on the golf course.

When the topic came up, Grady got up from his chair and headed to his liquor cabinet. He grabbed a rocks glass, threw in a few ice cubes, and reached for the Johnny Walker Red. It was getting close to happy hour and scotch always gave him some creative ideas. "What's on your mind?" he asked. "Try to make it quick. I've got a party to go to."

"I want to get rid of him. It's my last big score and I don't want him in the middle of it," Lew stated matter-of-factly.

"That's not what the agreement spells out," Grady admitted.

"How can I get out of the agreement?" Lew spat his venom across the room.

"Is that what you really want to do?"

Lew nodded. There was a way out of everything. He felt that as long as he had the most money and the most staying power, then he would be able to win every confrontation.

Grady was torn. The implication was clear. He could see that J Dub was going to get the short end of the stick. Yet, Lew was his client and always had a retainer on deposit. "It will create problems."

"What kind?"

"He might sue you."

"He doesn't have any money," Lew declared. "I'll bury him in court. That's if he can even find a lawyer to represent him."

"Why open up that can of worms? You're going to sell the place. Why not just sell it to him? He's been a good partner for you all of these years," Grady pleaded.

"I don't want to. I want to sell it to someone else."

Grady knew better than to ask who. He shook the glass, let the ice rattle, then took a healthy swig. "I gather that you've already started what you wanted."

"And I want to make sure that I can legally get away with it," Lew persevered.

Grady nodded his head. "J Dub doesn't have any rights. He's in a minority position. You can force him out if you want to. You've already told him that. All that is left to do is for you to do it."

Lew wanted to check and double-check what rights J Dub possessed. "And his only recourse is to sue me?"

Grady bobbed his head up and down. He took another swig of scotch, stuck his lower lip out, and placed his chin in his hand.

"What are his chances of beating me?" Lew continued.

"Think about it. He doesn't have any money to fight you. How's he going to win?" Grady offered.

Lew's ego could not accept any sort of defeat. "I want to make damn sure I'll win, if that happens."

"Force him out if that's what you feel is necessary. But you better protect yourself," Grady urged.

"What do you mean?"

"If you think that you might get sued, then you better take out a liability insurance policy to cover yourself," Grady suggested.

"Can I do that?" Lew's interest was piqued by the very thought of that idea.

"Sure you can. If he sues you, then you will have to spend some money to defend yourself. You can recover those fees if you have liability insurance," Grady explained.

The thought of having someone else pay his legal fees was exactly what Lew wanted to hear. "Then I can't lose," Lew reasoned. "I can take the chance of forcing him out of the agreement, stand to take all of the gains, get sued, and have someone else pay my defense bill."

"I guess in a perfect world it could happen like that," Grady assured Lew.

"How much do I have to give him to make him happy?" Lew inquired.

"You mean so that he won't sue you?" Grady corrected.

Lew shrugged.

"He's going to say his percentage is worth x number of dollars and you're going to claim it's worth nothing. Any judge in the county will say to split it down the middle. Especially if it is a partnership matter like this is. Then deduct attorneys' fees."

"Everybody I talk to says about thirty cents on the dollar is fair," Lew stated.

"Yeah, probably. We'll have to get some disclaimers and waivers signed," Grady added.

"If he's not a shareholder in the corporation, then I won't have to split anything with him, right?"

Grady nodded his head in agreement. "Why do you want to do that to the kid?"

"What difference does it make why? I want to get as much as I can. Let him sue me. I'll play the odds. Besides, I owe somebody a favor," Lew said maliciously.

"It could be costly," Grady warned.

"If I've got the insurance policy, then it won't cost me anything more than the premium," Lew rationalized. "Sometimes you don't have to play fair to win. That's the chance I'll take."

Chapter Seventy-Nine

The Week between Christmas and New Years, 1997 . . .

The King Air B200 made its descent onto the island of Tortola in the British Virgin Islands. Lew was a stickler for flying in luxury. Privately, he was scared to death to fly. The thought of someone else in control of his life made for a lot of nervous moments.

A few years before, Lew had reached a comfort level with a pilot that assured him that the King Air B200 would provide the luxury and safety needed to fly across the vast expanse of water. The aircraft could cruise at thirty-five thousand feet, had twin engines, and sat seven passengers comfortably.

It was Lew's customary routine to fly out of Ft. Lauderdale, Florida. The King Air B200 could go nearly two thousand miles on a full tank of gas. The trip into the Virgin Islands was a little over a thousand miles so Lew's fear of flying was put at ease. He had no friends to take with him so he would always rent the plane for his sole benefit.

Lew didn't care if it was the week between Christmas and New Years. It was his intention for Lois to stay back. When he went to the Virgin Islands, it was on his own time. What he did there was no one else's business.

As the aircraft readied for touchdown Lew's anxiety was tempered. Gone were the restless moments over the sea. Gone were the thoughts about an engine conking out. Gone were the fears that the pilot would have a heart attack and die in flight. He was happy to be back on land.

George Pierce greeted Lew in the baggage claim area. His suntan magnified his snaky look. After closing down FARMBELT ABSTRACT AND TITLE COMPANY he fled to Tortola with a boatload of proceeds that should have gone to the Morton heirs. George loved to sail and the islands offered him a tremendous opportunity to fulfill those desires. George also loved perfect weather. The average temperature was in the low to mid eighties. The humidity was next to nothing. The eastern trade winds provided a comfortable breeze.

In his own mind George Pierce had found heaven on earth. He had abandoned his claustrophobic fears of island life by taking to the sea. He had no yearning to move back to the States and face possible criminal charges. The island of Tortola was now his home.

Lew had funded the construction of a home on the island. It was his hideaway a couple of times a year when the weather got too cold in the States. George was the beneficiary of the good fortune the rest of the year.

The drive from the airport followed the coastline. The blue sky and the billowy, cumulus clouds were the perfect backdrop for the aquamarine waters. Sailboats dotted the ocean like stars on the American flag and the view became more scenic as the road wound its way up the volcanic slope to Lew's second home.

This was going to be a short trip for Lew. He and George needed to conduct some business. Neither could think of a better place to talk than on Lew's veranda overlooking an island sunset. "How's the place holding up?" Lew inquired.

"As long as we don't have a hurricane blow through, there's not much to worry about," George replied. He still had a fondness for his roots. "Is everything fine back home?"

"You remember the hooker, don't you?"

"How could I forget?" George reacted. "That was a telling night in all of our lives."

They looked at each other and studied each other carefully. They both had crossed over the line and each knew that time had ended their sleepless nights. Their eyes turned back to the orange ball that seemed to float on top of the water.

Lew snorted and grinned devilishly. "We traded a black hooker for a dumb college kid. One loser led to another."

"The body is gone, isn't it?" George asked somewhat fearfully.

Lew knew he had the upper hand and he intended to enjoy it for a moment or two. George was living the good life. Lew wanted to make him sweat for a second. He gave George a tight-lipped smile. Then he reached into his pocket and pulled out a gold-capped tooth.

A sense of relief overwhelmed George. He could not forget the events of that night. The fog had been blinding. The approaching car made everyone's heart pound. The stashing of the body into the back of the station wagon was a knee-jerk reaction.

The four guys were drunk. They sped through the murky haze at speeds that could have instantly killed all of them. Walter had suggested a wooded area for them to find. They clawed and scrambled to dig a shallow grave. All of them were covered in mud.

The expressionless face on the black hooker was etched in his memory. The gold-capped front tooth stuck out like a nugget in the sand at Sutter's mill. Yet they threw the body into the hole. The makeshift grave was covered with leaves and broken limbs.

George had spent many nights waking up in a cold sweat. He never knew if an animal would uncover a bone or an article of clothing would tip off an intruder. The night was forever carved into his memory. It seemed like only yesterday, but in reality much of his adult life had passed.

"The remains were barbecued," Lew said with a sinister smirk plastered across his face.

"No traces left?"

Lew shook his head. "Gasoline makes for a hot fire."

"Everything's gone?"

Lew nodded. "Except for what I just showed you."

"Good. Now I'll sleep better."

"I doubt if you worried about it too many nights over here," Lew replied. "But I do think that it's time for your brother to buy the property."

"Norman's been chomping at the bit for that ground."

"It's nice cash flow. He better be ready for it," Lew countered.

"You know what our deal was," George said in an effort to jog his memory.

George and Norman had been partners in FARMBELT ABSTRACT AND TITLE COMPANY. The Pierce brothers would do anything to get ahead. After George closed several deals with the Morton Estate, the partners closed the offices of the title company and George fled the country. Norman stayed behind to develop land and build homes.

"A deal is a deal. I'll honor what we agreed on," Lew admitted. "That's why I came down here."

George found it hard to believe that Lew Zerrmann would honor a handshake agreement that the two had made a generation before. "Is everything under control?"

"I might have some problems, but I'm big enough to bury J Dub," Lew declared, his malicious nature showing.

George was confused. "Bury who?" The last thing that he wanted was to be mixed up with another dead body.

"My partner," Lew admitted. "He can't keep up with me financially. I'll bury him in court if he tries to challenge me."

"What is going to happen?"

"I'll force my partner out of the business. He might sue me, but he won't be able to stay up with me on the legal bills," Lew explained.

"So after all of these years you really are going to deliver on your long-term promise?" George still couldn't believe what he had heard.

Lew nodded.

George was stunned. "You know, we've waited nearly twenty years to get that property. Why are you going to sell it to us after all of these years?"

"I had a talk with Norman. He's giving me the opportunity to develop the property with him. We can make millions. I assume that you will be involved in it, too."

"I knew that there had to be a reason that was more important than out of the kindness of your heart," George deadpanned.

"I mean, what the hell, you figured it all out way back when," Lew stated as he patted George on the back.

George grinned from ear to ear. His teeth shined brightly against his dark, tanned face. "The signature has held up for all of these years?" George inquired.

"Nobody knows squat," Lew bragged. He was proud of the fact that they had pulled off a swindle and had gotten away with it.

"What's next?"

"The sale is only a few months away." Lew conceded. "I found a way out of the buy/sell agreement. I squeezed all I could out of my partner. Screw him," Lew proclaimed.

"How quickly are you prepared to close?" George inquired.

"Sixty days. The next golf season is only a couple of months away," Lew explained. That should give us plenty of time for the legal work and financing . . . and the title work."

Lew's sinister grin jogged George's memory. He raised a question to Lew. "You don't think that the title company will challenge the chain of title, do you?"

"They haven't up to now. Why would they?"

"We both know why. What the hell, you've gotten over fifteen good years out of it," George stated.

"And some great cash flow," Lew admitted with an eerie sneer. "You never know, maybe after Norman closes I'll buy a yacht and cruise over next time." His fear of flying resurfaced.

Only a sliver of the reddish ball remained above the ocean horizon. Mary Jean Graham stepped out onto the veranda with a tray of drinks. After offering drinks to the men she placed the tray down and lit candles. The smoke served as a nice detraction to the bugs that swarmed after daylight.

When George fled to Tortola he brought Mary Jean with him. They had married. She had aged very well. The island climate had helped her to stay youthful and healthy. George had definitely done a good job keeping her happy. She was a nice catch on his arm.

Mary Jean possessed the same chirpiness that she had in her younger days. "Thanks for letting us house-sit your retreat," she said with a smile toward Lew.

"It's nice to get down here a few times a year," Lew admitted. "Now if I could only have you in my bedroom." Lew had no scruples when it came to sex. Every female was fair game for him in spite of who they were attached to.

The comment caught George and Mary Jean off-guard. George made light of the uneasiness. "If you were thirty years younger you might have a chance at that."

Mary Jean seized her chance to retaliate. "You know, this island life has changed me. I like the young, dark, island boys now."

"Don't you bring any mandingos up to my place," Lew shouted.

The years had educated Mary Jean. Gone was her naiveté and dinginess. "You haven't changed a bit. You'd love to watch," Mary Jean said with a smile as she called his bluff. Then she quickly backed off. "I was just kidding." The three sipped their drinks and laughed at Mary Jean's feisty sense of humor.

George changed the subject and queried Lew. "You don't think that the title company will ever find out, do you?"

"Everything has been destroyed," Lew answered, "and I don't remember a thing."

Mary Jean scribbled her hands through the air. It was as if she was writing through the dusk. "Both of you should be very grateful that Mary Jean and Margaret begin the same way." She laughed heartily as she walked over and hugged George. Her part in the scheme had been a well-kept secret.

"No doubt about it. You did some quick work, Babe," George said as he kissed his wife. "Look what it got us."

CHAPTER EIGHTY

First Few Days of January 1998 . . .

For years J Dub had gotten up between four and four-thirty in the morning. The winter months would allow for him to sleep in a little later. The sun wouldn't appear as early during those months. An item that he needed to deal with during the winter months was the warmth that was created by the sun. If the weather was nice, the chances were high that frost was on the greens. The golfers couldn't go out and play until the iciness burned off.

Nevertheless, the automatic alarm clock ran inside his body. Rain or shine, winter or summer, he was an early riser.

The atmosphere that surrounded the business had deteriorated badly after the meeting in Walter's office. J Dub felt as if he was in a lame-duck situation. He had a job to do, but he didn't think that he was necessarily going to benefit by doing the job, other than earn his weekly paycheck.

When the alarm went off a little after four, J Dub quickly silenced it. He had been tossing and turning in bed for an hour. Marcia was asleep and he didn't want to awaken her. He began his normal routine which started with a shower and shave. After throwing on a pair of casual slacks and a golf shirt he leaned over and gently kissed his wife. Marcia usually stirred a little when the shower became silent. This morning was no exception. Marcia was a little groggy when J Dub bent over to kiss her goodbye. "Going into work right now is about as tough as trying to make a downhill fifty-footer with a double break," he whispered. He referenced one of the toughest feats that the two of them had accomplished together.

She smiled even though she was still half asleep. It was obvious to Marcia that J Dub could still keep a nice disposition despite all of the negatives that had surrounded him. "The last time you did that you put yourself in a hole. Don't do it again," she said affectionately.

He gave her a loving squeeze. "I guess things will work out for the best."

"As long as you get away from the idiot, then I'll be happy," she whispered to him. J Dub grinned in the dark. He left the bedroom and headed for the kitchen. The winter darkness gave him the opportunity to eat at home and read the morning newspaper for a while.

After killing some time at the breakfast table, J Dub headed for the garage. The drive to the golf course was the same as it had been for years. J Dub always beat the rush hour traffic and this morning was no different. His home was less than ten minutes away from the golf course so the drive was normally uneventful.

The wind howled through the pre-dawn sky. Snow flurries suggested that the golf business would be slow. As he pulled into the golf course parking lot, J Dub was uncertain as to whether or not the inclement weather was going to hold off. Rain, snow, or shine, he knew that he needed to prepare the golf course for business.

He parked his pickup truck by the cart barn and, out of habit, set out to perform the duties that he had for so many years. He unlocked the cart barn and an eerie feeling enveloped him. Normally he was greeted by Bogey. However, that was not the case any more.

Over the years he had gotten used to the welcome that Bogey would give him every morning. The little guy would rush over to him and jump up his leg. His tail would be wagging. Many mornings J Dub would pick him up and Bogey would give him a lick on the face. Those days were over.

J Dub paused a moment to reflect. On this day, instead of filling Bogey's bowl with food and water, he noticed that the two bowls sat empty by the wall. He bent over to pick them up with the intention of putting them on a shelf. The wind whistled through the metal barn.

Out of the darkness jumped Fricke and Frack. Each was wearing a stocking hat. They brutally jumped on J Dub, threw him to the ground, and kicked at him. While one held him down, the other worked him over. "This trip is to the hospital," mumbled Fricke.

"The next one is to the morgue," added Frack.

For what seemed like an eternity, J Dub tried to cover his head and body from the vicious blows. If he covered his head, they would kick at his groin or his ribs. If he lowered his arms, then they would pummel his head and face.

J Dub was completely outmatched. He tried to fight back, only to be manhandled. He attempted to roll away but found a boot to the head. He made an effort to get on his feet but took a knee to the ribs.

"Watch your step asshole."

As quickly as they appeared, the two men slipped into the darkness and disappeared. J Dub had been knocked unconscious. He was left bloodied and bruised on the gravel floor of the cart barn. Wind and snow and sleet pelted his body.

Since the passing of Easy Earl, Fred was normally the first one to arrive at the pro shop. After working the night shift, he would clock out, stop for doughnuts, and drive over to the course. Right after daybreak Fred entered the parking lot. Everything seemed normal. He parked his used Cadillac and went to the door of the pro shop. He found that it was still locked.

Fred noticed that J Dub's pickup truck was parked by the cart barn. He hurried over to the barn to make sure that everything was alright. On the floor, J Dub was balled up into a fetal position.

"J Dub, what happened?"

"Help me, Fred."

Fred knelt down to administer aid to J Dub. He grabbed some towels, wetted them with water, and dabbed at J Dub's brow. "Tell me what happened."

"Two guys mugged me," J Dub mumbled as he grimaced in pain.

"Were you robbed?"

"I don't think so."

Fred could see that J Dub was in a world of hurt. "Let me call an ambulance and the police. We need to get you some help."

Within minutes an ambulance pulled up to the cart barn. Paramedics rushed to assist J Dub. The police arrived. "What's going on over here?" one of the cops asked.

"He said that two guys jumped him," Fred answered.

"Did they steal anything?"

"He didn't know, but the pro shop was locked when I pulled up," Fred replied. "Heck, it is January. There's no cash around here now. I stopped by to wish him a Happy New Year and find this."

"We'll look around and see what we can find."

"We're going to get him to the hospital as quick as we can," one of the paramedic's said. They loaded J Dub onto a stretcher, placed him in the ambulance and took off for the emergency room.

CHAPTER EIGHTY-ONE

J Dub was treated for multiple contusions around his face. He had a blackened eye, his nose was broken and at least two ribs were cracked. The punishment that his body sustained was like being in a head-on traffic collision at thirty-five miles per hour.

He knew who had sent the message. Lew was behind the beating. It would make it even harder to trace to him since he was out of town. J Dub was familiar with the way Lew operated. His tactics included intimidation. Lew had always gotten what he had wanted by negotiating from a position of strength. J Dub felt in his heart that this was a way that Lew would force him to do something that he really didn't want to do.

J Dub was confident that the police would not be able to get to bottom of what really happened. The business hadn't been robbed, so theft wasn't a motive. It was merely a case of being at the wrong place at the wrong time. The chances were great that the culprits would never be identified.

After being treated in the emergency room, J Dub was wheeled into a private room. His face was bandaged. He needed some strong painkillers to ease the throbbing from the battering that he took. The nurses hooked him up to an IV. A monitor showed a healthy heartbeat.

Marcia rushed to the hospital once she was notified. Not knowing the severity of the injuries to J Dub, she gathered Gail, Carrie, and Nick and brought them with her. She also placed a call to Curt and arranged to meet him at the hospital.

When they arrived, J Dub was under a heavy dose of anesthetics. He was resting comfortably. Yet Marcia lost control of her emotions when she saw the terrible shape that he was in. The massive wrapping around his head scared her.

She reached back into her memory to recall how they had first met. It was on a blind date in college. A fraternity brother had been going out with Marcia's older sister. He fixed the two of them up so that they could go on a double date to a football game. After the game the four of them went to a pizza parlor and shared a few pitchers of beer. Later that night they went to a fraternity party and danced until the sweat poured out of them.

Marcia knew then and there that J Dub was the guy that she was going to marry. They got along so well. He was truly a nice guy, well-mannered, and polite. He was also personable with all the people he came into contact with.

She was instantly attracted to his goals and dreams. At the time, he had been working hard on his golf game. After college he wanted to head to Florida, play the mini-tour, and try to qualify for his PGA card. He always used to tell Marcia that you only live once. J Dub felt that if he was going to take a chance in life, then the time for that would be right out of college before the complexities of life took over.

J Dub's dream didn't turn out the way that he had hoped but the new path that he took wasn't all that bad either. He had a loving wife, a stable relationship, great health, and three beautiful children. The career opportunity that had served as a replacement for his dream had also showed enduring promise.

Nevertheless, it all seemed to be such a waste as she stood there and looked at her husband lying motionless on a hospital bed. Deep down, Marcia also knew who was behind the pounding. The business negotiations weren't going as wonderfully as they had both hoped. The friction that surrounded the relationship between Lew and J Dub had been boiling to a climax.

Her first reaction was to comfort and console J Dub. However, the more she reflected back on their life, the angrier she became. Marcia wanted to get to the bottom of what happened. She wanted to be as supportive to her husband as she could so that the two of them could give Lew Zerrmann a good dose of what he deserved. Together, she intuitively knew, that they would have the strength to get over this and get to the bottom of what happened.

J Dub must have subconsciously felt the presence of his family in the room. He slowly opened his eyes and focused on his wife and the kids. Marcia could literally feel the pain that he was in and the disappointment that he was enduring.

"They jumped you, Honey," Marcia whispered.

J Dub nodded his head. "It was two of them."

Marcia reached for a towel and wiped his brow. She wanted to soothe his suffering the best that she could. She grabbed his hand and squeezed lovingly. "Please get away from him," she pleaded.

"He's trying to take everything from us," J Dub cried.

"Don't let him take your life, Hon."

"He's not strong enough to knock the will out of me," J Dub insisted. She bent over to kiss his forehead.

"He and I are playing two different games," J Dub rambled. "Mine is the game of life and his game deals with silly ego battles."

"I want you to look around this room," Marcia begged.

J Dug focused on his children and forced a weak smile. He recognized Curt and gave him a wink.

"What you're doing isn't worth it," Marcia implored.

J Dub squeezed her hand. He looked squarely into her eyes and shook his head. "No. Each and every one of you is why I'm doing it," he replied. "Somebody has to stand strong and battle the guy. I finally stood up to him and I'm going to stay with it."

Each child came forward and hugged their dad. They realized that he was a fighter and that he was battling for them. Curt reached over and squeezed his brother's calf. Curt led the children out of the room. Marcia was alone with her husband. "This nonsense has gone far enough!"

"I'm not throwing away fifteen years," J Dub said sternly.

Marcia grabbed an ice bag and applied it to his head. J Dub grimaced as the cold ice hit a tender area of his head. "Then don't throw away the next fifteen. We've got kids!" Marcia shrieked.

"Is that what you want? Do you want to start all over?"

"Maybe we should," Marcia rationalized. "Sometimes I don't think that all of this is worth it!"

"Come hell or high water, I'm going to make this situation right," J Dub declared. "He may think that he has won, but . . ."

"Don't leave all of your family stranded!" Marcia pleaded.

She clutched his hand. Her frustration with the entire state of affairs of buying the business had reached a peak. Marcia turned and stormed out of the room.

As she was leaving, she bumped into Booker. He had heard about the beating and had come over to talk to J Dub. In Marcia's mind, Booker was part of the reason that all of this happened to J Dub. She glared at him.

Aside from the investigation, Booker liked J Dub as a person. When he heard of the attack his first impression was that Lew probably had something to do with it. He rushed to the hospital as quickly as he could. "Are you sure that you're not ready for that protection we can provide for you?" Booker inquired.

"Do you think that Lew was behind all of this, too?" J Dub asked in return.

Booker raised his eyebrows and rolled his eyes. "It's hard to tell, but if they didn't take anything then I think that someone was trying to send you a message."

"I didn't think that it would come to this," J Dub responded.

"Desperate people do desperate things," Booker explained.

"How is the investigation coming along?" J Dub inquired. If this was what he was going to have to go through to help catch someone with their hand in the cookie jar, then he at least wanted to hear that his efforts were not for naught.

"I can't talk about the specifics of that," Booker stated, "but you know as well as me that we needed to get someone to talk or it would just be a circumstantial case."

"You've got mountains of evidence," J Dub replied. "Surely there is enough there to get him."

Booker nodded in agreement. "Dan and I sure think so. So did the U. S. Attorney. She was pursuing him aggressively."

"She's still on his tail, isn't she?"

"There are problems with that, too."

"What now?" J Dub asked. Booker threw the morning newspaper onto J Dub's lap. "What's it say? I can't bend my head that far."

The headline read: HACKETT RESIGNS AMID INVESTIGATION

"The U.S. Attorney resigned," Booker blurted.

"What?" J Dub asked incredulously.

"Someone tipped off the higher-ups in Washington," Booker started. "She had turned the home that she owned in this district into a rental and moved across the river so that she could put her kids in a better school district."

"How stupid was that?"

"If she had to do over again I'm sure that she would have made different choices," Booker confessed.

"That's crazy."

"Yeah, but that wasn't really what sealed her fate," Booker continued.

"What else could there be?"

"According to the article, she was having an affair with Peter Dooley."

"What? He's married with a litter of kids!"

"That's debatable. His wife has filed for a divorce," Booker offered.

J Dub couldn't get the questions out fast enough. "How long has that been going on?"

"It was news to me," Booker explained. "Evidently they went on a seminar or some sort of trip together and shared the same room. They were sleeping together on government money."

"That doesn't mean that they were having an affair." Booker raised his eyebrows. "Well, you know what I mean . . . it's only circumstantial," J Dub clarified.

Booker gave further details. "There was more to it than that. Someone started checking expense accounts, and phone logs, and then a set of pictures turned up."

" . . . For crying out loud."

"I know how you feel. We've been on this case for nearly three years."

"What's the status?"

"She was the one that was really pushing it," Booker spelled out.

" . . . But now she's gone?"

Booker shook his head and broke the disheartening news. "There is no way that we can prove intent without her. She's the whiz kid when it comes to that stuff."

J Dub thought the news that Booker had just delivered was incredible. "They're going to walk away from this thing after looking at it for three years?"

Booker shrugged his shoulders. "I hope not, but I don't know how we're going to keep the case."

J Dub's ire hit the ceiling. He nearly came out of the bed. "That really puts the screws to me!" he fired back.

"I can't talk about the case and the decisions that might be made," Booker maintained.

"I need you!" The pounding intensified in J Dub's head as the words left his mouth. He paused to gather his thoughts. "It's kind of like playing in a scramble tournament on the golf course. After you see a few putts, you can see the line. I was hoping that the evidence that you turned up would help me in court at some point in time."

Booker worked for the government and couldn't let personal relationships interfere with privileged information. "You'll have to force me to talk."

J Dub stared at Booker with an incredulous look. The events of the last few minutes had been beyond what he could ever imagine. In fact, the events of the entire morning had been off of the chart.

Booker broke the silence in the room. "Right now it looks like you're on your own."

J Dub studied Booker to see if there was a hidden message. He searched to read something between the lines. Booker turned and left. J Dub tried to clench his jaw only to grimace in more pain.

CHAPTER EIGHTY-TWO

J Dub spent one night in the hospital. It was mainly for observation. His nose would be sore, but it would heal okay. The ribs would be tender and he would feel uncomfortable for a while. The doctor prescribed a healthy dose of painkillers to ease the soreness. There wasn't much that medicine could do to take care of a bruised and battered ego.

Aside from the helpless feeling that he had from the ambush, his chief concern was what Lew was going to do next. It didn't take very long to find out. A few days after he returned from the hospital, Hank Lowery called. He had received a fax from Grady Patterson outlining the terms of the sale of stock from J Dub back to Lew. Since J Dub was in no mood to travel too far from his house, it was agreed that Hank would come over to J Dub's house and meet with J Dub, Marcia, and Curt.

"How bad is his offer?" J Dub started. It hurt for him to speak, let alone move ever so slightly.

"It's what we expected," Hank offered.

"But I don't want to sell," J Dub complained. "I'm a buyer of the business, not a seller."

"He doesn't have to sell to you," Hank explained. " . . . And it doesn't appear as if he is. Lew doesn't care. He has you backed into a corner. He is basically telling you to go ahead and sue him," Hank conceded.

"I can't do that!" J Dub shouted. He quickly grabbed his side as a twinge of pain rattled through his ribs.

"He knows that," Hank stated. "It's a pure power play on his part. He's going to force your hand."

Not only did J Dub's entire body ache from the beating, but now he was feeling sick to his stomach. He buried his forehead in his hand.

"Just take what you can and get away from the guy," Marcia urged.

"I'm not going to give away fifteen years of my life on a lousy business deal," J Dub anguished.

Hank stopped and thought before he spoke. It was the typical pause from a lawyer as minutes on the bill ticked away. "Well, you can choose to sign it . . ."

" . . . and it becomes a bad business deal for me," J Dub interrupted.

"Or you can choose not to sign it . . ."

" . . . and we'll get nothing," Marcia butted in.

"Or you can choose to counter his offer," Hank clarified. "But he will probably reject it."

"He's got the deck stacked against me," J Dub granted.

"I'm afraid so," Hank agreed. "All things considered, it's better to get it resolved now."

"And take a lousy deal," J Dub whined.

"Welcome to the world of minority shareholders," Hank said in an understatement. "You don't really have anything. The market for your shares is closed. He can pull a fast one on you if he wants."

"Oh, this is wonderful," J Dub moaned as he put his hand to his brow. "We've got some major family decisions to make."

"They would like an answer tomorrow," Hank added.

"That's a typical move from Lew. He'll back you into a corner and pounce on you," J Dub revealed.

"He holds the trump card," Hank admitted.

Not only did J Dub's entire body throb, but his heart and soul was aching. He felt hurt and betrayed. "It sounds like he has me over a barrel. Let us alone to talk about things."

Hank got up to leave. "That's fine. It's a big decision."

"Is there anything else we need to know?" J Dub asked.

"As I said, he is offering you thirty cents on the dollar to what your interest is valued at," Hank repeated.

"That's not any good . . . ," J Dub grumbled.

" . . . And there also is what we refer to as a 'hold harmless' clause in the offer," Hank added.

"What is that?" J Dub queried.

"He wants you to hold him harmless for anything that occurred between the two of you the entire time that you were partners," Hank continued.

"What!" J Dub shouted as he went into a mild state of shock. "I'm not about to agree to that!"

"Then he'll probably not give you anything and force you to sue him," Hank deadpanned.

"That really puts my backside up against the wall," J Dub whimpered. J Dub placed his hands on his face and rubbed his eyes. He was seething.

"I'll let you folks talk," Hank said on his way out the door.

"Any more surprises?" J Dub asked a final time.

"That probably gives you enough to think about. Call me tomorrow," Hank stated as he headed out the door.

~ ~ ~

The Next Day . . .

Time had run out for J Dub. He got squeezed by a ruthless, dishonest partner who prided himself on being a good businessman. It appeared that the playing field was going to be altered from green grass made plush by a sprinkler system to the stale mahogany walls of a courtroom. Any chance for survival would have to come from legal challenges that would have to prove that Lew had breached his fiduciary duty and had committed fraud against him.

J Dub had a wife and family and had to think of them first. After fifteen years at Prairie Winds he would go against his heart and take the most attractive offer that was placed on the table. After a sleepless night and an open discussion with Marcia, he decided to cut his losses. Early in the morning J Dub called Hank Lowery informing him that he would accept thirty cents on the dollar and sign the "hold harmless" clause. He had no choice.

Hank got in touch with Grady Patterson. The deal was signed and faxed with overnight delivery of the original documents.

Lew didn't say thank-you or even shake J Dub's hand. The buyout was done through lawyers. He stayed true to form and exhibited his narcissistic, sociopath behavioral patterns. It was all about him.

J Dub didn't get to go into the pro shop to say goodbye to the boys or Julie. Lew literally forced a minority partner squeeze out on J Dub and made arrangements to sell the property to another buyer. He told J Dub to get off of the property and stay off of the property and let it be known that he was no longer welcome at Prairie Winds. The clock had struck twelve. It was over.

CHAPTER EIGHTY-THREE

February 1998...

As one door in J Dub's life closed, another one opened. The fear, trepidation and uncertainty that came with the loss of a job as well as income smacked him right between the eyes. J Dub entered an arena that was unfamiliar to him. His new playing field consisted of law offices, coats and ties, conference rooms, and boxes of documents. Instead of going into a mild case of shock, J Dub relented and let Curt do the preliminary leg work of finding an interested law firm to handle his affairs.

J Dub was in the kitchen chopping vegetables for Marcia while she was shopping for specialty items for her next catering job. Out the window he saw Curt pull up in his car and motioned for him to let himself in.

Curt lumbered in looking dejected and drained.

"I can't believe how tough it is to get somebody to represent you," Curt complained. J Dub, Marcia, and Curt had devised a short list of law firms to contact. Curt sat down in a heap at the kitchen table while J Dub opened a soda from the refrigerator and set it in front of his brother.

"Have they seen the financials and the appraisal and tax returns?" J Dub asked.

"They've looked at the whole file," Curt replied between swallows of Coke.

"What seems to be the problem?"

"Robby Gregg at MARSILIO, MOLINA & MASSONE had a conflict of interest," Curt responded.

" . . . With who? The mob?"

"Somebody over there did some legal stuff for Walter Hancock once," Curt stated. "They couldn't even look at the case because of that."

"What about Aaron Boyd?" J Dub inquired. "Hank referred us to him."

"BERRY & BOYD doesn't think there is enough meat on the case. They say that it only has a fifty-fifty chance of winning," Curt continued.

"That's better than nothing," J Dub countered.

"From what I've been able to find out, law firms want to have a huge chance of winning or they're not willing to take the case on a contingency basis," Curt explained.

"Who else have you talked to?"

"Jack at BASDEN, HOWARD, CREIGHTON & MILLER won't tackle the 'hold harmless' clause," Curt made clear. "He said that it's next to impossible to get the courts to even listen to a case where one partner has absolved the other of any wrongdoing."

"Even if possible fraud was involved?" J Dub grumbled.

"He said that there were stronger cases out there. He didn't want to mess with it."

"You'd think that with all we have to gain that there would be some interest somewhere," J Dub pleaded.

"That's what I thought too," Curt agreed. "Thom Binger operates a one-man firm and said that his plate was way too full to even look at anything new. I think that he was more concerned about getting the hair transplant to take on his bald head."

"Don't these firms want to try to make a few bucks?" J Dub wondered out loud. "I mean the business supposedly had a value of five million dollars and on top of that was the new course and possibly some ground to be developed for home sites. There might be as much as twenty to thirty million dollars of developed property over there."

"I know," Curt agreed.

"Somebody taking this thing might be able to make themselves several million dollars," J Dub reasoned.

"That's the same way that I am thinking. Jim McCormick at HARRIS, MONTANARO, McCORMICK & OLSON said that his firm was only looking at class action lawsuits where they could obtain a multi-million dollar judgment. They were going after large corporations," Curt muttered.

"For crying out loud," J Dub moaned. "We have a case that might render a judgment of several million dollars."

"Yeah, but it's not against some big corporation," Curt rationalized.

"What do these guys want?"

"They want a case handed to them on a silver platter," Curt shouted. "They're all nothing but a bunch of whores."

"Are there any other options?" J Dub queried.

"K. T. Gill at VASQUEZ, GILL, TEESON & SUTHOFF said that their firm wasn't into the white-collar crime area. Their expertise wasn't in accounting documents and fraudulent papers," Curt cried.

"At least they were honest about that and didn't waste too much of your time," J Dub conceded.

"Mal at LYNCH & STROUD said that his firm lacked the expert litigator needed to win the case," Curt continued. "Basically that was his way of telling me that they weren't interested. It sounded to me like it might have caused a conflict with happy hour."

"You've got to be kidding. These are the responses that we're hearing?" J Dub complained.

"But it gets even more amazing," Curt declared. "Jim Reed at REED, MORGENSON, CORDES & FRANKLIN has a conflict of interest with the Pierce brothers. They have represented Norman in the past."

J Dub was exasperated. "What's new? It's starting to sound like I'm calling out foursomes to start off the first tee."

"Regina Blair at PERRY, MILBOURN & SIMPSON won't touch it because they are booked up with divorce litigation," Curt continued. J Dub stopped for a moment looking puzzled at the mention of the law firm.

"I've never heard of them . . . are they new?" J Dub inquired.

"No, but all the partners are female. Apparently, divorce litigation is their specialty. They represent ex-wives and gang up on men. How bad is that?" Curt responded nonchalantly.

J Dub started to smirk, "You mean to tell me you went into an all-female law firm with the initials of 'PMS'?"

Curt began to choke on swallows of Coke. The laughter was causing the fizz to back up through his nose. "Maybe that was why they had complimentary candy dishes filled with Midol in the reception area. I did notice that a lot of the attorneys were wearing Birkenstocks now that you mention it."

J Dub spit his coke back into his glass as the two laughed to relieve the stress that had been building. "That sounds to me like it is the perfect firm to take on Lew. We need some pit bulls to go after that slimeball."

Curt was in hysterics as he finished his story. "J Dub, you should have seen the Midol. Each one was stamped with 'PMS, $_{LLC}$'." The brothers laughed and laughed until it was out of their systems.

"Oh, Curt, thank you for that. I can't remember the last time I laughed that hard," J Dub offered. "Okay, back to business. Who else did you see?"

Curt pulled out his notes and reviewed them. He wanted to make sure that he hadn't left out any of the places that he had called on. "AHERN, JOHNSON & GUNTHER represented Lew before. They have a conflict."

"Is anybody left in town?" J Dub asked.

"The phone book is full of attorneys. There are seventy-nine pages in the yellow pages of the phone book," Curt deadpanned.

"Are any of them any good?" J Dub inquired.

Curt was ready with an answer. "You've got the divorce attorneys, the ambulance chasers, the DUI specialists, the workmen's comp guys . . ."

" . . . and none of them have an accounting background," J Dub groaned.

"It just appears that the good ones have a conflict with either, Lew, Walter or the Pierce brothers," Curt quipped, "or just men in general."

"The old saying is true," J Dub conceded.

"What is that?"

"It takes money to make money," J Dub muttered.

"It sure looks that way right now," Curt agreed.

J Dub was flustered and discouraged. Getting good legal representation was going to be next to impossible. Lew was way too connected. "What's the next move?"

"ROLAND, WILHITE, KEEGAN & ROWE will take the case if you put up a fifty thousand dollar retainer," Curt offered.

"I bet they will! Are you out of your mind?" J Dub roared. "Marcia will throw a fit. That's not an option."

"Then let's put our heads together and come up with an alternative plan," Curt suggested.

"Why don't I throw in the towel and become a stockbroker?" J Dub commented.

"You're good with people little brother but I doubt if you'd last a day and a half in that racket," Curt smirked.

"Maybe I can go back to the driving range and give lessons," J Dub proposed. "At least I can be good for something."

Curt offered his opinion. "From where you've been that's taking a couple of steps backward."

J Dub threw out an idea. " . . . How about real estate sales? That's how Lew made his money."

Curt shook his head. "Don't worry about anything. Something will turn up. You've got a five year window on the Statute of Limitations for fraud," Curt informed.

"I sure the heck hope that something happens before that," J Dub moaned.

An idea popped into Curt's head. "Hey, I've got a thought."

J Dub was getting tired of thoughts. He wanted some action. "I've had a few of those lately too but they don't seem to go anywhere."

"What about that guy that represented the Morton Estate in their lawsuit against the course?"

J Dub was mystified. "I don't even remember his name."

"Do you think that you can find out?" Curt asked. "He has to know something more than what we know."

"A copy of the lawsuit has to be around in one of these boxes."

"Let's give him a call. If he sued Lew and the course, then he won't have a conflict with Zerrmann," Curt rationalized.

"Why didn't we think of him before now?" J Dub asked.

"Maybe we just had to go through some three putt greens before we started dropping some one putts," Curt summarized.

Vim and vigor returned to J Dub's face. He could relate to the golf analogy. "I'll find his number. It doesn't hurt to give him a call." They clicked soda cans in agreement.

CHAPTER EIGHTY-FOUR

Raymond Parsons knew how to play his cards and he got it right. It was no wonder that he continued to be victorious in his district. On election day he normally won by the widest margin in the country. That was pretty good for a Midwestern guy with modest roots and run-of-the-mill aspirations.

After the resignation of Ellie Hackett, Ray followed with a keen interest the happenings in and around the U. S. Attorney's office. All kinds of names were being thrown around as to who her successor was going to be. In fact, the whole office was going to be overhauled. Ellie wasn't the only one that needed to be replaced. Peter Dooley had been fired and an Assistant U. S. Attorney needed to be hired.

In the beginning, speculation was that someone from within the office would be promoted. However, in the end, the government decided to bring in an outsider. They reached to the East Coast and appointed a fair-haired, lily-white lad that had gotten his feet wet with some local smuggling rings.

Donald Stokes was in his early forties and looked the part. He could have passed as a poster child for the clean and friendly. The government hoped that he could be stern and straightforward in a district known for its corruption. Only time would tell.

Ray took it upon himself to welcome Donald to town. He scheduled an appointment to meet him on his turf. Because of new safety regulations the three-story office building had been erected behind a wrought iron security fence. Electronic gates and video surveillance prevented unwanted traffic and unauthorized vehicles from the parking lot. A metal detector in the lobby further strengthened security of the building.

Times had changed. Criminals were so brazen now that every precaution was taken to keep them from entering the premises and taking justice into their own hands. It was an intimidating fortress to penetrate. The government wanted to do everything in its power to protect the "good" guys.

Ray made it past the maze of safety features and found himself in front of Donald Stokes. "Congratulations on your appointment, Don."

"Thank you."

Raymond knew that the best way to get someone to warm up was to get them to talk about themselves. "Now where is it you're coming in from?"

"Virginia," Don replied.

"What a pretty part of the country. I've spent a lot of time there on my travels to the Capitol," Ray continued.

"We got our start there," Don apprised. He referred to his family when he made the comment. He had married his college sweetheart and the "Old Dominion State" had been the birthplace of both of his sons.

Don's credentials were very impressive. He had done his undergraduate work at Duke University in Durham, North Carolina and had been accepted to Law School at the University of Virginia in Charlottesville. The government took notice and moved him right into the fast track.

"That's quite a different world than what we live in back here," Ray said with a chuckle.

"I'm sure that we'll adapt very nicely," Don commented. "I hear nothing but good things about the people in this part of the country."

"Some of the best that you'll ever run into," Ray added. "What are you into for enjoyment?"

Don couldn't help but laugh. "Is there any time for that? It seems that I work well past the eight-hour day."

"You have to like to hunt or fish or boat," Ray said as he stretched for any sort of common ground between the two.

"Seeing as I've had the opportunity to fish and go boating, I guess that I'd like to go hunting if the occasion ever presented itself," Don stated.

"Have I got just the place for you!" Ray exclaimed. "We've got one of the best duck hunting areas in all of the country. It's right down on the Mississippi River."

"That would be a new one for me," Don said with a twinge of excitement.

"The property is owned by a very good friend of mine," Ray offered.

"I'd like to do that," Don stated as he eagerly accepted the invitation.

"There's really nothing to it, you know," Ray continued. "I've been around these parts all of my life and have been serving the people in this area for over thirty years now."

"You have to be getting senior tenure in the House," Don added.

Ray smiled. "A good way to get your career around here off to a healthy start might be to get politically involved with the right people."

"I'm not here to play party favorites," Don interrupted.

"I'm not here asking for that," Ray said as the freckles on his face blushed. He ran his hand through his wavy, reddish-blonde hair. "I just wanted to let you know that there are plenty of nice folks to meet and wonderful things to do around here. I'm here to throw down the welcome mat and assist with that."

"That's thoughtful, Ray."

"Of course, if you think that you've been righted, then . . ."

"What do you need, Ray?" Don interrupted. He had been around the block. He knew what direction the conversation was headed.

"Well, you know that duck hunting site that I was talking about?" Ray stammered.

Don nodded.

"The gentleman that owns that is a very, very good political friend of mine. Your predecessor has been after him for well over three years in what could be termed a witch hunt. I'd like for you to take a good, long, hard look at the evidence and see if there is anything there." He got the feeling that Donald Stokes was going to be much better to work with than the uncooperative female that held the position before him. Raymond got up, shook Donald's hand, and left with a satisfied look on his face.

CHAPTER EIGHTY-FIVE

Booker and Hayden assumed the worst, but hoped for the best. For the better part of three years they had been working in close association with Ellie Hackett and Peter Dooley. When the call came from the U. S. Attorney's office to sit down and provide an update on the Zerrmann investigation they licked their chops in anticipation.

Their first impression of Donald Stokes was favorable. He seemed like an all-around good guy. His style was in stark contrast to the manner in which Ellie approached a case. She shot from the hip and went from the gut. Don played by the book.

Stokes needed an indoctrination period. Once the apprenticeship in the new area was complete, then it was down to the business at hand. His first priority was the existing files that were being investigated. He needed to cut through the chaff and get up-to-speed in a hurry.

Not everyone that was being investigated by the U. S. Attorney's office was going to be brought to justice. Some would fall through the cracks. The time and expense of an investigation was costly so the government wanted to make sure that those brought to trial were going to be convicted. Don had a keen eye for the law and which cases might be stronger than others.

Booker and Hayden were eager to keep their momentum in the investigation of Zerrmann and Hancock. They walked into Don's office well prepared for an informative conference.

"Sorry it's taken me so long to have you fellows come in," Don started.

"What's another day or two?" Booker chuckled. "We've been on this investigation for quite awhile."

"It's my understanding that it hasn't gone very smoothly," Don declared.

"Not so much that," Booker answered, "but it's an extremely complex case."

"We haven't been able to get the targets to talk," Hayden added.

"Everything is circumstantial," Booker responded. "We've tracked the evidence and cross referenced the documentation. I've developed a very accurate timeline that details all of the deception."

"It's our opinion that with the overwhelming amount of deceit and trickery that these two characters pulled off, a jury will convict," Hayden replied.

"In reading the summary report, the legal team sees some possible holes in our case," Don countered.

"There's no doubt that it's a tricky case," Booker admitted, "but with the right litigator on our side we think that the evidence will be crushing."

Don had never met Booker and Hayden. He had no idea how much work they had put in on this investigation. Nor did he care. "We've got a case that the jury won't understand. The defense team can put up a very good case for avoidance that will shoot the heck out of our evasion theory."

Booker and Hayden had known that Ellie was going to go to bat for them and roll the dice on a favorable jury decision. She was going to tackle the odds. It appeared that her successor was not willing to go down that road. He was going to walk away from a difficult situation and not fight for them. That made Booker hostile. "What are you talking about?"

"We're closing the file. I'm making a recommendation not to prosecute," Don informed the two. True to form, Stokes was playing by the book. He wasn't going to take any chances on an acquittal.

"We've got three years of hard work into that investigation," Booker complained.

"And what you did came up short," Don chastised them.

"I beg your pardon!" Hayden shouted. He was the one that did all of the forensic accounting work to connect the dots.

"It's going nowhere," Don calmly explained.

"The circumstantial evidence is overwhelming!" Booker urged.

"Based on the evidence and testimony and depositions, we cannot prove with a one hundred percent chance of certainty that they intended to evade taxes," Don maintained.

"The case is ready to go to trial," Booker argued.

"It won't fly," Don said adamantly. "I want this office to keep its unblemished record. I don't want to take a chance of losing my first case in this district."

"That's bullshit!" Booker yelled. The curse word slipped out. He had put his standing with the agency in jeopardy, but he was clearly frustrated.

"We'll have none of that talk in my office," Don stated as he lowered the boom. "The file is closed with a recommendation not to prosecute."

"These two guys had a racket going for a number of years and we can prove it," Hayden declared.

"As far as I'm concerned it is a civil case between the IRS and the taxpayer," Don announced.

"You know as well as we do that, the chance of us going after a taxpayer without a criminal conviction is slim," Booker pleaded.

"I don't know how your agency works," Don proclaimed.

"I'll tell you how it works," Hayden persisted. "We just wasted three years."

"Look, my decision is final. We've spent three years on this guy and nearly a half of million dollars on this investigation," Don continued.

"We've got nearly four million in back taxes, penalties, fines and interest to gain," Booker begged.

Don shook his head. "No. Enough is enough." He closed the file and got up. "I've got other things to do."

CHAPTER EIGHTY-SIX

March 1998 . . .

J Dub and Curt found their way into the rehabbed, historic part of town. They walked up the same steep and creaky steps that Lucille Morton and her son, Matt, had walked several years earlier. The stencil on the frosted window read Dennis K. Sneed, Attorney at Law.

The two middle-aged men couldn't help but shake their heads after they knocked on the door and entered the law office. Life had traversed from the gentle, tranquil and serene setting of a golf course environment to the slow-moving, high-risked, uncertain path known as the United States legal system. J Dub felt at home with a driver, sand wedge, or putter in his hands. He wasn't quite as familiar with a conference room in a law office, a deposition and a court reporter.

Denny was on the phone when they entered. He motioned with his head for them to enter. Neither one of the men could take a seat. Stacks of papers covered both of the chairs that were across from Denny's desk. The pictures on the wall suggested that Denny's family was the product of an interracial marriage. They saw what appeared to be an Eastern Indian wife, an Asian daughter and an African son.

In one of the photos Denny wore what looked like a white robe but was actually an Achkan suit with a Nehru collar. An impressive array of prayer beads dangled from his neck. J Dub and Curt glanced at each other. They wondered if they should have taken off their shoes and looked for a pillow to sit on.

As Denny ended the phone conversation, J Dub spoke. "Where are the candles?"

"And the incense," Curt added.

"That's a fine way to meet," Denny said as he rose to shake their hands. "Go ahead and put those papers on the floor."

"Nice filing system," J Dub blurted.

"Don't worry about that. I know where everything is," Denny said apologetically.

"That's reassuring," J Dub muttered. "I'm about to talk to you about something that's very important to me. I hope that you're organized enough to handle it."

"Don't let this bother you," Denny exclaimed. "How can I help?"

"Like we talked on the phone, we might be in a situation where we can help each other," J Dub started. "I need an attorney and you were the one that was involved in suing PRAIRIE WINDS GOLF COURSE."

"That's right. For some out-of-town clients," Denny verified.

"I just got caught in a squeeze play buyout, but I think that I was defrauded," J Dub explained.

"His ex-partner and the accountant for the business were under investigation by the IRS for tax evasion," Curt added.

"You're kidding me!" Denny cried out. "You mean Zerrmann? That's news to me."

"Yeah, he and our accountant, Walter Hancock, have been the targets of an IRS investigation into tax evasion." J Dub admitted.

Denny was extremely curious to hear that bit of news. "How is that progressing?"

"Heck if I know. But it seems like I've been answering questions from them for about three years," J Dub admitted.

"You know that Lew is an unscrupulous character," Denny volunteered as he leaned back into his chair.

"So I am finding out. I got caught holding the bag," J Dub groaned. "If nothing else, then there might be some information that I can provide to you."

"In return we're hoping that there might be some information that you can share with us," Curt included.

Denny certainly thought that his other clients had been shortchanged. Now, he would snoop into J Dub's situation. "How do you think that you were defrauded?"

"I think that the books were cooked," J Dub admitted.

"His partner had created a fake expense account and was funneling all the profits out of the company," Curt chimed in.

"You mean Zerrmann, right?" Denny asked with interest.

Both men nodded.

"I've been investigating him for several years," Denny volunteered. He paused, thinking for a long time. J Dub thought that Denny looked constipated and would need the bathroom at any minute. The delay in speaking made both of the men antsy.

"What are you doing?" J Dub inquired.

"I'm thinking," Denny responded.

"It looks like you need a laxative," J Dub quipped.

Denny smiled. "My thoughts are that you may want to talk to my other clients," Denny proposed.

"What good would that do?" J Dub asked. "He forced me out of the business and didn't let me exercise my option or my first right of refusal. I literally lost the farm when he wouldn't allow me to buy it."

"Count your blessings," Denny stated matter-of-factly.

"Why do you say that?" J Dub probed.

"You'll see once I let you in on what I know," Denny replied.

"The guy is unethical," Curt added. "He had been skimming a couple hundred thousand dollars a year out of the business."

Denny's ears perked up as he leaned forward. "That's something interesting that the heirs and I weren't aware of. It sure is a statement about his character if we can prove it."

"Nothing made any sense when we looked at the books," J Dub declared.

"If he would have gotten a loan and the business went upside down, then the bank could have come back at him for bank fraud," Curt ranted.

"Does he still own the business?" Denny asked.

"As far as I know," J Dub answered. "I think that he wanted me out of there so that he could sell it to someone else."

"Who is that?"

"As far as I have been able to find out, it's Norman Pierce. There is talk about the two of them developing the property into home sites or something," J Dub replied.

Denny was on the edge of his seat. "George Pierce's brother?"

"Yeah," J Dub blurted.

"Oh come on!" Denny shouted. "You need to talk to my clients."

"Why is that so important?" J Dub inquired.

"You're a golfer, right?"

J Dub nodded. "It's the gentleman's game," he said with a smile.

"Well, I hate to be the one to inform you, but I don't think that your ex-partner counts all of his strokes," Denny mumbled. He was proud of his analogy.

"The more that I learn, the more I tend to be of the same opinion," J Dub said as he shook his head in agreement. "Keep using those golf terms. I can relate to them."

"Do you want to try to beat him at his own game?" Denny queried.

"I wouldn't be here unless I wanted to try to get back at him," J Dub said.

"Get even," Curt corrected.

Denny beamed. His mind was going a thousand miles an hour. Perhaps this was the break that he had been hoping he would get for a number of years. "I've been on to him for quite a while," Denny started. "He's as slippery as an eel, or, should I say, as elusive as a hole-in-one?"

J Dub grinned. He was starting to really like the guy.

"We've had nothing but delay after delay. It seems like we have battled technicalities for at least a decade or so," Denny continued.

" . . . A decade? I know that he will use whatever he can to his advantage, but ten years is ridiculous," J Dub admitted.

"He's good at it, too," Denny concurred. "But he's also as dirty as they come."

"What do you know?" J Dub asked. His curiosity was piqued.

"Enough to know that a lot of people can't stand him," Denny cried out. "He's the biggest crook on this side of the river."

"Then he must have nine lives," J Dub joked.

"There are some things that we can do to take a few birdies out of his round. These new analogies have my mind in fifth gear," Denny stated.

J Dub forced a smile. "Like what?"

"First off," Denny asked, "would you be interested in having my law firm take your case?"

"We've gone to everyone in town," Curt revealed, "and I *do* mean everyone." Curt shot J Dub a quick glance.

"Nobody is interested because the case is too bizarre or complicated," J Dub added.

"But they don't know what I know," Denny countered, "and you might be able to fill in some blanks for me."

"I need someone to take it on a contingency basis," J Dub confessed.

"That's no problem. Just cover your expenses like court costs and copying charges. The estate has a nice retainer on file," Denny explained.

"So you have money to live on?" Curt guessed.

Denny nodded. "But you two can help the case."

"But can you help me?" J Dub countered.

"I think so," Denny theorized. "But I need you to talk to the principals of the estate."

"You said that they were out of town. Where are they?"

"Florida. West Palm Beach."

"I could use a trip out of town . . . after that, then what?" J Dub asked.

"They are committed to getting back what they lost. You need to talk to them. If they can get back what they've lost, then you might be able to retrieve what you've lost," Denny explained vaguely.

J Dub turned to Curt. "What have we got to lose?"

"If it turns out to be a wild goose chase, at least we'll be in Florida," Curt rationalized. "No other lawyer has seemed too enthusiastic about this case."

"I'll call them and arrange everything," Denny urged. "The two of you together might be a lethal combo."

"I hope you mean that in a good way," J Dub said with a smirk.

Denny's mind was still working overtime. He smiled in agreement. "Sort of like a birdie and an eagle, back to back. In the meantime, I want you to help me take out a little insurance."

J Dub knew enough to know that a back to back birdie and eagle meant that they were on a roll. "Like what?"

Denny had already moved to the next step. He was ready to start gathering evidence. "What can you provide to me in the form of documentation?"

"Tax returns, financial statements, partnership agreements, contracts, and an appraisal," J Dub replied.

"Can you run around and check on some things for me?"

J Dub shook his head up and down. "Within reason," he said.

"Good." Denny reached for his notepad and jotted down some instructions. "Here are some things that I'm going to need for you to do." He handed the note to J Dub. "There may be an opportunity for all of us to correct a mess that happened a long, long, long time ago."

CHAPTER EIGHTY-SEVEN

In the meantime, Lew had been partying up a storm. The spring of '98 had nothing but good fortune coming his way. Wherever he turned, big bucks followed.

First off, he had filed an insurance claim on the motorcycle that he had backed over. He had gotten a dozer that he owned and scooped up the wrecked bike. It was loaded into the back of his pickup truck. Late one night Lew met Monty on the local supermarket parking lot.

Monty had two friends with him that just happened to be named Fricke and Frack. The four of them unloaded the cycle onto the lot. Lew then called the police and reported that the motorcycle had been run over by someone when he had been inside the store.

The proceeds of the insurance settlement were enough to cover the cost of a brand new Harley-Davidson. There was even a little left over for a nice cash bonus for the three accomplices.

Shortly after that Lew received a letter via registered mail. It was a message from Donald Stokes at the U. S. Attorney's office. The letter informed him that he and Walter Hancock, who had been targets of a federal investigation for tax evasion, had been more-or-less exonerated. After an extensive examination it was decided that the government would not press charges.

Lew was ecstatic. He naturally picked up the phone to congratulate Raymond Parsons and Monty on a job well done. He assured Raymond that a nice sized packet would be delivered his way.

Another snippet of good news was that Grady Patterson had gotten the "hold harmless" agreement signed. Once Hank Lowery had forwarded the original over to Grady's office, Lew sent Monty to pick up the document. By Lew's account he made nearly three-quarters of a million dollars the day he forced J Dub out as a shareholder. The profits of the upcoming sale to Norman Pierce would not have to be distributed to anyone else. That was the difference between what J Dub stood to gain and what he ended up taking as a settlement.

Later on that night Lew took Lois and Monty out for an exquisite steak dinner. Afterwards, he threw a party for himself and Lois and Monty that lasted through the weekend. He bought two gorgeous female guests for entertainment. A limo delivered them in luxury for a three-day sex party in the dungeon.

Once the squeeze-out of J Dub was complete, Lew became free to negotiate with Norman on the sale of the golf course. The two of them decided that the best route to take would be for Norman to buy the golf course. The two of them could then enter into a joint venture to develop the surrounding property into home sites. They decided that the land near the highway could subsequently be rezoned for commercial use. By structuring the deal in that manner Lew stood to make well in excess of twenty million dollars.

For an old bachelor in his seventies that was more money that he could ever hope to spend.

Needless to say, when he stopped in to see Walter, Lew was in good spirits. "I told you we'd get out of that mess we were in," Lew chirped as Walter nervously tapped his pencil on the desk.

"I'm not supposed to talk to you," Walter advised.

Lew was puzzled. " . . . Why not?" Lew asked. "You got the letter from the U. S. Attorney's office saying that they were not going to press charges, didn't you?"

"Yes I did. It made Nora very happy and may have saved my marriage," Walter answered.

"I told you that we didn't do anything wrong," Lew gushed. His self-confidence was oozing out of his pores.

"All it means is that they couldn't catch us right now." Walter's tone suggested that they had merely gotten a par on the first hole and that there was plenty of golf left in the round.

"What do you mean? It's over and done with," Lew babbled like a craps player on a roll.

"That doesn't mean that we may not have civil charges at some later point in time," Walter explained. "Besides they might keep looking at me and some of my other clients. Listen I can't talk to you."

"Why? Dammit! We're home free." Lew clearly wanted to continue the celebration that he was on. "After three years of worrying about being cuffed and hauled off to prison we've got it made now."

"Maybe you do, but I still have the civil suit from the Morton Estate to deal with," Walter cried.

"Didn't Judge Rowland's court throw that case out?" Lew asked.

"They did for you, but not for me. As executor of the estate, I had a fiduciary responsibility to them," Walter confessed.

Lew pried further. "How is that going?"

"It's hard to say. We've tried every legal maneuver and stalling tactic that we can, but we can't seem to shake them," Walter replied.

"Then let me give you a big piece of advice," Lew stammered.

"That's okay. I'll listen to my lawyer. Just go away," Walter clearly wanted Lew to walk out the door. His wife and attorney had both told him not to pay any attention to one thing that would come out of Lew's mouth.

Lew acted like his feelings were hurt. "You don't want my business anymore?"

"Maybe since you're selling the golf course, we can end our association," Walter pleaded. He couldn't wait to get Lewferd E. Zerrmann out of his life for good.

"Just do like we did against the feds," Lew advised.

"What was that?"

"Keep your mouth shut!" Lew yelled. He glared at Walter.

"Pleading the Fifth may have worked against the feds when we had criminal charges, but it doesn't quite work that way in a civil suit!" Walter shouted back.

"How is that?" Lew probed.

"Think about it!" Walter screamed. He was visibly stressed. "We don't have to answer questions in a criminal case if we think that we might incriminate ourselves. In a civil case all the opposition has to show is a preponderance of evidence to gain a victory!"

"A jury still needs to give a favorable verdict for the estate," Lew rationalized.

"But it's a helluva lot easier to prove!" Walter shrieked.

"Are you scared?" Lew wondered out loud.

Walter flew off the deep end. He stood up and said, "Look, dammit! Things aren't going so good! And I sure as hell shouldn't be talking to you! Now get out!"

"I thought that we were together on this thing," Lew grumbled.

"It may not turn out that way," Walter admitted. The estate had been turning up the heat and his trial date was rapidly approaching.

Lew got up and walked to the door. "If that's the way you want it, then I guess we'll have to make it every man for himself."

"Hasn't it always been that way?" Walter took a deep breath and calmed himself down. "Do you and me both a favor," Walter said coolly. "Just leave."

CHAPTER EIGHTY-EIGHT

April 1998 . . .

The Boeing 737 touched down at Palm Beach International Airport in West Palm Beach, Florida. J Dub and Curt never thought in their wildest dreams that they would be traveling to the "Sunshine State" to pursue an interest in a golf course located in Illinois.

Denny had lined up a meeting for them with Lucille Morton and her son, Matt. It was going to be a quick trip for the two brothers. They were to meet Lucille and Matt in an airport coffee shop for a few hours after which they were to board a late afternoon flight and return home.

The flight was uneventful. After arriving in Florida and feeling the weather in the mid-eighties, they both wished that they had brought their golf clubs and had enough time to play a quick round. That wasn't to be the case this time however. This trip was to try to gather some information and see if there was a way for J Dub to recoup the recent losses that he had incurred. It was critical for his economic survival.

As planned, J Dub and Curt sat in a lounge off of Concourse A. Both of them wore "Tommy Bahama" shirts so that they would be easily recognized. Matt and Lucille were aware of what time their flight was to land and showed up right on time. "Greetings from South Florida," Matt said as he extended his hand. "Meet my mother, Lucille."

Lucille was a gracious woman, assured and elegant in her trendy sportswear. She was tan, physically fit and as warm as the South Florida sun.

"These did a pretty good job," J Dub joked as he pulled at the sleeve of his shirt.

"We couldn't miss them for the world," Matt laughed.

"Denny wanted us to meet," Lucille started. "He's been working with us for nearly ten years."

"It looks like we both got the shaft," Matt added. "With the new turn of events we may have common ground by combining forces."

"One thing that is in my favor is that my Statute of Limitations still has nearly five years remaining," J Dub volunteered. "But what happened to you?"

Lucille had lived a nightmare. She was ready to tell her story. "In some ways it is our own fault," she began. "Daddy died and mother was getting senile. Before his death, Daddy had hired Walter Hancock to be the executor of his estate. We assumed that with Walter on the payroll, our affairs would be handled accurately."

"But we found out otherwise," Matt announced.

"One of the things that he got my mother to do before her death was sign a tax form for the government," Lucille continued.

"I'm going to correct you, mom," Matt interrupted. "They forged that document."

"No, Matt, the signature on the tax form was not forged. They forged the signature on the power of attorney form," Lucille stated steadfastly.

Matt realized his original statement had been confusing. "Technically, that's right. They took the original signature off of the tax form and forged it onto the power of attorney form. With that signature, Walter, who was the executor of the estate, and the guy with the title company . . ."

" . . . That would be George Pierce," J Dub interrupted.

"Yes, George Pierce," Lucille agreed. She was thankful that J Dub had brought that name to her attention. "Mother would never have signed all of those contracts. George Pierce and Walter used the power of attorney form. Anyway, without our knowledge, the two of them started to sell off our real estate."

"They hid behind the power of attorney document," Matt pressed, "which we have determined with the help of a handwriting expert was a forged document."

"The golf course changed hands and we didn't even know about it," Lucille stated.

"We thought that we still had control of it but that a different management company was operating it," Matt proclaimed.

"That would have been Lew and me," J Dub acknowledged.

"Yes," Lucille admitted, "and when we found out that it wasn't still in our name we filed a lawsuit to try to get it back."

"But it was thrown out of court on a technicality," Matt added. He wasn't aware of the connection between Judge Troy Rowland and Lew.

Curt felt the need to run an idea by the group. "Weren't you folks looking at the financial statements that Walter was generating on behalf of the estate?"

"That was what I was referring to when I said that in some ways it is our own fault," Lucille confessed. "Walter was up there and we were down here. We were busy living our life. Daddy had a lot of property and we were paying Walter to manage it and watch over it for us."

"And then when we started to check on some things a few years later, we found that he had been disposing of all of it," Matt said.

"What did you find out?" J Dub inquired.

"Here is where the story gets a lot harder to believe," Lucille continued. "We found that he had been selling our property and we weren't getting any money for it."

J Dub and Curt wondered how it could be possible to lose several million dollars and not even be aware of it. "What?" J Dub exclaimed. "How can that be?"

Lucille grabbed a handkerchief out of her purse. She started to gently cry. "The best that we could trace, with Denny's help, was that the money was going to George Pierce's title company at closing," she said with a sniffle. "And he was keeping the money!"

"I know that we paid for it," J Dub stated matter-of-factly. "We went to the bank and got a loan."

"But the money went to the title company to be disbursed," Matt claimed, "and George Pierce kept it instead of giving it to Walter, and ultimately, us."

"The golf course was only one of the properties that he did that to us on," Lucille said as she started to sob. "We had farm acreage, apartment buildings, commercial strip centers and hotels." Lucille started bawling. She covered her face with her handkerchief. Matt put his arm around his mother to comfort her.

"Our family had property in Illinois, Kentucky, Oklahoma, and Nebraska as well as California, Colorado and Florida," Matt confessed.

"And the two of them sold it all out from underneath us," Lucille sobbed.

Curt and J Dub looked at each other in amazement. They couldn't believe what they were hearing. "Let's all take a break for a minute or two," Curt offered. "What would everyone like to drink?"

Curt rounded up the beverages for the group. Matt consoled his mother. J Dub took the occasion to visit the men's room. "I'm at a loss for what to say," J Dub said upon his return. "What am I involved in?"

"It sounds like a fraud," Curt said as a mild understatement.

"And fixing it is going to take an unbelievable amount of effort," Matt conceded.

"How can we help?" J Dub offered.

"We obviously feel that J Dub was victimized, too," Curt stated.

"But not nearly to the degree that you got it," J Dub agreed.

Lucille had composed herself. "Zerrmann has been taking steps to sell the property to Norman Pierce."

"You know that for a fact?" J Dub questioned.

"Yes. He's been working on that for some time," Lucille admitted.

J Dub was flabbergasted and beside himself as to what he didn't know. He had only heard through the grapevine that Lew was planning on doing that.

"When George Pierce did the title work twenty years ago he did not include a five acre piece of land that was split off of the farm as an old homestead," Matt declared.

"We've paid taxes on it for all of these years," Lucille disclosed.

"Lew knew about that, too," J Dub revealed. "It was over on hole number fifteen."

"We've been fighting him in court about that for the last several years," Lucille divulged.

"But it looks like the courts are going to award that to him under an adverse possession action," Matt announced.

"He's claiming that he has cared for that property for all of these years and that he is entitled to that as well," Lucille disclosed.

"So that's another piece of ground we won't get any money for," Matt whined.

"And then he will be free to sell the entire property to Norman," Lucille said with a whimper.

"We think that this was part of the original plan," Matt suggested.

"What was part of the original plan?" J Dub queried.

"To sell the property to Norman all along," Lucille proposed. "He and George knew about this way back when they owned the title company together."

Matt filled in more blanks. "We think that Lew made a deal with Norman way back then. Lew agreed to sell the property to Norman when it came time to sell it."

"That is wild," Curt exclaimed.

"It sure goes a long way in explaining why he has treated me the way that he has," J Dub declared.

"And you bring a lot of value to our situation," Lucille acknowledged.

"Denny has told us that the corporation that was operating on that property may have been operating fraudulently," Matt admitted. "That's where you come in under a different capacity."

"He's been under federal investigation for tax evasion," J Dub conceded.

"Not only did a group of dishonest businessmen pull a scam on us several years ago, but now we might be able to show that they operated an illegal enterprise over nearly two decades," Matt theorized.

"Denny feels as if all of you have been defrauded," Curt advocated, "and he feels as if Lew, at the very least, breached his fiduciary duty to J Dub."

"I have done the most research that I can do," Lucille declared. "Under contract law it appears that a transaction can be voided if no consideration was ever given . . . and we got no consideration. No money. Nothing!"

"And since we didn't receive any money for our property we are going to try to get it back," Matt maintained.

"What you've just told me is almost too bizarre to believe," J Dub admitted.

"It's true. It really happened," Lucille said.

"And there is another thing that you need to be made aware of," Matt continued. "Don't trust the U. S. Attorney's office, the FBI or the IRS. We've been trying for over a decade to get them to do something. They don't care about you or us . . ."

" . . . Or justice," Lucille butted in. She reached again for her handkerchief as tears formed in her eyes. "Trying to get the government to help is a total waste of time."

"All the prosecutors want to do is get slam dunk cases to protect their perfect records and further their own personal careers," Matt said angrily.

J Dub leaned back in his seat and stretched his arms. "What you've just told us is incredible!" he exclaimed. "This is unbelievable!"

"If nothing else, it sounds as if we'll be able to fill in some blanks for you," Curt offered, "and you'll be able to fill in some blanks for us."

"We think, along with Denny, that by joining forces we might be able to put a strong case together," Lucille suggested.

"We have some forensic accounting people dissecting the financial statements," J Dub added.

"And I have some contacts with title companies that can run a title search," Curt proposed.

"Then let's put the legal work in Denny's hands," Matt advised.

"That's fine by me as long as he'll work on a contingency basis," J Dub stated.

"He will for you," Matt answered. "We've put a sizable retainer up. You are more than welcome to join in our pursuit of this injustice."

"I see no reason why we can't help each other," J Dub agreed. "I feel terrible for what has happened to you."

"We lost a lot," Lucille stated. "I think more than anything else we don't want to see dishonest people prosper."

J Dub thought long and hard for a minute. "In a twisted sort of way, I'm sitting on both sides of the fence," he started. "On one side of the fence I was part of the group that may have committed fraud against you. That occurred when we bought the property. On the other side of the fence, I knew nothing about what you have just relayed to me. Therefore, Lew and Walter and George have defrauded me."

Lucille and Matt nodded their heads.

"Can I have assurances from you that you won't come back after me?" J Dub asked.

"If you can help us recover what we have lost, then we will most certainly not hold you responsible for any wrongdoing," Lucille promised. "Denny has already talked to us about waiving any conflicts of interests."

The group ended their discussion. J Dub and Curt were speechless. It was certainly going to be an interesting flight home.

CHAPTER EIGHTY-NINE

In the coming days, J Dub scheduled another appointment to meet with Denny. He wanted to talk about the various options that were available to him and try to determine some sort of strategy. Since the decisions that were going to have to be made included his family, J Dub wanted to make sure that not only Curt, but Marcia was present.

The three of them arrived at Denny's office and even though she had been forewarned, the condition of Denny's office appalled Marcia. Papers and files were scattered everywhere and Denny had not taken the time to clean off the chairs so that his clients would have a place to sit. To Marcia it was obvious that he normally conducted business in this haphazard way and she found it repugnant.

"This is my wife, Marcia," J Dub said as he introduced Marcia to Denny.

Denny extended his hand. "Are you allergic to filing?" Marcia asked curtly.

"I've been working on some projects," Denny explained. "We can go into the conference room."

"One can only hope that we can actually open a door without a mountain of papers collapsing on us." Marcia quipped. "You know, this isn't the best way to make an impression."

Denny gave her a look of disdain and then glanced at J Dub and grinned. "At least the chairs will be cleaned off in the conference room."

"Oh, are they visible to the naked eye?" Marcia sarcastically replied. She gave J Dub a look of '*We better not be wasting our time with this guy*'.

He led the three to a separate room behind his office. It was easy to see why Denny said what he had said. Located in the room were a folding table and four folding chairs. The four of them had to open a chair just to sit around the table.

Marcia glared at J Dub. "Can you handle a case like ours?" she said in a condescending manner to Denny. Marcia was sick and tired of fooling around with Lew; she didn't want to spend any more money than necessary with lawyers and she wanted to make sure that if she was going to pursue a legal avenue that she would have a decent chance of winning.

"There are some issues that we need to overcome," Denny started. "But I'll fight for my clients and I think that we have the law on our side."

"Forgive my bluntness but I don't want to get us into a situation where we mail you a check every month," Marcia blurted. "We simply don't have the money to fund an attorney that is on a wild goose chase."

"That won't be the case. I've been working with the heirs of the Morton Estate for about ten years," Denny declared.

"Ten years!" Marcia exclaimed. "We don't want to waste that kind of time."

"In some ways the work that I have done will benefit you," Denny said. "I'm a lot farther along in the research and I think that your addition to the case will strengthen it."

"What kind of time frame are we looking at?" J Dub asked.

"Realistically, probably six to eight years," Denny answered. "With any luck, then we may be able to get it done within eighteen to thirty-six months."

"Knowing Lew, he will put up all kinds of resistance. He'll fight us on every little technicality," J Dub warned.

"He already has. I think that your name on any lawsuit will surprise him. The people you will be hooking up with are substantial, despite all that they have lost," Denny maintained. "We can cause problems for him . . . and well we should. He hasn't been truthful."

"Six to eight years eats up a good portion of our adult life," Marcia suggested.

"I don't think that anyone is too enthused about that," Denny replied, "but that is the way the system operates. Of course, that is before any appeals."

Marcia turned to J Dub. "This is ridiculous. Is all of this really worth it?"

"Matt and Lucille made it clear that they were doing what they were doing just so that dishonest people would not continue to prosper," J Dub clarified. "This is not the only piece of property that they lost."

"Before I agree to anything," Marcia started, "I want to know what is involved and how much it is going to cost us. That guy has already disrupted our family life. The last thing that I want is to be married to him for another decade in court . . . especially when we're footing the bill." She looked at Denny. "And I certainly don't want the clock to start on the fees until your butt hits the seat."

Denny could see that Marcia was going to be an uncompromising client. "The agreement that I have structured is that the estate will take care of the retainer for my fees. You'll only have to pay your costs for filings and copying charges."

"I can't imagine that you'll work for nothing," Marcia disputed.

"You can pay me a contingency fee if we win a judgment."

Marcia's mood began to soften. "What will that be?"

"A third of what we collect."

"What are our chances?" Marcia pried.

After some hesitation Denny said, "Fifty-fifty . . . actually it's more like seventy-five, twenty-five."

"That doesn't sound very good," Marcia responded.

Curt had listened to the exchange and felt the need to explain some things further. "Most lawyers in town won't touch a case on a contingency basis unless they have at least a ninety percent chance of winning," he said.

"Then why does he want to take a case like this?" Marcia queried Curt.

Curt demurred to Denny. "After hearing the story that the Morton heirs relayed, my heartfelt interests entered the picture. I am a lawyer that wants good to triumph over evil . . . ," Denny put into plain words.

" . . . To the tune of a lot of money. That sort of sounds self-serving," Marcia rebutted.

Denny called her bluff. "You don't have to join the heirs if you don't want to. You are free to pack your bags and drive into the sunset. Go ahead and start all over in life if you'd like."

J Dub wanted to press forward and take a shot at recovering his losses. He turned to Marcia. "It's not going to be easy, Hon. This gives us a good opportunity to hold our up-front costs down and strengthen our case."

Marcia weighed all of the information that had been discussed. Three pairs of male eyes stared at her with the hopes that she would put her good graces onto whatever action that Denny deemed necessary. Deep down Marcia couldn't tolerate Lew at all. She wanted to see him pay a handsome price for unsettling their life. "What have we got to lose?" Marcia asked. She turned to J Dub and smiled. "I know how much this means to you. Let's make sure that we're going to win!"

Marcia's blessing was a relief to them. After hearing the tale that the Morton heirs told, the men felt that a fraud had occurred. The main concern for J Dub was that he was going to have to enter a playing field that was foreign to him. "What did you find out over the last couple of weeks?" J Dub asked Denny.

"It's not good."

"What happened now?"

Denny hated to be the bearer of bad news especially after the conversation that had just taken place with Marcia. "My sources told me that the U. S. Attorney's office has decided not to press charges on the tax evasion situation that the IRS was investigating."

J Dub sighed. "I can't say that it has come totally unexpected. Booker told me that it would be tough if Hackett resigned. Ellie was the main force that wanted to pursue his conviction. Plus, I haven't heard from him in a few weeks."

Denny enlightened the group. "It would have been nice to piggyback behind the criminal charges."

"But then any attorney in town would have hopped on this case," Curt jumped in.

"There are some things that we can do. We have a lot of the same information that the IRS was utilizing," Denny added.

"Have you decided what way to take this thing?" J Dub asked.

"Not yet. The nice thing is that we have several avenues that are available to us."

"Which way are you leaning?"

"I'm leaning toward federal court," Denny began. "A tax fraud has no state boundaries. It is a federal condition."

"What does that mean?"

"Basically we can file a lawsuit in any federal court," Denny replied. "So, I've been researching federal law."

Curt was interested in hearing what the research indicated. "What did you turn up?"

"Obviously fraud," Denny answered, "but because the deception involved so many people and lasted for such a long time, I'm thinking that other violations may have occurred."

"What sort of violations?" J Dub probed.

"Maybe some sort of conspiracy to commit a crime. An unjust enrichment charge might have sufficient grounds. Things like that," Denny replied. "What's interesting is that there are elements of a conspiracy here. The skimming lasted for a number of years which means that it might have been an ongoing illegal activity between Walter and Lew."

"The U. S Attorney's office said that it wasn't," J Dub countered.

Denny defended his thoughts. "They said that from a criminal standpoint. All we have to do is to prove that the skimming was ongoing over a number of years for the purposes of a civil lawsuit."

J Dub's interest was piqued. "Where does the conspiracy come in?"

"Lew did it with the help and aid of Walter," Denny declared. "He was your tax man. Even though the IRS couldn't prove that they acted together, I think that we'll be able to show that Walter was an agent for the corporation and the two of them acted in conjunction."

"Will it hold up?"

"Who knows what a judge and jury will say?" Denny replied. "Walter was also an agent for the Morton Estate. The sale of the property may have involved the efforts of several of them too. We know that Lew's name was on the contract and that George Pierce's title company closed the transaction. Walter was also involved in the sale since he was the executor."

J Dub wanted to learn as much as he could about the legal battle that was going to ensue. " . . . Anything else?"

"The lesser charge of breach of fiduciary duty may apply. We can't go after too much. We'll need to keep things simple for the jury," Denny advised.

"What's the time frame to start all of this?"

"The Morton heirs want to keep the hammer down. It looks like Lew, with the help of Grady Patterson, will beat them on an adverse possession claim. That will open the door for Lew to sell the property to Norman Pierce. In fact the sale might already be closed. I think that we will document everything, continue our investigation and launch the lawsuit when the time is right," Denny said as he spelled out his strategy.

"When is that to take place?"

"Who knows? Keep you ears open."

"What federal court do you want to use?"

"I want to take the case across the river. Let's get a new venue," Denny offered. "Walter has offices over there and the estate already has a lawsuit pending in state court over there."

"But all of the property is in Illinois," J Dub countered.

"It's a chance we'll take," Denny suggested. "But it may also be something of a trial balloon for us. I want to see exactly how these guys react and plan on defending themselves."

J Dub fired the questions as fast as he could think of them. "What are we talking about for damages?"

"In looking at the appraisal and all of the lot development and commercial possibilities, the retail value of the property is around forty million dollars," Denny theorized.

"And it should have been mine," J Dub lamented, "or at least the rights to it."

"Remember though, that the estate feels that it should be theirs. The beauty of the punitive damages is that the jury can decide what your injuries were," Denny explained.

"What's that?"

"Any damages that the jury decides might very well get tripled," Denny spelled out.

Marcia was astonished. "Are you talking about one hundred and twenty million dollars?" Marcia shouted.

Denny looked straight at Marcia and nodded. He meant business. "This has been going on for far too long. We want to get the property back for the estate. And in the process you've been damaged too. For anything close to that though we'll have to keep it in federal court."

"What sort of arrangement will we make with the estate?" J Dub asked.

"You two can discuss that," Denny proposed. "They don't want to come after you. We'll have the two of you sign a conflict of interest release. They only want to get Lew and the people that worked with him to defraud them."

Marcia looked around the room. The monetary figure that preoccupied her mind was numbing. "Are you sure that you aren't leading us down a path of no return?" Denny shook his head back and forth. "One hundred and twenty million dollars is like winning the lottery," she continued.

"We're not going to mess around with these characters," Denny assured her. "What they've done and gotten away with up until this point in time is heinous."

CHAPTER NINETY

Via a quiet title judgment a judge awarded Lew possession of the five-acre tract of land that the Morton heirs had disputed. As incredible as it was, the adverse possession claim that Lew had made survived the justice system. His old friend Grady Patterson had gotten it done.

With the title work cleaned up, Norman closed on the property. Monty was instrumental in drawing up the documents as well as any and all agreements that Lew and Norman would live by in the coming years. The golf course property would be sold to Norman who would then form a corporation to operate the golf course business. Lew and Norman entered into a joint venture agreement to develop the surrounding property into home sites and a shopping center.

The closing occurred late in the day on a Friday afternoon. A celebration followed and the cocktails flowed well into the night. A limousine whisked Lew, Monty and Norman off to dinner and eventually back to Lew's place for a night of debauchery with a few hired playmates.

It was a major coup for the businessmen. Lew pocketed several million dollars worth of cash. Norman had acquired enough property to keep his homebuilding company busy for the next decade. Monty loved the action and whatever remnants of cash that would fall into his lap . . . not to mention the evening that was enjoyed with the hired entertainment.

In the meantime, a slew of people had been working behind the scenes to head the culprits off at the pass. Denny continued his research into the law and the various rights that his clients possessed. The Morton heirs persisted with their efforts to supply as much documentation to Denny to support their claims. J Dub, Marcia and Curt worked with a local title company to obtain a title search as well as a detailed chain of title on the property.

Sean McVoy was a young man in his mid-thirties. He had gotten an opportunity many years earlier to become a partner in FARM and HOME TITLE COMPANY. It turned out to be the perfect occupation for his personality. Not many people possess the ability to research deeds in intricate detail. Hours and hours of exploratory examination at the County Recorder's Office are needed to ensure a thorough job. Sean always wore a white business shirt and sloppily-tied tie. Even though everyone at the Recorder's Office knew him, he insisted on wearing a name tag so that he would be easily identifiable. His glasses looked out of date. His words would slobber out of his mouth.

Despite his physical idiosyncrasies, Sean's work was meticulous. J Dub had heard that no one in the area could research title as well as Sean McVoy, so a detailed order was placed. The results were forthcoming.

"We had heard through the grapevine that some hanky-panky had occurred down there on that piece of property," Sean started as J Dub took a seat in the conference room of the title company.

J Dub had reached the point in his life when he felt like an inquisitive ten-year old. It seemed like he had a question for every new person that was entering his life. "What sort of hanky-panky?"

"A long time ago we had heard that a questionable transaction had taken place down there," Sean relayed.

"How so?"

"Oh, you know, someone had pulled a fast one and they had gotten away with it," Sean reiterated.

"What do you mean?" J Dub pried further.

"The scuttlebutt was that some guys had ripped off an absentee ownership group," Sean continued. "It was a hot topic when I first started here but the rumors were swept under the table pretty quickly. I haven't heard another thing about it until you walked in here a few weeks ago and placed the order with us."

"Is there any truth to the rumor?"

"What a mess!" Sean said as the words drooled out of his mouth. "How are you involved in it?"

"I was a partner in a group that purchased that property back then," J Dub volunteered.

"Sorry it took me so long," Sean said apologetically. "There has been a lot of back and forth movement on that property."

"How can that be?" J Dub inquired. "We've had it in the corporation for a long time."

"The deeds on the property don't indicate that," Sean rebuked. He threw a large stack of deeds onto the conference table. "Here's your chain of title."

"All of this stuff is a title search?" J Dub commented as he flipped through the massive stack of paperwork. "Why would one or two transactions cause all of this?"

"Because there were more than one or two transactions," Sean replied. He rolled out a map that consisted of several colored overlays. "This is a great diagram that will help you understand. Let's use this. It's kind of like playing Monopoly."

J Dub studied the plastic, color-coordinated visual aid. It was obvious that Sean had scrupulously prepared a detailed map. "What in the world have you done?"

"Going through all of those deeds is so confusing. I thought that I would help both of us out by tracking all of the transactions in color. That way it is a little easier to actually see all of the activity that occurred down there," Sean clarified.

"I'll try to follow you the best that I can," J Dub stated.

Sean flipped the first plastic overlay into place. Several parcels of property were covered with yellow acetate. "The yellow indicates all of the property that originally was owned by the estate."

"How many acres is that?"

"Well over four hundred."

"That should be correct," J Dub agreed. That was what Lew said that he originally had under contract. We added some acreage later as we made money."

"Here's where it starts to get tricky," Sean said. He could barely hide his enthusiasm. It was as if he had discovered the pot at the end of the rainbow.

Another overlay dropped on top of the yellow acetate. "There was no consideration given for the property in orange."

"When you say 'no consideration' what do you mean?" J Dub inquired. "We paid for the property."

Sean handed J Dub a deed. "No money was given for this acreage. This parcel is two-hundred and fifty acres. Here is the deed that says that no consideration was given for this property. It's stamped right on the deed."

"That's the property that Lew said that he bought from the estate. The golf course turned around and bought it from him several years later," J Dub declared puzzled.

"Then he made a big profit on it because he didn't give them a dime for it," Sean maintained.

"How can he get away with that?" J Dub asked.

"Your guess is as good as mine. It looks like he gave the contract to a lawyer or a title company and they simply transferred title over to him," Sean put into plain words. "Why they would have done that without collecting any money is beyond me."

"That's like stealing it!" J Dub exclaimed.

Sean looked above his glasses and snuck a peek at J Dub. "I can't disagree." He flipped another overlay into place. The acetate was covered in green. "You said that you got a loan for the golf course, right?"

'Yeah, sure we did."

"The green represents the property that was offered as security on the loan," Sean indicated.

"You mean the collateral?"

"Yes."

Sean slid another plastic piece of acetate into place. Red markings covered the grid. "You said that you refinanced the business on several occasions, right?" Sean questioned J Dub.

J Dub nodded his head in agreement.

"The deeds indicate that. Evidently Lew altered the legal descriptions of the collateral. With every refinancing, deeds of release appear to have been issued and recorded. They indicate that different collateral was in place for the different loans."

J Dub was in a mild state of confusion. "How can the bank let that happen?"

"Once again, your guess is as good as mine. They either didn't know or didn't care or maybe didn't even look at it," Sean speculated. "And it gets better."

"More surprises, huh?"

"The last overlay is what's going to knock your socks off," Sean said as the saliva started to dribble out of his mouth. He reached for the final overlay. "Evidently, when Lew received the deeds of release from the bank and the collateral was changed, he then quit-claimed the property from the golf course to himself. All of the black represents property that Lew has titled in his personal name."

Virtually the entire map was black.

"Oh no! Say it isn't so!" J Dub shouted.

"I wish that I could."

How can that be?" J Dub yelled.

"All I do is research at the Recorder's Office. This was what was indicated," Sean explained.

"Where did the money go?" J Dub pried.

"We know that it didn't go to the estate. The tax stamp that indicates 'No Consideration' tells us that," Sean started.

"Help me out a little," J Dub begged. "We got a bank loan. What's going on?"

"I don't know what happened. Unless the money was going to the title company for disbursement and the title company was keeping it. That is so unheard of . . . that it is either stupid or ballsy."

"What do you mean?"

"Let's think this through. If you say that the loan was made by the bank, then the money had to go to the title company to be paid to the sellers. But it clearly says on these deeds that nothing was given for the property," Sean theorized.

"That would mean that the title company kept the money," J Dub implied. "That was George Pierce."

"And this evidence confirms the rumors that I heard a long time ago," Sean deduced.

"Lew got the land, George Pierce got the money, and the estate got nothing!" J Dub shrieked. J Dub gathered the overlays and picked up all of the papers that indicated the chain of title. "This is mind-boggling! I've got to get this to my lawyer."

"Go to the Recorder's Office and Assessor's Office and cross reference this information," Sean advised. "The very thought is so brazen."

J Dub headed for the door. "When you really think about it, why rob a bank?"

It was Sean's turn to ask a question. "What are you getting at?"

"Why take a chance by hitting a Brinks driver on Friday afternoon at the local bank? You can get a heckuva lot more by doing it like this," J Dub hypothesized.

"That's a valid point. A person's gain could maybe be twenty times as much. And up to now they've gotten away with it," Sean concurred.

"Pretty disgusting, isn't it?" J Dub commented as he gathered up the colored maps and headed for the door.

CHAPTER NINETY-ONE

The Recorder's Office was located in the County Courthouse, an old three-storied, red-bricked building surrounded by a town square. It seems like every county seat across mid-America looks the same with its Civil War cannon out front. Majestic oak trees shaded the manicured bluegrass. Pansies and daffodils in the spring were replaced by a variety of multi-colored chrysanthemums in the fall.

J Dub needed to check to see if Sean had omitted anything. Taking Sean's advice was a good start he thought. He arrived at the courthouse around mid-morning and promptly stumbled up to the counter in the Recorder's Office. "Can someone please help me?"

A tight-lipped, female clerk named Delores sauntered over. She looked like a housewife that wanted something to do after her children either went off to college or left home to start a family. She had a turned-up nose that made her look snooty. "How can I help?" she offered.

"I've got a lot of legal descriptions and parcel numbers," J Dub began. "Can we check the rightful property owners?"

"It's all here on the computer."

"Can you look up Prairie Winds Golf Course?" J Dub asked.

Delores typed several keystrokes onto the keyboard. Nothing seemed to come up on the screen. "That's funny. Nothing seems to come up for Prairie Winds Golf Course," she said.

The questions had started to become a habit for J Dub. "How can that be? Are you sure you typed it in correctly?"

She typed a few more words. "Yes, but I'll recheck." A minute or two elapsed as she studied the monitor. "Wait, here's a past entry."

J Dub could smell a dead animal on the side of the road. "Could you do me a favor?"

"Sure, I'll try."

"Could you look up Lewferd E. Zerrmann and tell me what sort of property he has?"

Delores typed on the keyboard. Six pages of entries popped up on the monitor. "He owns lots and lots of property."

J Dub muttered under his breath. "It's all public knowledge, isn't it?"

" . . . Of course."

Rubbing his face in exasperation, J Dub asked "Could you give me a copy of all of his property and when it was titled in his name?"

"Sure," Delores stated. "We have to charge ten cents for every page."

"I'll wait," J Dub informed her. "Copy everything. I need to know when, where and how he titled property in his own name."

Delores nodded her head and began the task.

J Dub hit the vending machine a few times. He was on his third candy bar and second beverage when Delores informed him that she was finished. "Here it is," she declared. "It looks like the property was recently sold. There is a pending transaction that needs to be recorded."

"Who was it sold to?"

"It looks like N and P Enterprises."

J Dub thought out loud. "Who is that?"

"You can contact the Secretary of State's office. They have the principals of every corporation on file."

"You said N as in Norman and P as in Pierce, right?" J Dub surmised. Delores nodded. "Copy that too," J Dub advised. "I need all of it."

J Dub was getting angrier by the minute. *Jeez my knees! This is like peeling an onion with all the shady work that has been going on right under my nose!* However, his anger inspired him to get on a mission. Not only had he provided a wealth of information to Denny in regard to the financial affairs of the corporation, but now he had gathered important data that supported a fraudulent transfer of property. He headed straight to Denny's office.

"Here's a lot of documentation that supports what the Morton heirs have maintained all along," J Dub began as he placed the box of deeds on Denny's desk.

"Where have you been?" Denny pried.

"Some of the information is from the title company that details the chain of title. The other documents are from the Recorder's Office," J Dub answered.

"Good," Denny said. "You're doing your homework."

"I had no idea what was going on," J Dub acknowledged. "It's sickening to know that they could do that to the estate and get away with it for so long. I just know that I am hearing the same names over and over when it comes to these transactions on the chain of title."

"Hey, you're a victim too," Denny implied. "You ran a business that you thought was operating on the up and up. Plus, you thought that your future was protected with the option to purchase the property."

"Can you imagine if Lew would have sold me the property?" J Dub thought out loud at the irony of the situation. "You'd be suing me now on behalf of the estate."

"And you'd be in a bigger mess. Be glad that you didn't buy it," Denny suggested.

"What's the plan from here on out?" J Dub asked.

"I want to put the finishing touches on the lawsuit in the next couple of weeks. Then we'll try to get them all served over the same weekend," Denny explained.

"Who are we going after?"

"I want to serve Lew, Walter Hancock, George Pierce, and Norman Pierce," Denny responded. "Lew has been successful in getting one lawsuit dismissed that the estate has filed. He also beat them in court on the adverse possession claim. Plus, he's dodged a bullet against the U. S. Attorney's office not once, but twice. It's time to put a stop to what he is doing."

"Nobody else was willing to help me since the 'hold harmless' document was signed," J Dub stated. "Can we get around that?"

"I think that we can if it was fraudulently induced," Denny claimed. "There's case law that supports that theory."

J Dub was fired up and anxious to get the ball rolling. "I'm ready whenever you are."

"The estate has a pending suit against Walter. That case should be going to trial soon," Denny informed J Dub. "After damn near six years they can't stall any more. It's ready to go to court."

"Will that case help our cause?"

"It should," Denny admitted. "Walter's deposition testimony could be very damaging."

The questions rolled out of J Dub's mouth once again. "Why is that?"

"He admitted under oath that, as the executor of the estate, he did not receive any money for the property," Denny told J Dub.

"That should cook him, don't you think?" J Dub stated.

"We're hopeful," Denny explained, "but I want to wait and serve everyone at about the same time that that case is going to trial. That should be another surprise that they aren't counting on."

CHAPTER NINETY-TWO

The Fall of 2000 . . .

It had been almost three years since Lew had forced J Dub out of the corporation. Just like the morning of the raid, all hell broke loose over a weekend that was better suited for riding across the countryside looking at the changing of the leaves. Lew, Walter, and Norman were all served with papers that indicated that they were being sued by the heirs to the Morton Estate and J Dub. George Pierce was nowhere to be found, but it was believed that he was out of the country. The heirs to the Morton Estate had last traced him to the Virgin Islands.

Denny had been true to his word. He kept the lawsuit simple. The lawsuit alleged four counts of wrongdoing: fraud, breach of fiduciary duty, unjust enrichment and breach of contract. Despite all of the evidence it was going to be tough to prove.

Walter and Norman wasted no time either. Both of them were immediately on the phone to Lew. They demanded that he tell them what this latest lawsuit was all about. The three of them agreed to meet in Walter's office later that weekend. "What in hell have you got me involved in this time?" Walter demanded of Lew.

"I haven't done anything. When everything gets sorted out, you'll see that none of us have done anything wrong," Lew said defensively.

"Does this have anything to do with the tax investigation?" Walter shouted.

"It beats me," Lew insisted. "The IRS looked at us for a few years and said that we didn't do anything unlawful."

"Just because we didn't break the law doesn't mean that what was done didn't injure anyone civilly," Walter claimed.

"Then make them prove it," Lew countered.

"Prove it my ass!" Walter yelled. "I want the damn thing dismissed and all of this crap to go away!"

"Doesn't the estate already have a lawsuit pending against you?" Lew asked Walter.

"Yes they do, dammit!"

"Isn't that what is called double jeopardy?" Lew inquired.

"No, it's on stuff that is different from these charges," Walter shrieked.

Norman was finished with listening. "I don't know what the two of you have been up to but I don't appreciate being dragged into this mess."

"We haven't done anything," Lew stressed again. "The U. S. Attorney's office and the IRS said that we have operated within the scope of the law. That was years ago."

"Why was the lawsuit filed in federal court across the river?" Norman asked.

"As executor of the estate they are claiming that the whole mess started with me," Walter explained. "Since I have an office over there, I guess they figured that they would file the paperwork in Missouri."

"As far as I'm concerned we're all over in Illinois and so is the property. I want to get the thing transferred over here," Norman insisted.

"It's that damn Sneed character," Lew ranted. "I've had enough of him! This is about the third time that he's sued me on behalf of the estate!"

"What have you done?" Norman asked.

" . . . Nothing!" Lew answered. "And it wouldn't surprise me if he isn't behind the tax investigation either!"

"They must have something on you two to keep coming after you," Norman hinted.

"J Dub can't come after me. He signed a release saying that he would hold me harmless for everything that we were associated with," Lew boasted.

"That doesn't do the two of us any good," Walter begged to differ.

"The best thing to do is for all of us to get our own attorneys," Norman proposed. "Let's work on getting this thing over where it belongs."

Lew couldn't agree fast enough. "That a good idea. We need to get the lawsuit back over on our home turf where we can do something about it."

"The sooner the better," Walter stressed. "I've got my other trial starting in a week or so."

"I'm tired of this crap. I'm going to teach J Dub and that Sneed fella a lesson or two," Lew promised.

"In the meantime, let's get our attorneys on this thing," Norman concluded.

CHAPTER NINETY-THREE

Being in court was not one of J Dub's favorite activities. He had lost his job, he had taken a financial beating, and his life appeared to be headed into limbo for the unforeseeable future. He fought a myriad of emotions from failure to helplessness to hope . . . and the hope was for a miracle.

From their very first meeting, Denny had warned J Dub that the legal process would not go quickly. He suggested that J Dub find another job and try to keep busy doing constructive activities. Denny did his best to prepare J Dub for a long and lengthy battle.

After a half-hearted attempt as a night manager of a fast food facility and a three-day trial period sitting behind a desk as a stockbroker trainee, J Dub migrated back to what he knew best. He returned to the golf business and took a position at a local driving range. It was quite a step down financially in the middle part of his life but it enabled him to do what he loved. He had ample opportunity to teach the game of golf to children and the athletically challenged. The emotional rewards were worth every cent that the paycheck couldn't reimburse.

In the meantime, the lawsuit put the brakes on any sort of development plans that Lew and Norman had planned. Norman didn't know bluegrass from zoysia or a gang mower from a greens mower. Nor did he care. Consequently, the business at Prairie Winds Golf Course dropped off due to the lackluster effort by the new ownership. The regulars didn't like what had happened to J Dub and they found another golf course to play.

Each battle in court was similar to a yellow light on a main thoroughfare . . . hurry up and stop. The wrangling went back and forth. Every action called for a thirty day response and a new court date. Frivolous motions were constantly filed. Lew either tried to delay the inevitable or get the lawsuit dismissed or be victorious on a minor technicality. All of his tactics were within the scope of the law and subsequently forced interruptions in moving the case forward.

From the beginning J Dub felt overwhelmed. After a while he sensed that his side was severely overmatched. J Dub and the Morton heirs had one lawyer while Lew, Walter, and Norman each had their private counsel.

Denny was dressed in a suit that looked like it was purchased at the local discount house. The attorneys for the opposition wore tailored suits and shirts with cuff links. Denny wore shoes with rubber soles and dried mud on the edges. The opposing attorneys wore leather footwear that appeared to be spit-shined. Denny would show up in court with ruffled hair and a shoddy appearance while the attorneys for the defendants were manicured perfectly.

It was apparent that the battle was going to be uphill despite whatever rights J Dub and the Morton heirs thought that they possessed.

In the end, after eight months of squabbling, the gavel came down. The judge transferred the lawsuit over to the federal court in Illinois. The defendants were victorious in getting a change of venue back to their home turf. The lawsuit was assigned to the court of a familiar acquaintance of Lew Zerrmann . . . none other than an avid duck hunter named Judge Troy Rowland.

The Morton heirs had flown up from Florida to be present for the ruling. Denny quickly assembled a meeting with J Dub, Marcia, Curt and the Morton heirs. "What the heck are we going to do now?" J Dub inquired.

"We can't be in court over there," Denny urged.

"It's not our first choice but we have to stay the course," J Dub stressed.

"We can't be in Judge Rowland's court," Matt interjected.

"Why?" J Dub asked.

"He's already ruled against us in a previous case against Lew," Matt explained.

Denny nodded his head and substantiated Matt's comment. "That was one of the reasons we wanted to file across the river."

"What are we going to do now?" J Dub repeated.

"My thoughts are to drop the lawsuit," Denny suggested.

"We can't do that, can we?" J Dub asked. "I don't want to throw in the towel and give up."

"We can fight them in their own backyard," Denny proposed. "We'll just take the case into state court instead of federal court."

J Dub was still in an inquisitive mode. "Can we do that and have a chance?"

"Sure," Denny stated. "Not all of the decisions are going to go our way."

"That's not the end of the world, is it?" Marcia asked.

"No," Denny confirmed, "not at all. In a way it is sort of a blessing. We have one year to re-file the lawsuit. It will give us a little more time to prepare our case and obtain more evidence. The heirs still have a pending suit against Walter that should be concluded by then."

"The element of surprise will still be there," Matt maintained. "I think that they realize that we're not going away."

Within forty-eight hours of the judge's ruling Denny filed a motion to have the lawsuit dismissed without prejudice. If Judge Rowland accepted the motion, then the plaintiffs would be allowed to file a new suit on the same claims in a different venue.

Denny's advice was right on the mark. Since the motion was filed so quickly after the judge transferred the case to federal court in Illinois, the judge granted the lawsuit to be dismissed without prejudice. The plaintiffs were free to file a new lawsuit within twelve months. They had some more work to do.

The defendants went into a celebratory mode once they were informed that the lawsuit had been dropped. Lew immediately invited Norman over for a few cocktails and live entertainment in the dungeon. Monty was also present. He had become as much a part of the dungeon as the bondage equipment.

Walter, on the other hand, was having the fight of his professional life against the heirs on the charges that he did not accept any money for the sale of the property. Despite instructions from his attorney to cease all communication with Lew, Walter called for another meeting in his office with Lew and Norman. "I told you that we would bust their asses!" Lew gushed. "We haven't done anything wrong!"

Walter stared at Lew. "Do you only think about yourself?" Walter sighed. He had a much more difficult time accepting the good fate. "I'm not out of the woods yet."

"You'll be fine," Lew said with an air of encouragement.

"My position with the estate is a little different than yours," Walter informed Lew. "And I'm getting real concerned."

"What did you do?" Norman pried.

"It goes way back to when George was in town," Walter informed Norman, "and I have a feeling that you know exactly what we did."

"Hasn't the Statute of Limitations expired?" Norman inquired. "That was over fifteen years ago."

"It's based on the last predicate act and subsequent action," Walter advised. "These court challenges have been constant since the beginning. Besides it might be forty years with real estate."

"Is George involved?" Norman probed. He wanted to find out whether or not his brother might be liable for any wrongdoing. The fact that George left the country and stayed away suggested that he might be up to his elbows with legal problems.

"My guess is that you know what he did. You were partners in the title company with him," Walter reminded Norman.

Norman finally started getting a little apprehensive. "Can they come back against me, too?" Even though Norman didn't have an active role in the title company, he was listed as an officer in the corporation.

"They're going after George. If they get him, then they'll probably keep going and go after you, too," Walter alerted Norman.

"I'm going to stop all of the bullshit," Lew spoke up. "The best defense is an aggressive offense."

Walter rolled his eyes. He had gotten terribly tired of Lew and many of his ideas. In fact, he wanted the guy to get out of his life. "What do you have in mind now?"

"I've already informed Grady to file a counter claim against the heirs to the Morton Estate, J Dub, that Sneed character that thinks he's a lawyer, as well as his law firm," Lew boasted.

"Don't jump the gun," Walter pleaded.

"I'm going to put an end to this crap. I'm going to teach all of these people what capitalism is all about," Lew persisted.

"And what is your interpretation of it?" Walter probed.

"Prey on the weak! They can't stay with me. My pockets are too deep for them," Lew insisted.

Walter repeated a familiar saying. "Let sleeping dogs lie."

"Look, I'm not getting any younger. I want to get on with my life. These folks are holding me hostage. Norman and I can make over thirty million dollars on that project!" Lew yelled.

"You've got more money than you can spend during the rest of your life! How much is enough?" Walter asked.

"You can never have enough!" Lew insisted. "I'm going to take all of them down for the count! They can't outlast me!"

Walter glared across the desk into the eyes of a true narcissist. Lew's wrath and hostility was profound. He lived in a "me" world and alienated the sane people that surrounded him. His insecurities nibbled away at his grandiose self-image. Any breakdowns of the lifetime wall of protection would sink him into chaotic incoherency. In some ways Walter wanted to be defeated by the heirs so that justice would finally be served on a platter to Lew.

"You know, if they take me down," Walter stated calmly, "it will lead directly to you. You better think before you act selfishly."

"Screw them! I want to recover my legal fees. I'm going after the title company for messing up that five-acre tract. Plus I'm going after the liability insurance company to recover the costs to defend myself," Lew bellowed across the room. "I'm tired of all these people messing with me and my money!" Lew was intoxicated with power.

At seventy, Lew had defiantly decided to spend the remaining years of his life paying lawyers to stay in a courtroom. He paid attorneys to defend him against the IRS. He paid attorneys to clean up the title work. And he paid attorneys to sue J Dub, the Morton heirs, Dennis Sneed as well as the parent title company.

Walter was sick of hearing how Lew had always been a victim. "If you didn't have a lawsuit going, then I don't think that you'd be able to sleep at night. Is that all that you have to do?" he asked Lew.

"I haven't done anything wrong. I want my money back!" Lew countered.

Chapter Ninety-Four

Summer of 2001 . . .

Grady Patterson could try with all of his might to give Lew sound legal advice. Yet, Lew had a mind of his own. Grady advised Lew not to file a counter claim against the parties that had sued in civil court. The advice fell on deaf ears just as it had when he had given his opinion not to sue the title company. Lew had turned into a desperate "wrecking ball" that was content on living in a litigious world.

Within a week of the dismissal of the civil lawsuit Lew made sure that the Morton heirs, J Dub, Denny Sneed and Sneed's law firm were served with papers demanding reimbursement of his legal fees along with punitive damages. For good measure,

302

Lew also sued Curt and Marcia for slander and defamatory remarks. To take things one step further, he filed a claim with the liability insurance company. He wanted to be reimbursed for the legal fees that he had spent obtaining the change of venue.

Within days of filing the claim against the liability insurance company, the insurance company filed suit against Lew, Walter, Norman, the Morton heirs and J Dub. They wanted to get the facts of the fraud charges. One of the provisions in the liability insurance policy stated that if Lew had misrepresented any facts, the insurance company would not have to pay the claim. So Lew had to hire Grady again to defend him in that lawsuit. It was a vicious circle that kept Lew's ego puffed up with power.

If the facts weren't going to come out in any of the depositions, then they were never going to come out. Lew had a title company and an insurance company that wanted to know what was going on. Both of those entities smelled a rat. They were prepared to go to great lengths and spend countless dollars to find out the truth.

The last comment that he made to Grady before he walked out of Grady's office was, "Make sure that they know what it's like to spend money that they don't have to defend themselves! I'm going to bury them!"

"You really don't know what you're talking about," Grady warned. "The title company, the insurance company and the Morton heirs are going to get to the bottom of what you have done. They can all outspend you!"

"Let them try!" Lew yelled with abundant self-confidence.

"If you want to fight, then I hope that you're ready to pay for my legal fees," Grady argued.

"You bet I am. After I'm exonerated I plan to recover them anyway," Lew insisted.

"What have you done, by the way?" Grady probed for an answer.

" . . . Nothing!" Lew insisted.

"You're as clean as a baby's ass after a bath?" Grady asked.

"You better believe I am," Lew said adamantly.

"You can bet your ass that they are going to find out. You better be right or you're going to pay out the tail," Grady warned Lew again. "Am I getting through to you?"

Lew was telling Grady what to do instead of the other way around. All of the defendants were served within an hour or so of each other. It was a surprise for J Dub to hear the pounding on his front door. He wandered to the front door to see what all of the commotion was about. A rough looking character asked for J Dub to identify himself. He then handed over a forty some-odd page document informing J Dub that he had been sued by Lewferd E. Zerrmann.

Lew achieved the desired effect that he sought. The notice caused J Dub to ride the roller-coaster ride of sensations. He was shocked, scared, mad, frustrated, and most of all concerned. The first order of business was to break the news to Marcia. He then picked up the phone and called Denny. A meeting was hurriedly scheduled for the next day in Denny's office. "You never told me that he could do this," J Dub addressed Denny.

Marcia had progressed past the point of tears. She was livid. "I don't know what strategy we have up our sleeve, but this was one event that I wasn't counting on!"

"Okay. Everybody calm down," Denny started.

"I'm glad he came after me," Curt butted in. "I'm going to be the idiot's worst nightmare!" Denny smiled. "Now I can be on my brother's side and take an active role," Curt continued. "And when it's all said and done I'm going to go after his backside!"

"Let's look at what he is trying to do," Denny carried on calmly. "For everyone's information, in case you missed it in the affidavit, I got sued, too."

"He's trying to intimidate," J Dub reasoned. "In all my years as his partner I've seen it all too many times."

"It looks to me like he's trying to break up our alliance," Denny suggested. "We all got served, including Curt and Marcia."

"Yeah, what's that all about?" Marcia demanded.

"He might think that we'll all have to get separate counsel otherwise we will have a conflict of interest with each other," Denny informed.

"It's a way for him to put us on our heels and make us defend ourselves," Curt declared.

"I don't fully understand what Grady is doing," Denny persisted. "Surely he advised his client that we have the right to re-file a lawsuit against his client."

J Dub spoke up. "I know Lew. This is an attempt by him to bully us. He doesn't care if we can file another suit against him. This is his way of threatening us . . ."

" . . . And try to get his beloved money back," Marcia interrupted.

"In some ways he might be successful," Denny informed the group.

A distraught look enveloped J Dub's face. His life had come unraveled at the time that he should have been able to enjoy the good years of his life. "What are we faced with?"

Denny buried his head into his hand. It looked like a trip to the restroom was imminent.

"And how do we deal with it?" Marcia added.

The annoying pause that Denny reverted to when his mind was deep in thought invaded the room. The small group stood motionless staring at Denny for something, if anything that they could cling to. They had come too far to let it all go. After an excruciating silence of several minutes passed, Curt finally blurted "Just say something!"

Denny placed his forefinger and thumb on each side of his nose. He pressed on the pressure points located at the confluence of his eyes and nostril. His head rose and he looked at the group. "Okay, here's what we have to do."

"It better be good," Marcia coaxed.

"He's a formidable opponent," J Dub added.

"Look, he's trying to get me off the case. If he gets rid of me, then he knows that you folks can't get an attorney," Denny began. "If he separates you from the estate then he realizes that your staying power is gone."

J Dub glanced at Marcia. It was obvious that what Denny was saying was hitting home.

Denny continued with his line of reasoning. "I believe in this case. After finding out all of the intricacies of deception, it is my professional opinion that you folks have a solid case, but we're going to have to go our separate ways to some degree."

A look of despair shrouded J Dub and Marcia.

"I'll be able to get my insurance company to provide a malpractice attorney to defend me. That will not help you. So what I'll do is get the very best defense lawyer that I can find for you. There are some excellent attorneys that will take up this fight."

His words started to offer the assurances that J Dub, Marcia, and Curt were searching for. He knew that it was his responsibility to find someone that would go to battle for them.

"In fact, all of this might backfire into Lew's face. We can go into his neighborhood and find someone that is worthy. I'll find someone that owes me a favor on a referral. I'll get good representation for you," Denny assured the clients.

"What I'll also do is make a few phone calls and try to find a high-powered law firm that wants to take a look at this case on a contingency basis. I'll find someone that has the resources to outlast Lew. We have a wealth of incriminating evidence. Some firm out there will gamble on the work that we have accomplished. I can guarantee you that," Denny continued.

J Dub rose from his chair. He extended his hand to Denny. "That little so and so never knew when enough was enough. We're behind you one hundred percent."

"We're not about to quit halfway through the fight," Curt concurred.

Perhaps it was from meditation. Perhaps it was from yoga. A sense of relaxation prevailed over Denny. He forced a tight-lipped smile. "When you stop and think about it, in the long run, this might be the best thing that ever happened to us."

"Getting sued?" Marcia questioned. "That's something I never wanted, nor would have wished on anybody."

"No. No. No. Not at all," Denny carried on. "Who knows? Maybe I was in over my head," he admitted. "This suit might finally allow for us to get some top-notch lawyers involved in this case. If we can get the right attorneys working on this, then I think that we're going to have a decent chance at bringing these guys down."

"We've always known that it was a house of cards," J Dub maintained.

"If we could just loosen that first brick away from the mortar . . ." Curt started.

" . . . Then the whole wall might just start tumbling down," J Dub finished.

"Walter's case is going to trial real soon. He can't get any more extensions," Denny stated enthusiastically. "Give me a few days to make a couple of phone calls. There are a few heavy-duty friends of mine that owe me a favor. I'll be getting right back to you."

CHAPTER NINETY-FIVE

The Fall of 2001 . . .

The legal game was on and it wasn't anything like the game of golf with which J Dub was much more familiar. The deception, deceit, delays and dishonesty that pervaded the courtroom were so different than the way people conducted themselves on the golf course.

Lew had decided to flex his muscles and spend the remaining days of his life writing checks to attorneys. In the process, he brought a lot of people into the entanglement. His intimidation tactics may have worked in other endeavors in his life but in this particular battle, the truth was going to come out and the course of action was going to be very expensive. Lew truly believed that his aggression would surely weaken his foe.

In tough times unpredictable things happen. Denny worked overtime on the phone. He felt like he was responsible for putting the Morton heirs, J Dub, Marcia and Curt into a dire predicament. From an outsiders' perspective it sure seemed like he had messed up the legal maneuvers and had cost his clients dearly. Yet, the underdogs strengthened their resolve.

Denny had a productive telephone discussion with Eldie McLaughlin and met him the next day. McLaughlin was the principal partner in the most influential and politically connected law firm in the county where Grady Patterson had filed the summons on behalf of Lew. If Lew was serious about going through with his complaint, he was going to have his hands full. McLaughlin was connected and wouldn't back down to anyone.

J Dub was elated that Denny had found someone so quickly that had taken an interest in his dilemma. Not only had McLaughlin decided to represent J Dub but he had also agreed to defend Marcia, Curt and the Morton heirs against the lawsuit that Lew had instigated. It became apparent early on that not even Raymond Parsons would be able to help Lew against McLaughlin. The judge assigned to the case, Judge William Kimbeaux, was a good friend of McLaughlin's. Perhaps J Dub's prediction to Marcia would come true after all. It appeared that the scales of justice had started to tip a little bit.

Denny's work was not complete. He really couldn't represent the heirs and J Dub any more. To some degree Lew's strategy of breaking up a motivated alliance had succeeded. The clock was ticking. Denny felt that he had ten years worth of investigative work to give to a lead attorney. But he needed to find the right one to help his clients and soon. He sensed that whoever he did find would be able to take him on as co-counsel behind the scenes to complete the job.

As luck would have it, Denny ran into Dominic Miles, a retired judge. Denny had done a few favors for Judge Miles when the latter had served on the bench. They shared a cup of coffee and reminisced about some odd court cases that the judge had listened to while putting in duty as a public servant. "When you're up there in the robe, you hear everything," Judge Miles laughed.

"I'm involved in one like that right now," Denny commented.

"What's so odd about it?" Judge Miles.

"I'm representing the plaintiffs and the defendant is exceptionally tough. It looks like I might get knocked off the case as lead counsel and I need a high-powered firm to take over," Denny explained.

"You knew that I retired from the bench, didn't you?" Judge Miles mentioned.

The comment caught Denny completely by surprise. "No!" Denny exclaimed. "What are you doing these days?"

"I started back with the family firm," Judge Miles indicated.

MILES & MILES & MILES, P.C. was the most politically connected law firm in the St. Louis metro area. Six generations of fathers, sons, brothers, cousins, uncles, and nephews had passed through the doors of MILES & MILES & MILES. It was a closed fraternity. Only male family members were invited.

Way back before Dominic was born, one of the Miles' was Governor. He also had a great-uncle that had been a U. S. Senator. In fact, Dominic's brother, Brett, had been a recent U. S. Attorney. If there was ever a family to be involved with that was politically connected, then it was the Miles family. "What sort of work are you doing?" Denny pried.

Judge Miles dropped a bombshell. "With my experience I want to represent plaintiffs in civil litigation complaints. My years on the bench should serve me well in private practice."

Denny literally burned his tongue when he took a sip of his coffee. "Do you have anything brewing?" he probed.

"Heck, I just started back last week. I've got one malpractice case that I'm looking at," Judge Miles offered.

"Have I got a story for you," Denny started. "Do you want to look at another?"

"Why, of course," Judge Miles stated. "Let's go up to my office and talk with my brother Chad. He runs the firm these days."

The elevator ride to the top of the high-rise forced Denny's heart to beat erratically. He couldn't believe the stroke of luck that had just befallen him. If he could talk Judge Miles into taking this case, then the scales of justice would balance out in a split-second.

It was like old-home week for Denny after he had walked into the firm. He and Chad had attended college together. Of course their paths didn't cross much after that but they did have a few beers together back in their law school days.

"Hey, Denny!" Chad said enthusiastically. "How have you been?"

"Just trying to stay one step ahead," Denny replied.

"I'll never forget those parties we had at Mount Boysenberry," Chad said with a laugh. Mount Boysenberry was an affectionate nickname for an ancient, two-story house that housed a half dozen law students. It was located off-campus on a three-acre lot. "Those were the days. I'd take care of the kegs and your band would rock into the night."

"We didn't know how good we had it," Denny laughed. "Wouldn't we like to do that all over again?"

An hour later Denny emerged from the elevator with a smile that covered his face. He couldn't wait to get on the phone and call J Dub and the Morton heirs. Chad Miles had approved taking the case on a contingency basis. Dominic Miles had embraced the case so heartily that he immediately scheduled a modest cruise with the Morton heirs off of the east coast of Florida.

J Dub, Marcia, and Curt rushed over to Denny's office after he had left urgent messages for them. "The new lead counsel in the case would like to meet you," Denny started.

"Did you find someone to help you with the case?" J Dub asked. He could feel the excitement in Denny's voice.

"You bet I did!" Denny shouted. "Maybe we finally caught the break that we needed."

J Dub was dying to find out who Denny had met. "Who is it?"

"Dominic Miles," Denny said with a grin.

" . . . Of MILES & MILES & MILES?" Curt asked. Everyone in the area had heard of the Miles clan. Denny grinned again and nodded his head. It was as if he was the cat that had run off with a canary. "How did you pull that off?" Curt probed. "That's quite a coup."

"It was a chance meeting. One thing led to another," Denny explained. "He picked up the phone and called Lucille when I was sitting across the desk from him!"

Marcia was only somewhat impressed. She was still quite skeptical. "Something tells me that this isn't over yet."

"Oh, not by any means," Denny concurred. "But at least we have someone that will command a lot of respect in the courtroom. He's an ex-judge."

"What sort of deal will we be on?" J Dub inquired.

"They agreed to take it on a contingency basis," Denny responded.

"Thank God," Marcia said with a heavy exhale. She instantly approved that arrangement.

"He wants to meet with you as soon as he gets back from Florida," Denny stated.

"Let us know when and where," J Dub said. "We'll be there the minute he calls." Denny's enthusiasm had infected the entire room.

J Dub, Marcia, and Curt went into a holding pattern. They anxiously awaited the next move from Dominic Miles. Time crawled along at a snail's pace and they all wondered whether or not the meeting would live up to their expectations. J Dub couldn't wait to meet Judge Miles. He was hopeful that all of the pieces would finally mesh and that he could put this chapter of his life behind him.

A few weeks later . . .

On the day of the appointment, Marcia let her husband represent the family. She felt better after the meeting with Denny and wanted to stay away. She loathed all of the legal wrangling anyway. J Dub met Curt in the lobby of the office building and together they rode to the top floor.

The solid wood doors that served as the entrance to the law firm appeared to be twenty feet tall. The lobby was filled with exquisite art and leather furniture. The receptionist immediately asked if she could serve them a beverage. J Dub and Curt instantly thought that the environment was an upgrade from having to take papers off of a chair seat.

The ex-judge was prompt. "Dominic Miles," he said as he extended his hand. "I understand that you've got yourself in quite a predicament." J Dub and Curt instantly recognized the sincere look in the eye of Judge Miles as well as the confidence in his voice.

"I think that what I am in is a life-altering mess," J Dub joked.

Judge Miles led the men into his office and shut the door. Denny had already assumed a seat on the sofa. "And what is your role?" Judge Miles asked Curt.

"I'm a guy that has been trying to help his brother," Curt explained. "I had the time to chase all of this stuff down for him."

"I'm normally stuck in the pro shop," J Dub added.

"I understand," Judge Miles stated. "Let me say something if I could."

"Please do," J Dub murmured. Everyone in the room anticipated what the ex-judge was going to say next.

"I've met with the heirs to the Morton Estate. We spent three days together, day and night on a short cruise." He paused to look out the window toward the Gateway Arch and the Mississippi River that flowed below. "What has happened to you is wrong!" Judge Miles yelled. "If there is anything that gets my juices flowing in the morning . . . the one thing that really makes me want to get out of bed, then it's catching bad guys. I abhor what has happened to all of you in this case."

"Denny has filled me in on the details of the case. I've been down to meet with Lucille and Matt," Judge Miles continued. "I want to make sure that justice is served in this case. If all of the evidence is what you say that it is, then we have two legs up on these guys right now."

Denny helped Judge Miles occasionally. "Do you want to tell them about the smoking gun?"

The judge looked at Denny. "They don't know?" Denny shook his head. "We have evidence that the original contract that was signed has a forged signature on it," Judge Miles bellowed. "We're also fortunate enough to have one of the best known handwriting experts in the country living right here under our noses."

"Won't they just deny that the contract was forged?" J Dub asked.

"We expect them to," Judge Miles replied. "But we've ordered an affidavit of authenticity from Dr. G. G. Browne. He's the handwriting expert . . . and he is the best that there is in this part of the country. He's maybe one of the five best in the nation."

"I would think that they would get their own expert to dispute things," Curt suggested.

"In this part of the world, it's a horse race to see who can get to Dr. G. G. Browne first. We've already won the race. He's our expert witness," Judge Miles declared. A smile came over his face. "We'll have the affidavit that we need next week."

J Dub was back at it with the questions. "What's our new plan?"

"If the contract was forged, as we claim, then that means that this Zerrmann fellow has unlawfully detained possession of the property for damn near the last twenty years," Judge Miles clarified.

J Dub pried further. "What are the consequences of that?"

"The legal result is that the property has to revert back to the original owner," Judge Miles stated.

J Dub turned to Curt. "Lew will blow a gasket."

Judge Miles was not finished. "The kicker is that the courts also say that all money that has been earned on that property for all of the years that it was unlawfully detained must also be forfeited."

"That's probably long gone," J Dub suggested.

"But we can obtain a judgment for that amount that was earned. Then we can file liens on any and all assets that are owned by the parties that unlawfully detained the property," Judge Miles clarified.

The news of what Judge Miles had delivered took a minute to register with J Dub. With a gasp he said, "That will clean him out."

" . . . And well it should. Crime doesn't pay!" Judge Miles shouted.

"What about Norman?" J Dub continued.

"Who is he?" Judge Miles asked.

"He's the guy that owns it now."

"I wouldn't want to be his banker," Judge Miles joked. "We're going to go in and get that property back."

Denny waited until the time was right to comment. "If the property goes back to the estate, then Norman will have to pay his loan to the bank. But he won't be able to do that. So, it is safe to assume that the bank will sue Norman for the amount of their loan. And then Norman will have to sue Lew for the money that he paid to get the property."

"But we expect that the money is long gone," Judge Miles interrupted. "I'm sure that this Zerrmann character has moved it out of the local banks."

"In the meantime we will have them fighting amongst themselves," Denny advised.

"Where will the title company come in?" J Dub probed some more.

"Lew has filed suit against the title company," Denny informed. "We just found that out."

"Then you need to contact them and get them on our side," Curt hinted.

Judge Miles nodded his head in agreement. "We think that's a good idea. I've made contact with their attorney and informed him of the forged signature on the original contract. Needless to say, he was extremely interested in what we could bring to the table."

"It makes sense. They have the deepest pockets and would have a vested interest in correcting a bogus title transfer that happened under their nose," Curt added.

"Our hopes are, that once we give them a copy of the affidavit from the handwriting expert, then that will give the title company the ammunition that they will need to defeat this Zerrmann guy," Judge Miles thought out loud.

J Dub was concerned about his role in the lawsuit. "If the estate gets the property back, then how will I get compensated?"

"You were defrauded from the start. We'll go after a monetary judgment for you," Judge Miles stated matter-of-factly.

"I don't think that the estate wants the ground up here. They live in Florida," Denny interceded. "I'm sure that they would agree to sell it to you at a favorable price. They realize your role in the scam. In talking to them it sounds like you both are concerned about the well-being of the other."

"How quickly will all of this happen once we get the affidavit?" J Dub questioned the group again.

"We'll re-file the lawsuit for you and the Morton heirs very soon," Judge Miles announced. "I would think that we will be able to get some sort of resolution within eighteen to thirty-six months. That's our hope anyway."

J Dub glanced at Curt. "I guess that for as long as I've been involved with the guy, that's a short period of time."

"Just live your life. It'll be here and gone before you know it," Curt responded. J Dub and Curt finally felt that progress would be made. It was nice to see that they could force a little grin at each other.

CHAPTER NINETY-SIX

Late Spring of 2002 . . .

The events of the next several months occurred very similar to the way that Judge Miles had described them. MILES & MILES & MILES, PC was a powerful law firm that was not the least bit concerned about going over into Lew's territory. Dominic Miles went to Illinois and filed a lawsuit. It was now time for Lew and Walter and Norman to be served again by the process server. By now, he had gotten their habits down.

Walter was about at the end of the rope. The Morton Estate case against him was coming to trial any day. He had managed to get the trial delayed further due to a medical emergency from his legal counsel. With the current complaint, he faced possible civil liability to J Dub. His pockets were not nearly as full as Lew's pockets. His legal bills were boxing him into a corner. Walter wanted the entire dilemma to get over. Nora was bitching at him every day.

Norman also had a couple of lawsuits filed against him. If he knew what his brother, George, had done, then he was not tipping his hand. He had title to a lot of property and was too greedy to get to the truth of the situation. It was his opinion that he was going to force the burden of proof on J Dub and the Morton heirs.

Lew, once again, employed Grady Patterson. The case was assigned to Judge Walter O. Bremsky. As expected, Lew and Grady pulled their usual shenanigans in court. Right off the bat, they asked for a change of venue. Judge Bremsky quickly denied that motion. Their strategy all along seemed to delay the process and challenge every court decision. It was the same tactics that they had used before. Grady didn't mind. He kept collecting his fees.

The next ploy that they tried was to ask for a motion to dismiss. After hearing arguments from Dominic Miles, Judge Bremsky did something that no one expected. He said that he did not have enough information to make that decision. He did not accept the motion to dismiss, nor did he deny the motion to dismiss. Judge Bremsky stayed the motion to dismiss.

He ordered the parties to go through the discovery phase. He also ordered Dominic Miles to depose the defendants before making his decision. Lew and Walter and Norman vehemently opposed the order to be deposed. Their arguments went on deaf ears. They were on the clock that Judge Bremsky had imposed. It was one hundred twenty days and counting.

The days clicked off and nothing happened. The stalling techniques that Lew had successfully used in the past seemed to be working this time around too. Judge Bremsky did not intend for those same techniques to fly in his court. When Lew and Norman and Walter did not cooperate with discovery, Judge Bremsky was livid. The favorable court decisions that Lew had enjoyed for so many years seemed to disappear. He had done an adequate job of angering the judge.

Walter's day in court, on the separate suit that the estate had filed, rapidly approached. Dominic Miles had taken over that case from Denny as well. They tried to get Walter to admit his wrongdoing in exchange for civil leniency. Walter went against the wishes of his wife, Nora. He battled the estate in civil court and was eventually held civilly liable for inappropriately handling the affairs of the estate. The civil judgment against him wiped out all of his errors and omissions insurance plus some. Nora filed for divorce.

"That's the first card to fall in this house of cards," Denny proudly said to J Dub in a follow-up phone call. Needless to say, the estate was ecstatic. Finally after well over a decade of wrangling in court they prevailed.

It had been too long of a process and too frustrating for J Dub to get very excited. "One down and a few more to go," J Dub responded. "Let's see what happens with Lew."

"We'll keep our fingers crossed that it turns out in our favor," Denny stated. "If we stay the course, then we should be okay."

The handwriting affidavit from Dr. G. G. Browne was submitted as official evidence during the discovery phase of the process. It was difficult for Lew and Walter and Norman to combat that piece of evidence. Shortly thereafter the deposition testimony of Walter's separate suit with the estate was entered into evidence. J Dub was clearly starting to make some progress down the stretch.

Those two documents were both entered into evidence in the title company lawsuit as well as the case that the liability insurance company had filed. Without a doubt, the tide had turned. Lew was in court facing adversaries that were bigger and stronger than him. They were after the truth and were not going to stop until they got it. Grady tried unsuccessfully to get Lew to cut his losses, but Lew adamantly refused his advice.

The Fall of 2002 . . .

After staying the motion to dismiss, the day had finally arrived for Judge Bremsky to rule on the motion that Grady had filed on behalf of Lew. To everyone's surprise Judge Bremsky dropped a bombshell. He granted the motion to dismiss. No reason was given, only simple instructions for the clerk to notify all attorneys. Abruptly, it appeared that the end of the road had come for J Dub and the Morton heirs. Lew claimed that a prior court decision with which he had been victorious over the Morton Estate prevented any further legal action because the previous decision had been deemed final.

Hurriedly, a meeting between Denny Sneed, Dominic Miles, J Dub, and the heirs to the estate was called. "How can that happen?" J Dub asked.

"If you read between the lines, the narrative behind the decision doesn't hold any water," Denny explained, "because there was no narrative."

"What good does that do us now?" J Dub went on to ask.

"It means that we have an excellent chance of being victorious in the Court of Appeals," Denny went on to say. "We'll file an accelerated appeal. It's the easiest way for us to win there."

" . . . And how long is that going to take?" J Dub pried.

"Anywhere from six to twelve months," Denny replied.

"There's another setback to the middle part of my life . . . and then what?" J Dub asked.

Denny chose to break the news as gently as he could. "That's our last chance. If we lose there, then we are done."

"For crying out loud," J Dub shouted. "They are accomplishing exactly what they wanted to accomplish."

"The delays are working in their favor," Lucille chimed in. "We've been delayed in this legal process for nearly two decades."

"Welcome to our American system of justice," Dominic stated.

"I guess what they say is true," J Dub said with a tone of resolve in his voice.

"What's that?" Denny asked.

J Dub pondered his next statement. "We've got boxes of evidence. It's not what you know, it's who you know."

"Or maybe how much money you have. Somebody had to get to the judge," Matt offered. "Can he make a decision like that?"

"Judges like to play God," Denny stated. "They can do what they want."

" . . . But they have to have legal justification," Dominic Miles butted in.

"It would be interesting to see if either Lew or Grady contributed to Bremsky's political campaign," Matt argued. "It looks to me like Judge Bremsky owed a favor to someone."

"With the documents that we have the whole process smells of corruption," Lucille offered.

"I'm absolutely sure that Lew and his buddies exercised their influence over the judge," J Dub stressed. "Somebody had to get to him."

"On the surface it may appear like that," Denny countered. He didn't want to insinuate that the justice system in America worked in the way that J Dub and the heirs were suggesting. Denny turned to Dominic Miles for more clarity.

"We think that Judge Bremsky is giving them a false sense of security. His narrative was non-existent and had no legal support," Dominic stated. "We think that the decision will be overturned in the Court of Appeals."

"What makes you so sure?" J Dub inquired.

"First of all, we have the law on our side," Denny said matter-of-factly.

Dominic Miles picked up where Denny left off. " . . . And secondly, a lot of the appellate judges are . . ." Dominic stopped and weighed his response carefully. "Let's just say that I was a judge for a long time earlier in my career."

A collective grin broke out among them. J Dub's words suddenly took a familiar ring. "I guess it's a no-brainer," he offered as he read between the lines. "Let's wait the necessary time and hope for a favorable reversal."

Six Months Later During the Spring of 2003 . . .

The appellate court for the Southern District of Illinois was housed in an ancient two-story building in Mount Vernon about an hours' drive from St. Louis. What appeared to be at least a dozen coats of white paint had white-washed the brick building. A black wrought iron fence surrounded the property which at one time most certainly had been the hub of the town. Oak trees flourished and forsythias bloomed a radiant yellow backdrop to rows of contrasting red tulips. A horseshoe shaped staircase that once provided access to a second story entrance had been closed and now only one ground-level entrance was available to the public.

As they walked onto the grounds and across the red brick sidewalk J Dub commented to Curt, "I can't believe that we're down to the eleventh hour on this thing. These oral arguments better go well."

Curt marveled at the history that surrounded them. "Look at this place! I bet Abraham Lincoln has been here before. That would have been over a hundred and fifty years ago."

"Then let's hope that his ghost is looking after our side," J Dub offered as a last resort. The thought of being down to the wire had unnerved him.

The two brothers entered the building and passed through a portable metal detector. During heightened security that didn't seem abnormal even though Mount Vernon was a small town and it appeared that many of the residents probably didn't even lock their doors at night. They made their way to the second floor courtroom and promptly grabbed two of the twenty or so seats. Lucille and Matt entered a few minutes later and sat nearby. Their case had been placed second on the docket for the days' business.

A buzzer startled all in attendance. "All rise!" the bailiff shouted. He had probably been on the state payroll for thirty years, but looked like he had the employment history of a weekend rent-a-cop. His tie was six inches above his belt and stained with vegetable beef soup. There was yellow mustard on his shirt.

Three appellate judges entered the courtroom and assumed their seats behind the bench. The judge seated in the middle said, "The first case to be argued today is Catamaran versus Catamaran which had been dismissed from Judge Bremsky's court."

Curt stuck his elbow into J Dub's ribs. "I can't believe it," he whispered.

"What?" J Dub inquired.

"I thought the guy at the end looked familiar," Curt said softly.

" . . . The little Mexican looking guy?" J Dub asked.

"Yeah, that's Alvarez Catamaran."

"Who's that?"

"He was the local jockey that was called up as a substitute four or five years ago to ride in the Derby. They put him on a long shot and he brought the horse home," Curt murmured. "His nickname is Alley Cat. He rides at the track and when the racing card is over he goes to the bars until closing looking for the easy marks. His wife filed for divorce."

"So," J Dub naively shrugged.

Curt rubbed his thumb and forefinger together. "You just heard the judge. It was thrown out by Judge Bremsky. He must be a money hungry SOB."

"That's not good," J Dub sighed. "We might be in for trouble."

"Order in the court!" the bailiff shouted as he stared at Curt and J Dub.

"Unless the appellate judges look at the law and can't be bought," Curt whispered.

"Let's hope that there is justice in this world," J Dub said softly.

"Right now, we just need it in the State of Illinois," Curt said in an understatement. The two brothers stared at each other.

CHAPTER NINETY-SEVEN

"Now what's going to happen?" J Dub blurted to Denny and Dominic Miles as the whole group gathered for lunch after the oral arguments were heard.

"We scored a lot of points in front of the appellate judges today," Dominic stressed.

"If I would have been a juror I would have voted for the other side. I thought that we got killed," Matt stated vehemently.

"Not really," Denny bickered, "you don't know how this system works."

"I think that we got a pretty good idea during the first case that was argued today," Curt disputed.

"Yeah, open your wallet and peel off the cash," J Dub added. "It looks like all of the judges are out for themselves . . . especially Judge Bremsky."

"Look, I've been a judge," Dominic squabbled. "That's not how the system works. At the appellate level they are way above that. The law comes into play."

"Believe me, we scored some points today," Denny included. "The law is on our side on this one."

"Then how long is it going to take for them to make a ruling?" J Dub asked.

"Maybe another six to twelve months," Denny answered.

"There's no way!" J Dub hollered. "I can't stand to be controlled for this length of time and held hostage by the court system."

"They will take their time to make sure that they get it right," Dominic assured the group.

"You know J Dub, Lew held you hostage for a lot longer than that," Curt said in a consoling tone. "Just hang in there."

~   ~   ~

Well Over a Year Later During the Summer of 2004 . . .

The voice on the other end of the line said, "J Dub, why don't you and Curt and Marcia be at my office later this afternoon. I've got some news to tell you."

"Is it good?" J Dub inquired.

"I'd rather tell you in person," Denny continued.

A few hours later J Dub and Curt climbed the same staircase that they had so many times in the past. Marcia had been sick of the situation for years and let the guys go by themselves. Fear and trepidation occupied every step until J Dub stuck his head into Denny's office.

"How bad is it?" J Dub blurted as he got right to the heart of the matter.

"Here's the ruling," Denny stated as he raised a brief into the air. "The appellate court reversed Judge Bremsky's decision."

"Hallelujah!" J Dub shouted. The three men traded high-fives and hugs. A genuine feeling of success invaded the office. "Where do we go from here?"

"Judge Bremsky is under strict orders from the appellate court to hear the case. We'll get our day in front of a jury." Denny enjoyed being the messenger of the good news.

"Finally!" Curt exploded.

"You know, it's been over six years," J Dub added. "Let's get 'em!"

~   ~   ~

Over Two Years Later During the Fall of 2006 . . .

After the three appellate judges reversed Judge Bremsky's order the case was sent back to his court with strict orders to hear the case. A jury was convened. The legal proceedings continued. Lew and Grady had used up all of their stalling techniques. Denny Sneed and Dominic Miles were ready for the action and felt that the evidence would clearly sway the judge and jury this time.

The statute that dealt with property that was unlawfully detained originally came on the scene as a tool to help landlords evict tenants that failed to pay rent. In this particular case, Lew had unlawfully possessed the property because of the forged contract. He had entered into a contract with the estate based upon a forged power of attorney document. The fact that none of the money that he had given to George Pierce ever made it's way to the Morton Estate was icing on the cake. That meant that no consideration had been given for the property either.

Dominic Miles presented another theory to Judge Bremsky and the court. He argued that since the forged document had occurred nearly two decades earlier, a continuing tort situation existed. A continuing tort would be a crime that went on and on. He used that to counter any Statute of Limitation problems that the estate might encounter.

The evidence and deposition testimony that had been entered into evidence was damaging. Dominic Miles asked Judge Bremsky's court to grant a court order so that the heirs could regain title to their property and retain possession of the property. After that was granted, Judge Bremsky also determined that the heirs to the Morton Estate were entitled to any money that had been earned on the property from the time that it was unlawfully detained. To add insult to injury, the court ruled that the heirs were also entitled to punitive damages plus court costs and interest.

Judge Bremsky's court did not take this matter lightly. The fact that the property had been unlawfully detained for nearly twenty years and that the forgery had continued for such a long period of time made the case qualify for priority status. When everything was said and done the property was awarded back to the Morton heirs. They also received a multi-million dollar judgment. J Dub received a significant monetary judgment from Lew and Walter due to the shoddy accounting. Norman was ordered to forfeit all of the golf course property.

On the day that the decision occurred, Lucille and Matt Morton were in the courtroom. J Dub, Marcia and Curt were also in attendance. When the gavel came down the victims jumped for joy and truly felt vindicated after all of the years of deceit. During the congratulatory handshakes, Judge Miles turned to J Dub. "They've got another surprise coming."

"What could top this?' J Dub asked.

"Nothing for you personally," Judge Miles acknowledged. "But you remember what I said in my office, don't you?"

" . . . About what?" There had been so much legal language that had been said that had confused J Dub. He was at a loss for what was next.

"About what gets my juice flowing," Judge Miles said with a smile.

J Dub beamed. "You said that catching bad guys does it for you."

A wry grin came over the face of Dominic Miles. "If this wasn't enough of a blow to these guys, then I want to let you know that I contacted my brother, Brett," Judge Miles whispered.

"And, what is he going to do?"

"That group of U. S. Attorneys is a small fraternity. It's even a smaller fraternity than the Miles family," Judge Miles murmured.

J Dub grinned. "You didn't, did you?"

The smile on the face of Dominic Miles wouldn't go away. "We gift-wrapped a criminal case for them. Lew and Walter and Norman have got another surprise on the way . . . and if we can figure out a way to get to George Pierce, then he'll get a shocker too."

J Dub exchanged handshakes with Denny and Dominic. "I want to thank both of you for taking the case when no one in town would touch it. You were willing to work through the complexities and get to the bottom of what happened," J Dub said. "Anything that you make on the deal is well deserved. Every other lawyer in town wanted the case handed over to them on a silver platter. No one wanted to work on it." The three men hugged. It was highly likely that they would be business partners in the coming years.

CHAPTER NINETY-EIGHT

The Summer of 2007 . . .

The estate received the court order and swiftly took possession of the property. The appeal process didn't appear to have much traction behind it. A by-product of the courts' decision paved the way for a flurry of lawsuits. The title company, which Lew had sued, filed a countersuit that included George Pierce, Norman Pierce, and Walter Hancock as accomplices to the forgeries. The bank that had granted the loan to Norman Pierce filed a civil lawsuit against him to recover the money that they had loaned to him to purchase the property. Norman, in turn, sued Lew, who had sold the property to him.

Lew could not accept defeat. He felt as if he had been victimized by the actions of George Pierce and Walter Hancock. He turned around and sued both of them for forging the signature on the power of attorney that had been used to close on the original contract. The irony of the situation was that Lew had knowledge of the inventive scam in the first place.

Acting on the information that was provided by Dominic Miles, the feds quickly re-opened the investigation that had abruptly ended several years before. George Pierce was in the Virgin Islands and seemingly protected since he was out of the country. Norman, however, had been a partner in the title company. The investigators were all over him.

The walls closed in on Lew this time around. It didn't look like anybody was going to be able to help him out. After Lew had sold the golf course he had bought a yacht with the money that he had received from Norman. After the dismissal of the charges by the U. S. Attorney's office, the IRS had instructed Special Agent Booker to keep tabs on all the financial transactions that Lew Zerrmann had made. Booker had traced the flow of money from the sale of the golf course through Lew's bank account and to the purchase of a yacht. The yacht was docked at Harbour Town Marina off the coast of South Carolina, in Hilton Head.

Through the grapevine it was learned that Lew had prepared to leave the country. The feds had traced George Pierce to Tortola in the Virgin Islands. Getting him out of there was another thing. They also learned that he had been staying in a home that was owned by Lew Zerrmann. It made sense that Lew would attempt to flee to that destination and probably use the yacht as transportation.

Wiretaps revealed that Lew planned to leave Hilton Head with Monty. The government wanted to prevent that from happening. J Dub got wind of the plan from Booker. After being in a partnership with Lew for the length of time that he had, J Dub had a vested interest in having a final word with Lew.

The plane that Lew and Monty chartered landed just before dawn at Savannah/Hilton Head International airport. It was right after daybreak on a muggy morning in June when the two of them jumped into a rental car and hop scotched over to I-95 in South Georgia. Within ten minutes they were over the Savannah River and into South Carolina. After traveling another eight miles they took a right onto US-278 for the twenty-five minute ride to Sea Pines Plantation on Hilton Head Island. The live oaks that were draped with Spanish moss, and the banyan trees, pines, and palmettos provided a canopy over the road. In a matter of minutes they had parked the car and strolled past the various shops at Harbour Town. The cloudless sky indicated that another brutally hot day was in store for the people on Hilton Head Island.

The marina itself seemed to take the shape of a key lock. For the most part, it was circular with an opening onto Calibogue Sound. All of the docks were concrete with ramps that led to individual slips. Virtually all of the boats at the marina were backed into their individual locations. Harbour Town's various gift shops, condominiums and multi-family units surrounded the marina. The infamous Harbour Town Lighthouse marked the entrance to Calibogue Sound as the boats exited the marina.

Lew and Monty strolled around the circular dock toward Lew's new, eighty foot Hatteras Motor Yacht. The vessel was gorgeous and its interior was elegant with wood paneling and crown molding in all its staterooms. Every new and modern electronic convenience in the world was standard. Marble flooring and ebony cabinets added ambience. The master bedroom and bath featured a king-sized bed and whirlpool jets in the hot tub. A global positioning satellite system tracked its whereabouts.

As they walked leisurely, Lew turned to Monty. "I don't know what in the world Grady was doing. He wouldn't listen to me. He sold me out, Monty. I haven't done anything wrong."

"Hey, at least nothing came out about the hooker," Monty rationalized. He wanted to make sure that his tail was covered.

"Those bastards may have gotten a judgment, but they'll need a lifetime to collect," Lew announced to Monty. "They're going to need to find me first."

"Fat chance of that," Monty declared. "In another thirty minutes we'll be in international waters." The entrance to Harbour Town Marina dumped into Calibogue Sound just minutes from the Atlantic.

"This screwed-up country of ours," Lew started. "A guy works his ass off for all of his life and then the courts come and take every last penny away."

"It doesn't seem right, does it?" Monty did his best to ingratiate his friend.

"Can you believe that ridiculous court decision?" Lew ranted. "I didn't do anything wrong."

"I can't believe the disrespect that the judge and jury gave toward a successful businessman like you," Monty agreed.

"I'm fed up with this country," Lew fumed.

Monty looked toward the sky. The slight breeze tempered the rapidly rising heat. "It's a beautiful day to hit the seas."

"I'll never be back," Lew stammered.

"Why do you say that?" Monty asked. "You seem so bitter."

"They took it all. It's not right," Lew stated with his own twisted interpretation of events.

"But you killed someone and got away with it. I took the fall for you on the money laundering and kept you out of prison. You've had all of the toys that money could buy," Monty rationalized. "It's been a good run for you."

"Who gives a rat's ass. Let's beat them to the punch and get out of here," Lew urged. "I've had enough of this country."

Monty jumped onto the rear of the yacht and continued to the front. Lew walked to the rear of the yacht. Before boarding, Lew stopped. He was about to leave American soil for good. He looked at Calibogue Sound and then at the yacht. He nodded his approval. "It doesn't get any better than this," he yelled to Monty right before he leaped onto the rear of the yacht.

J Dub walked around the circular dock from the opposite direction. He wanted to come face to face with the guy that didn't even have the guts to thank him for all of the years of hard work. In fact, they hadn't spoken since the day in Walter's office when Monty had done Lew's dirty work. Even on that day, Lew didn't say a word.

"Are you going to run to the islands since you didn't win?" J Dub yelled to Lew. He continued to walk right up to the rear of the yacht.

The voice startled Lew. It was a voice that he recognized from the past. He turned to stand face to face with J Dub. "It's business, J Dub, just business."

"I've heard that one before. You were the one that taught me the ropes in business and how to win," J Dub said coolly.

Lew laughed in his face. "I used you like a mule."

"You're going to run now and try to hide, aren't you?" J Dub asked.

Lew did not reply.

J Dub fired one question after another. "What's wrong? Don't you like to be on the losing side? Can't you take a little of your own medicine?"

Lew's temper started to boil. "You haven't collected a dime yet."

"I'll go to hell before I let you leave," J Dub hollered.

"Screw you!" Lew retaliated as he pulled a gun out of his pocket and pointed it squarely at J Dub.

A calm look and tranquil feeling enveloped J Dub. He started to cackle quietly at Lew and the absurdity of the situation. Booker had told him how he had laughed in Lew's face when Lew threatened him on the morning of the IRS raid at Lew's house. As J Dub peered at the revolver, he did what he had wanted to do for years. He taunted Lew. "Put that down. You're a bully and a crook, not a killer."

"Get out of my life, kid, before I blow your head off!"

J Dub called his bluff. "You don't have the guts to pull the trigger." J Dub stood steadfastly with both feet firmly planted on the dock. "You never have been much of a man."

Lew glared at J Dub. "You're taking a big chance," Lew stressed. Other than the day in the pro shop, this was the only time that Lew could remember that J Dub had stood up to him.

J Dub snickered again. "No bigger chance than going into business with you."

"Your problem was that you never could figure out how to gain control," Lew chastised his ex-partner. He steadied the gun at J Dub.

J Dub stood strong and erect. "But I learned how to win. I decided a long time ago that I wasn't going to lie or cheat or steal to succeed like some people I know."

A momentary pause froze the two men in time. They stared into each others' eyes. The silence was broken by a voice out of a loudspeaker. " . . . Stop! Hands up! . . . FBI . . . IRS. You're under arrest for obstruction of justice and tax evasion!"

An endless number of uniformed agents pounced out of nowhere with guns drawn. All of the weapons were trained on Lew. The commotion startled Lew. He had his sights on fleeing the country. The sudden turn of events shocked him.

J Dub laughed out loud at Lew. "But I learned my lessons well. One of the things that you taught me was to always have backup," J Dub sneered.

Special Agent Booker appeared on the dock. Beside him was Lois. She had worn a dark pair of sunglasses to apparently hide her eyes from the glare. Lois removed her shades to reveal eyes that resembled a raccoon. She had been beaten about the face. Her eyes were nearly swollen shut. Her face was puffy.

"You lied under oath, Lew! Drop it!" Booker yelled.

Lois screamed at the top of her lungs. "There is no way you're getting out of here! Take a good look at what you did to me, you pig!"

Lew was still in a daze. He was trapped. Agents surrounded him. He peered out to the water. He returned his eyes to J Dub. Lew glared back at Booker. The gun dropped from his hand onto the deck of the yacht. Agents started to scurry about.

Booker shouted again. " . . . Lew! . . . Lew!"

Lew had quickly reached into his pocket. He seized the black velvet covered pill box. With catlike quickness he grabbed the pills and popped them into his mouth. They were swiftly ingested. He threw the pill box across the deck of the yacht. It contained the gold-capped tooth of the hooker. "If you're so smart, get your monkey-ass, tar-baby brain to figure that one out!"

Booker had no idea what Lew had thrown. He remembered back to the time that they had confronted each other in the confines of Lew's home. He smiled and chuckled. "You just don't get it, do you Lew?"

"More than you can ever imagine," Lew replied.

J Dub wasn't surprised. In fact, he had privately mentioned to Marcia and Curt that if Lew ever got cornered he would pop the cyanide pills and do himself in. Cyanide poisoning can be rapid. Lew had always made it a point to carry a dose that would be heavy enough to finish the job. Hitler had always been Lew's idol. He had mentioned that to J Dub on many occasions.

Within a few seconds Lew underwent contractions in his chest cavity. He experienced a shortness of breath. His body went into mild convulsions. Inside a couple of minutes he slumped over and slid into unconsciousness. His breathing ceased. He literally died within three minutes.

It was over that quickly.

J Dub looked at Booker and smiled. The early morning chill had forced him to wear a sweatshirt over his golf shirt. He proceeded to take off a bullet-proof vest that was hidden underneath. As he handed it to Booker he said, "This came in handy after all. Thanks for the advice."

CHAPTER NINETY-NINE

The weather for Lew's funeral cooperated for the few people that were in attendance. It was bright and sunny, much better than what Lew deserved.

J Dub and the boys didn't bother going to the memorial service. They sat in the coffee shop a few doors down from the church and waited for the hearse to drive by on its way to the cemetery. When the procession went by only five cars followed the hearse. That came as a mild surprise to the boys. No one knew that Lew had that many friends.

The boys scurried out the door and piled into their cars as hastily as they could. Not a one of them wanted to miss the casket's final descent into the ground.

Julie jumped into a car with J Dub and Curt. This was another event that Marcia had planned to miss. Elia, Paco, and BT shared a vehicle. Paul, Rollie, and Fred hopped into another car.

At the grave site the pastor made the eulogy short and concise. He had finished his final words only moments before the boys had arrived.

Ray and Monty walked away from the coffin as J Dub and the group approached. "J Dub, let me know if I can provide any help to you," Ray offered. He and Monty walked to their car.

J Dub stood in disbelief. He glanced at all of the guys and shook his head.

Julie broke the silence. "There's another loser."

"Can you believe that guy?" J Dub replied. The group stopped to gaze at the casket. The realization that it was over finally hit home. J Dub turned to the boys. He was in a celebratory mood. "What do you say we go to the course and play a round of golf, guys?"

"I couldn't think of a better way to enjoy this day and have a good time," Fred said with a grin.

"Maybe we can get them to throw that noisy piece of junk motorcycle in the hole, too," Paco stammered.

"He sure was appropriately named," Paul stated.

"Julie and I always joked that Lew was short for loser," J Dub replied.

"What a chicken. He couldn't stand the heat and took the easy way out," BT added. "He turned out to be the ultimate loser." His words took a minute to sink in. Everyone nodded in agreement.

"Before we go and play, we need to do what they do in the old country," Elia mumbled in his Middle Eastern accent.

"What's that Elia?" J Dub asked.

"It's an old Middle Eastern custom to do this to people that have done you wrong." Elia stood with a grin and reached for his zipper. "Piss on him!" J Dub and all of the boys stepped forward and relieved themselves on the coffin.

CHAPTER ONE HUNDRED

In the days that followed, J Dub was all over the golf course shaking hands and making the golfers feel welcome. He and Dominic Miles had made a deal with the heirs to the Morton estate to purchase the golf course. The pro shop was for Julie to operate. Marcia popped in a lot more regularly to see her husband and deliver lunch.

J Dub always made it a point to make sure that Easy Earl's tree got plenty of water. He would repeatedly go and sit in the shade of that tree and remember his trusted friend.

One of the items that got priority on J Dub's agenda was the acquisition of a golf course dog. He wanted a bull terrier that would make the surroundings feel like home. Yet, after looking around, he couldn't decide on one. So, after a little thought, he decided to buy the whole litter. They were appropriately named Bogey, Birdie, Eagle, and Ace.

It was a common sight to see J Dub pounding balls on the driving range. He had finally gotten back home to the place where he belonged. On many days, Curt would join him.

"You know Curt, I've made lots of birdie putts to win matches, but I had to stand over this one for a few years, give it a good read, and then drop it," J Dub said.

"We had some help along the way," Curt replied.

"Thank goodness because he sure didn't play by the rules," J Dub added.

"We were lucky that the government paid for a lot of the investigation," Curt stated with a grin, "and the estate funded the lawyers."

"All it took was a few years of patience . . . something that the great game of golf has taught me," J Dub smiled. "Besides, I had a lot more time left on my clock than him."

"That pathetic loser wanted to rush things and play hard ball. He didn't give you much of a choice," Curt agreed.

"That made my decision easier," J Dub acknowledged. "I just wish that George Pierce didn't get off."

"Snakes can slither away."

J Dub switched gears. "You know, Booker really surprised me."

" . . . How's that?"

"I finally figured out why Booker couldn't talk. The government was waiting to put their final plan into action. The obstruction of justice charge was a lot easier for them to prove than tax evasion," J Dub said with a grin.

"I guess that they had enough invested in the guy to make sure that justice was done," Curt responded. "In a sick, demented way, Lew's greed helped you."

"What do you mean?"

"If he would have sold it to you, then you would have had to fight the estate," Curt explained. "You would have had to turn the property back over to them."

J Dub stared into his brother's eyes. "Denny had warned me about that. We always knew that the land would survive Lew. I just didn't know if all of us would make it through the process."

"It sure ate up a lot of time," Curt said as he looked to the heavens. "Somebody sure is looking over you."

J Dub allowed for the minute of reality to settle in. "It was a lot better for us to have the estate on our side rather than going against them in court. We would have never made it." J Dub peered out to the range and reflected on his youth. "You know, dad was always right."

" . . . About what?" Curt pried.

"He always told me under the shade of that old oak tree at the range to stay patient. He told me to apply the principles that I learned from golf to everyday life," J Dub put into plain words. "Dad always told me to slow down, be honest with myself, and commit."

"It looks like you learned your lesson well."

J Dub smiled. "You know, Curt, all things considered I probably should have hit the nine-iron." J Dub slowly pulled his driver back, uncoiled his body, and launched a drive into the crystal clear blue sky. "Who knows what's going to happen next?"

"Wow," Curt said as he marveled at his brother's swing, "especially if you keep hitting shots like that."

J Dub grinned. "You never know. We're not getting any younger. If I can keep my cool, stay within myself, and finish the round strong, then there's always the senior tour."

#   #   #